The Quran Speaks

BAHIS SEDQ

This edition published by
Dog Ear Publishing
4010 W. 86th Street, Ste H
Indianapolis, IN 46268

www.dogearpublishing.net

ISBN: 978-145751-887-4
This book is printed on acid-free paper.

Printed in the United States of America

*This book is dedicated to the hope and vision
of a world undistracted by religious divisions—
a truly wonderful world!*

CONTENTS

Author's Note

The Quran is perhaps the most influential book of all time. In addition to that, it also contains critical information about Muhammad, who in his own right is amongst the most dominant personalities in history. On either score, the Quran is a "must-read."

The fact that it is in a language unfamiliar to most* could pose a problem, but there are plenty of translations in virtually all languages. The real challenge is to identify the more authentic amongst the translations. This was the first task to confront the author; which translations should be trusted? After much deliberation, I chose the following.

- **Syed Abul Ala Maududi:** *The Meaning of the Qur'an*[1]

  Maududi is the founder of the Jamaat-i-Islami† in British India but is influential in other parts of the globe as well—particularly the Arab world and amongst Muslims living in the West.[2] He stands out for providing a most readable translation of the Quran, assisted by a detailed commentary. Maududi's work thus was a fairly obvious choice.

---

* Even Arab Muslims find it hard to understand the Quranic Arabic, as it is quite different from the everyday spoken Arabic.

† The Islamic Party

- **Abdullah Yusuf Ali:** *The Meanings of the Holy Quran*[3]

  Yusuf Ali also qualifies with ease, as his translation is possibly the most widely known in the English-speaking world. He is popular across the board, but particularly amongst moderate Muslims who see him as representing the liberal face of Islam.

  We shall rely on Yusuf Ali's original translation, but it may be mentioned that there is also a recent revision that makes changes to the original work to bring it "within the current understanding and interpretation of the Qur'an."[4] We shall occasionally refer to the latter as well.

- **Mohammed Marmaduke Pickthall:** *The Koran*[5]

  Pickthall, an Englishman who converted to Islam while in the service of the Nizam of Hyderabad, too has delivered a translation that is highly regarded. Additionally, he brings the perspective of a Westerner who converted to Islam. I therefore feel that he should also be included in the list.

- **Muhammad Taqi-ud-Din al-Hilali and Muhammad Muhsin Khan:** *Translation of the Meaning of the Noble Qur'an in the English Language*[6]

  This translation is sponsored by the Saudi government and is distributed free. Because of such patronage, it has become quite popular in recent years. It is therefore not easy to ignore this translation, either—though it is not the most popular amongst liberal Muslims.

Apart from being well regarded, these translations carry the attribute that they cannot be considered anti-Islamic and may be consulted without fear on this score. The other advantage is that, together, they represent varying shades of the spectrum, from the conservative to the more liberal, and one therefore hopes to capture all colors.

I would have liked to engage all translations in every discussion, but recognizing that this would overly burden the dialogue—particularly because all four translations are in agreement on most verses—I found that some compromise was necessary. Keeping this in perspective, the book adopts the following approach: It uses Maududi's translation throughout and often also refers to his commentary. Without exception, however, Yusuf Ali's translation is also carried in the endnotes or in the main discussion. On the more critical issues, particularly where there is any mentionable disagreement amongst the translators, all four translations are consulted. Where that is not the case, translations by Pickthall and Hilali-Khan of all verses quoted in the book can be found in the appendix. This should demonstrate that in a vast majority of cases, the conclusion in this text is not dependent on any particular translation.

*

To assist the reader, this book at times draws attention towards the more relevant aspects of a quoted text through appropriate emphasis. Unless specifically stated otherwise, all such emphasis is provided by me and is not part of the original text.

*

Lastly, I would like to inform the reader that this book is written under a penname meaning "seeker of the truth". In resorting to this technique, I do not mean to doubt that an overwhelming majority of Muslims would allow me the license to express the views noted in this book, which in any case are founded on the Quran.

1

THE QURAN SPEAKS

*Read in the name of your Lord Who created. Created man
from a clot of congealed blood. (96:1–2)[1]*

These are the first verses of the Quran—placed in chapter 96, as
the Quran is not arranged in chronological order.[2] It seems fitting
that we begin our journey with these same verses.

They inform us that man is created from a clot of congealed
blood. This requires explanation, considering that a zygote, the
earliest form of an embryo, actually results from the fertilization
of the ovum by the sperm, neither of which involves blood. The
zygote then goes through various stages, and even the point at
which the embryo develops blood comes much later. The
biological fact thus is that blood has little to do with conception
or the phases that follow conception.[3]

Could the Quran have got it wrong at the outset? One
explanation could be that the above verses are referring to
Adam—that he (not his progeny) was created from a clot of
congealed blood. But that would contradict many other verses of

the Quran that tell us that Allah created Adam from clay,[4] and it therefore seems implausible.

The more plausible explanation is that the Quran did not mean to be scientifically accurate in this regard but only to communicate with its audience on the basis of what they happened to believe. Based on the fact that menses stops in pregnancy, or the fact that a miscarried embryo may give the appearance of "a clot of congealed blood"* during certain phases of its development (though in the mother's womb, the embryo would not involve congealed blood), the Arabs may well have believed that there was some connection between blood and conception—along the same lines as Aristotle, who considered menstrual blood to be the "actual generative substance."[5]

It is only recently, of course, that we have acquired the exact knowledge about conception and the phases that follow conception, which makes the first verses of the Quran (or their accepted translations, at least) seem a little odd. But that notwithstanding, the fact truly is that nearly a billion and a half people—almost 25% of the globe's population—firmly adhere to the Quran's message. Islam is not only the fastest growing religion but also possibly the one with the lowest exit rate.

This begs the question, what makes Islam so appealing to its adherents today? The "magnificence" of the Quran is one reason. Muslims believe that the Quran is at once a scientific miracle; a system of laws and justice *par excellence*; a comprehensive moral code that addresses complex situations in a simple, elegant, and balanced manner; and much more—all expressed in matchless literature so brilliant that it can only be the word of Allah and certainly beyond the abilities of an illiterate person!†

---

* or a "*leech-like* clot of congealed blood," according to Yusuf Ali's revised translation

† The fact that not many have read the Quran in a language they understand (even Arab Muslims do not fully understand the Quranic text) and that fewer still have attempted or been able to comprehend it fully (the fact that the Quran is not compiled chronologically or by subject means that it remains inaccessible to a vast majority of its believers) suggests that most Muslims do not have firsthand knowledge of these attributes. But they do believe that the Quran reflects them all.

The other factor that binds Muslims to their faith is the aura of Muhammad. Muslims believe that he was perfect, or very nearly so. They thus find it hard to believe that, when a man of his impeccable character certifies that he is Allah's Messenger and the Quran His book, doubts should still be expressed about his prophethood.

For Muslims, at least, the question is not whether the Quran is the word of Allah; it unquestionably is. For them, the task is to ascertain the Quran's true meaning. The initial expectation is that this should be straightforward. Allah's word cannot be unclear. This also happens to be the Quran's promise:

> We have sent down to you Revelations that clearly expound the Truth, and none but the disobedient reject them. (2:99)

> *Alif Lam Ra.* These are the verses of the Book that makes its object perfectly clear.(12:1)[6]

What is surprising is that no one seems to understand the meaning of *Alif Lam Ra* (A.L.R) or similar prefixes such as *Alif Lam Mim* found in many chapters of the Quran.* We are told "these letters are one of the miracles of the Quran and none but Allah (alone) knows their meaning."[7] Why, then, should these

---

* According to Muslim scholars, these letters were prevalent in Arabic literature at the time the Quran was revealed and no one therefore questioned their use. Muslim scholars are also dismissive of the possibility that the letters found their way into pre-Islamic Arabic literature as references to deities worshipped by the Arabs. Maududi, for instance, notes:
> Letters of the Arabic alphabet like *Alif, Lam, Mim,* called the *muqatta'at,* which are pre-fixed to a number of the Surahs of the Quran, were in common use in the Arabic literature of the period when the Quran was revealed. The poets and rhetoricians made use of this style, and instances of this can even be found in the pre-Islamic prose and poetry which has survived. *As their significance was appreciated by all concerned, none objected to or questioned their use, because it was no enigma to them. Even the bitterest opponents of the Quran, who never missed an opportunity, did not raise any objection against their use.* But as their use was abandoned with the passage of time it became difficult for the commentators to determine their exact meaning and significance. An ordinary reader, however, need not worry about their meanings because they make no difference as far as the Guidance of the Quran is concerned. (Maududi: *The Meaning of the Qur'an,* note 1 to *Surah Al-Baqarah,* Volume 1, pp. 51–52)

letters find mention in a verse that professes to make "its object perfectly clear"?

Before we seek the explanation in the Quran, let us note that the claim that the Quran makes "its object perfectly clear" is also tested by other verses, such as the following:

> By the dawn, and the ten nights, and the even and the odd, and the night when it departs! Is there in it an oath for a man of sense? (89:1–5)[8]

Even though the Quran is confident that the meaning of the above verses would be self-evident to a "man of sense," the reality as noted by Maududi is that there are no less than thirty-six interpretations of just one aspect of the above verses!

> Much difference of opinion has been expressed by the commentators in the commentary of these verses, so much so that in respect of "the even and the odd" there are as many as 36 different views.[9]

This brings us back to the question of how to reconcile the Quran's claim that it makes its "object perfectly clear" with verses like *Alif Lam Ra* and the above. The Quran explains:

> There are two kinds of verses in this Book: *muhkamat* (which are precise in meaning) they are the essence of the Books and the other kind is *mutashabihat* (which are ambiguous). Those, who are perverse of heart, always go after the *mutashabihat* in pursuit of mischief and try to interpret them arbitrarily, *whereas in fact, none save Allah knows their real meanings!* (3:7)[10]

Why were the *mutashabihat* (the ambiguous verses) revealed at all? Perhaps to identify the "perverse of heart," who would interpret them arbitrarily and would thus be exposed, but because the Quran does not exactly identify the verses about which "none save Allah knows their real meanings," it is possible that even the more steadfast believers may unknowingly focus on such ambiguous verses and end up in disputes regarding the interpretation of the Quran.

This explains the murder of Uthman, the Prophet's son-in-law and the Third Caliph, at the hands of Abu Bakr's son (Muhammad), on the charge that Uthman was deviating from the

Quran! The resulting battle (known as the First Fitna) between Aisha (the Prophet's widow) and Ali, in which many believers were killed* and which has contributed much to the Shia–Sunni schism,[11] is also similarly explained. Neither conflict would have arisen if the protagonists, all dear associates of the Prophet, had focused instead on the *muhkamat* (the precise verses), such as the following:

> And do not be like those, who became divided into sects and got involved in differences of opinion *even after receiving clear teachings*. (3:105)[12]

In which category should one place the following verses, though?

> O Believers, do not take the Jews nor the Christians as your friends: they are one another's friends only. If anyone of you takes them as friends, surely he shall be counted among them; indeed Allah deprives the wrong-doers of His Guidance. (5:51)[13]

> Let not the Believers make the disbelievers their friends and take them into their confidence in preference to the Believers. *Whoever will do this shall have no relation left with Allah*; however your show of friendship towards them will be pardonable, if you do so to guard against their tyranny. (3:28)[14]

Many believers find these verses to be "precise in meaning" and decline to take Jews, Christians, and other disbelievers as friends—lest they be deprived of Allah's Guidance, or "shall have no relation left with Allah."† This is problematic, as there are sizeable Muslim communities living amongst Christians, Jews, and other religious groups in different parts of the world who are

---

* Ali, who succeeded Uthman as Caliph but by now was married to Abu Bakr's widow (and was thus the murderer's stepfather), is reported to have made Muhammad b. Abu Bakr the governor of Egypt. This drew Aisha (Prophet's widow and half-sister to the murderer) in conflict with Ali, resulting in a full-fledged battle between the two.

† The argument that the scope of these verses should be restricted to Jews, Christians, and the disbelievers of the Prophet's time does not convince all believers, considering that there is no such qualification stated in the referred verses.

prevented by the above verses from integrating. The worst manifestation, however, is the plight of minorities living in Muslim countries; they often live as humbled second-class citizens, as the Quran is understood by many of its adherents to dictate that the believers must not treat these people as friends.

Religious minorities, however, are not the only ones to feel uneasy in Muslim societies. In most non-Muslim countries, certain personal freedoms are now taken for granted, even if they are opposed to the religion of the majority. The underlying principle is that each person, man or woman, is entitled to equal respect, which means that the society must not interfere with his or her personal choices. The consensus is that each individual must be extended the maximum possible liberty compatible with equal liberty for others[15] and that, so long as one stays within such confines, the society has no right to punish one's personal choices.[16] On the basis again that all persons are equal, it is concluded that slavery is absolutely impermissible; there can be no discrimination on the basis of sex alone; each person is entitled to freedom of expression and freedom of religion and none can be punished for choosing or changing their religion; and so on. A corollary to the aforesaid is that there can be no limits on consenting adults freely associating with each other, particularly in the privacy of their homes.

The Quran, however, seems uncomfortable on some of these scores. As we shall discuss in later chapters, it does not always treat women as equal to men, it does not extend freedom of religion and expression of the kind that the above principle demands, and it makes the exercise of certain personal freedoms punishable, as evident from the following verse:

> The woman and the man guilty of fornication, flog each one of them with a hundred stripes, and let not any pity for them restrain you in regard to a matter prescribed by Allah, if you believe in Allah and the Last Day, and let some of the believers witness the punishment inflicted on them. (24:2)[17]

Does this suggest that Islam is out of touch with today's world? There is a level of incompatibility between Islam (as practiced) and modern thinking—this much is difficult to dispute.

And because the Quran also commands that the "Guidance and the Right way" prescribed by it must "prevail over all other ways,"[18] it is felt by some that there are all the elements of a conflict—termed by Huntington "The Clash of Civilizations." Therefore, either the world must be transformed to fit the Islamic framework (the agenda of Islamic extremists as well as missionaries, though they adopt entirely different approaches) or a fresh interpretation is required to adapt the Quranic message to modern living (the approach adopted by moderate Muslims).

But as the extremists, the missionaries, and the moderates pursue their respective visions, it is imperative that we engage them all on a more fundamental question, too: Is the Quran the word of Allah? The question is of relevance not just to Muslims but to all those interested in Islam. This book explores the answer.

For a fair inquiry into this question, the source of information needs to be impeccable. We shall rely fundamentally on the Quran itself—what better choice! Whether or not one believes in the Quran's divine origin, it is generally accepted (by its followers at least) that the Quran is very nearly (if not entirely) in its original form. We shall therefore consult the Quran to test the claim that it is beyond human ability to have authored a book like this. We will also rely on the book to discover the truth about Muhammad. It is worth noting that although we know remarkably little about the Prophet prior to the advent of Islam,[19] from that point onwards, all significant events in his life are documented in the Quran. The Quran thus provides a priceless opportunity to see Muhammad closely.

What translations should be used, though? In the Author's Note, we observed that each of the following translators is highly regarded in Islamic circles: Maududi, Yusuf Ali, Pickthall, and Hilali-Khan. This book will therefore engage them all, in the following manner: Maududi's translation will be the one generally quoted (as in this chapter), while Yusuf Ali's translation will be placed in the endnotes and at times even in the main discussion. The other two translations will also be included in the discussion from time to time but can otherwise be consulted in the appendix. The object is to present as fair an understanding of the Quran as possible, without placing excessive reliance on any one interpretation. What the reader may also discover upon consulting these translations is that, regarding a vast majority of issues taken up in this book, the conclusions are not affected by any particular translation, as all tend to agree.

With these observations, it is time that we let the Quran speak.

2

THE CONTRADICTIONS CHALLENGE

*Do they not ponder over the Quran? Had it been from any
other than Allah, surely there would have been many
contradictions in it. (4:82)*[1]

Allah's word cannot of course be contradictory, but, that said, it
goes to the Quran's credit that it is not hesitant to embrace the
above challenge.

To assess the claim, we shall split the discussion into three
categories: internal inconsistencies, mathematical deficiencies, and
scientific discrepancies. Absolutely none of these contradictions
can be attributed to Allah. One therefore expects the Quran to
clear the hurdle with ease.

INTERNAL INCONSISTENCIES

Internal inconsistencies are particularly embarrassing, as they tend
to show that the author has not presented his ideas coherently
enough, or even that he lacks the ability. No such errors are
expected from the Quran, but let us take some instances where it
appears to come perilously close to crossing the line.

- ### *"A day with your Lord"*

The Quran tells us:

> He administers the affairs of the world from the heavens to
> the earth, and the report of this administration ascends (to be
> presented) before Him in a Day whose length, according to
> your reckoning, is a thousand years. (32:5)[2]

It seems surprising that the affairs of the world should take a
thousand years to be presented to Allah,* but this timeframe is
repeated (albeit in a different context) in the following verse:

> These people are demanding of you to hasten the
> chastisement. Allah will never fail to fulfill His threat, but a
> day with your Lord is equal to a thousand years as you reckon.
> (22:47)[3]

This verse was revealed in response to taunts by disbelievers
who could not understand the delay in the punishment they were
threatened with.† They were informed that a day with Allah is
equal to one thousand years and so they must wait! But what is
perplexing is that this timeframe undergoes a dramatic change in
the following verse:

> A demander has demanded a torment (the torment) which
> must befall. It is for the disbelievers. There is none to avert it.

---

*   According to Yusuf Ali (who is somewhat supported by Hilali-Khan, but
not by Pickthall who agrees with Maududi) this verse refers to the affairs
being presented to Allah "in the end."

†   Regarding verse 22:47, even Yusuf Ali and Hilali-Khan do not suggest that
the timeframe mentioned in the verse has relevance to the affairs being
presented to Allah "in the end."

It will come from that God who is the Owner of the Steps of Ascent. *The angels and the Spirit ascend to His presence in a day whose measure is fifty thousand years.* So have patience, O Prophet, a graceful patience. (70:1–5)[4]

Apart from having to reconcile the two divergent timeframes disclosed by the Quran, the question also is: Why should it take the "angel and the Spirit" fifty thousand years "to ascend to His presence"? Particularly when the Quran also tells us:

And if My servants ask you, O Prophet, concerning Me, tell them that I am quite near to them. I hear and answer the prayers of the suppliant, when he calls to Me. (2:186)[5]

Is this a contradiction, or is the Quran simply being playful?*

•   *Believers versus nonbelievers*

The Quran expresses the confidence that just twenty believers with fortitude are sufficient to overcome two hundred nonbelievers and that a hundred of them will overpower a thousand:

O Prophet stir the believers to the fight. If there be twenty men among you who show fortitude, they will overcome two hundred men, and if there be a hundred such men of you, they will overcome a thousand of the deniers of the Truth, for they are a people who lack understanding. (8:65)[6]

What is a little surprising, though, is that this ratio changes significantly in the very next verse:

Now that Allah has lightened your burden, He has noticed that you are still weak; so if there be a hundred steadfast men among you, they will overcome two hundred men and if there be a thousand such men, they will overcome two thousand by

---

* Elsewhere, the Quran informs us that those who defied Allah's commands in the past were visited with chastisement. Could it be that they suffered for crimes committed a thousand years earlier (that being the timeframe for the affairs of the world to be presented to Allah)? Or possibly fifty thousand years earlier (that being the time "the angels and the Spirit" take to "ascend to His presence")?

Allah's permission. But Allah is with those people alone who show fortitude. (8:66)[7]

One may try to explain the apparent discrepancy on the basis of the words "Now that Allah has lightened your burden, He has noticed that you are still weak," but the fact is that both verses deal with the steadfast believers (i.e., those who have fortitude). Had verse 66 referred to the ordinary believers and verse 65 to the more steadfast believers, one may have more readily appreciated the significant imbalance.

It may be that the two verses were revealed on different occasions and put together at the time the Quran was compiled, on account of the fact that they cover the same subject. The Quran may not have come up with both in the same breath.

• *Inheritance shares*

The Quran is not expected to address all situations regarding inheritance. It therefore focuses on only a few, which then form the cornerstones of the Islamic law on inheritance.

One scenario specifically addressed by the Quran is that of the person who "leaves no children and no parents behind" but is succeeded by one or more siblings:

> ... And if the deceased, whether man or woman (whose property is to be divided as inheritance) leaves no children and no parents behind but has one brother or one sister alive, each of the two will be entitled to one-sixth of the whole but in case the brothers and sisters are more than one then the total share of all of them will be one-third of the whole after the fulfillment of the will and the payment of the debt (if any) provided that it is not injurious (to the heirs).* This is the Commandment of Allah and Allah is All-Knowing and Lenient. (4:12)[8]

This verse allows no doubt. The inheritance shares it identifies can be stated with exactitude:

The words "provided that it is not injurious (to the heirs)" suggest that the maximum aggregate share of 1/3 can stand further reduced, which exacerbates the contradiction with verse 4:176 (discussed below).

- If only one brother survives: 1/6
- If only one sister survives: 1/6
- If more than one brother/sister survives: 1/3

Does this verse apply only to half brothers and half sisters from the side of the mother alone? There is absolutely no mention of that in the above verse, but Muslim scholars are adamant that this is how it needs to be read. Maududi, for instance, informs us:

> All the commentators are agreed that in this verse brothers and sisters refer to *half* brothers and *half* sisters *from the side of the mother alone.*[9]

Mohammed Pickthall goes a step further and adds the limitation in the translation itself (albeit parenthetically, which is a technique employed to signify words that are not part of the Quranic text):

> And if a man or a woman have a distant heir (having left neither parent nor child) and he (or she) have a brother or a sister (*only on the mother's side* then ...).

Why so? And could the Quran not have made the addition itself?* The following verse at least answers the first question:

> People seek your verdict on (the inheritance left by) a childless person. Say, "Allah gives His verdict: *if a person dies childless and leaves behind a sister, she shall get half of his inheritance, and if the sister dies childless, her brother shall inherit her property; and if the deceased leaves behind two sisters, they shall inherit two thirds of the inheritance; and if the number of the brothers and sisters is more than two, the share of each brother shall be double that of each sister.* Allah makes His Commandments plain to test you lest you should go astray. Allah has perfect knowledge of everything." (4:176)[10]

Like verse 4:12, which was quoted earlier, this verse addresses inheritance in the context of a childless person and spells out the

---

* For instance (taking Maududi's translation as template): "And if the deceased, whether man or woman (whose property is to be divided as inheritance) leaves no children and no parents behind but has one *half* brother or one *half* sister alive *from the mother's side*, each of the two will be entitled to one-sixth of the whole ..."

shares of brother(s) and sister(s) who may survive the deceased. Let us see how it compares with 4:12, however.

Surah An-Nisa	Inheritance share if one brother survives	Inheritance share if one sister survives	Collective inheritance share if more than one brother/sister survives
Verse 12	1/6	1/6	1/3
Verse 176	The whole	1/2	2/3 or the whole*

The incompatibility between the two verses is too glaring to be missed. They clearly dictate shares contradictorily to one another, and significantly so.†

This thus explains the difficulty faced by Muslim scholars, who must make adjustments to avoid the contradiction. These scholars therefore have reached some kind of consensus that verse 4:12 refers to "half brothers and half sisters from the side of the mother alone." The fact that there is no mention of "half brothers and half sisters" in the Quran poses a difficulty but at least avoids the glaring contradiction. Moreover, if one is at all to read words into the Quran, it makes sense to ensure that the end result would not contradict yet other verses. Based on this sound principle, Muslims scholars had to clarify not just that verse 4:12 applies to half brothers and half sisters but also that they should be "from the side of the mother alone."

---

* Two-thirds applies if only sisters survive the deceased, but if there should also be a brother among the survivors, then the whole property (and not just 2/3 of it) would be inherited by the brothers and sisters.

† Verse 4:12 then also includes the feature, which is missing in verse 4:176, that the deceased should have no surviving parents—which makes things more complicated, considering that verse 4:176 reserves a larger share for brothers and sisters (even though the parents may also possibly be alive) than does verse 4:12 (which applies when the parents do not survive the deceased). This only compounds the difficulty.

But where does this leave the Quran? Revered by many as a masterpiece of articulation!

This difficulty would not have arisen but for verse 176, which was revealed in response to a specific question posed to the Prophet: "People seek your verdict on (the inheritance left by) a childless person." This does explain Quran's annoyance with needless questioning:

> O Believers, do not ask questions concerning such things which, if made known to you, would only vex you, but if you will ask such questions at the time when the Quran is being sent down, they will be made known to you. (5:101)[11]

And though the Quran also explains on another occasion that it has been sent down piecemeal rather than all at once so that "whenever they brought to you an odd thing (or a strange question) We sent its right answer to you in time and explained it all in the best manner,"[12] on this occasion at least, it seems to have fallen short of "the best manner."

• *Creation of the heavens and the earth*

The Quran announces the order in which the universe was created, first the earth and then the heavens:

> O Prophet, say to them, "Do you deny that God, and set up others as equals with Him, Who created the earth in two days? He indeed is the Lord of all creation. He set mountains over the earth (after its creation) and bestowed blessings on it, and provided in it means of sustenance adequately according to the needs and demands of all those who ask. This was done in four days. *Then he turned to the heaven, which was only smoke at that time.* He said to the heaven and the earth: 'Come into being whether you like it or not.' They both said: 'We do come in submission.' *Then in two days He made the seven heavens*, and in each heaven He ordained its law, and We adorned the lower heaven with lights and made it fully secure. Such is the design of the One who is the All-Mighty, the All-Knowing." (41:9–12)[13]

The sequence is repeated in verse 2:29[14] but is somehow reversed in the following verses, which tell us that the earth was created after the heavens:

> Are you (O men,) harder to create, or is the heaven? Allah built it: He raised its vault high and gave it balance, and covered its night and brought forth its day. *After that He spread out the earth from within it.* He brought out its water and its pasture, and set the mountains in it, as a means of sustenance for you and your cattle. (79:27–33)[15]

Maududi is aware of the discrepancy* and offers the following explanation:

> Among the earliest commentators the dispute has been going on for ages as to what was created first according to the Quran, the earth or the heavens. One group of them argues on the basis of this verse and verse 29 of *Al-Baqarah* that the earth was created first. The other group argues from verses 27–33 of *An-Nazi'at* that the heavens were created first, because there it has been clearly stated that the earth was created after the heavens. But the fact is that nowhere in the Quran has the mention of the creation of the universe been made to teach Physics or Astronomy, but while inviting towards belief in the doctrines to *Tauhid* and the Hereafter, like countless other Signs, the creation of the heavens and the earth also has been presented as food for thought. For this purpose it was not at all necessary that the chronological order of the creation of the heavens and the earth should have been presented, and it should have been told whether the heavens were created first or the earth.[16]

---

* In contrast, Yusuf Ali evades the issue by use of the word "moreover" (instead of "then" and "after that") in the referred verses, but is not supported by Hilali-Khan or by Pickthall, who agree with Maududi's translation. Interestingly, the revised translation based on Yusuf Ali's interpretation (as noted in endnote 14) reads: "It is He Who hath created for you all things that are on earth; *Then* he turned to the heaven And made them into seven firmaments." (2:29) But even in the original translation, the sequence in which the creation of the earth and the heaven is narrated does differ between verses 41:9-12 and 2:29, on the one hand, and verses 79:23-33, on the other. So the discrepancy is visible in Yusuf Ali's original translation as well, though not as pronounced!

One may, however, empathize with Muslim scholars who seem perplexed, and have been for ages, whether, according to these Quranic verses, the heavens or the earth came into existence first. The debate would not have arisen but for a clear contradiction within the Quran.

• *Destruction of Lot's tribe*

Lot was Abraham's brother and a prophet in his own right. The Quran tells us that his tribe was destroyed for practicing homosexuality. The following verses narrate the encounter between Lot and the angels who were tasked to carry out the destruction. The angels had presented themselves in the form of attractive men.

> Afterwards when these envoys came to the house of Lot, he said, "You appear to be strangers." They answered, "Nay, but we have come to you with that concerning which these people had doubts. We tell you the truth that we have come to you with the truth. You should, therefore, depart with your people in the last hours of the night and you yourself should follow them in their rear; let none of you turn round to look behind; go straight where you are being bidden." And We informed him of Our decree that they shall be utterly destroyed by the next morning. And the people of the town rushed rejoicing to the house of Lot. He said, "Brethren! These are my guests: therefore do not dishonor me. Fear God and do not put me to shame." They replied, "Have we not forbidden you to plead for all and sundry?" At last Lot pleaded, "Here are my daughters, if you are bent on it." By your life, O Prophet, they were at that time so intoxicated with lust as to be quite beside themselves with passion. (15:61–72)[17]

According to this account, the angels disclosed their identity, the purpose of their visit, and the command that Lot must depart with his people in the last hours of the night, before the people of the town arrived at Lot's residence. Surprisingly, though, this sequence changes in the following narration:

And when Our Messengers came to Lot, he was greatly perturbed and distressed in mind because of their visit and said, "This is a day of woe!" (No sooner did the visitors come to him than) his people spontaneously rushed towards his house, for they had previously been addicted to wicked deeds. Lot said to them, "O my people, here are my daughters, who are purer for you. So fear God and don't degrade me by committing evil to my guests. What! Is there not a single good man among you?" They replied, "You know it well that we have no need of your daughters, and you also know what we want." Lot cried, "I wish I had the power to set you right or I could find some strong support for refuge." *Then the angels said, "O Lot, We are messengers sent by your Lord. They shall not be able to do you any harm. So depart from here with the people of your household in the last hours of the night. And look here: none of you should turn round to look behind; but your wife (who will not accompany you) shall meet with the same doom as they.** The morning has been appointed for their destruction—the morning has almost come." Accordingly, when the time of the execution of judgment came, We turned the habitation upside down and rained on it stones of baked clay, and each one of these stones had been specifically marked by your Lord. And such scourge is not far from the workers of iniquity. (11:77–83)[18]

The Quran may possibly afford it, but this kind of variation would be fatal to a witness's credibility in a court of law.

• *Iblis (Satan): an angel or jinn?*

It may not ultimately matter whether Iblis is an angel or jinn, or perhaps both at the same time, but it is interesting to see how the Quran unfolds the truth. We may start with the following verses.

Just recall the time when your Lord said *to the angels*, "I am going to appoint a vice regent on the Earth." They humbly

---

*   In contrast, verses 15:61-72 do not mention that the angels informed Lot that his wife would meet the same doom. Interestingly, verses immediately preceding 15:61-72 tell us that before visiting Lot, these angels visited Abraham and disclosed that Lot's wife would suffer the same fate as his tribe, but when recording the encounter with Lot, verses 15:61-72 omit this aspect, which is at variance with verses 11:77-83.

enquired, "Are you going to appoint such a one as will cause disorder and shed blood on Earth? We are already engaged in hymning Your praise, and hallowing Your name." Allah replied, "I know what you do not know." After this he taught Adam the names of all things. Then He set these *before the angels* and asked, "Tell me the names of these things, if you are right (in thinking that the appointment of a vice regent will cause disorder)." They replied, "Glory be to You. You alone are free from defect. We possess only that much knowledge which You have given us. Indeed, You alone are All-Knowing and All-Wise." Then Allah said to Adam, "Tell them the names of these things." When Adam told them the names of all those things, Allah declared, "Did I not tell you that I know those truths about the Earth and the Heavens which are hidden from you? I know what you disclose and what you hide." *Then we commanded the angels, "Bow yourselves to Adam." All bowed but Iblis refused to do so; he waxed proud and joined the defiers.* (2:30–34)[19]

The Quran appears to suggest in these verses that Iblis is an angel. Why else would a command addressed to the angels apply to him? This impression is then confirmed by the following verses, for much the same reason.

And remember when *We commanded the angels* "Bow yourselves before Adam," *all bowed down but Iblis.* He replied, "Should I bow before the one whom you have created of clay?" (17:61)

Recall to mind the time when *We said to the angels*: "Bow yourselves to Adam," then *all bowed down except Iblis*, who refused. (20:116)[20]

The following account then introduces a slight variation by mentioning that Allah "created jinn from the flame of heat" but does not say that Iblis is one of them. He is still depicted as an angel.

We created man from dried clay of rotten earth, *and before that We had created jinn from the flame of heat*. Then recall to mind the time *when your Lord said to the angels* "I am going to create a man from dried clay of rotten earth. When I have brought him to perfection and breathed of My spirit into him, you should bow down before him all together." *Accordingly all the angels bowed down except Iblis*: he refused to join those who bowed down. The Lord said "O Iblis! What is the matter with you that you have not joined those who have bowed down?" He replied, "It does not behoove me to bow down before this man whom you have created from dried clay of rotten earth." (15:26–33)[21]

Another notable twist emerges in the following accounts, in which Iblis claims that he is created from fire, but he is still clubbed with the angels:

Indeed, We planned your creation, then We shaped you, and then We said to the angels "Bow yourselves before Adam." Accordingly all bowed save Iblis who did not join those who bowed themselves. Allah said "What prevented you from bowing down when I commanded you?" *He replied "I am better than he; Thou created me of fire and created him of clay."* (7:11–12)

Accordingly, the angels prostrated themselves, all in obedience, but Iblis assumed arrogance, and became one of the disbelievers. The Lord said, "O Iblis, what has prevented you from prostrating yourself before him whom I have made with both my hands? Are you assuming arrogance, or are you one of the high ones?" *He replied, "I am better than him: You have created me from fire and him from clay."* (38:71–76)[22]

Finally, though, the Quran discloses that *Iblis* is actually one of the jinn:

Remember! When We said to the angels, "Bow down before Adam." They bowed down but Iblis did not. *He was one of the jinns,* so he chose the way of disobedience to his Lord's Command. (18:50)[23]

The question is: Why did the Quran resort to such material variations, while describing one and the same occurrence? As for the status of Iblis (whether an angel or jinn), there may not be any necessary contradiction, if the jinn are but a subspecies of angels.

MATHEMATICAL ERRORS

The Quran is not expected to contradict the fundamentals of mathematics, such as the fundamental that it is not possible to divide a pie in shares that add up to more than one. We look at the Quran's discussion of inheritance shares again to see if it does

> As regards inheritance, Allah enjoins you concerning your children that: The share of the male shall be twice that of female. In case the heirs be more than two females, their total share shall be two-thirds of the whole and if there be only one daughter, her share shall be half of the whole. If the deceased has children, each of his parents shall get one-sixth of the whole, but if he be childless and his parents alone are his heirs, the mother shall have one-third of the whole. If the deceased has brothers and sisters also, the mother shall be entitled to one-sixth of the whole. The division of all these shares shall take place only after fulfilling the terms of the will and after the payment of the debt (if any). As regards your parents and your children, you do not know who is more beneficial to you. Allah has apportioned these shares and most surely Allah is All-Knowing, All-Wise. And you will get half of what your wives leave behind, if they be childless; but if they leave children, then your share shall be one-fourth of what they have left, after the fulfillment of their will and the payment of their debts (if any). As for them, they will be entitled to one-fourth of the inheritance left by you, if you are childless; but in case you leave behind children, their share will be one-eighth of the whole after the fulfillment of your will and payment of your debts (if any). ... (4:11–12)[24]

It is interesting to see how this works in the case of a deceased man who is survived by his mother and father, three daughters, and one wife.* The above verses spell out the following shares:

Daughters: "Allah enjoins you concerning your children. ... In case the heirs be more than two females, their total share shall be *two-thirds of the whole.*"

---

* We assume that he leaves neither a will nor a debt, so the entire property is available for distribution amongst the heirs.

Parents: "If the deceased has children, each of his parents shall get *one-sixth of the whole.*"
Wife: "As for them (wife), they will be entitled to one-fourth of the inheritance left by you, if you are childless; but in case you leave behind children, their share will be *one-eighth of the whole.*"

In other words:

Daughters: 2/3
Parents: (1/6 + 1/6) = 1/3
Wife: 1/8

But doesn't this add to more than one, exactly what we concluded is not mathematically possible to achieve?

This distribution has understandably caused disagreements among Muslim scholars. Some propose that the wife and the parents must be given their full Quranic shares and the daughters would get what is left.

Others (including some prominent schools) give an interesting solution. Recognizing that the total adds up to more than one and realizing that the Quran gives no indication about who is to yield (as all three categories are entitled to the prescribed share "of the whole"), they offer the solution that all must get ratably less. In other words, in the situation described above, no one shall get the share prescribed by the Quran; this is a perfectly legitimate solution, except that it also acknowledges the stark deficiency in the Quranic articulation!

Is this an isolated instance, though? One certainly does not expect the Quran to routinely yield shares that exceed one in aggregate. Let us revisit verses 4:12 and 4:176 to find the answer. This time, we consider the case of a childless woman who is succeeded by her husband and one full brother. Here are the shares prescribed by the Quran:

Husband: "And you will get half of what your wives leave behind, if they be childless." (4:12)
Siblings: "If a person dies childless and leaves behind *a sister*, she shall get half of his inheritance, and if the sister dies childless, *her brother* shall inherit her property, and if the

deceased leaves behind *two sisters*, they shall inherit two thirds of the inheritance." (4:176)*

If the husband is to inherit one half (according to verse 4:12) and the full brother is to inherit the whole (in terms of verse 4:176), doesn't the total exceed one? The problem is barely avoided when only the husband and one full sister survive. They both inherit one half each, which adds to exactly one, but the equilibrium is disturbed once again if two full sisters along with the husband should survive the deceased woman. The following applies in that case: "and if the deceased leaves behind *two sisters*, they shall inherit two-thirds of the inheritance." Can the husband be given one half and the sisters two-thirds at the same time?

This may also explain why Muslim scholars disagree so fiercely on inheritance shares, with different schools proposing entirely different solutions. There would be complete unanimity if the Quran were consistent with the fundamentals of mathematics.

SCIENTIFIC DISCREPANCIES

There are Muslim scholars who insist that the Quran is an absolute scientific miracle. We shall assess the claim at some length in Chapter 4, but for the moment, let us consider it unimaginable for God's word to contradict established scientific facts. Let us see if it does.

• *Man created from a spurting fluid*

In Chapter 1, we noted the very first verses of the Quran, which seem scientifically inaccurate in telling us that man is created from a clot of congealed blood. Interestingly, the Quran then informs us:

---

* Recall that to avoid conflict, Muslim scholars have restricted the applicability of this verse to full brothers and sisters and the applicability of verse 4:12 (i.e., the portion quoted earlier under the sub-heading "Inheritance Shares") to half brothers and half sisters from the mother's side only. Staying within the categorization suggested by Muslim scholars, we are taking the case of full brothers and sisters, to which verse 4:176 is said to apply.

Then let man at least consider from what he is created. *He is created from a spurting fluid that issues forth from between the backbone and the breastbones.* (86:5–7)[25]

This is intriguing. There is first the issue whether man was created from a clot of congealed blood or from a spurting fluid (sperm). But once past that, the suggestion that sperm is emitted "from between the backbone and the breastbones" poses an additional challenge, considering that if one draws a line between any part of a man's breastbones and any part of the backbone, the organs that actually produce and emit this fluid are missed every which way.[26]

We must, though, rule out the possibility that Maududi (and not the Quran) got it so wrong. Following are translations by Yusuf Ali and Hilali-Khan:

Now let man but think from what he is created! He is created from a drop emitted. *Proceeding from between the backbone and the ribs.* (Yusuf Ali)

So let man see from what he is created! He is created from a water gushing forth. *Proceeding from between the backbone and the ribs.* (Hilali-Khan)

Both translations agree that according to the above verses, sperm issues forth from "between the backbone and the ribs/breastbones." Interestingly, Pickthall translates the same verses as follows:

So let man consider from what he is created. He is created from a gushing fluid. That issued from *between the **loins** and the ribs.*

A closer look, however, reveals that Pickthall only cleverly hides the error—by resorting to an English word (loin) that covers within its range of meaning both the backbone and the genitals. The dictionary meaning of this word includes "the part of the body of a human or quadruped on either side of the backbone and between the ribs and hips" in addition to the more commonly understood meaning, namely "the reproductive organs."[27] Pickthall is thus able to make the Quran look scientifically more accurate in English, but is he honest in doing so? Even the gain is marginal, for it is still inaccurate to suggest that the fluid issues forth "from between the loins and the ribs." As a matter of fact, the fluid issues forth only from the loins (i.e., the reproductive organs), and the organs all the way up to the ribs (which are quite needlessly implicated by the Quran) have little involvement.

It is to Maududi's credit that he is not shy of confronting this embarrassing reality:

> "*[S]ulb*" is the backbone and "*tara'ib*" the breast bone, i.e. the ribs…. although different parts of the body have their own separate functions, no part can perform its function by itself but only in coordination with the other parts. No doubt the seminal fluid is produced by the testes from where it is emitted through a particular channel. But if the stomach, liver, lungs, heart, brain, kidney etc. are not performing their respective functions rightly, the system of the production of the seminal liquid and its emission cannot work by itself.[28]

The problem with the above verses is twofold. First, they inform us that sperm is emitted from organs that are actually unconnected with the whole process. Maududi tries to explain this particular deficiency, though if we are to accept his argument, it could just as well be said that the fluid is emitted from the brain or the heart—both, after all, are deeply involved in the larger scheme of things, as are many other organs. Second, the above verses omit mention of the organs that in fact are most directly involved. Maududi's explanation does not address the latter issue at all.

• *Sex of the fetus*

The Quran informs us how the embryo develops. According to it, determination of sex takes place after the limbs have been fashioned:

> Does man think that he will be left to himself to wander at will? Was he not a mere sperm drop, which is emitted (in the mother's womb)? Then he became a blood clot then Allah formed him and fashioned his limbs in proportion; *then from it*

He made two kinds, male and female. Has he not then the power to give life to the dead. (75:36–40)[29]

It is of course true (as is apparent from miscarriages as well) that limbs are fashioned just before the embryo gives the first *outward* appearance of sex in the form of genitals. On this basis, it was believed for a long time that the sex of the fetus is determined after the limbs have been formed. We now know, however, that sex is in fact the first thing to be determined—at the very moment of conception, instantly upon the ovum being fertilized by the sperm. It is therefore interesting that the Quran chose to go with the belief of the time!*

- **Hearts to think**

For a long time, thinking and understanding were functions attributed to the heart, which may explain why the Quran too draws the same association:

> Say to them, "Allah it is Who created you, and gave you the faculties of hearing and sight *and gave you the hearts to think and understand,* but you are seldom grateful." (67:23)[30]

> It is Allah Who has endowed you with the faculties of hearing and seeing and *given you hearts to think,* but you do not show any gratitude. (23:78)[31]

> And this is a fact that there are many jinns and human beings whom We have created (as if) for Hell. *They have hearts but they do not think with them;* they have eyes but they do not see with them; they have ears but they do not Hear with them. (7:179)[32]

---

* It needs to be noted, though, that other translators are slightly less forthright. Consider Yusuf Ali's translation, for instance:

> Does man think that he will be left uncontrolled, (without purpose)? Was he not a drop of sperm emitted (in lowly form)? *Then* did he become a leech-like clot; *then* did ((Allah)) make and fashion (him) in due proportion. *And of him He made two sexes, male and female.* Has not He, (the same), the power to give life to the dead?

Even according to the above translation, however, the sequence clearly reveals that sex is determined after the limbs have been formed.

In the same vein, the Quran also repeatedly tells us that the disbelievers will not understand, as their hearts (not minds) are sealed.[33]

Is the Quran metaphorical? Possibly so, but it has to be said that the point could easily have been made without reference to hearts at all, which would then have avoided any contradiction.[*]

What is also interesting is the extent to which the other translators go in order to resist this association between thinking/understanding and the heart, only to yield in the end. Yusuf Ali, for instance, translates verses 67:23 and 23:78 without reference to the heart. In contrast, Hilali-Khan and Pickthall translate the same verses by omitting reference to thinking or understanding (except parenthetically in one case), while mentioning the heart—in other words, the exact opposite of Yusuf Ali—but all agree that in verse 7:179, the Quran is referring to "hearts wherewith they understand not."[34]

• *Creation in pairs*

Some Muslim scholars find it incredible that the Quran knew so long ago that plants depict male-female variation. They rely on the following verses to make the point:

> He has created in pairs *every* kind of fruit, and He covers the day with the veil of night. Surely there are great Signs in these for those who reflect upon them. (13:3)

> Glorified is He Who created in pairs *all* species, whether of the vegetable kingdom or of their own (i.e. human) kind, or of those things of which they know nothing. (36:36)

> And We have created *everything* in pairs; may be that you learn a lesson from it. (51:49)[35]

The Quran does, of course, state that Allah has created *everything* in pairs, but is this accurate? It is instructive to note the following facts:

---

[*] For instance: "Say to them, 'Allah it is Who created you, and gave you the faculties of hearing and sight *and thinking and understanding*, but you are seldom grateful.'"

o A vast majority of plants do not have male and female distinction but are bisexual, in that they have male and female organs on the same plant.

o There are plant species that are entirely asexual.

o It is not true that every kind of fruit has male and female distinction (with the male fruit resulting in a male plant and the female fruit resulting in a female plant). Only fruits from plants that depict male-female distinction carry the attribute.

o Because the Quran tells us that Allah has "created everything in pairs," including also the animal kingdom, it is relevant to mention that even in this category, there are species that do not have males and females and that adopt the asexual form of reproduction and multiplication.

The following passages from *Encyclopaedia Britannica* substantiate the above facts:

Among lower animals and plants, it [reproduction] may be accomplished without involving eggs and sperms. Ferns, for example, shed millions of microscopic, non-sexual spores, which are capable of growing into new plants if they settle in a suitable environment. Many higher plants also reproduce by non-sexual means. Bulbs bud off new bulbs from the side. Certain jellyfish, sea anemones, marine worms and other lowly creatures bud off parts of the body during one season or another, each thereby giving rise to population of new, though identical, individuals. At the microscopic level, single-celled organisms reproduce continually by growing and dividing successively to give rise to enormous populations of mostly identical descendants.[36]

In most plant groups both sexual and asexual methods of reproduction occur. Some species, however, seem secondarily to have lost the capacity for sexual reproduction.[37]

Individual plants may be either bisexual (hermaphroditic), in which male and female gametes are produced by the same organism, or unisexual, producing either male or females gametes but not both.[38]

Asexual reproduction (i.e., reproduction not involving the union of gametes) ... occurs only in invertebrates, in which it is common, occurring in animals as highly evolved as sea squirts, which are closely related to vertebrates. ... Hermaphroditism, in which one individual contains functional reproductive organs of both sexes, is common among lower invertebrates; yet separate sexes occur in such primitive animals as sponges, and hermaphroditism occurs in animals more highly developed—e.g., the lower fishes.[39]

Biologists have so far "found some 2,000 living species in which they haven't seen a trace of sexual behavior,"[40] when just one such species would have been enough to refute the Quranic claim.[41] This is in addition, of course, to the vast majority of plants, which are bisexual (hermaphroditic) and do not therefore fit the statement that every kind of fruit and all species in the vegetable kingdom have been created in pairs.

People may not have known these facts at the time the Quran was revealed, but they are all well established today.

Regarding the question of how the Quran knows that some plants at least have males and females (even if it inaccurately extrapolates that to include all plants), the answer lies in the fact that date palms (the plant best known to the Arabs) carries this variation (see Chapter 4 for further discussion). This explains why the Arabs (incorrectly) thought that all living things, whether in the animal kingdom or among the plants, had male-female distinction.

*

The above discussion is not exhaustive of contradictions and discrepancies visible in the Quran but is perhaps enough to provoke thought. To close the discussion, it is worth reminding ourselves of the Quranic challenge that got us started in the first place. This time, we rely on Yusuf Ali's translation:

> Do they not consider the Qur'an (with care)? Had it been from other than Allah, they would surely have found therein much discrepancy. (4:82)

3

MUHAMMAD: THE LAST PROPHET

O Prophet, We have made lawful to you your wives ... and those women who come into your possession out of the slave girls granted by Allah, and the daughters of your uncles and aunts, who migrated with you, and the believing woman who gives herself to the Prophet. ... This privilege is for you only, not for other believers ... so that there may be no hindrance to you; and Allah is All Forgiving, All Merciful. (33:50–51)[1]

Muhammad, unquestionably, is amongst the most influential personalities in history. Many analysts would even place him at the very top.[2] To his followers, though, he must also be acknowledged as the finest ever.

It is pertinent, therefore, to see Muhammad through the eyes of his present-day followers. This is how they tend to view him:

- *Sadiq and Ameen:* Even before prophethood, Muhammad was widely regarded as *sadiq* and *ameen*—The Truthful and The Trustworthy.

- *Steadfast:* After being rewarded with prophethood, Muhammad tirelessly spread the word of Allah, unfazed by the unbearable hardship thrown his way.

- *Last Prophet:* Even Allah acknowledges Muhammad's exceptional qualities, by choosing him to be the last prophet—clearly a case of the best being reserved for last!

- *Selfless:* Muhammad selflessly served the cause of Islam for 23 years, never once using the platform for personal gains.

- *Leader par Excellence:* Muhammad commanded unparalleled respect amongst his companions and followers, exactly as one would have expected.

- *Gentle and Forgiving:* Despite facing hostility in the spread of Islam, Muhammad remained gentle and forgiving—more so than any other person in history.

- *Miracle Powers:* Some of Muhammad's followers (but not all) also believe that Muhammad had certain signs/miracles, which were meant to prove his prophethood.

- *Perfect:* Last but not least, it is believed that Muhammad was not just a great leader but was also perfect in his personal life, particularly in his dealings with the holy wives.

This is an impressive list, which explains the absolute hold that Muhammad commands over his followers today, but is it also true? We must consult the Quran to find out. Fortunately, there are enough traces in it for one to reconstruct Muhammad as he really was. The other advantage, of course, is that the authenticity of the Quran as a source in comparison to other accounts cannot be doubted.

Let us then take these attributes one by one and test them against disclosures made by the Quran.

SADIQ AND AMEEN

Muslims believe that Muhammad was regarded as The Truthful and The Trustworthy even before he declared his prophethood.*

---

* They believe that when Muhammad was to declare his prophethood, he first asked his tribe (the Quraysh) to certify that they considered him *sadiq* and *ameen* and only once they confirmed did he announce that Allah had chosen him to spread the message of Islam. His followers hence believe that

They ask, can a person with such immaculate reputation be expected to lie that he was the messenger of Allah?

This is based on what Muslim historians have recorded, but does the Quran also confirm that Muhammad was regarded as *sadiq* and *ameen*? As a matter of fact, it doesn't. This on its own may not have attracted attention, as the Quran was not expected to state facts known to all, but what makes the omission notable is that the Quran states other facts that also were well known—such as that Muhammad was illiterate[3] and that the Quran is written in Arabic (which is repeated numerous times). When seen in this particular light, the omission to state that Muhammad was regarded as The Truthful and The Trustworthy becomes more meaningful.

But there is also perhaps a more positive indication in the Quran that Muhammad may not have been regarded as *sadiq* and *ameen*.

They say, "Why was not this Qur'an sent down to one of the great men from the two cities?"* Is it they who distribute the mercy of your Lord? (43:31–32)[4]

One suspects that the disbelievers may not have spoken in this manner if Muhammad had carried the aforesaid reputation. The Quran at least should have retorted by reminding the disbelievers that Muhammad was indeed the best amongst them, that they themselves regarded him as The Truthful and The Trustworthy— provided, of course, it was true. That the Quran made no such attempt leaves one in some doubt.

Knowing, as well, that despite preaching in Mecca for thirteen years, Muhammad (as disclosed in the Quran) managed only a few supporters, one wonders if this too may have been different had Muhammad carried the reputation now attributed to him. It may

Muhammad commanded this reputation even before he was chosen to be Allah's messenger.

The "two cities" are understood by Muslim scholars to refer to Mecca and Ta'if (as noted in the translation by Hilali-Khan, for instance).

thus be that Muhammad only posthumously came to be regarded as *sadiq* and *ameen*.*

It is also important to make the point that even if Muhammad was truly regarded as *sadiq* and *ameen*, it does not follow that the Quran must therefore be the word of Allah. The following possibilities must also be considered.

- Muhammad may have viewed himself as a reformer who understood that any transformation he may present as his own would be rejected. Aware of the fact that lasting imprints were left by those who claimed to be prophets, he may have opted for a "noble lie."

- Muhammad may have had genuine visions of Gabriel delivering to him the "word of Allah," without there being any objective reality to it. Many people report similar experiences, though we treat them less charitably.

- Muhammad may have presented himself as the prophet of God for personal gain.

In principle, all these possibilities need to be weighed alongside the one that Muhammad was truly Allah's messenger. We defer assessment as to which is the most plausible possibility until Chapter 11.

HARDSHIP IN THE WAY OF ISLAM

The proposition put forward by his followers is that Muhammad would not have endured intolerable pain to spread the message of Islam unless he was truly the messenger of Allah. One is not sure whether to agree, considering that the adversity a person is prepared to face is indicative at best only of how strongly he pursues his views. It is no guarantee that the views are correct.†

---

* This should explain why Abu Talib, Muhammad's uncle and benefactor, never converted to Islam and preferred to die a pagan. Earlier to that, he may also have turned down Muhammad's proposal for his daughter Fakhita. (Armstrong: *Muhammad: A Biography of the Prophet*, p. 79)

† Muhammad's opponents also fought for their faith, and many of them even died in the process. Are we to hold that they too were divinely inspired?

It should also be informative to reconstruct the exact troubles Muhammad confronted. We shall do so by placing reliance on the Quran. Our focus will be on the thirteen (largely barren) years Muhammad spent preaching in Mecca before migrating to Medina, which is where he found success. Let us see what the Quran documents.

• *Forbidden from praying at the Ka'ba*

Amongst the first troubles faced by Muhammad and documented by the Quran is that he was forbidden to pray at the Ka'ba: "Have you seen the one who forbids a servant when he prays?" (96:9–10).[5]

The reference here is to Abu Jahl, a leader of the Quraysh, who forbade the Prophet. Abu Jahl must have found it objectionable that, despite abandoning the religion of the Quraysh and speaking foul against their gods and goddesses, Muhammad was still praying in their revered compound—which at the time was home to 360 idols. But then, people across the globe like to keep their places of worship "pure." Non-Muslims today are not even allowed to enter the holy cities of Mecca and Medina.

One is thus not sure whether this is truly a hardship worth mentioning.

• *Slander*

We learn next that Muhammad may also have been slandered occasionally.

> Abu Lahab ... was doomed to utter failure. ... Certainly he shall be cast into a blazing Fire, and (along with him) his wife too, *the bearer of slander.* (111:1–4)[6]

Incidentally, the italicized words are an interpretation, and the actual words—"carrier of the wood"—may hold other meaning too.* Assuming the Quran meant to refer to slander, it does

---

* Maududi includes the following explanation:
The words in the original are *hammalat al-hatab*, which literally mean:

appear odd that Abu Lahab and his wife should be doomed to utter failure and should be cast into a blazing fire just for that!

We learn that Abu Lahab was Muhammad's uncle and also father-in-law to two of his daughters. Muslim historians have recorded that when Muhammad started preaching Islam, Abu Lahab instructed his sons to divorce the wives, which they did.[7] That may possibly be the true reason why Abu Lahab finds special mention in the Quran. The charge of slander alone appears insufficient.

•   *Ridicule*

The Quran also mentions that the disbelievers used to ridicule the believers:

> The culprits used to laugh at the believers in the world. They would wink at one another when they passed by them. When they returned to their kinsfolk they returned jesting and when they saw them, they would say, "These are the people gone astray", although they had not been sent to be guardians over them. Today the believers are laughing at the disbelievers, as they recline on couches and gaze at them. Have not the

---

'carrier of the wood'. The commentators have given several meanings of it. Hadrat 'Abdullah bin 'Abbas, Ibn Zaid, Dahhak and Rabi` bin Anas say: She used to strew thorns at the Holy Prophet's door in the night; therefore, she has been described as carrier of the wood. Qatadah, Ikrimah Hasan Bari, Mujahid and Sufyan Thauri say: She used to carry evil tales and slander from one person to another in order to create hatred between them; therefore, she has been called the bearer of wood idiomatically. Sa`id bin Jubair says: The one who is loading himself with the burden of sin, is described idiomatically in Arabic as: Fulan-un Yahtatibu ala zahri bi (so and so is loading wood on his back); therefore, hummalat al-hatab means: 'The one who carries the burden of sin.' Another meaning also which the commentators have given is: she will do this in the Hereafter, i.e. she will bring and supply wood to the fire in which Abu Lahab would be burning. (Maududi: *The Meaning of the Qur'an*, note 4 to *Surah Al-Lahab*, Volume 6, pp. 619–620)

However, Hilali-Khan also support Maududi's interpretation: "And his wife too, who carries wood (thorns of Sadan which she used to put on the way of the Prophet, *or used to slander him*)."

disbelievers been duly rewarded for that they used to do? (83:29–36)[8]

These verses reassure the believers that they will have the last laugh when they are rewarded in the Hereafter for forbearing the ridicule. Note, however, that the Quraysh inflicted no more than gentle ridicule—*laughing, winking, and jesting*!

•   *Exile*

We move next to a more serious charge against the polytheists of Mecca—that they banished the Prophet from their city. Muhammad did migrate to Medina after preaching in Mecca for thirteen years, but the question is whether this was voluntary or forced.

The following verses are the first to draw our attention in this regard. They were revealed in Mecca.

> And these people have persistently been trying to uproot you from this land and exile you from it, but if they do so, they will not be able to stay here much longer. (17:76)

> These people (i.e. the disbelievers of Makkah) are devising some plans, and I, too, am devising a plan. So leave the disbelievers, O Prophet; leave them to themselves for a while. (86:15–17)[9]

These verses record that the Quraysh were "trying to uproot ... and exile" the believers and were "devising some plans," but would the Quran have stated it thus had the plans been implemented? It is also worth noting the evidence on the basis of which the Quran concludes that the disbelievers were devising such plans: nothing more than eavesdropping by angels!

> Have they decided to contrive a plan? Well, we too, shall contrive. Do they think that We do not hear their secret talk and their whisperings? *We hear everything and Our angels at their sides are recording it.* (43:79–80)[10]

Could it even be that the fears were largely imaginary? Certainly, had the Quraysh made any concrete efforts to displace

Muhammad, the Quran may not have relied on angels to prove the plans.*

Also instructive are certain verses that were revealed after the Prophet's migration to Medina. The Quran could now definitively document all the torture suffered in Mecca, as this was a matter of the past. Instead, it notes only the following:

> It is worthwhile to remember the time when those who rejected the Truth, were *making plots* against you *to capture you or to slay you or to exile you.* They were plotting their plots and Allah was devising His schemes: and Allah's schemes are most effective of all. (8:30)[11]

The Quran does not clarify whether the plot was to capture or slay or exile, but, more importantly, even in hindsight, the Quran accused the Quraysh only of "making plots," not of implementing them. This proves that even if such plots were devised (which is speculative), they were not implemented. The Quran would otherwise have stated things differently.

The following verse revealed in Medina is equally telling. It also confirms that despite thirteen years of preaching in Mecca, Muhammad found only a few followers.

> Recall to mind that time *when you were few in number* and were regarded as weak in the land *and were fearful lest the people should do away with you*; then Allah provided you with a place of refuge, strengthened you with His succor and bestowed pure and good provisions upon you so that you may be grateful. (8:26)[12]

The Quran reminds believers of the time when they were "few in number" in Mecca and "were fearful lest the people should do away with you." While such anxiety is quite natural—many minorities live under similar fears—the question is: would this have been stated thus if the Quraysh actually had done away with the believers? Or even some of them? This was also the perfect occasion for the Quran to list the violence committed by the

---

* We will see in Chapter 8 that exactly the same kind of evidence was employed to banish the Jewish tribe Bani Nadir from Medina. The charge in that case was that they were conspiring to kill Muhammad.

Quraysh, but it mentions only that the believers "were fearful"—not that what they feared ever materialized!

Objectively speaking, the Quraysh may not perhaps have been so antagonistic towards the believers as is commonly assumed. The Quran corroborates this assessment by mentioning that the believers, even after migrating to Medina, remained on friendly terms with the disbelievers of Mecca:

> O you who have believed, if you have come out (from your homes and emigrated) in order to fight in My way and to seek My goodwill, then do not make friends with My enemies and your enemies. *You show them friendship even though they have refused to believe in the Truth that has come to you, while they drive out the Messenger and you away only because you believe in Allah, your Lord. You send them friendly messages secretly, whereas I know full well whatever you do secretly and whatever you do openly.* Whoever from among you does so, has indeed gone astray from the right way. (60:1)[13]

> He only forbids you to take for friends those who fought you in the matter of religion, and drove you out of your homes, and cooperated with others in your expulsion. Those who take them for friends are indeed the wrongdoers. (60:9)[14]

This, too, shows that the Quraysh may not have been so ruthless.[15]

• *Murder attempt*

Muslim historians, however, insist that the Quraysh even attempted to murder Muhammad, specifically on the night he planned to leave for Medina, and that only Allah's help saved the Prophet.*

Maududi explains:

This plot was made at the time when the Quraysh realized that the Holy Prophet also was going to migrate to Al-Madinah. They felt that if he succeeded in emigrating from Makkah, he would be out of their reach and become formidable. Accordingly they held an urgent meeting of their chiefs in Dar-un-Nadvah (Council House) to discuss the matter and come to a final decision in regard to him. Some were

It is fair to note certain facts before concluding that the Quraysh did attempt to kill the Prophet. For instance, it is noteworthy that Muhammad lived amongst the Quraysh for thirteen years, during which he openly preached the message of Islam that was less than charitable to the religion practiced by the Quraysh, and yet there is absolutely no suggestion, whether in the Quran or in the accounts recorded by Muslim historians, that there was ever an attempt on his life prior to this last evening. The Quran does not even testify that any of his companions were ever killed or physically tortured.[16] It seems unlikely, therefore, that the Quraysh would have attempted to kill Muhammad on the very night when, dejected by lack of success in Mecca, he himself planned to leave.

Equally significant is that Muhammad left his family, including his wives, daughters, and Ali, in Mecca. If the Quraysh were intent on killing or capturing Muhammad, they could have used the family to force him to return. They did nothing of the sort, indeed

---

of the opinion that he should be chained and imprisoned for life. But this plan was not approved for it was feared that his Companions would go on working for the mission and would do their best to release him, even at the risk of their own lives, as soon as they would gain some power. The others proposed that he should be exiled from Makkah for that would at least relieve them of the "disorder" he was creating among them. Then it would not matter for them where he lived and what he did. But the chiefs rejected this plan, saying, "This man possesses the art of a charming speech and of winning hearts. If he leaves this place, he may go to the other Arab clans and win them over to his side, and then after gaining power, he may attack Makkah." At last Abu Jahl, putting forward his plan, said, "Let us select from each of our families one strong, stout and smart young man of high rank. They should all attack Muhammad at one and the same time and kill him. In this way, the responsibility for his blood will be divided equally among all the families of the Quraysh, and it will not be possible for Banu 'Abd Manaf, the family of Muhammad, to fight with all of them and they will be forced to accept blood-money for him." They approved this plan unanimously and nominated young men to kill him at the appointed time. Accordingly, the would-be murderers reached their places on the night fixed for the crime, but the Holy Prophet, throwing dust in their eyes, escaped safely from Makkah. Thus their plot ended in utter failure at the eleventh hour. (Maududi: *The Meaning of the Qur'an*, note 25 to *Surah Al-Anfal*, Volume 2, pp. 139–140)

even allowing the family to join him in Medina a few months later—except for his daughter Zaynab, who chose to stay in Mecca until after the battle of Badr![17]

Most decisively, however, it is the Quran itself that refutes the charge that the Quraysh attempted to murder Muhammad. Consider the following verses, which were revealed long after the Prophet's migration to Medina:

> If you do not help your Prophet, (it does not matter): Allah did help him before *when the disbelievers forced him to go away from his home*, and he was but the second of the two, when the two were in the cave. (9:40)

> Will you not fight such people who have been breaking their solemn pledge, *who conspired to banish the Messenger* and were the first to transgress against you? (9:13)[18]

The Quraysh are accused in these verses of breaking pledges, of conspiring to banish the Prophet, and of being the first to transgress against the believers—but not of conspiracy or attempting to kill the Prophet![19] It is thus fair to conclude that the charge regarding attempted murder is not well founded. The Quran at least does not corroborate it, and even gives indications of the contrary.

• *Ibn Ishaq on hardship suffered by Muhammad*

The above assessment is based on Quranic disclosures, but even according to Ibn Ishaq (the earliest biographer of the Prophet), the worst that Muhammad ever faced at the hands of the polytheists of Mecca is as noted below:

> Yahya b. Urwa … on the authority of his father … told me that the latter was asked what was the worst way in which the Quraysh treated the apostle. He replied: "I was with them one day when the notables had gathered in the *Hijr* and the apostle was mentioned. They said that they had never known anything like the trouble they had endured from this fellow; he had declared their mode of life foolish, insulted their forefathers, reviled their religion, divided the community, and cursed their gods. What they had borne was past all bearing, or words to

that effect." While they were thus discussing him the apostle came towards them and kissed the black stone, then he passed them as he walked round the temple. As he passed they said some injurious things about him. This I could see from his expression. He went on and as he passed them the second time they attacked him similarly. This I could see from his expression. Then he passed the third time, and they did the same. He stopped and said, "Will you listen to me O' Quraysh? By Him who holds my life in His hand I bring you slaughter." This word so struck the people that not one of them but stood still or silent. ... on the morrow they assembled in the *Hijr* again, I being there too ... while they were talking thus the apostle appeared, and they leaped upon him as one man and encircled him, saying "Are you the one who said so-and-so against our gods and our religion?" The apostle said, "Yes, I am the one who said that." And I saw one of them seize his robe. Then Abu Bakr interposed himself weeping and saying, "Would you kill a man for saying Allah is my Lord?" Then they left him. *That is the worst that I ever saw the Quraysh do to him.*[20]

*

To sum up, it is apparent that, apart from Muhammad's being forbidden to pray at the Ka'ba, receiving occasional ridicule, and possible banishment from Mecca, the Quran does not document any significant hardship imposed on Muhammad or his followers. Even regarding banishment, the more plausible possibility is that Muhammad chose voluntarily to leave Mecca, perhaps under the impression that the Quraysh were conspiring to banish him, but largely because he had not succeeded in developing a sizeable following despite thirteen years of preaching. He may have reckoned it was time to move on.

The Quraysh may not have been entirely friendly, of course. The Prophet, after all, was preaching against their religion, and it would be natural for them to practice some kind of social isolation, which is probably what the Quran is referring to when it says that the believers were forced to leave their homes. But on relative scale, considering what the world has seen through the ages and even in recent times, this kind of persecution is hardly worth listing.

It is difficult, therefore, to concede that Muhammad endured unbearable hardship of the kind that only a true prophet could.* Ironically, the above discussion may even show that the Quraysh were a rather tolerant lot. Muhammad's own approach towards other religions will be discussed in Chapters 7 and 8.

THE LAST PROPHET

Muslims firmly believe that Muhammad is not only a prophet but the very last prophet.[21] This belief exalts his stature above all other prophets—the inference is that Allah must surely have reserved the absolute best for last! The following verse is quoted as decisive of the issue:

> (O people) Muhammad is not the father of any of your men, but he is the Messenger of Allah and the last of the Prophets and Allah is the knower of everything. (33:40)[22]

Interestingly, when one consults the full context of the above verse, one finds that this critical declaration, that Muhammad is "the last of the Prophets," emerges in the midst of a discussion that is otherwise entirely about Muhammad's marriage to the divorced wife of his adopted son.† This is not the best setting one

---

* In fact, just in recent times, Nelson Mandela (who suffered twenty-six years of imprisonment) and Bobby Sands (who, for reasons good or bad, starved himself to death) endured far more to make their respective points. Neither declared himself to be divinely inspired.

† Verses 33:37–40 (also discussed later in the chapter in a different context): O Prophet, remember the time when you were saying to the man, whom Allah as well as you had favored "Keep your wife and fear Allah." You were at that time keeping hidden in your heart that which Allah intended to reveal; you were fearing the people, whereas Allah has a greater right that you should fear Him. So when Zaid had fulfilled his desire of her, We married (the divorced woman) to you so that there remains no hindrance for the believers in regard to the wives of their adopted sons when they have fulfilled their desire of them. And Allah's Command had to be carried out. There is no harm for the Prophet to do a thing which Allah has ordained for him. The same has been the way of Allah with regard to all the Prophets who

would recommend for such a vital announcement. Other verses
do provide a more suitable setting—for instance, the one that
mentions that Muhammad was a messenger who appeared after a
long time,[23] or the one that points out that he appeared after
many messengers before him.[24] These latter verses provided a
more natural context to state that Muhammad was the last
prophet and that there would be none after him. The opportunity,
however, was not availed.

One also discovers that what is interpreted by Maududi
(together with Hilali-Khan) as "the last of the Prophets" should
more accurately be translated as "Seal of the Prophets" (which is
how Yusuf Ali and Pickthall translate it).[25] The exact words used
by the Quran are *khaataman-nabiyyiin*, and because the word
khaatam is also used in other verses, such as the following, we can
get an exact feel of what it means.

> If Allah were to take away your hearing and your sight and set
> a *seal* upon your hearts ... (6:46)[26]

The exact translation, therefore, is "Seal of the Prophets," which
does not have the same connotation (not necessarily, at least) as
"the last Prophet."

There is, at best, enough doubt for the matter to also be
looked at in light of the following.

•   *Could the Quran have been clearer?*

It has to be said that the Quran could certainly have been clearer
in stating that there shall be *no other messenger* after Muhammad. It
is surprising that more trivial matters (such as how to perform
ablution) have been expressed with greater precision.[27] The fact
that the critical issue of Muhammad being the final messenger has

---

have gone before, and Allah's Command is an absolute settled
decree. (This is the way of Allah for those) who convey His
messages, who fear Him alone and fear none but One God: Allah is
enough to take account. *(O people) Muhammad is not the father of any of
your men, but he is the Messenger of Allah and the last of the Prophets* and
Allah is the knower of everything.

been addressed so casually in comparison suggests that the Quran did not consciously declare Muhammad as the last prophet.

• *Lack of emphasis*

The Quran is not shy of repetition. Whether regarding the Oneness of Allah or the instruction to establish *salat* and *zakat* or to fast during the holy month or to perform *hajj*; regarding the stories of Moses, Lot, or Abraham; or regarding the assertion that Allah has created everything in pairs, messages are repeated many times. In absolute contrast, however, when it comes to the declaration that Muhammad is the last prophet, not only is the language vague and the context unnatural, but the message is not repeated—not even once.

• *Told in Arabic*

The Quran repeatedly announces that it is sent down in Arabic so that the Arabs should "understand it well."* It even explains:

---

* For instance, *Surah Yusuf* verse 2, *Surah Ar-Raad* verse 37, and *Surah Ta-Ha* verse 113:

> We have sent it down as Quran in Arabic so that you (Arabs) may understand it well. (12:2)
> It is with this instruction that We have sent this Command in Arabic to you. (13:37)
> And, O Muhammad, thus have We sent this down as an Arabic Quran and have given therein warnings in various ways, perhaps these people may be saved from the perverseness or that this may help arouse understanding in them. (20:113)

Yusuf Ali's translations follow:

> We have sent it down as an Arabic Qur'an, in order that ye may learn wisdom. (12:2)
> Thus have We revealed it to be a judgment of authority in Arabic. (13:37)
> Thus have We sent this down—an arabic Qur'an—and explained therein in detail some of the warnings, in order that they may fear Allah, or that it may cause their remembrance (of Him). (20:113)

The same point is then made in *Surah Ash-Shuaraa* verses 193–195, *Surah Az-Zumar* verse 28, *Surah Ha-Mim As-Sajdah* verse 3, *Surah Ash-Shura* verse 7, and *Surah Ad-Dukhan* verse 58.

> Had We sent this Qur'an in a foreign tongue, the people
> would have said, "Why have not its verses been well
> expounded? What! The scripture in a foreign language
> and the listeners are Arabs?" (41:44)[28]

But with such naked focus on the Arabs, are we to conclude that
the Quran truly meant to depict itself as Allah's last word for all of
mankind?[29]

• *Indication of prophets to come*

The following verse, targeted at the Jews, also throws some
informative light on the issue:

> Give the good tidings of a painful chastisement to those *who
> reject Allah's revelations and slay His Prophets unjustly* and are
> deadly against those who rise up from among the people to
> enjoin right and justice. (3:21)[30]

There are two ways to interpret this: *either* the Quran holds the
Jews of Arabia blameworthy for the slaying of prophets that must
have occurred centuries earlier (considering that the Quran itself
mentions that no prophet had appeared to guide mankind for a
long time before Muhammad)—which of course would be
unreasonable, as the Jews who lived alongside Muhammad may
have been guilty of rejecting Allah's revelations (i.e., the Quran)
but not of slaying His prophets—*or* the verse is extending a
warning to those who may in the future "slay His Prophets
unjustly." In that case, could Muhammad be the last Prophet?

• *Kalima*

Finally, reference may be made to the *kalima*, which is recited to
mark a person's entry into the Islamic faith. This is how it reads:

> None has the right to be worshipped but Allah, *and
> Muhammad is the Messenger of Allah.*[31]

There is no mention, however, of Muhammad as the last prophet.

*

What this shows is that Muhammad may not have presented himself as the last prophet, and that this credential may perhaps have been added to his attributes after his death.*

A SELFLESS MAN

Muslims hold Muhammad in high esteem for serving Islam with total selflessness. Even if true, it should not necessarily mean that he was the messenger of Allah and the Quran His word. However, we must also find out through the Quran whether Muhammad was really as selfless as believed by his followers.

• *Entitlement to spoils of war*

The battle of Badr, the first in the name of Islam, provides a useful starting point. This took place soon after the Prophet's migration to Medina. Accounts corroborated by the Quran[32] tell us that the Prophet was planning to raid a trade caravan of the Quraysh returning from Syria that was led by Abu Sufyan. Because similar raids had taken place in the past, Abu Sufyan suspected the designs and sent for help.† Thus provoked, the

---

* There are accounts that after Muhammad's death, others made claims of their own prophethood but were swiftly put to the sword by Abu Bakr. It is possible that this is when Muhammad came to be regarded as the last prophet.

† Ibn Ishaq records the story as follows:

Then the apostle heard that Abu Sufyan was coming from Syria with a large caravan of Quraysh, containing their money and merchandise, accompanied by some thirty or forty men. ... When the apostle heard about Abu Sufyan coming from Syria, he summoned the Muslims and said, "This is the Quraysh caravan containing their property. Go out to attack it, perhaps God will give it as a prey." The people answered his summons, some eagerly, others reluctantly because they had not thought that the apostle would go to war. When he got near to the Hijaz, Abu Sufyan was seeking news, and questioning every rider in his anxiety, until he got news from some riders that Muhammad had called out his companions against him and his caravan. He took alarm at that and hired Damdam and sent him to Mecca, ordering him to call out Quraysh in defense of their

Quraysh decided it was time to take decisive action against the "caravan raiders." According to Muslim historians, the Quraysh gathered an army of about 1,000 that was confronted by 300 or so believers (though the Quran says that the disbelievers were twice the number of believers, which shows that the disparity recorded by Muslim historians is exaggerated).[33] All accounts are, however, agreed that the believers were victorious in the battle.

The question thus arose regarding the entitlement of spoils. The Quran initially declared that these belonged to Allah and His Messenger.[*] This may not have satisfied the believers, though, who appear to have demanded a definite share as well. The Quran clarified in a succeeding verse of the same *Surah*:

> And know that whatever spoils you have got, *the fifth of these is for Allah and His Messenger and for the relatives and the orphans and the needy and the wayfarers.* (8:41)[34]

The revised formula now allocated four-fifths of the bounty to those who participated in the battle and one-fifth to the Prophet and *"the relatives* and the orphans and the needy and the wayfarers."[†] This was definitely a more acceptable division for the believers and also provided them the incentive to participate in future expeditions, which may have numbered between thirty-eight and sixty, according to Muslim historians. Very few of these expeditions were defensive in nature.

More relevantly, the Prophet also secured a good enough share in the revised formula—even if not as healthy as the one the

---

property, and to tell them that Muhammad was lying in wait for it with his companions. (Ibn Ishaq, *The Life of Muhammad*, p. 289)

[*] *Surah Al-Anfal* verse 1:

They ask you concerning the bounties? Say, "The bounties belong to Allah and His Messenger. So fear Allah and set things aright among yourselves; obey Allah and His Messenger, if you are true believers." (8:1)

Yusuf Ali's translation:

They ask thee concerning (things taken as) spoils of war. Say: "(such) spoils are at the disposal of Allah and the Messenger. So fear Allah, and keep straight the relations between yourselves: Obey Allah and His Messenger, if ye do believe."

[†] It is not entirely clear why the Prophet's relatives should have deserved this privilege, though.

Quran had initially declared. To compensate for this reduction, on the odd occasion when the enemy surrendered without putting up a fight, as in the case of Bani Nadir,* the Quran increased the share of the Prophet and "the kinsfolk and the orphans and the needy and the wayfarers" to 100%.[35]

It is from such spoils that Muhammad thenceforth made his living. He did not indulge in any other trade or profession. Indeed, as more battles were fought and won—though the primary purpose of such battles must have been to spread Islam—the disposable income of the Prophet gradually increased. There is, however, a contrary indication in the following verse that some battles and raids may have had a different purpose. This is addressed to those who declined to accompany the Prophet on a certain occasion,† and the punishment prescribed for them was that they would not be allowed to accompany the Prophet when he set out to take spoils:

> *When you set out to take the spoils*, those who were left behind, will surely say to you, "Allow us too to go with you." They wish to change Allah's decree. Tell them plainly, "You shall not come with us. Allah has already said this before." (48:15)[36]

Does this suggest that there were battles and raids meant only for taking spoils, and not so much for the spread of Islam?

In any case, there is evidence that Muhammad's financial position improved perceptibly with time. As recorded by Ibn Ishaq:

> When the apostle distributed the captives of B. *al-Mustaliq*, Juwayriya fell to the lot of Thabit, or to a cousin of his, and she gave him a deed for her redemption. She was a most beautiful woman. She captivated every man who saw her. She came to the apostle to ask his help in the matter. ... He said,

---

* Bani Nadir and Bani Qainuqa were two of the three main Jewish tribes living in Medina. Their banishment is discussed in Chapter 8 (The Jews of Medina).

† When he went for *umrah* in 6 AH, resulting ultimately in the peace treaty at Hudaybya, a number of believers declined to accompany him, perhaps fearing that there would be a war with the Quraysh.

"Would you like something better than that? I will discharge your debt and marry you," and she accepted.[37]

The Prophet had accumulated enough resources to pay Juwayriya's ransom and could also afford this addition to his household—which may explain why "the relatives and the orphans and the needy and the wayfarers," who had a share together with the Prophet in one-fifth of the spoils, were not always happy with the division, as we shall see later.

• *Restriction to four wives*

Muhammad soon accumulated enough savings from the banishment of Bani Qainuqa and Bani Nadir and from other raids to sustain an expanded household. The problem in taking additional wives was not financial anymore; it was that the Quran placed a limit of four wives, which Muhammad had reached. The following verses were revealed at this stage to remove the bar from the Prophet:

> O Prophet, We have made lawful to you those of your wives, whose dowers you have paid, *and those women who come into your possession out of the slave girls granted by Allah*, and the daughters of your paternal uncles and aunts and of your maternal uncles and aunts, who migrated with you, and the believing woman who gives herself to the Prophet, if the Prophet may desire to marry her. *This privilege is for you only, not for other believers. We know what restrictions We have imposed on other believers concerning their wives and slave girls. (You have been made an exception) so that there may be no hindrance to you; and Allah is All Forgiving, All Merciful.* You are granted the option that you may keep aside any of your wives you please, and keep to yourselves any of them you please, and call back any of them you had set aside; there is no blame on you in this regard. Thus, it is expected that their eyes will be cooled and they will not grieve, and they will all remain well satisfied with whatever you give them. Allah knows whatever is in your hearts and Allah is All-Knowing, All Forbearing. *No other women are lawful to you after this, nor are you allowed to have other wives instead of them, even if their*

beauty may be very pleasing to you. You may however have slave girls.
Allah is Watchful over everything. (33:50–52)[38]

Although these verses (ostensibly) place limits on women
lawful to the Prophet—which may have been to placate the holy
wives who must have resented the continual erosion of their
status as other spouses were added to the household—it is the
exceptions to the rule that are more intriguing. Muhammad, in
addition to keeping slave girls, could take as many wives as he
liked from the following categories:

- o "women who come into your possession out of the slave
  girls granted by Allah"
- o maternal and paternal cousins "who migrated with you"
- o "the believing woman who gives herself to the Prophet"

Muhammad availed himself of all three categories, too.* As
recorded by Ibn Ishaq, he married thirteen times in all.[39]
Resultantly, Muhammad's wives must have lived in perpetual
anticipation of new additions. Ibn Ishaq records an interesting

---

* As noted by Maududi:

> Besides making the fifth wife lawful for the Prophet, Allah in this
> verse also granted him the permission to marry a few other kinds of
> women.
>
> (1) The women who came into his possession from the slave girls
> granted by Allah. According to this the Holy Prophet selected for
> himself Hadrat Raihana from among the prisoners of war taken at
> the raid against Bani Quraizah, Hadrat Juwairiyah from among the
> prisoners of war taken at the raid against Bani al-Mustaliq, Hadrat
> Safiyyah out of the prisoners of war captured at Khaiber, and
> Hadrat Mariah the Copt, who was presented by Maqauqis of Egypt.
> Out of these he set three of them free and married them, but had
> conjugal relations with Mariah on the ground of her being his slave
> girl. In her case, there is no proof that the Holy Prophet set her free
> and married her.
>
> (2) The ladies from among his first cousins, who ... had migrated in
> the way of Allah for the sake of Islam. The Holy Prophet was given
> the *chance* to marry any one of them he liked. Accordingly, in A.H. 7
> he married Hadrat Umm Habibah. ...
>
> (3) The believing woman who gives herself to the Prophet ... On
> account of this permission the Holy Prophet took Hadrat
> Maimunah as his wife in A.H. 7. (Maududi: *The Meaning of the Qur'an*,
> note 88 to *Surah Al-Ahzab*, Volume 4, p. 124)

account regarding the last illness of the Prophet. He notes this in the words of Aisha:

> The apostle of Allah returned from the cemetery to find me suffering from a severe headache and I was saying, "O my head!" He said, "Nay, Aisha, O my head!" Then he said, "Would it distress you if you were to die before me so that I might wrap you in your shroud and pray over you and bury you?" I said, "Methinks I see you if you had done that returning to my house and spending a bridal night therein with one of your wives." The apostle smiled.[40]

Muhammad died shortly afterwards. Aisha, barely nineteen at the time and already married for thirteen years, would remain a widow for another fifty-six years,[41] as "Mothers of the believers" (as the holy wives are designated) were not permitted to marry again.

•   Marriage to Zaynab

Amongst Muhammad's thirteen wives was his cousin Zaynab, earlier married to his adopted son Zayd. According to Arab custom, the divorced wife of an adopted son fell in the prohibited category. The Quran, however, removed the bar just before Muhammad was to marry Zaynab:

> Allah has not put two hearts in a persons [sic] body ... *nor has made your adopted sons your real sons.* These are the things which you utter from your mouths, but Allah says that which is based on reality and He alone guides to the Right Way. *Call your adopted sons by their father's [sic] names, this is more just in the eyes of Allah.* (33:4–5)[42]

Muhammad proceeded to marry Zaynab, but objections were raised. The Quran stepped in to categorically state that Muhammad had acted under Allah's command. The believers were also assured that, unlike some other privileges, this one was not confined to the Prophet—they too could avail themselves of it:

> *O Prophet, remember the time when you were saying to the man, whom Allah as well as you had favored "Keep your wife and fear Allah." You*

were at that time keeping hidden in your heart that which Allah intended to reveal; you were fearing the people, whereas Allah has a greater right that you should fear Him. So when Zayd had fulfilled his desire of her, We married (the divorced woman) to you *so that there remains no hindrance for the believers in regard to the wives of their adopted sons when they have fulfilled their desire of them. And Allah's Command had to be carried out. There is no harm for the Prophet to do a thing which Allah has ordained for him.* The same has been the way of Allah with regard to all the Prophets who have gone before, and Allah's Command is an absolute settled decree. (This is the way of Allah for those) who convey His messages, who fear Him alone and fear none but One God: Allah is enough to take account. (O people) Muhammad is not the father of any of your men, but he is the Messenger of Allah and the last of the Prophets and Allah is the knower of everything. (33:37–40)[43]

These verses were clearly intended to address the objections against Muhammad's marriage to the divorced wife of his adopted son, but they raise a more important question: What was the Prophet hiding? Had he secretly desired Zaynab while she was still married to Zayd? The following incident is recorded by Muslim historians:

> One afternoon Muhammad had gone to visit Zayd, who happened to be out. His wife Zaynab opened the door and because she was not expecting visitors was very lightly clad. Zaynab was now in her later thirties but was still said to be extremely beautiful and on this occasion Muhammad succumbed to her charms. He turned away hastily, muttering something that sounded like, "Praise be to God who changes men's hearts."[44]

According to these accounts, Zayd, upon learning of the incident, offered to divorce Zaynab so the Prophet could marry her. Muhammad declined initially but then relented and married Zaynab.

The account seems corroborated by the Quran: ("O Prophet, remember the time when you were saying to the man, whom Allah as well as you had favored 'Keep your wife and fear Allah.' You were at that time keeping hidden in your heart that which

Allah intended to reveal.") It is difficult to make sense of these words except in the context of the above incident. The occurrence must also have been widely known for the Quran to refer to it so openly.

Maududi, however, is unable to accept that the Prophet could desire a married woman:

> Some people have misconstrued this sentence to mean this: The Holy Prophet desired to marry Hadrat Zainab and wanted that Zaid should divorce her. But when Zaid came to the Holy Prophet and said that he wanted to divorce his wife, the Holy Prophet stopped him only half-heartedly. At this Allah said: "You were keeping hidden in your heart that which Allah intended to reveal." The real meaning however is contrary to this.[45]

He offers the following explanation:

> Allah had hinted to His Prophet [in order to remove a social evil pertaining to adoption] that when Zaid had divorced his wife, he would have to marry the divorced lady. But since the Holy Prophet knew what it meant to marry the divorced wife of the adopted son in the contemporary Arab society, and that too at a time when apart from a handful of the Muslims, the entire country had become jealous of him, he was hesitant to take any step in that direction. That is why when Hadrat Zaid expressed his intention to divorce his wife, the Holy Prophet said to him, "Fear Allah and do not divorce your wife." What he meant by this was that Zaid should not divorce his wife so that he was saved from facing the trial, otherwise in case the divorce was pronounced he would have to comply with the command, and thus provoke a severe storm of criticism and vilification against himself. But when the Holy Prophet deliberately forbade Zaid to divorce his wife so that he himself might be saved from what he feared would cause him defamation, Allah found this below the high position that He wanted His Prophet to enjoy, whereas Allah intended to effect a great reform through this marriage of the Prophet. The words "You were fearing the people, whereas Allah has a greater right that you should fear Him," clearly point to the same theme.[46]

Maududi's explanation is problematic. To begin with, it is entirely speculative and contrary to accounts recorded by Muslim historians. Maududi then suggests that the words "You were at that time keeping hidden in your heart that which Allah intended to reveal; you were fearing the people, whereas Allah has a greater right that you should fear Him" disclose the Prophet's reluctance (not his desire) to marry Zaynab. If so, the Quran cannot be commended for clarity. Most significantly, however, Maududi's explanation suggests that Muhammad dared play games with Allah—that he instructed Zayd not to divorce Zaynab in order to evade a situation *decreed by Allah*, simply because that would have proven embarrassing!

One also wonders whether adoption was really such a critical "social evil" to require instant corrective action at the hands of the Prophet, when other issues far more demanding of intervention were left entirely to Muslim jurists to fight. The Quran does not, for instance, bar slavery, as we shall see in Chapter 5. It is intriguing as well that the above-quoted verses address the case only of adopted sons, not of adopted daughters. Could this be because Muhammad's situation did not demand a verdict regarding the latter? The end result at least is that there is no clear bar regarding adoption of girls, though the "social evil" should be equivalent.

• *Entitlement to prisoners of war*

As noted above, Muhammad was allowed to marry "women who come into your possession out of the slave girls granted by Allah," and also to additionally "have slave girls" (33:50–52). There was also no restriction on numbers, as noted by Maududi:

> This verse explains why one is permitted to have conjugal relations with one's slave girls besides the wedded wives, and there is no restriction on their number. ... Here, of course, the Holy Prophet is being addressed and told: "It is no more lawful for you to take other women in marriage, or divorce any of the present wives and take another in her stead; slave girls, however, are lawful." This shows that no restriction has been imposed in respect of the slave girls.[47]

Muhammad availed himself of this license, too. Mention may particularly be made of Rayhana and Safiya, who were both admitted to the Prophet's household as slave girls, though Safiya would later marry Muhammad.

Rayhana belonged to Bani Qurayzah, the unfortunate Jewish tribe whose story is documented in the Quran and narrated in Chapter 8. After the Battle of Trench, all adult men of the tribe, including Rayhana's husband, were slaughtered and the women and children enslaved. While distributing the spoils, Muhammad chose for himself Rayhana, who remained his slave until the end.*

Safiya was the wife of Kinana, the chief of the Jewish tribe of Khaybar. Her account as recorded by Ibn Ishaq follows:

> When the apostle had conquered al-Qamus the fort of B. Abul Huqayq, Safiya d. Huyayy was brought to him along with another woman. Bilal who was bringing them led them past the Jews who were slain; and when the woman who was with Safiya saw them she shrieked and slapped her face and poured dust on her head. When the apostle saw her he said, "Take this she-devil away from me." He gave orders that Safiya was to be put behind him and threw his mantle over her, so that the Muslims knew that he had chosen her for himself. I have heard that the apostle said to Bilal when he saw this Jewess behaving in that way, "Had you no

---

*   Ibn Ishaq notes:

    Then the apostle divided the property, wives and children of B. Qurayza among the Muslims ... and took out the fifth. ... Then the apostle sent Sa'd b. Zayd with some of the captive women of B. Qurayza to Najd and he sold them for horses and weapons.

    The apostle had chosen one of their women for himself, Rayhana d. Amr, one of the women of B. Qurayza, and she remained with him until she died, in his power. The apostle had proposed to marry her and to put the veil on her, but she said: "Nay, leave me in your power, for that will be easier for me and for you." So he left her. She had shown repugnance towards Islam when she was captured and clung to Judaism. So the apostle put her aside and felt some displeasure. While he was with his companions he heard the sound of sandals behind him and said, "This is Tha'laba b. Sa'ya coming to give me the good news of Rayhana's acceptance of Islam" and he came up to announce the fact. This gave him pleasure. (Ibn Ishaq: *The Life of Muhammad*, p. 466)

compassion, Bilal, when you brought two women past their dead husbands?" ... When the apostle married Safiya in Khaybar or on the way, she having been beautified and combed, and got in a fit state for the apostle by Umm Sulaym d. Milhan, the apostle passed the night with her in a tent of his. Abu Ayyub, Khalid b. Zayd passed the night girt with his sword, guarding the apostle and going round the tent until in the morning the apostle saw him there and asked him what he meant by his action. He replied, "I was afraid for you with this woman for you have killed her father, her husband and her people, and till recently she was in unbelief, so I was afraid for you on her account."[48]

When Safiya was initially admitted to the Prophet's household as a slave girl, her husband was still alive. It was only subsequently that he was captured and killed. The Quran, however, ensured that this did not create a legal hurdle:

And forbidden to you are the wedded wives of other people, *except those who have fallen in your hands (as prisoners of war).* (4:24)[49]

*

What is remarkable, perhaps, is that Muhammad is still credited with serving Islam with total selflessness.

IN THE EYES OF THE COMPANIONS

From the absolute hold Muhammad commands over his followers today, it is but natural to conclude that this must also have been the case with his companions—those who were privileged to live alongside him. It should therefore be interesting to see what the Quran has to reveal.

• *Routine interactions*

In routine interactions, at least, one learns from verses revealed long after the Prophet migrated to Medina that the companions did not extend Muhammad any special respect. They treated him like any other and would even address him in raised voices.[50] To similar effect are verses revealed at the time the believers were preparing for the battle of Trench[51] and other verses[52] in which the believers are coaxed to respect the Prophet. Muhammad thus seems not to have commanded respect on his own—the Quran had to instruct the believers.

- ### *Secret consultations*

Matters get a bit more serious when the believers are accused of secret consultations against the Prophet:

> *Have you not seen those who were forbidden to hold secret consultations, yet they persist in what they were forbidden? They converse secretly together of sin and transgression and disobedience to the Messenger.* And when they come to you, they greet you in a way in which Allah has not greeted you, and say to themselves, "Why does Allah not punish us for what we say?" Hell is enough for them: they will become its fuel. What an evil end! *O you who have believed, when you talk secretly together, then do not talk of sin and transgression and disobedience to the Messenger but talk of virtue and piety, and fear the God before whom you shall all be mustered together. Conspiring secretly is the work of Satan.* This is done in order to cause grief to the believers, whereas it cannot harm them at all unless it be by Allah's leave. And let the believers put their trust in Allah alone. (58:8–10)[53]

One may think that these verses refer to the hypocrites,* but the Quran does state: "O you who have believed, when you talk secretly together, then do not talk of sin and transgression and disobedience to the Messenger." This suggests that some true believers must also have been suspected of indulging in the practice. What is also significant is that these verses were revealed after the Battle of Trench, a good eighteen years after the declaration of prophethood. It seems that Muhammad still did not command anywhere near the kind of reverence he receives today.

---

* The hypocrites are a convenient punching bag for Muslim scholars every time something goes wrong, whether at Uhad or during the Tabuk expedition or the slander incident, as we shall see below. It is always the hypocrites who are held responsible.

The other possibility is that Muhammad was simply paranoid and that the believers did not hold any secret consultation against him. This idea is not flattering, either, but it does at least help one understand the following command against backbiting:

> Do not spy, nor should any one backbite the other. Is there any among you who would like to eat the flesh of his dead brother? (49:12)[54]

This command is perhaps best understood as reflective of the Prophet's mistrust of the believers, as one would not normally place backbiting on par with eating a dead brother's flesh.

- ### *Warfare*

Did the believers show greater respect to Muhammad during times of war?

Our first inquiry in this regard relates to the Battle of Uhad.* It is reported that 1,000 men of Medina initially committed to join the Prophet in the battle but 300 of them withdrew at the last moment under Abdullah bin Ubbay. Only the more steadfast went to the battlefield.

Muslim historians record that once the Prophet reached Uhad, he assigned fifty archers to protect a strategic location to prevent the enemy attacking from the rear. He also instructed the archers to guard their position no matter how the battle turned.† These

---

*   This was the "revenge match" staged by the Quraysh, who lost the first battle at Badr and challenged the believers to a sequel—though there are accounts that this too was in response to continuing raids on Meccan trade caravans. (Rogerson: *The Prophet Muhammad*, pp. 153–154)

†   Ibn Ishaq records:

> He *[the apostle]* put his camels and army towards Uhad and said, "Let none of you fight until we give the word." ... There were 50 archers, and he said, "keep the cavalry away from us with your arrows and let them not come on us from the rear whether the battle goes in our favor or against us; and keep your place so that we cannot be got at from any direction." The apostle then put on two coats of mail and delivered the standard to Mus'ab b. 'Umayr. ... Then God sent his help to the Muslims and fulfilled His promise. They slew the enemy with the sword until they cut them off from their camp and there was an obvious rout. ... There was nothing at

archers, however, upon seeing that the believers had made some initial gains, disobeyed the command and left the spot. This allowed the enemy to attack from the rear, resulting in a massive defeat for the believers.

The Quran confirms that the believers suffered defeat and explains that this was "so that Allah may test from among you who were believers and choose the righteous witnesses of the Truth."[55] This seems fine, except that the Quran had earlier promised the believers: "Allah will help you with (not three thousand but) five thousand angels, known by certain marks, *in case of a sudden attack from the enemy.*"[56] But when the sudden attack did take place, the angels were slow to react, resulting in a major defeat for the believers.

The Quran also then tells us how the Prophet's companions behaved in the midst of the battle. Remember, the following account is regarding the more steadfast believers, as the hypocrites had already withdrawn before the battle.[57]

> Allah did fulfill His promise (of help) to you in the initial stage of the battle, it was you who were killing them by Allah's leave *until you lost heart and disputed about your duty and disobeyed your leader, when Allah showed you what (the spoils) you coveted, for there were among you some who hankered after the life of this world, and others who cherished the Life-after-death.* Then Allah caused your retreat before the disbelievers in order to test you, but the fact is that even then Allah pardoned you, for Allah is very gracious to the believers. *Recall how you were fleeing in such a panic that you did not even look back at one another, and the Messenger in your rear was calling out to you.* Consequently, Allah inflicted upon you one sorrow after the other so that you may learn this lesson for the future that you should not grieve for what you have lost and for any misfortune that might befall you: Allah is fully aware of all that you are doing. (3:152–153)[58]

These verses make the following important disclosures:

---

all to prevent anyone seizing them when the archers turned aside to the camp when the enemy had been cut off from it (T. making for the spoil). Thus they opened our rear to the cavalry and we were attacked from the behind. (Ibn Ishaq: *The Life of Muhammad*, pp. 373, 379)

o *The believers "disobeyed" the Prophet.* This is not something one expects from their successors today, which goes to show that Muhammad did not perhaps command the same respect amongst his own companions that he now does.

o *The believers had "disobeyed" because of the spoils.** This raises the question: Did the believers not trust the Prophet with equitable distribution? This, at least, is what the Quran suggests: "It is not conceivable that a Prophet should ever commit breach of trust" (3:161).[59] Maududi, too, clarifies in respect of this verse:

> This is the answer to the suspicion of the archers about the honesty of the Holy Prophet in regard to the division of the spoils. When they saw their companions plunder the enemy, the archers feared that the former would get the whole of the spoil and they would be deprived of it at the time of division; just because they had not taken part in the plunder. That is why they spontaneously deserted their posts.[60]

o *The believers fled while "the Messenger in your rear was calling out to you."* If there were any who stayed to defend the Prophet, the Quran does not mention them. Uthman, the third Caliph and twice the Prophet's son-in-law, is clearly listed by Muslim historians amongst those who fled.[61]

One may have thought that there was no greater honor for a believer than to embrace martyrdom in the very presence of the last Prophet, and yet they fled, those who lived alongside Muhammad, leaving the Prophet stranded!† The Quran tells us further that these deserters also subsequently doubted the whole strategy adopted by the Prophet.[62] It is absolutely unimaginable that today's Muslims would behave in similar fashion.

We move next to the last phase of the Prophet's career—to the *Tabuk* expedition against the "people of the Book," which is also mentioned in Chapter 7 (The Sword Verses). The Prophet needed

---

' As noted in the above verses: "when Allah showed you what (the spoils) you coveted, for there were among you some who hankered after the life of this world."

† According to historical accounts, the Quraysh left the battlefield under the impression that Muhammad had been killed.

a sizeable contingent to accompany him for the expedition to be successful, but many believers declined to go. *Surah At–Taubah* reports this:

> O *you who believed!* What was amiss with you that, when you were asked to march forth on the Way of Allah, you clung to the earth? What! Did you prefer the life of this world to the life of the Hereafter? (9:38)[63]

A long tirade spread over ninety-odd verses criticizes those who did not accompany the Prophet. Much of it is addressed to the hypocrites, but the true believers are not spared, either. The above verse, for instance, is clearly addressed to the believers, and there are other verses, as well.[64]

One can't help but note that today's misguided suicide bombers, who routinely kill themselves in the mere hope (admittedly false) that Muhammad will receive them as martyrs, at the gates of paradise, show far greater regard for the Prophet than did those who actually lived alongside him.

• *The Friday sermon*

The battlefield has its own dynamics, not always conducive to bringing out the best in people. One must not, therefore, be too critical of the believers who fled at Uhad and of others who failed to accompany the Prophet to Tabuk. But what about the Friday sermons that Muhammad used to deliver? They surely presented a very different setting. One would expect the believers to be totally immersed in the experience, catching each and every word uttered by the last Prophet. This is not exactly the picture painted by the Quran:

> O you who have believed, when the call is made to the Prayer on Friday, hasten to the remembrance of Allah and leave off your trading. This is better for you only if you knew. Then when the Prayer is over, disperse in the land and seek Allah's bounty, and remember Allah much; perhaps you may achieve success. *And when they saw some merchandise and sport they broke off to it and left you standing.* Say to them, "That which is with Allah

is far better than sport and business, and Allah is the best of all providers." (62:9–11)[65]

Maududi elaborates:

> This is the incident because of which the commandment pertaining to the Friday congregational prayer has been enjoined in the previous verses. ... A trade caravan from Syria arrived in Madinah right at the time of the Friday Prayer and its people started playing their drums to announce their arrival. The Holy Prophet (upon whom be Allah's peace) at that time was delivering the Sermon. Hearing the drum the people in the congregation became impatient and rushed out towards Baqi' where the caravan had halted, except for 12 men.[66]

If one goes by the other three translations (which are somewhat as follows: "But when they see some bargain or some amusement, they disperse headlong to it and leave thee standing"), it seems that the Quran is not referring to an isolated incident but a more regular feature.*

• *As judge and decision maker*

Despite the above discussion, one may not have imagined that the believers, after presenting their disputes to Muhammad for adjudication, would be resentful of his verdict. One expects, rather, that they would *always* have bowed to his decisions with total submission. The Quran has the following to say, however:

> Nay, O Muhammad, by your Lord, they can never become Believers until they accept you as a judge for the decision of disputes between them, and then surrender to your decision

---

* Maududi (see: *The Meaning of the Qur'an*, commentary to *Surah Al-Jumuah*) suggests that this incident must have taken place during the early period in Medina (when the believers were not so well trained), but if the remaining verses of this short *surah* (in which the Jews are severely criticized—this was never the case during the early period of Medina) are any indication, the incident took place much later. Most scholars, in fact, date the *surah*, or at least the rest of it, to the seventh year after migration.

with entire submission without feeling the least resentment in their hearts. (4:65)[67]

The above verse deals with disputes referred to the Prophet for adjudication. The following regards decisions by Muhammad generally:

> *It does not behoove a believing man and a believing woman that when Allah and His Messenger have given their decision in a matter, they should exercise an option in that matter of theirs,* and whoever disobeys Allah and His Messenger has indeed strayed into manifest error. (33:36)[68]

If one accepts this account, this means that the believers used to exercise options of their own even once Muhammad had given a decision in the matter! The practice must also have been common enough for the Quran to address it.

- ### *Distribution of* sadaqat

Sadaqat include *zakat,* spoils of war, and also, interestingly, the amount the believers were advised by the Quran to contribute (if they could) when seeking consultation with the Prophet: "O you who have believed, when you consult the Messenger in private, you should give something in charity before your consultation" (58:12).[69] Muhammad, as the head of the community, distributed the *sadaqat* amongst the deserving while keeping a share for himself as permitted by the Quran. Could this have raised the slightest suspicion or controversy? Absolutely not! (One would think.) The Quran, however, has the following to say:

> O Prophet, there are some who find fault with you concerning the distribution of *sadaqat* (*zakat* collection): if something is given to them thereof, they are pleased and if they are not given anything thereof, they become *angry.* (9:58)[70]

This seems a huge departure from the pagans of Mecca, who are said to have regarded Muhammad as *sadiq* and *ameen.* Could it be the special privileges extended to Muhammad by the Quran that ultimately took a toll?

• *The slander incident*

Mention must in particular be made of the "slander incident."
This relates to the Prophet's wife Aisha. Ibn Ishaq quotes Aisha in
this behalf:

> When the apostle intended to go on an expedition he cast lots
> between his wives which of them should accompany him. He
> did this on the occasion of the raid on B. al-Mustaliq and the
> lot fell on me, so the apostle took me out. ... When the
> apostle finished his [return] journey on this occasion he
> started back and halted when he was near Medina and passed
> a part of the night there. Then he gave permission to start and
> the men moved off. I went out for a certain purpose having a
> string of Zafar beads on my neck. When I had finished, it
> slipped from my neck without my knowledge, and when I
> returned to the camel I went feeling my neck for it but could
> not find it. Meanwhile the main body had already moved off. I
> went back to the place where I had been and looked for the
> necklace until I found it. The men who were saddling the
> camel for me came up to the place I had just left and having
> finished the saddling they took hold of the howdah thinking
> that I was in it as I normally was, picked it up and bound it on
> the camel, not doubting that I was in it. Then they took the
> camel by the head and took off with it. I returned to the place
> and there was not a soul there. The men had gone. So I
> wrapped myself in my smock and then lay down where I was
> knowing that if I were missed they would come back for me,
> and by Allah I had but just lain down when Safwan b. al-
> Muattal al-Sulami passed me; he had fallen behind the main
> body for some purpose and had not spent the night with the
> troops. He saw my form and came and stood over me. He
> used to see me before the veil was prescribed for us, so when
> he saw me he exclaimed in astonishment "The apostle's wife"
> while I was wrapped in my garments. He asked me what had
> kept me behind but I did not speak to him. Then he brought
> up his camel and told me to ride while he kept behind. So I
> rode it and he took the camel's head going forward quickly in
> search of the army, and by Allah we did not overtake them
> and I was not missed until the morning. The men had halted
> and when they were rested up came the man leading me and

the liars spread their reports and the army was much disturbed. But by Allah I knew nothing about it.

Then we came to Medina and immediately I became very ill and so heard nothing of the matter. The story had reached the apostle and my parents, yet they told me nothing of it though I missed the apostle's accustomed kindness to me. When I was ill he used to show compassion and kindness to me, but in this illness he did not and I missed his attentions. When he came in to see me when my mother was nursing me, all he said was, "How is she?" so that I was pained and asked him to let me be taken to my mother so that she could nurse me.

Aisha mentions that she learned of the slander while at her parents' house. She then continues her narration:

The apostle ... came in to see me. He called Ali and Usama b. Zayd and asked their advice. Usama spoke highly of me. ... As for Ali, he said: "Women are plentiful, and you can easily change one for another. Ask the slave girl, for she will tell you the truth." So the apostle called Burayra to ask her, and Ali got up and gave her a violent beating, saying, "Tell the apostle the truth,"* to which she replied, "I know only good of her. The only fault I have to find with Aisha is that when I am kneading dough and tell her to watch it she neglects it and falls asleep and sheep comes and eats it!" Then the apostle came in to me. My parents and a woman of the Ansar were with me and both of us were weeping. He sat down and after praising God he said, "Aisha you know what people say about you. Fear God and if you have done wrong as men say then repent towards God, for he accepts repentance from his slaves." As he said this my tears ceased and I could not feel them. I waited for my parents to answer the apostle but they said nothing. ... When I saw that my parents would not speak I asked them why, and they replied that they did not know what to answer, and by Allah I do not know a household which suffered as did the family of Abu Bakr in those days. When they remained silent my weeping broke out afresh and then I said: "Never will I repent towards God of what you

---

* This may explain the cause of the battle between Ali and Aisha a few years later, as referenced in Chapter 1.

mention. By Allah, I know that if I were to confess what men say of me, God knowing that I am innocent of it, I should admit what did not happen; and if I denied what they said you would not believe me." ... so I said "I will say what the father of Joseph said: 'My duty is to show becoming patience and God's aid is to be asked against what you describe.'"

And, by God, the apostle had not moved from where he was sitting when there came over him from God what used to come over him and he was wrapped in his garment and a leather cushion was put under his hand. As for me, when I saw this I felt no fear or alarm, for I knew that I was innocent and that God would not treat me unjustly. As for my parents, as soon as the apostle recovered I thought that they would die from fear that confirmation would come from God of what men had said. Then the apostle recovered and sat up and there fell from him as it were drops of water on a winter day, and he began to wipe the sweat from his brow, saying, "Good news, Aisha! God has sent down (word) about your innocence." I said, "Praise be to God," and he went out to the men and addressed them and recited to them what God had sent down concerning that (T. "me"). Then he gave orders about Mistah b. Uthaha and Hassan b. Thabit and Hamna d. Jahsh who were the most explicit in their slander and they were flogged with the prescribed number of stripes.[71]

Muslim scholars attribute the slander to the hypocrites. Only grudgingly do they concede that some true believers were also involved:

Besides the hypocrites, some true Muslims also had been involved in this campaign, and among them who took leading part in it, were Mistah, Hassan bin Thabit, the famous poet of Islam, and Hamnah, daughter of Jahsh and sister of Hadrat Zainab.[72]

As opposed to that, the Quran is more forthright:

Those who have invented the slander are some of your own people. You should not however regard this matter as evil, for it has good in it for you. Whoso took any part in this, he earned his share of the sin accordingly, and the one who had the greatest share of responsibility in it, shall have a terrible punishment. *When you heard of it, why didn't the believing men and the believing women have a good opinion of themselves, and why did they not say, "This is a manifest slander."* Why did the slanderers not bring four witnesses (to prove their charge)? Now that they have not brought witnesses, they themselves are liars in the sight of Allah. Were it not for Allah's grace and mercy towards you in this world and in the Hereafter, a painful scourge would have visited you because of the things in which you were involved (just think how erroneous you were) when you passed this lie on from one tongue to the other and uttered with your mouths that of which you had no knowledge. You took it as a trifling matter whereas it was a great offense in the sight of Allah. Why did you not, as soon as you heard of it, say, "It is not proper for us to utter such a thing? Glory be to Allah! This is a great slander." Allah admonishes you that in future you should never repeat a thing like this, if you are true Believers. Allah makes His revelations clear to you, and He is All-Knowing, All-Wise. (24:11–18)[73]

These verses are quite obviously addressed entirely to the believers. There is no mention of the hypocrites at all. It may be noted that the Quran does not mince words when it refers to the hypocrites; an entire *surah* in the Quran is thus dedicated to their conduct, but not so here. In this case, the Quran places the blame entirely and only on the believers: "Those who have invented the slander are some of your own people … why didn't the believing men and the believing women have a good opinion of themselves."

*

All the above accounts are unanimous that Muhammad's stature has risen with time. Those who lived alongside him may not have noticed some of the qualities his followers today are so acutely aware of. They also did not extend him the same respect and reverence that today's Muslims do. The most surprising aspect is that even in respect of an exceedingly sensitive matter, that of Aisha's honor, the believers treated Muhammad with no special regard.

A MAN OF MERCY

Unlike Jesus, who regularly interacted with lepers, or so we are told,[74] Muhammad may not have extended his sense of kindness this far. Ibn Ishaq records that one of his wives (Asma) was "found to be suffering from leprosy and so returned to her people."[75] The following verse may be referring to this incident (though open to alternative interpretation):

> You [the Prophet] are granted the option that you may keep aside any of your wives you please ... and call back any of them you had set aside; there is no blame on you in this regard. (33:51)[76]

But that aside, Muhammad is believed by his followers to be the most merciful man in history—who else would have announced a general amnesty upon the conquest of Mecca that those taking refuge in their homes or in the Ka'ba or with his sworn enemy Abu Sufyan would all be forgiven? His followers tend to believe that not a single person was resultantly executed, which stands at the heart of Muhammad's image as a forgiving man.

It is true that Muhammad did not treat the Meccans like he treated the Jews (as we shall see in Chapter 8), but then, the Meccans were his kith and kin. They may also not have been so ruthless towards the believers as is commonly believed.* It is not surprising, therefore, that the Prophet showed greater sympathy for them than for the Jews. As for Abu Sufyan, it is noteworthy that even he was by now amongst Muhammad's fathers-in-law. One must not therefore draw too much from the special privilege extended to him on the occasion.

The fact also is that not everyone was forgiven upon the conquest of Mecca. Maududi notes:

> At the conquest of Makkah, the Holy Prophet forgave all the people of Makkah except only a few men, and did not kill

---

* if the discussion in the earlier section "Hardship in the Way of Islam" has merit

more than three or four of even those who had been made an exception.[77]

Incidentally, the exceptions included women too, as we shall see in Chapter 5. The killings, moreover, were exactly as commanded by the Quran:

> The punishment of those who wage war against Allah and His Messenger and run about to spread mischief in the land is this: they should be put to death or crucified or their alternate hands and feet should be cut off, or they should be banished from the land. (5:33–34)[78]

The killings were also not unprecedented, as noted by Maududi:

> But since in this verse [*Surah Muhammad*, verse 4] it has neither been clearly forbidden to kill the prisoner the Holy Prophet understood this intention of Allah's Command, and also acted accordingly, that if there was a special reason for which the ruler of an Islamic government regarded it as necessary to kill a particular prisoner (or prisoners) he could do so. This is not the general law but an exception to it, which would be applied only when necessary. Thus, the Holy Prophet put to death only 'Uqbah bin AbiMu'ait and Nadr bin Al-Harith from among the 70 prisoners taken at Badr, and only the poet Abu Azzah from the prisoners taken at Uhad. *Since the Bani Quraizah had surrendered on the condition that they would accept whatever decision Hadrat Sa'd bin Mu'adh would give in their regard, and he had decreed that all the males of the Quraizah should be killed, the Holy Prophet had them executed.* From among the prisoners taken at Khaiber only Kinannah bin Abi al-Huwaiq was put to death because of his violating the agreement. At the conquest of Makkah, the Holy Prophet commanded in respect of only a few particular persons from among the inhabitants of Makkah that any one of them who was captured should be put to death. Apart from these exceptions, the Holy Prophet never killed prisoners of war, and the same also continued to be the practice of the righteous Caliphs.[79]

The case of Bani Qurayzah noted in the above passage is special. Because it finds mention in the Quran, it cannot be ignored. We defer full discussion until Chapter 8, but recall that

Rayhana belonged to this tribe and was admitted to the Prophet's household the same evening as her family was slaughtered.

Also listed in the above passage is Kinana (Kinannah), the husband of Safiya, who was taken into the Prophet's household (initially as a slave girl) when her husband was still alive. According to Ibn Ishaq, Kinana was ultimately captured and ordered by the Prophet to be tortured and killed.* His case does, though, stand at the very center of the following jurisprudential issue, arising from the verse that permits believers to have sexual intercourse with married women taken as prisoners of war. Based on the fact that Safiya was admitted to the Prophet's household before Kinana could be captured and killed, Muslim scholars have concluded:

> Those women who become prisoners of war, while their unbelieving husbands are left behind in the War Zone, are not unlawful because their marriage ties are broken by the fact that they have come from the War Zone into the Islamic Zone. It is lawful to marry such women, and it is also lawful for those, in whose possession they are, to have sexual relations with them. There is, however, a difference of opinion as to whether such a woman is lawful, if her husband is also taken a prisoner along with her. Imam Abu Hanifah and those of his way of thinking are of the opinion that the marriage tie of such a pair would remain intact but Imam Malik and Shafi'i, are of the opinion that it would also break.[80]

---

* Ibn Ishaq: *The Life of Muhammad*, p. 515:
  Kinana b. al-Rabi, who had the custody of the treasure of B. al-Nadir, was brought to the apostle who asked him about it. He denied that he knew where it was. A Jew came (T. was brought) to the apostle and said that he had seen Kinana going round a certain ruin every morning early. When the apostle said to Kinana, "Do you know that if we find you have it I shall kill you?" he said Yes. The apostle gave orders that the ruin was to be excavated and some of the treasure was found. When he asked him about the rest he refused to produce it, so the apostle gave orders to al-Zubayr b. al-Awwam, "Torture him until you extract what he has," so he kindled a fire with flint and steel on his chest until he was nearly dead. Then the apostle delivered him to Muhammad b. Maslama and he struck off his head.

Because Kinana was not captured "along with" Safiya, his case cannot be precedent for women in the latter category, and hence the disagreement amongst Muslim scholars on whether women whose husbands are also taken prisoners with them are permissible for sexual relations.

The Prophet did not have to wait the period of four months and ten days to marry Safiya (after her husband had been killed), as this waiting period is prescribed only for widows of the believers. Because Safiya did not fall in this category, there was nothing preventing her being instantly married to the Prophet, as she was.[81]

*

One must not be too harsh in judging the Prophet, though. Acceptance of the principle that noncombatants (particularly women and children) must be given special protection and that even prisoners of war are entitled to respect and dignity—which does not allow that they be subjected to sexual intercourse or torture—was centuries away. But, that said, it also seems inappropriate to consider Muhammad as the most forgiving or merciful man in history, as Rayhana and Safiya may have a different opinion.

MIRACLES

The Quran does try to tell us that Muhammad had no miracle powers:

> These people ask, "Why has no Sign been sent down to this Prophet from his Lord?" Say, "Allah is able to send down a sign but most of these people do not understand the wisdom underlying it." As regards Signs, just have a look at any of the beasts that move upon the earth and at any of the birds that fly in the air: they too are species like you. (6:37–38)

> They declare with solemn oaths by Allah that if a Sign (i.e. a miracle) comes before them, they will believe in it (your Prophethood). O Muhammad, tell them, "Allah alone can

show Signs." And what will make you (O Muhammad) realize that, even if the Signs come, they would not believe? (6:109)

As regards their saying, "Why has not a Sign been sent down to this Prophet from his Lord?" tell them "The unseen belongs wholly and solely to Allah. Well, wait (for it): I, too, shall wait with you." (10:20)

These people who have rejected your Message, say, "Why has no Sign been sent down to this person from His Lord." You are a warner only and every people has its guide. (13:7)

They say, "Why have Signs not been sent down upon this person from his Lord?" Say, "The Signs are with Allah: I am only a plain warner." Is this (Sign) not enough for these people that We have sent down to you the book, which is recited to them? (29:50-51)[82]

Despite these passages, within just a generation of Muhammad's death, there were accounts regarding how he caused an empty well to fill up with water, how he caused a bunch of dates to multiply until everyone present had their share, how a roasted lamb served to him was enough to feed hundreds of people, and so on. Miracles were also attributed to his birth and adolescence. Notably, many Muslims believe these accounts of miracles to be correct as well, the above verses notwithstanding.

Particular mention must, however, be made of the "splitting of the moon," as this finds mention in the Quran:

The Hour of Resurrection has drawn near *and the Moon has split asunder.* Yet whatever Sign these people may see they turn away and say, "This is current magic." They have denied (this too) and followed their own lusts. Ultimately, every matter has to reach an appointed end. (54:1–3)[83]

Two questions arise in this behalf. One, is the Quran presenting this as Muhammad's miracle (a sign conferred on him by Allah to prove his prophethood)? Two, did any such occurrence take place?

On the first, Maududi concludes that this is not presented as a sign of Muhammad's prophethood.* This seems the more

---

˙   Maududi notes:

acceptable approach, considering that if the incident took place at the instance of the Prophet and was meant to be a sign/miracle conferred on him, then either the verses quoted at the beginning of this section would have made mention of this or, if the occurrence took place after those verses were revealed, then the Quran would have clarified in other verses that this was the sign the disbelievers were always asking for. Moreover, if this were presented as a miracle belonging to the Prophet, the disbelievers would also then have demanded that it be repeated, but there is no evidence that they made such demand or that the moon was split another time.

On the second question, whether the occurrence took place at all, it is difficult for more objective readers to believe that it did. In fact, even the disbelievers denied it.* But if one is to consider the possibility that something like this may have happened,† it seems likely that the observers mistook Jupiter or Mars as a second moon. Both can look like small moons during certain phases in their orbits (when close enough to the earth, which happens rarely), and the onlookers may just have thought that the moon had been split.

Here, the question arises: What was the real nature of this incident. Was it a miracle that the Holy Prophet (upon whom be peace) performed on the demand of the disbelievers of Makkah as a proof of his Prophet-hood? Or, was it only an accident that occurred on the Moon by the power of Allah and the Holy Prophet had only called the peoples [sic] attention to it and warned them to mark it as a Sign of the possibility and nearness of Resurrection? A large group of the Muslim scholars regards it as among the miracles of the Holy Prophet and holds the view that it had been shown on the demand of the disbelievers. But this view is based only on some of those traditions which have been related from Hadrat Anas. Apart from him no other Companion has stated this. ... Above all, the Qur'an itself also is presenting this event not as a Sign of the Prophet-hood but as a Sign of the nearness of Resurrection. (Maududi: *The Meaning of the Qur'an*, note 1 to *Surah Al-Qamar*, Volume 5, p. 247)

* Though the above translation attributes to them the statement "this is current magic," the word actually used by the Quran is *sehr*, which also means "deception and fraud" (as we shall see in Chapter 9). This shows that the disbelievers totally disputed any such occurrence.

† Even though many mythical accounts in history have probably been created out of nothing at all.

THE PERFECT MAN

As there are Muslims who believe that Muhammad was absolutely perfect in every respect, it is worth noting that the Quran does record instances of imperfection, including occasional errors in the recitation of the Quran.[84] The Quran also instructs the Prophet to seek forgiveness for his errors,[85] which suggests that he may have made mistakes that could even be categorized as "sinful" (hence the direction to seek forgiveness). The incident of the "Satanic verses" comes to mind in this behalf—more about that in Chapter 10.

There is also the claim that Muhammad was perfect in his relationship with the holy wives. The issue possibly arises on account of the verse (noted in Chapter 6) that allows believers to marry multiple wives (up to four at a time), provided they can do justice to all. Although the Prophet was exempt from the restriction of four wives (and therefore married thirteen times), the expectation is that he would not have done so unless he was able to do justice to all the wives. His current followers therefore believe that he discharged this obligation with perfection.

The following verses containing a thinly disguised threat of divorce to the holy wives tell a different story:

> *O Prophet, why do you make unlawful that which Allah has permitted for you?* (Is it because) you seek the goodwill of your wives? Allah is All-Forgiving, All-Merciful. *Allah has already appointed a way to absolve you (people) from your oaths.* Allah is your Master, and He alone is the All-Knowing, the All-Wise. (And this also is noteworthy that) *the Prophet had confided a matter to a wife in secret. Then, when she disclosed the secret (to another) and Allah informed the Prophet (of the disclosure of the secret), the Prophet made known (to the wife) part of it and overlooked part of it.* So when the Prophet told her (of the disclosure) she asked, "Who informed you of this?" The Prophet said, "I was informed by Him Who knows everything and is All-Wise." If you both (women) repent to Allah, (it is better for you) for your hearts have swerved from the right path, and if you supported each other against the Prophet, you should know that Allah is his protector, and after Him Gabriel and the righteous believers

and the angels are his companions and helpers. *It may well be that if the Prophet divorces all of you, Allah will give him in your place better wives, who are true Muslims, who are believing and obedient, penitent, worshipping and given to fasting, be they previously married or virgins.* (66:1–5)[86]

One is intrigued to explore the background to this incident, but first, let us note the elements disclosed by the Quran:

- o The Prophet confided a matter to one of his wives in secret.
- o Also, he took an oath to abstain from something Allah had permitted him.
- o The wife to whom the matter was confided disclosed it to another.
- o The issue ultimately spread to all the wives, who seem to have united against the Prophet.
- o The holy wives were resultantly threatened with divorce and were also warned "that Allah is his protector, and after Him Gabriel and the righteous believers and the angels are his companions and helpers."
- o Allah reminded the Prophet as well that He "has already appointed a way to absolve you (people) from your oaths," thereby enabling the Prophet to withdraw from the oath.[87]

The question is, what may have caused such a serious breakdown between Muhammad and his wives? According to Maududi:

Although it has not been mentioned in the Quran as to what it was the Holy Prophet had forbidden himself, yet the traditionists and commentators have mentioned in this regard two different incidents, which occasioned revelation of this verse. One of these related to Hadrat Mariyah Qibbiyyah (Mary the Copt lady) and the other to his forbidding himself the use of honey.

The incident relating to Hadrat Mariyah is that after concluding the peace treaty of Hudaibiyah one of the letters that the Holy Prophet (upon whom be Allah's peace) sent to the rulers of the adjoining countries was addressed to the Roman Patriarch of Alexandria also, whom the Arabs called Muqawqis. When Hadrat Hatib Bin Abi Balta took this letter to him, he did not embrace Islam but received him well, and in reply wrote: "I know that a Prophet is yet to rise but I think he will appear in Syria. However, I have treated your messenger with due honor, and am sending two slave girls to you, who command respect among the Coptics." (Ibn Sa'd). One of those slave girls was Sirin and the other Mariyah (Mary). On his way back from Egypt Hadrat Hatib presented Islam before both and they believed. When they came before the Holy Prophet (upon whom be peace) he gave Sirin in the ownership of Hadrat Hussain bin Thabit and admitted Hadrat Mariyah into his own household. In Dhil Hijjah AH 8, she gave birth to the Holy Prophet's son, Ibrahim (Al-Isti'ab, Al-Isabah). ... One day the Holy Prophet (upon whom be peace) visited the house of Hadrat Hafsah when she was not at home. At that time Hadrat Mariyah came to him there and stayed with him in seclusion. Hadrat Hafsah took it very ill and complained of it bitterly to him. Thereupon, in order to please her, the Holy Prophet vowed that he would have no conjugal relation with Mariyah in future. According to some traditions, he forbade Mariyah for himself and according to others, he also swore an oath on it.

The other incident ... is as follows: The Holy Prophet (upon whom be peace) usually paid a daily visit to all his wives after the Asr Prayer. Once it so happened that he began to stay in the house of Hadrat Zainab bint Jahsh longer than usual, for she had received some honey from somewhere as a gift and the Holy Prophet was very fond of sweet things; therefore he would have a drink of honey at her house. Hadrat A'ishah states that she felt envious of this and spoke to Hadrat Hafsah, Hadrat Saudah and Hadrat Safiyyah about it and together they decided that whoever of them was visited by the Holy Prophet, should say to him: "Your mouth smells of maghafir." Maghafir is a kind of flower, which gives out an offensive smell, and if the bee obtains honey from it, it is also tainted by the same odor. They all knew that the Holy Prophet was a man of very fine taste and he abhorred that he should emit any kind of unpleasant smell. Therefore, this device was contrived to stop him from staying in the house of Hadrat Zainab and it worked. When several of his wives told him that his mouth smelt of Maghafir, he made a promise not to use the honey any longer.[88]

The latter explanation is not convincing. It suggests that the Prophet's wives deliberately lied to him as part of a planned scheme, which is not something one expects from ladies who are regarded as the mothers of the believers. It also does not appeal to reason that overstaying with one wife to taste honey would cause such resentment amongst the others so they would all gang up against the Prophet. They too could have acquired honey or waited until the favored wife ran out of supplies. Lastly, this account offers no explanation for the pronouncement "the Prophet had confided a matter to a wife in secret" but that "she disclosed the secret (to another)." The story is devoid of an element that fits this description.

In comparison, the Mariyah Qubiyyah story makes perfect sense and meets all the elements disclosed in the Quran. One can perfectly understand why Hafsah may have been upset to find the Prophet spending time with a slave girl, and in her quarters. It is plausible, as well, that the Prophet promised not to have conjugal relations with Mariyah in the future, to placate Hafsah, but desired that the whole affair should be kept a secret and that Hafsah, however, disclosed this to the other wives, who joined hands against the slave girl—she, after all, was not in the same league as them.

One also does not understand the reluctance to accept this version, considering that the Quran allowed the Prophet to have slave girls and it is an accepted fact that he did. In fact, Mariyah Qubiyyah even bore him a son (Ibrahim) who died at the age of a year and a half, so there seems no reason to reject this account, which perfectly fits the bill.

But it matters not what may have caused the relationship between Muhammad and his wives to breakdown. What is more significant is that it did—and to such an extent that the wives were even threatened with collective divorce! This much is recorded in the Quran and is therefore not open to debate, and although it is strange that the Quran should be burdened with this matter about Muhammad's dispute with his wives, what this does prove is that Muhammad was not entirely perfect—not even in his personal life.

*

The entire discussion in this chapter paints a picture that is different altogether from what Muslims tend to believe about Muhammad. Because it is based on disclosures made in the Quran, the truly perplexing question is, How did Muhammad get lost in history?

4

THE QURAN: A SCIENTIFIC MIRACLE

As for the one who presumes that Allah will neither help him in this world nor in the Hereafter, he should (if he can)* ascend the sky by a rope and cut a hole into it and then peep through it and see for himself whether any device of his can avert his doom, which he abhors. And We have sent down this Quran with clear teachings such as these, but Allah alone guides whomsoever He wills. (22:15–16)[1]

The Quran may not have intended so, if the above verses are any indication, but there are Muslim scholars who insist that the book is an absolute scientific miracle.† They cite the following as instances supporting the claim. The Quran:

- o discloses that plants have male and female pairing;
- o reflects awareness regarding the speed of light and the theory of relativity;
- o declares that the earth is round;
- o describes that the sun and the moon are both in orbits;

---

*   The words "(if he can)" are Maudidi's addition and not an exact translation.

†   The following may be taken for an example:

The scientific evidences of the Quran clearly prove its Divine origin. No human could have produced a book fourteen hundred years ago that would contain such sound scientific facts. (Naik: *The Quran and Modern Science: Compatible or Incompatible?* p. 66)

o informs us that all living things are created from water;

o informs us that 309 lunar years are equal to 300 solar years;

o documents that the moon reflects light emitted by the sun;

o matches modern geological research by telling us that mountains are like pegs firmly driven into the earth;

o mentions underwater currents as well as the fact that there is no light deep in the sea;

o describes the phenomenon of freshwater not mixing with seawater;

o is a mathematical wonder, as depicted by the "Miracle of 19";

o shows awareness that the tectonic plates cause the surface of the earth to shift over time;

o foretells the Big Bang theory regarding the origin of the universe; and

o depicts a scientifically accurate knowledge of embryology.

The list is impressive, no doubt, but is it accurate? Before we probe more deeply, it is useful to get a flavor of what mankind had already achieved—apparently without divine help—before Islam.

PRE-QURANIC DISCOVERIES

- ### *365 ¼-day solar year*

The Egyptian civilization has left many an indelible imprint on history, but one notable discovery regards the length of the solar year. They were perhaps the first to discover that it was 365 ¼ days:

> The one solid work that rested on the Egyptians' astronomy was the calendar. They were the first people to establish the solar year of 365 ¼ days and they divided it into twelve months, each of three "weeks" of ten days, with five extra days at the end of the year.[2]

It seems incredible that the Egyptians should have discovered this so long ago, but then, theirs was no ordinary civilization.

- ### *Moon reflects the light of the sun*

Anaxagoras, an Ionian who lived in Athens around 450 BCE (i.e., two generations before Aristotle), understood that the moon shines by reflected light. He also devised a theory of the phases of the moon. The doctrine was so dangerous that:

> the manuscript describing it had to be circulated in secret, an Athenian samizdat. It was not in keeping with the prejudices of the time to explain the phases or eclipses of the Moon by the relative geometry of the Earth, the Moon and the self-luminous Sun.[3]

- ### *Circumference of the earth*

Anaximander, a student of Thales, was one of the first to describe the earth as a sphere rather than a flat plane.[4] He discovered this in the sixth century BCE.

Despite that and many other remarkable achievements, one would not have expected anyone to calculate the circumference of the earth without modern instruments. It took an absolute genius to do so.

> The discovery that the Earth is a little world was made, as so many important human discoveries were, in the ancient Near East, in a time some humans call the third century BC, in the greatest metropolis of the age, the Egyptian city of Alexandria. Here there lived a man Eratosthenes. ... One day he read in a papyrus book that in the southern frontier outpost of Syene, near the first cataract of the Nile, at noon on June 21 vertical sticks cast no shadows. ... A reflection of the Sun could be seen in the water at the bottom of the deep well. The Sun was directly overhead. ... Eratosthenes asked himself how, at the same moment, a stick in Syene could cast no shadows and a stick in Alexandria, far to the north, could cast a pronounced shadow. Consider a map of ancient Egypt with two vertical sticks of equal length, one stuck in Alexandria, and the other in Syene. Suppose that, at a certain moment, each stick casts no shadow at all. This is perfectly easy to understand— provided the Earth is flat. The Sun would then be directly

overhead. ... But how could it be that at the same instant there was no shadow at Syene and a substantial shadow at Alexandria?

The only possible answer, he saw, was that the surface of the Earth is curved. Not only that: the greater the curvature, the greater the difference in the shadow lengths. ... For the observed difference in the shadow lengths, the distance between Alexandria and Syene had to be about seven degrees along the surface of the Earth; that is, if you imagine the sticks extending down to the center of the Earth, they would there interact at an angle of seven degrees. Seven degrees is something like one-fiftieth of three hundred and sixty degrees, the full circumference of the Earth. Eratosthenes knew that the distance between Alexandria and Syenes was approximately 800 kilometers, because he hired a man to pace it out. Eight hundred kilometers times 50 is 40,000: so that must be the circumference of the Earth. This is the right answer. Eratosthenes' only tools were sticks, eyes, feet and brain, plus a taste for experiment. With them he deduced the circumference of the Earth with an error of only a few percent, a remarkable achievement of 2,200 years ago. He was the first person accurately to measure the size of a planet.[5]

The list of discoveries above is not exhaustive of mentionable discoveries prior to the Quran, but those mentioned were chosen on account of relevance to the discussion that follows. It is worth noting that scientists who came upon these mindboggling conclusions relied neither on modern instruments nor on the divine word—just on the power of observation. The Quran would do even better, one may expect.

As we launch our inquiry, however, we must remain watchful of attempts to attribute credit where none is due, as, for instance, where the Quran is only narrating phenomena visible to all or stating the commonly held belief of the time. We must equally be vigilant of scientific miracles that turn out to be the exact opposite—i.e., scientific errors. With this caution, let us consider the miracles attributed to the Quran, one by one.

"WE HAVE CREATED EVERYTHING IN PAIRS"

That Allah has created everything in pairs is a claim we confronted in Chapter 2 as well. It is based on the following verses.

- "He has created in pairs every kind of fruit." (13:3)
- "He created in pairs all species, whether of the vegetable kingdom or of their own." (36:36)
- "We have created everything in pairs." (51:49)

We concluded, however, that these are scientifically incorrect. It is thus surprising that to some Muslim scholars, these very same verses reflect a scientific miracle. Naik premises his amazement regarding the above verses on the following:

> Previously, humans did not know that plants too have male and female gender distinction. Botany states that every plant has a male and female gender. Even the plants that are unisexual have distinct elements of both male and female.[6]

The fact, however, is that man has known for a very long time (for more than four thousand years before the Quran) that certain plants display male and female gender distinction. The following passage from *Encyclopaedia Britannica* is instructive:

> Illustrations on certain seals reveal that the Babylonians had learned that the date palm reproduces sexually and that pollen could be taken from the male plant and used to fertilize the female plant. Although a precise dating of these early records is lacking, a Babylonian business contract of the Hammurabi period (1800 BC) mentions the male flower of the date palm as an article of commerce, *and descriptions of date harvesting date back to about 3500 BC.*[7]

The date palm, incidentally, was also the plant most familiar to the Arabs.

Naik is thus quite wrong to suggest that at the time the Quran was revealed, "humans did not know that plants have male and female gender distinction." He is equally wrong that according to botany, "every plant has a male and female gender," when only a small percentage of plants observe this distinction, date palms being among them.*

The following facts, substantiated in Chapter 2, are again referenced to highlight the error in the Quranic verses noted above:

o Most plants are bisexual, in that they have male and female organs on the same plant and do not have separate male and female plants. They therefore diverge from the Quranic description.

o There are also plants that are entirely asexual, which too is contrary to what the Quran tells us.

o Even in the animal kingdom, there are species that do not have males and females and that adopt the asexual form of reproduction and multiplication. The Quran thus turns out to be wrong even regarding the animal kingdom.

The fact additionally is that sexual reproduction (or pairing) was a later development (in evolution). For hundreds of millions of years (possibly well over a billion years) after the emergence of life, sexual reproduction was simply unknown, and even today, it is not the only means of reproduction. What this shows is that Allah made many things in pairs, but clearly not everything. Thus, the absolute statements in the Quran (e.g., "We have created *everything* in pairs") are incorrect and should not be presented as scientific miracles.

SPEED OF LIGHT AND THEORY OF RELATIVITY

Some Muslim scientists insist that the Quran depicts an exact knowledge of the speed of light and also of the theory of relativity![8] Let us take a closer look.

---

* What is surprising is that Naik should make this observation, because in the immediately following sentence, he concedes that there are plants that have both male and female elements in the same plant. The latter is of course true for a vast majority of plants, but this contradicts his earlier statement as much as it contradicts the Quranic verses noted above.

• *Speed of light*

The view that the Quran spells out the speed of light is stated in the above-referenced source as follows:

> Moslems (Muslims) believe that angels are low density creatures, and that God created them originally from light. They move at any speed from zero up to the speed of light. It is the angels who carry out God's orders. ... In the following verse, the Quran describes how angels travel ... And the speed at which they commute to and from this Tablet turned out to be the known speed of light:
>
>> [Quran 32.5](Allah) Rules the cosmic affair from the heavens to the Earth. Then this affair *travels to Him a distance* in one day, at a measure of one thousand years of what you count.
>
> ... These people back then followed the lunar calendar and **counted 12 lunar months** each year. These months are related to the moon and not related to the sun. Hence in 1 day the angels will travel a distance of 1000 years **of what they counted (the moon)**. Since this verse is referring to distance, then God is saying that angels travel in one day the same distance that the moon travels in 12000 lunar orbits. Outside gravitational fields this speed turned out to be the known speed of light.*

Let us understand the proposition first. It draws on verse 32:5, particularly the words "travels to Him a distance,"† to argue that the Quran is referring to the distance traveled by the moon in one thousand lunar years. It is then suggested that this is the same distance as traveled by light in one day. From this, it is inferred that the Quran knew the speed of light (as it mentions both measures, namely "one day" and also "one thousand years," in the same verse).

The critical question, therefore, is whether there is indeed any consonance between the distance traveled by light in one day and

---

* The emphasis (the italicized and bold text) is contained in the original text.
† This, it turns out, is an incorrect translation, as we shall see below.

the distance traveled by the moon in its orbit around the earth in 12,000 lunar months. Here are the calculations:

Distance traveled by light in one day
299792.458 km/sec x 60 sec/minute x 60 minutes/hour x 24 hours = **25,902,068,371.2 km**

Distance traveled by the moon in its orbit around the earth in 12,000 lunar months
1.023 km/sec x 60 sec/minute x 60 minutes/hour x 24 hours/day x 29.5 days/lunar month x 12,000 lunar months = **31,289,068,800 km**

It is apparent that there is absolutely no consonance between the two. The moon clearly travels a far greater distance in 12,000 lunar months than light travels in one day. This difference is only exacerbated when we take into account the fact that the moon (together with the earth) is also orbiting the sun during this period. If one counts that distance as well, another 911,047,227,926.07 kilometers would need to be added.[*]

Incidentally, even the author of the above-referenced source is conscious that calculations do not match. To overcome this difficulty, the author attempts huge adjustments. First, the lunar month is reduced to 27.3 days—which is inconsistent with the translation noted above (as this is not how we count time based on the lunar cycle; we count it as 29.5 days). Second, rather than enhancing the distance traveled by the moon on account of its orbit around the sun, a reverse calculation is made—this on the pretext that distance should be measured outside the gravitational fields. One is not sure what exactly it means for the distance to be measured outside the gravitational field, or why this should be, considering that the earth and the moon have always existed, ever since their creation 4.6 billion years ago, within the gravitational field of the sun!

It then transpires that even the starting premise of the argument is (demonstrably) flawed. The words "travels to Him a distance," which are the foundation of the hypothesis, are entirely manufactured. Nothing of the sort is stated or implied by the

---

[*]   940,000,000km/365.25 days x 29.5days/lunar month x 1200 lunar months = **911,047,227,926.07 km**

relevant verse, as is apparent from translations we trust in this book.*

- ### *Theory of relativity*

More innovative still is the claim that the theory of relativity too is fully depicted in the Quran. We quote from the same source as referred above.[9]

> Moslems use Einstein's theory of special relativity with the following verse in the Quran to assert that angels indeed accelerate up to the speed of light:
>
> > [Quran 70.4] The angels and the Spirit ascend to Him in a day, the measure of which is fifty thousand years.
>
> Here angels will experience 1 day while humans will measure it as 50,000 years (time vs. time and not time vs. distance as the previous lunar verse). However, according to the theory of special relativity, given this time difference (time dilation), we can calculate the speed at which that object traveled. We can verify if those angels really accelerate up to the speed of light, as claimed by Moslems, or not. Outside gravitational fields it is:
>
> $$\Delta t = \frac{\Delta t_2}{\sqrt{1 - \frac{v^2}{c^2}}}$$

---

* He administers the affairs of the world from the heavens to the earth, and the report of this administration ascends (to be presented) before Him in a day whose length, according to your reckoning, is a thousand years. (Maududi)

He rules (all) affairs from the heavens to the earth: in the end will (all affairs) go up to Him, on a Day, the space whereof will be (as) a thousand years of your reckoning. (Yusuf Ali)

He directeth the ordinance from the heaven unto the earth; then it ascendeth unto Him in a day, whereof the measure is a thousand years of that ye reckon. (Pickthall)

He manages and regulates (every) affair from the heavens to the earth; then it (affair) will go up to Him, in one Day, the space whereof is a thousand years of your reckoning (i.e. reckoning of our present world's time). (Hilali-Khan)

(Where Δt_0 is the time measured for a mover by a mover; Δt is the time measured for a mover by a stationary frame; v is the velocity of the mover relative to the stationary observer):

Δt_0 is the time experienced by angels (1 day).

Δt is the time as measured by humans (50,000 lunar years x12 lunar months/lunar year x 27.321661 days/lunar month).

v is the velocity of angels in this case (which we intend to calculate and then compare to the known speed of light).

c is the nominal speed of light, 299792.458 km/s.

From the above equation we can solve for the unknown velocity:

$$\Rightarrow v = c \sqrt{1 - \left(\frac{\Delta t_0}{\Delta t}\right)^2} = c\sqrt{1 - \left(\frac{1}{50000 * 12 * 27321661}\right)^2} = c * 0.9999999999999981$$
$$= 299792.4579999994 \ km/sec$$

This time dilation (time difference) shows that angels indeed accelerate to relativistic speeds; outside gravitational fields this is the same speed calculated from the previous lunar verse also outside gravitational fields. … Moslems ask how could an illiterate man who lived 1400 years ago have figured out Time Dilation and the core of Relativity?*

One may not have imagined that a verse (70:4) that contradicts another (32:5), as discussed in Chapter 2, would yield a result so startling! This mindboggling finding is based on the following equation:

$$\Rightarrow v = c \sqrt{1 - \left(\frac{\Delta t_0}{\Delta t}\right)^2} = c\sqrt{1 - \left(\frac{1}{50000 * 12 * 27321661}\right)^2} = c * 0.9999999999999981$$
$$= 299792.4579999994 \ km/sec$$

---

* The emphasis (the bold text) is contained in the original text.

Before we celebrate, let us see how the result may change if, instead of 50,000 years noted in verse 70:4 and incorporated in the above arithmetic, we were to place some other figures in the equation. The following results emerge:

A billion years:　　　299792.457999999
A million years:　　　299792.457999999
One year:　　　　　　299792.457999999

The magic apparently lies not in verse 70:4 but in the formula!

SHAPE OF THE EARTH

We saw earlier that Anaximander discovered in the sixth century BCE that the earth is round. Eratosthenes even calculated the circumference of the earth with remarkable accuracy 2,200 years ago. The Quran thus would not be the first to declare that the earth is round, but it would be remarkable if it knew this fact. Some scholars, of course, insist that it does. Naik is among them.

> Consider the following Quranic verse regarding the alternation of day and night: "Seest thou not that Allah merges Night into Day and He merges Day into Night?" (31:29). Merging here means that the night slowly and gradually changes to day and vice versa. This phenomenon can only take place if the earth is spherical. If the earth was flat, there would have been a sudden change from night to day and from day to night.
>
> The following verse also alludes to the spherical shape of the earth: "He created the heavens and the earth in true (proportions): He makes the Night overlap the Day, and the Day overlap the Night."(39:5) The Arabic word used here is *Kawwara* meaning "to overlap" or "to coil"—the way a turban is wound around the head. The overlapping or coiling of the day and night can only take place if the earth is spherical.
>
> The earth is not exactly round like a ball, but geo-spherical, i.e. it is flattened at the poles. The following verse contains a description of the earth's shape: "And the earth, moreover, hath He made egg shaped." (79:30) The Arabic word for egg here is *dahaahaa* which means an ostrich-egg. The shape of an

ostrich-egg resembles the geo-spherical shape of the earth. Thus the Quran correctly describes the shape of the earth, though the prevalent notion when the Quran was revealed was that the earth was flat.[10]

Let us take these three arguments in turn.

As suggested in the first argument, it may perhaps be that if the earth were flat, the night would not merge into the day and the day would not merge into the night, but instead, one may see a more abrupt change from day to night and vice versa. But then, the Quran only describes what is visible to all—which is that the day gradually yields to the night and the night slowly merges into the day. How does one conclude that by merely describing the obvious, the Quran also understands the underlying phenomenon that this is because the earth is round?*

The next argument, that "overlapping or coiling of the day and night can only take place if the earth is spherical," is also misconceived. Day and night recur not because the earth is round but because it rotates on its axis. If it were flat but rotated on an axis so as to expose its two sides to the sun one after the other, day and night would still be caused (even if more abruptly than we see at present). The same would be the case if the earth were cylindrical or, for that matter, any other shape—provided it rotated on an axis.†

We come finally to the most persuasive argument put forward by Naik, the one based on the verse "And the earth, moreover, hath He made egg shaped" (79:30). The problem, though, is that this translation is absolutely unique—certainly in comparison to the ones we trust:

"After that He spread out the earth." (Maududi)

---

*   Also, why should one conclude that the Quran understands the earth to be spherical–why not cylindrical? That too would cause the day to merge into the night and vice versa.

†   The fact also is that the day does not overlap or coil the night, and the night does not overlap or coil the day as a turban is wound around the head. Overlapping and coiling require continuity, whereas the day that follows the night is entirely new and different from the previous one.

"And the earth, moreover, hath He extended (to a wide expanse)." (Yusuf Ali)

"And after that he spread the earth." (Hilali-Khan)

"And after that He spread the earth." (Pickthall)

Considering the obvious disparity between these translations and the one quoted by Naik, one is keen to know the source of the translation adopted by Naik. He adds the following note at the start of his work:

> References and translation of the Quran are from the translation of the Quran by Abdullah Yusuf Ali, new revised edition, 1989, published by Amana Corporation, Maryland, USA.[11]

What is interesting is that this source too contains the very same translation as we have noted above (and not what Naik quotes). Unfortunately, Naik neither discloses the source of the translation he uses with respect to verse 79:30 nor the reason why in this case he opts to ignore Yusuf Ali.

While considering whether the Quran truly understood the shape of the earth, the following verse also attracts attention:

> You are also permitted to eat and drink during the nights of the Fast months. Until you can discern the white streak of dawn from the blackness of night. (2:187)[12]

If the Quran knew that the earth is spherical, should it not have known that this rule would be unworkable for people living near the poles? Eratosthenes at least may have chosen a different measure to determine the duration of fasting.

THE SOLAR SYSTEM

Referring to verse 36:40, Naik informs us:

> This verse mentions an essential fact discovered only recently by modern astronomy, i.e. the existence of the individual orbits of the Sun and the Moon, and their journey through space with their own motion. ... One cannot help but be amazed at the scientific accuracy of the Quranic verses.

Should we not ponder over the question: "What is the source of knowledge contained in the Quran?"[13]

One is inspired to consult the referenced verse, which reads as follows:

Neither it is possible for the Sun to overtake the Moon; nor for the night to outstrip the day. *Each is gliding in its own orbit.* (36:40)[14]

It turns out, however, that this is not exactly the startling disclosure one anticipated! In fact, this verse seems to describe things exactly as an untrained eye sees them. An untrained eye observes the sun rise in the east every morning and set in the west in the evening. It also sees the moon undergo a similar motion. It thus concludes that the two are gliding in their respective orbits, neither overtaking the other—exactly what the Quran tells us. One therefore wonders what there is to glorify in this.

The picture becomes even clearer, though, when we look at the full context in which the above verse expresses itself:

Another sign for them is the night: We remove the day from above it, and they are covered in darkness. *And the Sun: it is moving to its place of rest.** This is the decree of the All-Mighty, All-Knowing God. And the Moon: We have determined stages for it till it again becomes like an old dry palm-branch. *Neither it is possible for the Sun to overtake the Moon; nor for the night to outstrip the day. Each is gliding in its own orbit.* (36:37–40)[15]

The following verses also address the same subject, so it is helpful to include them in the discussion too.

And We made the sky a safe canopy, but in spite of this they do not pay due heed to its signs. *And it is Allah, Who has made*

---

* Pickthall supports Maududi regarding the italicised wording, while Yusuf Ali (supported by Hilali-Khan) translates: "And the sun runs his course for a period determined for him." In the commentary to Yusuf Ali's revised translation, however, it is conceded that "a place of rest" is also plausible and not an incorrect translation (Note 3983, *The Meaning of the Holy Qur'an*, Eleventh Edition (1430 AH/2009 AC) Amana Corporation, Maryland, p. 1124). There is no dispute, in any case, that these verses mention the movement of the sun in the context of day and night.

the night and the day and created the sun and the moon; all of them are
floating, each in its own orbit. (21:32–33)[16]

The following points emerge from a reading of the above
verses.

o In both sets of verses, it is in the context of day and night that
the Quran refers to the sun and the moon gliding in their
respective orbits—exactly as an untrained eye would see things
as well. The untrained eye would associate the sun and its
apparent orbit with the day, and the moon and its orbit with
the night. The fact, however, is that night and day have
nothing to do with the (apparent) movement of the sun or the
moon, or any orbits they may glide in, but only with the
rotation of the earth.

o The Quran also associates darkness of night with the sun
"moving to its place of rest." Is there such a place? Isn't it
rather that the sun never rests[17] and is always showering the
earth with its rays? Once again, the Quranic description is
more consistent with how an untrained eye perceives the
phenomenon than with facts.*

o It is also quite noticeable that there is no mention in the above
verses of the earth's orbit. Considering that the Quran
specifically mentions that the sun and the moon glide in their
orbits (we shall see what that may mean in the case of the sun),
was it not appropriate for it to also mention the orbit of the
earth? This may not have been generally known at the time,
but the Quran could certainly have noted it.

o Coming next to the sun's orbit, does it truly have one? We
now understand that the entire galaxy (the Milky Way) goes
through a rotation, which takes about 250 million years. Is that
what the Quran is referring to? If so, the context at least is
odd, as this galactic rotation has absolutely nothing to do with
night and day, which is the precise setting in which the above
verses describe the sun's motion. Moreover, the earth too goes

---

* Even Yusuf Ali's translation ("And the sun runs his course for a period
determined for him") invites the question: Does the sun have such a course
that causes day and night?

through the same galactic rotation, in addition to orbiting the sun. Why not mention the earth as well?

That the Quran did not really mean to reveal the functioning of the solar system is also apparent from the following verses:

> And O Muhammad they ask you about Zulqarnain: tell them "I am going to recite to you an account of him." We had established his power on earth and had provided him with every kind of ways and means. At first he made preparations for an expedition (to the West and marched on) *till he reached the limit where the sun set, and found it setting in black waters,* and there he saw a people. ... Then he made preparations (for another expedition and marched on) *till he reached the limit where the sun rose. There he saw the sun rising on a people,* whom We had not given any shelter from sunshine. (18:83–90)[18]

But is it possible to reach the setting of the sun, or the place where it rises? Zulqarnain* seems to have found both!

Interestingly, the commentary to Yusuf Ali's revised translation states:

> "Reaching the setting of the sun" does not mean the extreme west as there is no such thing. West and East are relative terms. It means a western expedition *terminated* by a "spring of murky water."[19]

But if the Quran understood that there is no such thing as the extreme west, should it not have said simply: "till he reached the black waters"? Why add that Zulqarnain "reached the limit where the sun set, and found it setting in black waters"? Besides, while mention of the "murky water"† may perhaps be taken to signify the termination point of the westward expedition, how does one find a similar termination point regarding the eastward journey? We are told that Zulqarnain "reached the limit where the sun rose," and "he saw the sun rising on a people, whom We had not given any shelter from sunshine." Are there such people? And are they closer to the sun (to require shelter)?

---

*   According to some assessments, this refers to Alexander the Great.
†   using Yusuf Ali's translation

The impression one gets from the verses discussed in this section is that the Quran, if it knows the shape of the earth and the workings of the solar system, does not wish to reveal the secret; it is comfortable adopting the errors that marked the age before Copernicus. It is difficult, therefore, to accept that the Quranic discussion on the subject constitutes a miracle.

"WE CREATED EVERY LIVING THING FROM WATER"

While scientists ponder the origin of life, how the first living cell was created and learned to reproduce and mutate, and though there are several theories in this regard, including that life was transported from outside the solar system or that it originated deep in the crust of the earth and so on, the Quran is unconcerned with the debate. It announces that Adam was created from clay and the jinn created from fire.[20]

But what is perplexing is that it also then says, "(We) created every living thing from water" (21:30).[21] How can that be, if Adam was created from clay and the jinn from fire—unless, of course, the Quran only means to refer to procreation, as opposed to the original creation of man or jinn, and by water it means to refer to sperm, as in the following verses.*

> He began the creation of man from clay; then spread his progeny by an extract the nature of a *despicable water.* (32:7–8)

> And Allah created every creature from *a sort of water:* of them some one crawls upon its belly: another walks on two legs and still another on four; Allah creates whatever He wills for He has power over everything. (24:45)[22]

In that case, however, the Quran must not think of plants as living things, as their reproduction does not involve sperm! Moreover, even in the animal kingdom, there are species that undergo purely asexual reproduction and others that follow a form of sexual reproduction in which nothing like the sperm (water) is involved.

---

* It is difficult, though, to grasp how the procreation of the jinn should involve water or sperm!

Muslim scholars, however, tell us that this disclosure, "We created every living thing from water," too represents a scientific miracle:

> When we look at the verses concerned with the creation of human beings and living things, we clearly see evidence of a miracle. One such miracle is of the creation of living things from water. ... The words "Water is the main component of organic matter. 50–90% of the weight of living things consists of water" appear regularly in encyclopedias. Furthermore, 80% of the cytoplasm (basic cell material) of a standard animal cell is described as water in biology textbooks.[23]

The proposition is that because water constitutes a sizeable portion of the "standard animal cell," one can say that all living things are created from water. The problem, however, is that there are numerous living organisms (some forms of bacteria and virtually all forms of viruses) in which the "standard animal cell" is not employed at all—there is no cytoplasm in such organisms. Even with respect to organisms that do employ the standard animal cell, it is hardly correct to say that they have been created from water, because water is but one component and all the defining features of the organism (the DNA for instance) come from other elements.

That said, if we must give credit for the hypothesis that life is created somehow from water, it belongs rightfully to Thales, who was the first to come up with this thesis nearly a thousand years before the Quran:

> One of the earliest Greek philosophers, Thales of Miletus (c. 7th century BC), maintained that the universe contained a creative force that he called physis, an early progenitor of the term physics; *he also postulated that the world and all living things in it were made from water.*[24]

THE SOLAR YEAR AND THE LUNAR YEAR

The Egyptians (amazingly) discovered that the time it takes the earth to orbit the sun comes to 365 ¼ days. The lunar year, in contrast, is more easily calculated and comes to approximately 354 days. It takes simple arithmetic beyond this to conclude that 300 solar years are very nearly equal to 309 lunar years. Muslim scholars, however, believe that the Quran's knowledge of this fact constitutes another scientific miracle.* Let us consult the Quran to ascertain whether the claim is well founded.

The verse that contains this information was revealed in the context of a mythical story regarding a group that falls asleep in a cave and wakes up three hundred-odd years later.

> Some people will say, "They were three and the fourth was their dog," and some others will say, "They were five and the sixth was their dog." These are mere irrelevant guesses. There are still others who say, "They were seven and the eighth was their dog." Say, "My Lord alone knows best how many they were." There are a few people only who know their correct number: so you should not enter into discussions with them about their number except in a cursory way: nor ask anyone about them and never say about any matter, "I will do this tomorrow (for you cannot do anything) except that Allah wills it." If ever you inadvertently utter anything like this, you should at once remember your Lord and say, "I hope that my Lord will guide me in this matter with that thing which is nearest to the right way for me." *And some people say that they remained in their Cave for three hundred years and some others add nine more years (to the reckoning of the period).* O Prophet, say, "Allah knows best about the period of their stay there, for He is fully

---

* Consider, for instance, the following discussion:

> There is a difference of eleven days between the Hijri calendar and the Gregorian calendar, in which a year is the time it takes the Earth to orbit the Sun. Indeed, attention is drawn to this difference in another verse: *"They stayed in their Cave for three hundred years and added nine. (Qur'an, 18:25)"* We can clarify the time referred to in the verse thus: 300 years x 11 days (the difference which forms every year) = 3,300 days. Bearing in mind that one solar year lasts 365 days, 5 hours, 48 minutes and 45.5 seconds, 3,300 days/365.24 days = 9 years. To put it another way, 300 years according to the Gregorian calendar is equal to 300+9 years according to the *Hijri* calendar. As we can see, the verse refers to this finely calculated difference of 9 years. (Allah knows best.) *There is no doubt that the Qur'an, which contains such pieces of Information, which transcended the everyday knowledge of the time, is a miraculous revelation.* (www.miraclesofthequran.com)

aware of all that is hidden in the heavens and the earth." (18:22–26)[25]

What is quite apparent is that the Quran is not proposing to introduce knowledge previously unknown. It simply mentions "some people say that they remained in their Cave for three hundred years and some others add nine more years." The credit for any underlying miracle must therefore go to the people referred in the above verse, and not the Quran, as conceded even by Maududi:

> [T]he number of the years "300 and 309" have not been stated by Allah Himself but Allah has cited these as sayings of the people.[26]

Besides, the Egyptians had discovered several thousand years earlier than the Quran that the solar year was 365 ¼ days. How long should it have taken for this information to pass on to the Meccans, who regularly visited Egypt for trade? The rest was a matter of simple arithmetic.

THE MOON REFLECTS THE LIGHT OF THE SUN

Anaxagoras discovered as far back as 450 BCE that the moon shines by reflecting the sun's light. Does the Quran know this too? Some Muslim scholars insist that it does.[27] Consider the following discussion:

> The Arabic word for the sun in the Quran, is *shams*. It is also referred to as *siraaj* which means a "torch" or as *wahhaaj* meaning "a blazing lamp" or as *diya* which means "shining glory." All three descriptions are appropriate to the sun, since it generates intense heat and light by its internal combustion. The Arabic word for the moon is *qamar* and it is described in the Quran as *muneer* which is a body that gives *noor* i.e. reflected light. Again the Quranic description matches perfectly with the true nature of the moon which does not give off light by itself and is an inactive body that reflects the light of the sun. Not once in the Quran, is the moon mentioned as *siraaj*, *wahhaaj* or *diya* nor the sun as *noor* or *muneer*. This implies that the Quran recognizes the difference

between the nature of sunlight and moonlight. ... *The Glorious Quran and modern science, are thus in perfect agreement about the differences in the nature of sunlight and moonlight.*[28]

This thesis builds on the fact that the Quran uses different terminology to describe the moon (and its light) as compared to the sun (and the light emitted by it). But wouldn't most people do that, considering that the intensity of light from the two sources is not nearly the same? Additionally, the moon goes through phases that the sun does not, so it makes sense to use different terminology for the two bodies.

In order, then, to prove that the Quran understands that the moon has borrowed light, it is argued: "The Arabic word for the moon is *qamar* and it is described in the Quran as *muneer* which is a body that gives *noor* i.e. reflected light." Is the premise correct, though? The following verse tells us that it isn't.

Allah is the light of the heavens and the earth: His light (in the universe) may be likened (to the light of) a lamp in a niche: the lamp is in a glass shade: the glass shade is like a glittering star and lamp is lit with the olive oil of a blessed tree which is neither eastern nor western: its oil is (so fine) as if it were going to shine forth by itself though no fire touched it (as though all the means of increasing) light upon light (were provided); Allah guides to His light whomever He wills. (24:35)[29]

The word repeatedly used for light in the above verse is *noor*, which according to Naik is reflected light. The difficulty is that in the above verse, this same word is used to refer to light radiated by Allah! Is that also borrowed light?

The following verse only compounds the difficulty:

O Prophet, We have sent you as a witness, a bearer of good news and a warner, an inviter to Allah by His leave *and a luminous lamp.* (33:45–46)[30]

The words used here for the Prophet are *wa siraajan muneeran*. If we go by the argument noted in the above passage that *muneer/noor* is borrowed light and *siraj* is the real light, we end up concluding that Muhammad is at once radiating and reflecting light, whereas Allah only reflects light!

The fact, of course, is that the meaning attributed to *noor* by Naik is simply incorrect. It is difficult, therefore, to agree that the Quran understands that the moon shines by reflected light.

MOUNTAINS AS PEGS

The Quran describes mountains as "pegs."[31] One may have thought that this simile was used on account of the apparent resemblance between the two above the surface, but Muslim scholars tell us that the true cause lies much deeper:

> Modern earth sciences have proven that mountains have deep roots under the surface of the ground and that these roots can reach several times their elevations above the surface of the ground. So the most suitable word to describe mountains on the basis of this information is the word "peg," since most of a properly set peg is hidden under the surface of the ground. ... Modern geology has confirmed the truth of the Quranic verses.[32]

The fact is that "folds" (or "roots," as they are described in the above passage) are too irregular to resemble pegs underneath the surface of the earth—in most cases, at least—which means that although mountains somewhat resemble pegs above the surface (which is the complete explanation for why the Quran uses this description), they do not resemble pegs below the surface. Besides, there are mountains that lack folds or roots altogether. Dome and volcanic mountains, for instance, do not employ these at all—so how are they to be described as pegs underneath the surface?[33]

UNDERWATER WAVES AND DARKNESS IN THE SEA

The following verses have also attracted disproportionate attention.

(On the other hand,) the deeds of those who disbelieved, maybe likened to a mirage in a waterless desert, which the thirsty one took for water; but when he reached there he found nothing to drink; nay, he found there Allah Who settled his full account, and Allah is very swift at reckoning. Or (their efforts may be likened to those of a man trying to swim in) a deep dark ocean, covered with billows, one over the other, and above it a cloud: darkness upon darkness: so much so that if he stretches out his hand, he cannot see it. There is no light for the one whom Allah does not give light. (24:39–40)[34]

One may have thought the Quran was merely likening the disbelievers first to a mirage in the desert and then to the deep, dark ocean, wave upon wave of ignorance, compounded by further darkness from the clouds. Muslim scholars, however, read much more than that.

They hold that these verses refer to underwater waves, which are not visible to the naked eye, and hence a miracle.[35] But why do they think so, when there are waves on the surface of the sea that are not only visible to the naked eye but also perfectly fit the Quranic description? Why should we think that the Quran was referring to underwater waves while describing the state of the unbelievers to those who had absolutely no clue that such waves even existed?

Muslim scholars also conclude that these verses are referring to the fact that there is complete darkness in the sea, which they insist was not known to man, as there are limits on how deep one can go without modern equipment.[36] But doesn't the sea look absolutely dark when one views it from the outside? Does one really need to walk across to the other end of an unlit room to tell that it is dark?

TWO BODIES OF WATER WITH PARTITION

An attempt is made by some to argue that the following verse also reflects a scientific miracle:

And it is He, Who has let loose the two seas, one palatable and sweet, the other bitter and salty, and there is a partition between them, which is an insurmountable barrier. (25:53)[37]

The description fits that of an estuary. This is formed when "palatable and sweet" fresh water flows into "bitter and salty" seawater. The fresh water seemingly retains its distinctive color and character, and a pool of fresh water can be seen separate from seawater.[*] The phenomenon is visible in many different parts of the world, including where the Tigris, Euphrates, and Nile Rivers flow into the sea.

The first question is whether the mere mention of this by the Quran constitutes a miracle. It might be so if the phenomenon were not visible to the naked eye or were so uncommon that the Arabs would not be expected to know about it, but the fact is that it could be seen at multiple places not too far from Mecca; thus, the mere mention of it in the Quran cannot be considered a miracle.

The next question is whether the Quranic description is scientifically accurate. One discovers that it is not—there is no "insurmountable barrier" between the two waters that prevents their mixing. Even Naik grudgingly concedes that,[†] but to rely on a more authentic source, let us refer to the following definition of an estuary:

---

[*]   The size of the pool varies depending on the influx of fresh water, which shows that it is dependent on a constant inflow.

[†]   He notes, for instance (relying on Gross, *Oceanography*):

Modern science has discovered that in estuaries, where fresh (sweet) and salt water meet, the situation is somewhat different from where two salt water seas meet. It has been discovered that what distinguishes fresh water from salt water in estuaries is a "pycnocline zone with a marked density discontinuity separating the two layers." *This partition (zone of separation) has a salinity different from both the fresh water and the salt water.* This phenomenon occurs in several places, including Egypt, where the river Nile flows into the Mediterranean Sea. (Naik: *The Quran and Modern Science: Compatible or Incompatible?* p. 29)

There would be no "zone of separation" having salinity between that of fresh water and saltwater if there were an insurmountable barrier between the two waters.

a semi-enclosed coastal body of water, which has a free connection with the open sea, *and within which sea water is measurably diluted with freshwater derived from land drainage.*[38]

This clearly documents that there is in fact no impenetrable partition between the two waters. The Quran is thus wrong to suggest that there is an "insurmountable barrier" between the two waters, "one palatable and sweet, the other bitter and salty."[39]

THE MIRACLE OF 19

Some analysts are fascinated by the "miracle of 19"—this being the number of keepers of hell as disclosed in the Quran.[40] Although the Quran does mention other numbers too, it is this number that has attracted particular attention. The following are listed as miracles associated with 19:

- The first *surah* to be revealed has 19 verses.
- The last *surah* to be revealed has 19 words.
- The 50th *surah*, which begins with the letter *Qaf*, contains a total of 57 (19 x 3) letters *Qaf*. There are also 57 letters *Qaf* in the 42nd *surah* with a letter *Qaf* at the beginning. The 50th *Surah* contains 45 verses. Added together, these total 95 (19 x 5). There are 53 verses in the 42nd *surah*. These again total 95 (42 + 53).
- When we add together the number of times that the letter *Qaf* appears in the Qur'an, we reach a total of 798 (19 x 42). Forty-two is the number of another *surah* with *Qaf* among its initial letters.
- The letter *Nun* appears at the beginning of only the 68th *surah*. The total number of times it appears in that *surah* is 133 (19 x 7).
- The letters *Ya* and *Sin* appear at the beginning of *Surah Ya Sin*. The letter *Sin* appears 48 times in *Surah Ya Sin*, and the letter *Ya* 237 times. The total of these letters is 285 (19 x 15).[41]

What is surprising is that the verse (74:31) that mentions this number is not itself the 19th from either end of the *Surah* in which it finds mention; and even the *Surah* is not the 19th from the beginning or the end of the Quran. It would surely have been remarkable if that, too, were the case.

It may also disappoint Muslim scholars that similar permutations can be found regarding just about any work—the possibilities are virtually infinite[42]—but would they agree that as long as one can identify similar permutations, even regarding the number 19, any work that meets the challenge would qualify as the word of Allah? If so, one may want to put Rushdie's *The Satanic Verses* to the test!

THE TECTONIC PLATES

With so many miracles attributed to the Quran, it would be surprising if the Quran omitted mention of the tectonic plates and their movement.

> In one verse, we are informed that mountains are not motionless as they seem, but are in constant motion. *You see the mountains you reckoned to be solid going past like clouds. (Qur'an, 27:88)* This motion of mountains is caused by the movement of the Earth's crust that they are located on. The Earth's crust "floats" over the mantle layer, which is denser. It was at the beginning of the 20th century when, for the first time in history, a German scientist by the name of Alfred Wegener proposed that the continents of the Earth had been attached together when it first formed, but then drifted in different directions, and thus separated as they moved away from each other. Geologists understood that Wegener was right only in the 1980s, 50 years after his death.[43]

Did the author truly neglect to consult the other verses surrounding 27:88?

> And on the Day when the Trumpet will be blown, all those who are in the heavens and the earth, shall be struck with terror except those whom Allah shall be pleased to protect. And all shall present themselves before Him in submission. *Today, you see the mountains and think that they are firmly set, but on that Day they will be flying about like the clouds ... (27:87–88)*[44]

This only shows the extent to which some are prepared to go to prove miracles in the Quran.

THE BIG BANG THEORY

The argument that the Quran foretells the Big Bang theory is based on the following translations, which are not taken from sources we trust in this book.

> *Do not those who disbelieve see that the heavens and the Earth were meshed together* then *We ripped them apart?* And then We made of water everything living? Would they still not believe? (21:30)

> And the heaven, We built it with craftsmanship *and We are still expanding.* (51:47–48)[45]

These translations do capture some of the main elements of the Big Bang theory. Let us, therefore, take a closer look at the highlighted features of the above translations:

o *Do not those who disbelieve see that the heavens and the Earth were meshed together ...?*

It is, of course, a critical feature of the Big Bang theory that the heavens and the earth constituted one mass at the start. The above statement is thus consistent with the theory, but it seems that even the Arabs held the same belief. How do we know that? The quoted words themselves indicate so. The Quran adopts this style ("Do not those who disbelieve see") when referring to matters "known" to the addressee.[46] In contrast, when the Quran talks about matters that shall become evident at a later stage, it uses the words "Those who disbelieve will soon realize."[47] It is thus fair to conclude that the Quran only meant to state what the Arabs already believed in.*

o *... then We ripped them apart.*

This too is a feature of the Big Bang theory, that the formation of the universe commenced with a cataclysmic event. The above words capture that well enough. One must concede, as

---

* It was also quite natural for them to think that if there was an architect of the universe (and we shall see in Chapter 10 that they did believe in one), the heavens and the earth could not have existed on their own before being created. The Arabs seem therefore to have believed that the architect of the universe created the two from one piece, like a potter uses the same piece of clay to make different things.

well, that this could not possibly have been part of the Arab belief of the time and it is therefore remarkable that the Quran should mention this at all. The problem, though, is that these words are missing from translations we use in this book,* which all depict a more sedate happening: "We parted them"/"We clove them asunder." This milder terminology is consistent with the Arab belief of the time that the heavens and the earth were joined together until they were unpeeled by the Creator to make the universe—but it does not contain the additional dimension that this happened through a violent event.

○ ... *and We are still expanding [the heavens].*

The Big Bang theory tells us—as does the above translation—that the universe is still expanding. Again, this is quite remarkable, except that the more dependable translations do not make any mention of this.† They only describe the vastness

---

* Have not the people, who have disbelieved (the Message), ever considered this: the heavens and the earth were at first one mass; then *We parted them*, and created every living thing from water? Do they not acknowledge (that this is Our Creation)? (Maududi)

Do not the Unbelievers see that the heavens and the earth were joined together (as one unit of creation), before *We clove them asunder?* We made from water every living thing. Will they not then believe? (Yusuf Ali)

Have not those who disbelieve *known* that the heavens and the earth were joined together as one united piece, then *We parted them*? And We have made from water every living thing. Will they not then believe? (Hilali-Khan)

Have not those who disbelieve *known* that the heavens and the earth were of one piece, then *We parted them*, and we made every living thing of water? Will they not then believe? (Pickthall)

† And heaven—We built it with might, and We extend it wide. And the earth—We spread it forth; O excellent smoothers! (Maududi)

With power and skill did We construct the Firmament: for it is We Who create the vastness of space. And We have spread out the (spacious) earth: How excellently We do spread out! (Yusuf Ali)

With power did We construct the heaven. Verily, We are able to extend the vastness of space thereof. And We have spread out the earth: how Excellent Spreader (thereof) are We! (Hilali-Khan)

of the heavens, which is visible to all, but do not suggest that the universe is still expanding.

What the above translations do arouse, however, is the expectation that other verses would also exactly match the Big Bang theory; it cannot be that the Quran is so closely aligned with the theory at one point and out of step on other occasions. Let us therefore consult some other verses too, starting with the following:

> O Prophet, say to them, "Do you deny that God, and set up others as equals with Him, *Who created the earth in two days?* He indeed is the Lord of all creation. He set mountains over the earth (after its creation) and bestowed blessings on it, and provided in it means of sustenance adequately according to the needs and demands of all those who ask. *This was done in four days. Then he turned to the heaven, which was only smoke at that time.* He said to the heaven and the earth: 'Come into being whether you like it or not.' They both said: 'We do come in submission.' *Then in two days he made the seven heavens,* and in each heaven He ordained its law, and *We adorned the lower heaven with lights and made it fully secure.* Such is the design of the One who is the All-Mighty, the All-Knowing." (41:9–12)[48]

We learn from these that the earth was created first,[49] which took two days; Allah then set mountains and provided the earth with means of sustenance, which was done in another four days. Thereafter, He turned towards the heavens and created the seven heavens in two days. The entire universe, according to the above count, took eight days in all to be created.

This is incongruous, however, with what the Quran tells us elsewhere, which is that the universe was created in just six days.[50] To avoid this inconsistency, Muslim scholars conclude that the four days it took Allah to set up mountains and to provide the earth with means of sustenance, as noted in verses 41:9–12, must be taken as inclusive of the first two days it took to create the earth.

We have built the heaven with might, and We it is Who make the vast extent (thereof). And the earth have We laid out, how gracious is the Spreader thereof. (Pickthall)

Even still, how is that consistent with the Big Bang theory? Broadly speaking, the theory tells us that the creation of the universe was initiated by the Big Bang, which took place possibly between thirteen to fourteen billion years ago. Over the next several billion years, galaxies (billions in number and each containing billions of stars) were gradually formed. We also learn that while the Milk Way is amongst the oldest galaxies, the solar system comprising the sun and the earth (and other planets) did not actually form until about 4.6 billion years ago. The period between the Big Bang and the formation of the solar system is thus estimated to be nine billion years (and possibly more).

A number of discrepancies between the Big Bang theory and what the Quran describes in verses 41:9–12 are thus instantly visible:

o The Big Bang theory tells us that it took the universe billions of years, not just six days, to form.[51]

o The Big Bang theory also tells us that the earth was not created first and that much of the universe had already been formed before our solar system began to take shape.

o We also learn from the Big Bang theory that the proportionate time it took the earth to be formed as part of the solar system is nowhere near what the Quran suggests, which is that two-thirds of the time was spent only on creating the earth and one-third on the rest of the universe. This shows that the Quran gets it wrong not only in absolute numbers but also on relative scale.[52]

o It also seems odd that if it took the earth alone four days to be created, the entire universe comprising a hundred billion odd galaxies with billions of stars each and countless solar systems like ours should have been created in just two days.[53] Did the Quran not have a fair idea of how truly vast the universe is (in comparison to the earth, at least)?

o The Quran tells us that the universe is arranged as seven heavens, whereas our study of the ever-changing and expanding universe provides no such indication.

The demonstrable fact, therefore, is that the descriptions in these latter verses (41:9–12; 32:4; and 11:7) bear absolutely no resemblance to that of the Big Bang theory. The expectation aroused by the translations noted at the beginning of the section, which seemed so perfectly to fit the theory, is thus let down.

There are also other verses that tell us that Quran's discussion of the universe is far more reflective of the Arab belief system of the time than an accurate depiction of how the universe is actually structured.*

EMBRYOLOGY

We come finally to embryology. The claim regarding this is that the Quran's discussion on the subject is nothing but magical. Keith L. Moore is the one most extensively quoted in this behalf:

> The interpretation of the verses in the Quran referring to human development would not have been possible in the 7th century AD, or even a hundred years ago. We can interpret them now because the science of modern Embryology affords us new understanding. *Undoubtedly there are other verses in the Quran related to human development that will be understood in the future as our knowledge increases.*[54]

---

* *Surah Ar-Raad* verse 2, *Surah Luqman* verse 10, *Surah Ar-Rum* verse 25, and *Surah At-Tur* verse 38 may, for instance, be noted:
> It is Allah Who raised up the heavens without such pillars as you could see: then He sat Himself upon the Throne of His Kingdom (13:2)
> He created the heavens without pillars that you could see. (31:10)
> And of his Signs is this that *the Heaven and the Earth stand firm by His Command.* (30:25)
> Do they have a ladder by climbing which they overhear what goes on in heavens? Then let any of them who has overheard bring a clear proof. (52:38)

Yusuf Ali's translations:
> Allah is He Who raised the heavens without any pillars that ye can see; is firmly established on the throne (of authority). (13:2)
> He created the heavens without any pillars that ye can see. (31:10)
> And among His Signs is this, *that heaven and earth stand by His Command.* (30:25)
> Or have they a ladder, by which they can (climb up to heaven and) listen (to its secrets)? Then let (such a) listener of theirs produce a manifest proof. (52:38)

What is interesting is that even Moore seems to concede that there are verses that are inconsistent with our present knowledge, though he expresses the confidence that they too will be understood as our knowledge increases! The very first verses of the Quran ("Read in the name of your Lord Who created man from a clot of congealed blood") come to mind. There are others too, as we shall see below.

Going through the above-referred article, one discovers that Moore's confidence in the Quran is ultimately based on certain elements.

- Moore is fascinated that the Quran describes the embryo as a "leach-like structure," which he says is the correct description of the embryo between 7 and 24 days.[55]
- He is also amazed by the description "a chewed lump," which pertains to a slightly subsequent stage. This, too, he thinks is accurate.
- Lastly, he is impressed by the order in which the Quran describes the appearance of hearing, seeing, and understanding in the embryo. How could the Quran have known this so many centuries ago?

We shall see that each of these elements turns out to be spurious and inaccurate.

Moore draws the first two elements from Zendani's translation of verse 23:14[56]:

> Then We made the drop into a *leech-like structure*. Then of that leech-like structure, We made a *chewed lump*. Then We made out of the *chewed lump*, bones, and clothed the bones in flesh. Then We developed out of it another creature.

None of the translations we trust in this book agree with Zendani's, though. They translate the verse as referring to "a clot of (congealed) blood" and "piece of flesh"/"lump" instead of "a leech-like structure" and "chewed lump."* Two of the three

---

* Maududi's and Yusuf Ali's translations follow (the other two translations, which can be consulted in the Appendix, are along similar lines):
  [T]hen changed the sperm drop into *a clot of blood* and the clot into *a piece of flesh*: then turned the *piece of flesh* into bones: then clothed

elements constituting the mainstay of Moore's thesis thus disappear (if reliance is placed on the translators we trust).[57]

One is also not sure why Moore finds the descriptions "a leech-like structure" and "a chewed lump" so fascinating in the first place, considering that the various stages of embryos were visible through miscarriages and dissections (both of which were employed as means of observation by the Greeks, for instance) and that Moore himself concedes that as early as the fourth week, the embryo would be visible to the unaided eye and would resemble a leech-like structure. If it resembles a chewed lump* at a later stage, that too would be visible to the naked eye through miscarriages and dissections, so why the fascination?

We move next to the third element of Moore's thesis, namely the order in which the Quran (supposedly) describes the appearance of hearing, seeing, and understanding in the embryo. He draws this from Zendani's translation of verse 32:9:

---

the bones with flesh, and then brought him forth as quite a different creation (from the embryo). (Maududi)

Then We made the sperm into *a clot of congealed blood.* Then of that clot We made a (foetus) *lump*; then We made out of that *lump* bones and clothed the bones with flesh; then We developed out of it another creature. (Yusuf Ali)

Interestingly, Yusuf Ali's revised translation is as follows:

Then We made the sperm into *a leech-like clot.* Then of that clot We made a (foetus) *lump*; then We made out of that *lump* bones and clothed the bones with flesh; then We developed out of it another creature. (*The Meaning of the Holy Qur'an,* Eleventh Edition (1430 AH/2009 AC) Amana Corporation, Maryland)

The change seems to have been inspired by Moore's article—as the referenced source does state: "Revisions have been made in both the content and form of the original work. Where necessary, the content has been updated within the current understanding and interpretation of the Qur'an" (p. xi).

On the description "a chewed lump," even Moore is a shade tentative:

The Arabic word "mudghah" means "chewed substance or chewed lump." Toward the end of the fourth week, *the human embryo looks somewhat like a chewed lump of flesh.* The chewed appearance results from the somites which resemble teeth marks. The somites represent the beginnings or primordia of the vertebrae. (Moore: "A Scientist's Interpretation of References to Embryology in the Quran," pp. 15 16)

According to Moore, the human embryo looks "somewhat like a chewed lump"! One gets the impression that this may not be exactly so.

And He gave you hearing and sight and feeling and *understanding.*

Because understanding is a function of the brain, Moore assumes that the Quran must be referring to it and therefore includes the following discussion in his article:

This part of Sura 32:9 indicates that the special senses of hearing, seeing, and feeling develop in this order, which is true. The primordia of the internal ears appear before the beginning of the eyes, *and the brain (the site of understanding) differentiates last.*[58]

What Moore does not realize is that the verse 32:9 actually mentions "the hearts" and not "understanding."* Because the Quran incorrectly attributes the function of understanding to the heart (as discussed in Chapter 2), Zendani† exercises the license to translate the verse as though it is referring to understanding. Absolutely unaware of this huge leap, Moore takes it a step further and starts discussing the development of the brain in the embryo, much impressed that the verse is consistent with the scientific fact that "the brain (the site of understanding) differentiates last"!

Moore thus is misled by false translations, but his approach, too, leaves much to be desired. While referring to verse 23:13,[59] he notes:

The drop or *nutfah* has been interpreted as the sperm or spermatozoon, *but a more meaningful interpretation would be the zygote which divides to form a blastocyst which is implanted in the uterus.*[60]

Maududi, Hilali-Khan, and Pickthall translate the verse:
    ...and He gave you the ears, and the eyes *and the hearts.* (Maududi)
    ...and He gave you hearing (ears), sight (eyes) *and hearts.* (Hilali-Khan)
    ...and appointed for you hearing and sight and *hearts.* (Pickthall)
Yusuf Ali, in contrast, uses the words "and feeling (and understanding)," and we shall presently see why that may be the case.
    And He gave you (the faculties of) hearing and sight *and feeling (and understanding).*
†   As also Yusuf Ali.

It is apparent right away that Moore is looking for "a more meaningful interpretation" of the Quran, not an accurate depiction of what the Quran says.* The same zeal—i.e., the desire to make the Quran look better than it is—also inspires the following comment (in relation to the verse "He makes you in the wombs of your mothers *in stages,* one after another, in *three veils of darkness*"[61]):

> It is unlikely that they [doctors in the 7th century A.D.] knew that it [embryo] developed in stages, even though Aristotle had described the stages of development of the chick embryo in the 4th century B.C. The realization that the human embryo develops in stages was not discussed and illustrated until the 15th century.[62]

The statement "it is unlikely that they knew that it [embryo] developed in stages" is disappointing. Scientists in earlier days lacked modern instruments, but they had alternative means of observation. Galen, for instance, describes abortions and dissections as two sources of information. This may not have given them an exact understanding of how the embryo develops, but they knew that it develops in stages!†

Not surprisingly at all, Moore also avoids discussion of verses

---

* *Nutfah,* of course, means "the sperm or spermatozoon," whereas a zygote results from the fertilization of the ovum by the sperm. The two are entirely different. In any case, only the sperm drop is placed in a place of rest (the ovum is already there), so by no stretch can the verse be translated as referring to a zygote. One is thus entitled to ask: If *nutfah* means a sperm (which it unmistakably does and which Moore concedes), why should we allow "a more meaningful interpretation" to change that to "zygote"? Just to make the Quran more congruous with science?

† Regarding specifically the "three veils of darkness," Moore has the following to add:

> The three veils of darkness *may refer to*: (1) the anterior abdominal wall; (2) the uterine wall; and (3) the amniochorionic membrane. *Although there are other interpretations of this statement, the one presented here seems the most logical from an embryological point of view.* (Moore: "A Scientist's Interpretation of References to Embryology in the Quran," p. 15)

One can tell that there is no perfect fit between the above verse and biological facts. Moore tries to find a suitable fit but is forced to yield that other interpretations are possible, too—which means that the "veils of darkness" may not perhaps be three exactly!

that are problematic. He does not, for instance, discuss the verse that informs us that man is created from "a clot of congealed blood" (96:2).* As noted in Chapter 1, if the Quran means to tell us that blood has anything to do with conception, it adopts the same error as committed by earlier scientists who also drew an erroneous association between blood and conception (perhaps on the basis that menses stops in pregnancy). And if it means to tell us that the embryo, at any stage of its development, involves (or even resembles) "a clot of congealed blood," then, too, the description is inaccurate. Congealed blood (as in coagulated or frozen or solidified blood) never forms part of the embryo (i.e., in the mother's womb).†

Moore also then omits discussion of the verses noted in Chapter 2 that inform us that the sex of the embryo is determined after the limbs have been fashioned.‡ As we noted, this is the stage stage at which a miscarried embryo shows signs of his or her sex through the formation of the genitals but is not the moment when sex is actually determined. Again, the Quran replicates the error committed by earlier scientists.

Moore also does not include the following verses (encountered in Chapter 2) in his discussion:

> Then let man at least consider from what he is created. *He is created from a spurting fluid that issues forth from between the backbone and the breast bones.* (86:5–7)[63]

As noted in Chapter 2, if one draws a line between any part of a man's breastbone or ribs and the backbone, the organs that

---

*   It may be noted that even the revision to Yusuf Ali's translation mentions "leech-like *clot of congealed blood*" (see endnote 1 to Chapter 1).

†   The Quran may perhaps have thought so on account of the appearance of a miscarried embryo, if aborted during a certain phase of the embryonic development.

‡   For reference, the verses are noted below:
> Does man think that he will be left to himself to wander at will? Was he not a mere sperm drop, which is emitted (in the mother's womb)? Then he became a blood clot then Allah formed him and fashioned his limbs in proportion; *then from it he made two kinds, male and female*. Has he not then the power to give life to the dead. (75:36–40)

actually produce, store, and emit the fluid are missed out every which way.[64]

All told, there is no avoiding the fact that Moore's celebrated analysis is seriously flawed. The Quran's discussion on embryology is very far from being a scientific miracle; if anything, it is inaccurate.

*

We note from the discussion in this chapter that tall claims are made regarding scientific miracles in the Quran that turn out in the end to be hollow. What is disappointing is that often enough, such claims are based on incorrect and manufactured translations.

The fact is that the Quran is simply not a scientific miracle. It was perhaps never intended to be. Those who put forward the claim only end up drawing attention towards glaring deficiencies that can hardly be expected from Allah. Maududi, in contrast, takes the more prudent approach. He is of the view that the Quran does not mean to state scientific facts. Speaking incidentally in the context of embryology, he notes:

> This refers to the different stages of development of the child in the womb of its mother. *This description is based on observation and not on scientific research*, and there was no need for it for the purpose for which reference to this has been made here.[65]

Muslim scholars will perhaps serve their religion better if they too stick to this very pragmatic approach.

5

THE QURAN AND JUSTICE

Fiat justitia ruat caelum.*—Piso

It is difficult for one to disagree with John Rawls as he states the indispensible value of justice:

> Justice is the first virtue of social institutions, as truth is of systems of thought. A theory however elegant and economical must be rejected or revised if it is untrue; likewise laws and institutions no matter how efficient and well-arranged must be reformed or abolished if they are unjust. ...
> *Being first virtues of human activities, truth and justice are uncompromising.*[1]

The Quran too echoes much the same priority—though its focus in the following verses is narrower, applied to disputes involving individuals rather than laws and institutions:

---

* "Let justice be done though the heavens fall."

(O Muslims), Allah enjoins you to ... judge with justice, when you judge between the people. (4:58)[2]

There is thus little disagreement as far as the priority of justice is concerned—all are agreed that it should be foremost. It is when we come to what justice truly means that differences emerge. In this chapter, we familiarize ourselves with the Quran's understanding of justice.

One may have started with the caution that because each age has its own vision of justice, one must not expect the Quran to replicate ours, but there are Muslims, particularly the more moderate ones, who insist that it does. They maintain that, in contrast to man-made systems of thought, which are anchored in their respective times, the Quran transcends this limitation and is able to deliver a concept of justice remarkably consistent with our present-day understanding. They even demand that credit be given to the Quran for recent advances in moral philosophy. We must keep this claim in perspective as we take a closer look at the Quran's concept of justice.

SLAVERY

Slavery provides a useful starting point. Our contemporary sense of justice dictates that slavery is against the most basic human rights and is absolutely unacceptable. Article 4 of the Universal Declaration of Human Rights reflects the consensus in this regard.[*] In the same vein, many modern-day constitutions also spell out unambiguously that slavery shall not be permitted in any form.

As for the Quran's position on slavery, the following verses are noteworthy, in that they recognize slavery but also depict compassion for the slaves.

And if one slays a Believer by error, *he must set free one believing slave* as expiation. (4:92)

---

[*]   Article 4 states: "No one shall be held in slavery or servitude; slavery and the slave trade shall be prohibited in all their forms."

The expiation (of breaking such an oath) is ... *to free one slave.* (5:89)

And if those who are in your possession, ask for a deed of emancipation, execute the deed of emancipation with them, provided that you find some good in them. (24:33)[3]

Moderate Muslims argue that this is as good as banning slavery. They maintain that prohibiting the practice outright would have been disruptive in those days and that change needed instead to be introduced gently, which is what the Quran implements, but that one ought to be able to extrapolate from the compassion noted in the above verses that slavery is in fact illegal in Islam.

The purist, in comparison, is not satisfied that this critical issue should have been left to extrapolation. Why did the Quran not close the debate altogether? The purist is also troubled by the following verses:

Most certainly those Believers have attained true success who ... guard their private parts scrupulously, *except with regard to their wives and those women who are legally in their possession,* for in that case they shall not be blameworthy. (23:1–6)

But those people (are an exception) who are the performers of salat ... who guard their private parts. *Except with regard to their wives and those women who are legally in their possession,* for in their case they are not blameworthy. (70:22–30)[4]

These verses quite clearly permit sexual intercourse with the slave girls.* That being so, did the Quran really mean to ban slavery?

The purist also wants to know whether Muhammad's own household was free of slaves. The argument put forward by the moderates—that change needed to be introduced gradually—may have applied to other believers but surely not to the Prophet's own family. It is thus absolutely critical to the purist to establish that the Prophet's own household remained free of slaves, to

---

* These verses (and others like these) have encouraged the opinion (as we noted in Chapter 3) that "one is permitted to have conjugal relations with one's slave girls besides the wedded wives, and there is no restriction on their number." (Maududi: *The Meaning of the Qur'an,* note 94 to *Surah Al-Ahzab,* Volume 4, p. 131)

serve as a beacon for others. Did it? The following verse seems to provide the answer:

> There is no blame on the wives of the Prophet that they are visited in their houses by their fathers, their sons, their brothers, their brothers' sons, their sisters' sons, their family women *and their slaves*. (33:55)[5]

What is equally significant is that this verse was revealed in the fifth year after migration (5 AH)—i.e., eighteen years after the advent of Islam. Muhammad's own household ought to have been absolutely free of slaves by then, if the Quran intended to make slavery illegal.[6]

More perplexing still is the fact that even the Prophet was permitted by the Quran to keep slave girls:

> "O Prophet, We have made lawful to you … those women who come into your possession out of the slave girls granted by Allah … You may however have slave girls." (33:50–52)[7]

This was a concession he availed himself of, as well, as noted in Chapter 3.*

It is therefore difficult to agree with moderate Muslims that the Quran means to ban slavery. The Quran certainly shows greater resolve on adoption. Recall that the Prophet was commanded by Allah to marry his adopted son's divorced wife in order to discontinue the practice of adoption. The Quran could similarly have instructed the Prophet and his wives (at least) to remain free of slavery, but apparently, this was not a priority.

All said, it is difficult to hold that the Quran reflects our present-day commitment against slavery, which has inspired wars to be fought just to abolish the practice. It would be unfair to give the Quran any credit for this admirable spirit.

---

* Recall that one such slave girl, Mariyah Qubiyyah, even caused a souring of terms with the holy wives.

WAGING WAR AGAINST ALLAH AND HIS MESSENGER AND SPREADING MISCHIEF (*FASAD*)

Our contemporary sense of justice dictates that each person is entitled to practice and propagate the religion of his or her choice, which includes the right to renounce a faith. It is also felt that each person is entitled to express himself freely, even if the views are contrary to those of the majority, are against the religious convictions of any community, or are critical of religious personalities.

These rights also, incidentally, find reflection in the Universal Declaration of Human Rights.*

Islam, however, is distinctly uncomfortable with these propositions—particularly the right to renounce one's religion and the broad right to freedom of opinion and expression. That is why some Muslim countries have not accepted the Universal Declaration of Human Rights. Instead, one sees rather strict blasphemy laws in many Islamic countries making disrespectful remarks against the Prophet punishable with death.

The question is whether this kind of "intolerance" is based on the Quran. The following verses invite attention:

> The punishment of those who wage war against Allah and His Messenger and run about to spread mischief in the land is this; they should be put to death or crucified or their alternate hands and feet should be cut off, or they should be banished from the land. This is the disgrace and ignominy for them in this world and there is in store for them a harsher torment in

---

* *Article 18*:
  > Everyone has the right to freedom of thought, conscience and religion; *this right includes freedom to change his religion or belief*, and freedom, either alone or in community with others and in public or private, to manifest his religion or belief in teaching, practice, worship and observance.

  Article 19:
  > Everyone has the right to freedom of opinion and expression; this right includes freedom to hold opinions without interference and to seek, receive and impart information and ideas through any media and regardless of frontiers.

the Hereafter, except those, who repent before you have power over them for you should know that Allah is Forgiving and Compassionate. (5:33–34)[8]

These verses stipulate that waging war against Allah and His Messenger, and spreading mischief *(fasad)* is punishable with death, crucifixion, cutting off of alternate hands and feet, or banishment. Beyond that, the Quran does not provide any guidance on how these punishments are to be allocated amongst those found guilty.[*] Neither are the contours of this extremely serious offense sufficiently clarified. Thus, the fundamental requirement of justice that laws, particularly criminal laws, should admit of no doubt and that all persons must be informed of the exact limits beyond which they would be punished, as also the extent of the punishment, seems ignored.

Let us explore what could potentially be covered, however.

- **Warfare**

Waging physical war against Allah and His Messenger seems the most obvious offense covered by the above verses. As noted in Chapter 3, it is also the case that the Prophet ordered killings of prisoners of war (albeit selective) who were guilty of waging war against Allah and His Messenger.[†]

- **Blasphemy**

The verses are also broad enough to capture blasphemy, as ridiculing or criticizing the Prophet is tantamount to spreading mischief and waging war against Allah and His Messenger. This is the basis for many Muslim countries to legislate the offense of blasphemy.

---

[*]   In other words who should be killed, who ought to be crucified, who must suffer cutting off of alternate hands and feet, and who mere banishment.

[†]   With the Quran being a timeless command, is there any reason why this should not apply in today's world? That is how the Taliban justify killings of prisoners of war.

The Prophet himself set some early precedents, too. Ka'b Ibn Ashraf, a Jewish poet who used to make fun of the Prophet and the Quran, was the first to be killed in Medina on the specific orders of the Prophet.[9] This precedent was also followed after the conquest of Mecca. Amongst those ordered to be killed were al-Huwayrith and Sara both of whom had insulted the Prophet.[10] Mention may also be made of Asma d. Marwan, who used to make speeches against the Prophet:

> When the apostle heard what she had said he said, "Who will rid me of Marwan's daughter?" Umayr b. Adiyy al-Khatmi who was with him heard him, and that very night he went to her house and killed her. In the morning he came to the apostle and told him what he had done and he said, "You have helped God and His apostle, O' Umayr!"[11]

• *Apostasy*

What about apostasy? Can that be equated with waging war against Allah and His messenger? Relinquishing Islam is an act of defiance against Allah and His Messenger. If not suitably punished, it may encourage others to follow suit. There are also precedents from the Prophet's life that support the conclusion that apostasy is punishable under the above verses. Ibn Ishaq, for instance, records the following account regarding the conquest of Mecca:

> The apostle had ordered his commanders when they entered Mecca only to fight those who resisted them, except a small number who were to be killed even if they were found beneath the curtains of the Ka'ba. Among them was Abdullah b. Sa'd. The reason he ordered him to be killed was that he had been a Muslim and used to write down revelation; then he apostatized. Another was Abdullah b. Khatal. He had become a Muslim ... and apostatized. He had two singing girls Fartana and her friend who used to sing satirical songs about the apostle, so he ordered that they should be killed with him.[12]

- ### *Practicing a religion other than Islam*

As we shall see in Chapter 7, the Quran may view other religions as falling into two categories. There are the people of the Book (the Jews and the Christians) who are to be humbled but not destroyed. They are also permitted to practice their religion within the Islamic State, provided they pay *Jizya* (poll tax). As for the adherents of all other religions, they seem to fall in the category of polytheists, who are to be killed unless they convert to Islam.

When we look at verses 5:33–34 in this context, the following position seems to emerge:

- Practicing polytheism in itself constitutes war against Allah and His Messenger. Hence it is that polytheists are to be killed.
- People of the Book are permitted to practice their religion, but if they propagate it beyond their community, that may perhaps be to take it too far.

*

The principle that each person is entitled to the maximum possible liberty compatible with equal liberty for others,[13] which finds reflection in the Universal Declaration of Human Rights and constitutes the heart of modern liberal thought, does not seem to sit well with the Quran. This principle dictates that each person has the right to criticize Muhammad just as he and his followers had the right to ridicule the gods and religion of the Quraysh.[14] This principle also demands that each person be extended the right not only to practice and propagate his or her religion but also to renounce it, as did the believers who left paganism to join Islam in seventh-century Arabia and as do fresh converts to Islam today, but this goes beyond what the Quran seems to permit.

There is thus a visible divide between our present-day sense of justice and what the Quran allows regarding freedom of religion and expression. The divide becomes all too apparent when issues like Rushdie's *The Satanic Verses*, the Danish cartoons, and the movie *The Innocence of Muslims* surface, but it is there all along. It is wrong to deny it.

PERSONAL FREEDOMS

Modern liberal thought rests on the premise that there are certain inalienable rights that dictate that each person should be allowed a sphere where he is absolutely free to practice his choices and where society has no right to interfere. Interaction of virtually all kinds between consenting adults, particularly in the privacy of their homes, falls into this category. The majority cannot, for instance, impose its decision by making homosexual behavior punishable, as this is a matter that falls entirely within the sphere allocated to the individual.

Most religions, however, find such freedom troublesome,* Islam being no exception. The first verses in this behalf were revealed shortly after the Prophet's migration to Medina:

> If any of your women be guilty of indecency, call for four witnesses from among yourselves to testify against them: If they give evidence and prove the guilt, then confine them to their houses until death comes to them or Allah opens some other way out for them. And punish the two of you who commit this crime; then if they both repent and reform themselves, leave them alone, for Allah is generous in accepting repentance, and merciful in forgiving sins. (4:15–16)[15]

These verses dictate that the women guilty of "indecency" and "the two of you who commit this crime" are punishable. The punishment is spelled out in following verses:

---

* They prescribe strict limits on sexual conduct, which is generally permitted only within the bounds of marriage—the Quran is an exception in that it allows sex with slave girls as well. There is also a consensus amongst many religions regarding homosexuality that it is "unnatural" and therefore impermissible. There may indeed have been justifiable reasons for placing restrictions on sexual conduct in earlier times. This helped control sexually transmitted diseases and also tended to minimize doubts about parentage of children. However, now that there are foolproof methods for disease avoidance, birth control, and to the ability to determine parentage with precision (through DNA testing), some of the reasons for these restrictions seems to have been lost.

The woman and the man guilty of fornication, flog each one of them with a hundred stripes and let not any pity for them restrain you in regard to a matter prescribed by Allah, if you believe in Allah and the Last Day, and let, some of the believers witness the punishment inflicted on them. A man guilty of adultery (or fornication) shall not marry any but the woman guilty of the same or a *mushrik* woman, and none shall marry a woman guilty of adultery (or fornication) but the man guilty of the same or a *mushrik* man: such marriages are forbidden to true believers. (24:2–3)[16]

Interestingly, the Quran does not prescribe stoning to death for adultery, though there are accounts of the Prophet implementing this punishment.* If these accounts are correct, then either the Prophet felt that he could disregard the Quran or perhaps there were verses prescribing stoning to death that got omitted when the Quran was compiled (which happened after the Prophet's death). Certainly, the explanation given by some jurists that stoning applies to adultery after marriage and lashes apply when the offense is committed before marriage seems inadequate, as demonstrated by the following verse:

Whoever cannot afford to marry free Muslim women, should marry one of the Muslim slave-girls in your possession ... Then if they are guilty of indecency, after they have been fortified by wedlock, they shall be given half the punishment prescribed for free women. (4:25)[17]

If a slave girl "fortified by wedlock" is to be given "half the punishment prescribed for free women," who are to be stoned to death, how would that work? Verse 33:30 raises much the same issue:

---

* Maududi, for instance, notes:

  As regards the punishment for adultery after marriage, the Quran does not mention it, but it has been prescribed in the Traditions. We learn from many authentic Traditions that not only did the Holy Prophet prescribe the punishment of stoning to death for it verbally but also enforced it practically in several cases. (Maududi: *The Meaning of the Qur'an*, Note 2 to *Surah An-Noor*, Volume 3, p. 298)

Wives of the Prophet, whoever among you commits a manifest indecency, will be doubly punished.[18]

It is remarkable that the Quran even contemplated this possibility regarding the holy wives,* but the question also is, if wives of the Prophet were to be "doubly punished," how would that have worked in the context of stoning to death?

Whatever the exact measure of punishment (one hundred lashes or stoning to death), it is at least clear that there is little room in the Quran for personal freedoms of the kind allowed by modern liberal thought. What is perplexing, though, is that the Quran does not include any discussion on forced intercourse. It is absolutely silent on rape. Perhaps its intense focus on consensual sex (which we may not even consider punishable) allowed this "lesser" offense to go undetected.

Equally notable is the Quran's omission to prohibit sex with underage girls. Considering that girls used to be married young in the Bedouin culture (the Prophet's own marriage to Aisha is an example) and also that the Quran allows sex with slave girls (when children, too, could fall in that category) the issue was there to be addressed, but far from barring it, the Quran even endorsed the practice of child brides, as we shall see in Chapter 6.

MURDER

Murder is an offense recognized by all systems of law. The Quran is no exception. We take A. J. Arberry's translation of the verse that deals with it:

> O believers, prescribed for you is retaliation, touching the slain; *freeman for freeman, slave for slave, female for female*. But if aught is pardoned a man by his brother, let the pursuing be honorable, and let the payment be with kindliness. (2:178)[19]

One gets the impression that punishment for murder is dependent on the status of the person killed. In other words, if a

---

Perhaps this too (much like the command against backbiting, which was discussed in Chapter 3), is best explained as reflective of certain paranoia.

freeman has been murdered, a freeman needs to be put to death by way of retaliation. If a woman has been killed, then the compensation has to be in the form of a woman. And if a slave is killed, then a slave needs to be sacrificed or handed over in retribution. This is the message one draws from the words "freeman for freeman, slave for slave, female for female."

This was also the custom in tribal Arabia,[20] and it made sense in a system that did not recognize all to be equal. If one lost a slave, it was unfair to demand as retribution the life of the freeman who may have committed the murder. Adequate compensation required that a slave be killed or handed over in retaliation. In contrast, if a slave happened to kill a freeman, punishing the slave alone would hardly have restored the balance. Where all were not equal, justice demanded retribution according to the status of the slain.

This offends present-day sensibilities, however, as we treat all to be equal and firmly believe that liability for a crime rests squarely and only with the person who commits it. We therefore consider it unjust to punish a person who is not responsible for the crime. This raises the question: Could the Quran be so far removed from our present-day sense of justice, or does the fault lie in the above translation?

Maududi and Yusuf Ali translate the same verse differently:

O Believers, the law of retribution has been prescribed for you in cases of murder; if a free man commits a murder, *the free man shall be punished for it and a slave for a slave*: likewise if a woman is guilty of murder the same shall be accountable for it. But in case the injured brother is willing to show leniency to the murderer, the blood money should be decided in accordance with the common law and the murderer should pay it in a genuine way. (Maududi)

O ye who believe! the law of equality is prescribed to you in cases of murder: *the free for the free, the slave for the slave, the woman for the woman*. But if any remission is made by the brother of the slain, then grant any reasonable demand, and compensate him with handsome gratitude, this is a concession and a Mercy from your Lord. (Yusuf Ali)

Except for one slip by Maududi ("a slave for a slave"), both translations agree that it is the person who commits the crime who must be punished.*

If that is the message the Quran truly means to communicate, however, it could easily have communicated it in this way: "Prescribed to you is retribution for murder; the person committing it shall be punished for it." There was no need to include multiple parties (freemen, slaves, and women) in the equation, which lends itself to the contrary interpretation discussed above. Considering also that there was an existing tribal custom that required retribution according to the status of the victim, clearer articulation was required if that custom was to be set aside. One is therefore not sure if the Quran really intended to interfere with the existing practice.

Another problematic aspect is that of blood money: "But in case the injured brother† is willing to show leniency to the murderer, the blood money should be decided in accordance with the common law and the murderer should pay it in a genuine way." It seems odd that the murderer should be allowed to go free, without suffering the penalty, if only the brother of the slain is persuaded to forgive. But what if the brother himself (or someone dear to him) is the murderer? Equally, what about the situation in which the slain does not have a brother?[21] If we are at all to extend the concession, why should the murderer not have the same opportunity to pay blood money and secure pardon as he would if the slain did have a brother? And then, why should the brother be the one to take this critical decision—why not the son of the slain, or his father? All this seems a bit arbitrary.‡

---

* This conclusion seems to be based largely on extrapolation, though, rather than exact translation. For instance, the words "if a freeman *commits* a murder" (in Maududi's translation) are missing in the Quranic text. Likewise, the words "the law of *equality* is prescribed to you" (in Yusuf Ali's translation) seem an extrapolation.

† translated by Yusuf Ali as "the brother of the slain"

‡ If the language ("the injured brother"/"brother of the slain") is meant to include other relatives, this creates its own problem. Who, ultimately, would decide that the murderer should be pardoned?

The Quran's casual handling of murder is also evident in two Quranic accounts regarding Moses. According to the first, Moses deliberately kills a man and is not only forgiven by Allah but also rewarded with prophethood.[22] The second records an even stranger encounter Moses has with Khidr (who may have been an angel or a prophet—it is not clarified). It is best to set this out in full:

> There they found one of our servants whom We had blessed with special favor and had given him a special knowledge from Ourselves. Moses said to him, "May I accompany you, so that you may teach me also that Wisdom, which has been taught to you?" He answered, "You cannot bear with me, and you cannot have the patience with regard to that matter of which you have no knowledge." Moses said, "If Allah wills, you will find me patient and I will not disobey you in any matter." He said, "Well, if you want to accompany me, you should ask me no questions about anything until I myself mention it to you." So they proceeded on until they boarded a boat, and that person bored a hole in the boat. Moses cried out, "What! have you bored a hole in it so that all the passengers may be drowned? This is a grievous thing that you have done." He answered, "Didn't I tell you that you would not be able to bear with me patiently?" Moses replied, "Please do not rebuke me for my forgetfulness, and do not take me to task in regard to my conduct." *Then they journeyed on until they met a boy and that person slew him. Moses cried out, "Have you killed an innocent person, though he had killed nobody? Surely this is a horrible deed that you have committed."* He answered, "Didn't I tell you that you would not be able to bear with me patiently?" Moses said, "If after this, I ask anything of you, you may not let me accompany you. Well, now I have afforded you with an excuse from myself." Then they traveled on until they reached a certain habitation and requested its inhabitants to give them some food but they declined to entertain them. There they saw a wall which was about to fall down. That person set it up again. Moses said, "Had you wanted, you could have demanded payment for your labor." The other said, "That will do: we must now part company. Now I explain those things about which you could not keep patience. As regards the boat, it belonged to a few poor persons who toiled on the river. I

intended to damage it because further on there was the territory of a king who forcibly seized every boat. *As for the boy, his parents were true Believers and we feared lest he should trouble them with his rebellion and unbelief. Therefore we wished that in his stead their Lord may grant them another child who may be more righteous and filial.* As regards the wall, it belonged to two orphan boys, who reside in this city. A treasure for them lies buried under this wall. As their father was a righteous man, your Lord willed that when these children attain their maturity, they should dig out their treasure. All this has been done as a mercy from your Lord: I have not done anything of my own authority. This is the interpretation of those things about which you could not keep patience."(18:65–82)[23]

One is not sure what message the Quran means to deliver in these verses. Maududi is equally perplexed:

> In connection with this story, a very hard problem arises to which an answer must be found: Two of the three things done by Hadrat Khidr are obviously against those commandments of the Law which have always been in force since the creation of man. No law allows anyone the right to damage the property of another and kill an innocent person. So much so that if a man were to know by inspiration that some usurper would illegally seize a certain boat, and that a certain boy would be involved in a rebellion and unbelief, even then no law, sent down by Allah, makes it lawful that one should bore a hole in the boat and kill the innocent boy by virtue of one's inspiration. If in answer to this, one were to say that Hadrat Khidr committed these two acts by the Commands of Allah, this does not solve the problem, for the question is not this, "By whose command did Hadrat Khidr commit these acts?" but it is this: "What was the nature of these commands?" This is important because Hadrat Khidr did these acts in accordance with Divine Command, for he himself says that these acts of his were not done by his own authority, but were moved by the mercy of Allah, and Allah Himself has testified this by saying: "We gave him a special knowledge from Ourselves." *Thus it is beyond any doubt that these acts were done by the Command of Allah, but the question about the nature of the command remains there, for it is obvious that these commands were not legal because it is not allowed by any Divine Law, and the fundamental*

principles of the Quran also do not allow that a person should kill another person without any proof of his guilt. Therefore we shall have to admit that these commands belonged to one of those decrees of Allah in accordance with which one sick person recovers, while another dies: one becomes prosperous and the other is ruined. If the Commands given to Hadrat Khidr were of this nature, then one must come to the conclusion that Hadrat Khidr was an angel (or some other kind of Allah's creation) who is not bound by the Divine Law prescribed for human beings, for such commands as have no legal aspect, can be addressed to angels only. This is because the question of the lawful or the unlawful cannot arise about them: they obey the Commands of Allah without having any personal power. In contrast to them, a man shall be guilty of a sin whether he does any such thing inadvertently by intuition or by some inspiration, if his act goes against some Divine Commandment. This is because a man is bound to abide by Divine Commandments as a man, and there is no room whatsoever in the Divine Law that an act may become lawful for a man merely because he had received an instruction by inspiration and had been informed in a secret way of the wisdom of that unlawful act.[24]

Not surprisingly, though, the Taliban quote these very verses to justify attacks on and killings of little schoolgirls (who they feel would spread "rebellion and unbelief" if allowed to be educated). They believe that the Quran gives clear guidance that even children can be killed in anticipation of their future "errant" conduct!

It is difficult thus to resist the conclusion that, in respect of murder, at least, the Quran is deeply anchored in its times, far removed from ours.

THEFT

Hammurabi was the first to legislate the principle of an eye for an eye. This was in eighteenth-century BCE. The principle demands proportionality between the offense and retribution.

The Quran too is aware of this, in the context of the Jewish scriptures,[25] but opts for the following when prescribing punishment for theft:

> As for the thief, whether man or woman, cut off the hand of either of them: it is the recompense for what they have earned, and an exemplary punishment from Allah; Allah is All-Powerful, All-Wise. (5:38)[26]

Could this punishment apply even to trivial thefts (e.g., a mother stealing food to feed hungry kids)? The Quran does not exclude the possibility.

The Quran also seems unmindful of the possibility of human error, which is one major reason why capital punishment is opposed so vociferously by some. What if it transpires that a failure of justice has taken place? How do we rectify the error? Cutting a thief's hand poses a similar issue. Suppose it is discovered that a mistake was made—perhaps the "stolen property" was only misplaced and not stolen, or it turns out that somebody else took it, or that the witnesses lied for ulterior purposes. No doubt, even in the case of false imprisonment, we cannot restore the time a person may have lost, but he is at least able to live a full life after the mistake is recognized. Not so with his hand chopped off! He must carry that for the rest of his life. The punishment is also excessively harsh and disproportionate*—even barbaric, some would insist! That said though, it is wrong to accuse the Quran of inventing such punishment. This was the punishment for theft according to Arab custom.[27] The Quran only continued it.

*

One gathers from the above discussion that the Quran has its own sense of justice not always in accord with ours and more

---

* What makes it even harsher is that in those days, it would be highly likely that cutting the hand might result in death due to infections and blood loss. The Quran could at least have considered imposing lesser harm, such as cutting a finger and reserving the extreme punishment, if at all, for a hardened thief.

deeply entrenched in seventh-century Arabia than some Muslim scholars would have us believe. Just so, Piso's understanding of justice was anchored in his times and is therefore difficult for us to appreciate, but it made perfect sense to him:

> Seneca tells of Gnaeus Piso, a Roman governor and lawmaker, when he was angry, ordering the execution of a soldier who had returned from a leave of absence without his comrade, on the ground that if the man did not produce his companion, he had presumably killed the latter. As the condemned man was presenting his neck to the executioner's sword, there suddenly appeared the very comrade who was supposedly murdered. The centurion overseeing the execution halted the proceedings and led the condemned man back to Piso, expecting a reprieve. But Piso mounted the tribunal in a rage, and ordered the three soldiers to be executed. He ordered the death of the man who was to have been executed, because the sentence had already been passed; he also ordered the death of the centurion who was in charge of the original execution, for failing to perform his duty; and finally, he ordered the death of the man who had been supposed to have been murdered, because he had been the cause of death of two innocent men.[28]

Piso earned immortality by pronouncing, "Let justice be done though the heavens fall."

6

THE QURAN AND WOMEN

When women were viewed as inferior members of the human family and treated as property belonging to men, the Prophet Muhammad accepted women as equal partners in society, in business, and even in war. Islam codified the rights of women. The Quran elevates the status of women to that of men. It guarantees women civil, economic and political rights. —Benazir Bhutto[1]

Benazir Bhutto is not alone in expressing these views. She echoes the feelings of all moderate Muslims who believe that Islam revolutionized the status of women by giving them rights as far back as the seventh century CE that non-Muslim women have only recently begun to realize. The Quran, they insist, honors women more than any other political system does.

Muslim clerics representing the other end of the spectrum also agree that Islam honors women, though they occasionally bring a different perspective to the debate. Consider the following discussion carried by an Egyptian TV channel involving the cleric Sa'd Arafat.[2]

Anchor: Wife beating is a serious allegation. Let us examine this bit by bit.

Cleric: Allah honored wives by instating the punishment of beatings. Honored them with beatings? How is this possible! The Prophet Muhammad said: "Don't beat her in the face, and do not make her ugly." See how she is honored. If the husband beats his wife, he must not beat her in the face. Even when he beats her, he must not curse her. This is incredible! He beats her in order to discipline her. In addition, there must not be more than ten beating, and he must not break her bones, injure her, break her teeth, or poke her in the eye. There is a beating etiquette. If he beats to discipline her, he must not raise his hand high. He must beat her from chest level. All these things honor the woman. She is in need of discipline. How should the husband discipline her? Through admonishment. If she is not deterred, he should refuse to share the bed with her. If she is not repentant, he should beat her, but there are rules to the beating. It is forbidden to beat her in the face or to make her ugly. When you beat her you must not curse her. Islam forbids this.

Anchor: With what should he beat her? With his bare hands? With a rod?

Cleric: If he beats her, the beatings should not be hard, so that they do not leave a mark. He can beat her with a short rod. He must avoid beating her in the face or in places in the head where it hurts. The beating should be on the body and should not come one right after the other. These are all choices made during the process, but beatings are allowed only as a last resort. The honoring of the wife in Islam is also evident in the fact that the punishment of beating is permissible in one case only: when she refuses to sleep with him.

Anchor: When she refuses to sleep with him?

Cleric: Yes, where else could the husband go? He wants her, but she refuses. He should begin with admonishment and threats—

Anchor: Allow me to repeat this. A man cannot beat his wife… over food or drink.

Cleric: Beatings are permitted only in this case, which the husband cannot do without.

It would be interesting to see who on the status of women represents the true face of Islam—Benazir Bhutto or perhaps Sa'd Arafat. Before we consult the Quran for an answer, it may not be out of place to take a quick glance at how women were treated prior to Islam.

STATUS OF WOMEN BEFORE ISLAM

There were pre-Islamic societies in which women not only inherited property but inherited on equal footing with men. Pompeii, which was destroyed by a volcanic eruption in 79 CE, is one example. Though Roman law may not generally have been entirely favorable to women, "in the inheritance of her father's estate the daughter took an equal share with the son"—in certain circumstances, at least.[3]

There are also examples of societies in which women could rule. Queen Hatshepsut, for instance, was on the throne for about two decades in the first half of the fifteenth century BCE in Ancient Egypt—which was nearly two millennia before the advent of Islam.

Because our primary interest is the Bedouin culture of Arabia, it is worth noting that even amongst the Arabs of Mecca, women seem to have been well regarded. We know, for instance, that Khadija, Muhammad's first wife, was a wealthy businesswoman. She engaged Muhammad as her trading agent before marrying him. This indicates that women were entitled to hold property and to engage in businesses in their own right. Khadija must also have inherited property from her family or previous husbands[4] in order to be able to do so, which suggests that Islam did not bring any sea change by allowing Arab women a share in inheritance. Indeed, Quran may only have adopted the existing custom, as it did in many other instances.*

Particularly relevant in this regard is the fact (noted in the Quran) that there were a number of goddesses amongst the deities worshipped by the Arabs, some of which held prime positions in

---

* For instance, it adopted the same *hajj* rituals as were practiced by pagan Arabs prior to Islam.

the pantheon. This too is indicative of the position held by women in Arab society. Had women not commanded respect, the Arab pantheon may have consisted only of gods and no goddesses.

One also finds other indications of emancipation of women prior to the advent of Islam. The Quran accuses Abu Lahab's wife of slandering the Prophet,* which suggests that women were free to express themselves. One also learns from the Quran that the dress restrictions imposed by it on women were not the custom in Arabia, which shows that women were permitted to dress more liberally. Women were also not restricted from interacting with men and were not confined to their homes.

Although it may also be true that girls were occasionally buried alive upon birth,[5] the practice could not have been widespread, as there was no shortage of women in Arabia—the Quran would not otherwise have permitted four wives to each believer, in addition to slave girls.

This is not to suggest that women were equal to men, but it does seem that they were quite well regarded in the pagan culture of Arabia. One would expect their status to only improve further with Islam, considering that women are one half of the population and Allah could not therefore be unmindful of their well-being, and also the fact that Muhammad did not have any male heirs, which too should have attracted greater focus on them. In this perspective, let us see if the Quran "elevates the status of women to that of men," as Benazir Bhutto states in the opening quotation.

STATUS OF WOMEN AS REFLECTED IN THE QURAN

An initial flavor of the Quran's approach towards women is gathered from verse 16:72,[6] which mentions sons and grandsons amongst the blessings of Allah but completely omits to include daughters and granddaughters. The impression thus conveyed by the Quran—that daughters are lesser blessings (if blessings at all)—is then reinforced by a series of verses (addressed to the

---

*   According to some interpretations, at least.

polytheists, who considered certain goddesses to have the power of intercession with Allah) in which the Quran expresses annoyance: "Are the sons for you and the daughters for Allah? This would indeed be an unfair division!" (53:21–22).[7]

Verses 2:228 and 4:34 also do not disturb the balance. They clarify that "men are a degree above them [women] in status" as "Allah has made one superior to the other."[8]

It would be interesting to see if this changes when the Quran comes to discussing the following specific issues.

• *Inheritance shares*

In Chapter 2, we encountered verses from *Surah An-Nisa,* which give women half the share of men in inheritance. Whether it is the brother against the sister or the son against the daughter or the husband against the wife, the man gets twice the share of the woman, which is consistent with the proposition that men are a degree above them.*

Moderate Muslims feel uneasy with this grossly unequal division. The explanation they offer is that a woman also gets a dower from her husband, which makes up for the lesser inheritance shares. Let us consider this argument further.

The Quran does prescribe payment of dower "as an obligation of enjoyment of conjugal relations"[9]—which may seem a touch distasteful, as though conjugal relations are objects for sale, but the practice already existed among pagan Arabs, as recorded by the Quran.[10] That aside, the argument that a dower somehow makes up for the loss of inheritance is problematic. It does not address the case of many women who never get married or of those who get married to men who are unable (or decline) to pay adequate dower. How are fairness and equality extended to such women?

The question also is, If the lesser inheritance shares are meant only to restore equality in favor of men (due to the imbalance created by dower), would it not have been simpler and better to

---

* One exception is that the mother inherits equal to the father in the case of a child's death.

allocate equal shares in inheritance and do away with dower altogether?* This may also have been more respectful to women and given them the status of equal partners in marriage.

Moderate Muslims then resort to the argument that what the Quran implemented was nevertheless a huge advance in those times and must be viewed in that spirit. The difficulty with this argument is that even the pagans allowed inheritance to women. Can we be sure that the Quran took it forward, or perhaps even backward?

- ### Witnessing of documents

The Quran instructs the believers to record their debts in writing and to have the document witnessed:

> O Believers when you contract a debt for a fixed term, you should put it in writing. …. And let two men from among you bear witness to all such documents. *But if two men be not available, there should be one man and two women to bear witness so that if one of the women forgets the other may remind her.* (2:282)[11]

Does the Quran treat two women as equal to one man in the above context? Not quite, as at least one man must always witness the document—four women thus are not adequate replacement for two men. Moreover, in the case of wills, which also are required by the Quran to be attested to, women are excluded as eligible witnesses altogether.[12]

Such treatment may have made sense in seventh-century Arabia, when women were probably illiterate—by and large, at least—and not likely to be familiar with financial transactions. It was a pragmatic solution that if two men were not available, then one man and two women could witness the document. What the Quran did not anticipate, though, was that women one day would be equal to men. Marie Curie, for instance, won two Nobel Prizes (one for chemistry and the other for physics) and is the first person to achieve this distinction. There are countless other

---

* As it is, dower can be waived by agreement and does not therefore provide adequate protection, and it may even have to be returned if the woman wants to be free of the bond of marriage.

examples of women excelling men in virtually all fields, which makes this restriction absolutely archaic in today's world.

A better solution would have been to stipulate that two persons familiar with such transactions should be asked to witness the document. This would have emphasized the need for reliable witnesses who could understand the transaction, but without drawing a line on the basis of gender. The Quran, of course, does not adopt this more neutral approach. As things stand, therefore, women are forever barred from being equal witnesses. The fact that the woman may be an expert banker and the man totally illiterate doesn't change the equation!

This rule also unfortunately reinforces the message that women are somehow inferior to men.

• *Polygamy*

In light of the above discussion, one does not expect the Quran to restrict each believing man to just one wife—i.e., "one man one woman" is not the recipe one anticipates. In the case of polygamy, however, the ratio turns out to be even more skewed than in respects of inheritance and testimony. Each man is permitted to marry up to four women at a time:

> [You] may marry two or three or four women whom you choose. But if you apprehend that you might not be able to do justice to them, then marry only one wife or marry those women who have fallen in your possession. This would be the better course to avoid injustice. (4:3)[13]

Moderate Muslims are troubled by this, and stress that this license to marry multiple wives is conditional on the husband determining first that he is able to do justice to all wives and that because this is not ordinarily possible, the Quran in fact encourages monogamous relationships. But if the Quran truly meant to encourage monogamous relationships, could this not be better stated? And would the Prophet have married thirteen times? The problem also is that even when the Quran suggests "if you apprehend that you might not be able to do justice to them, then marry only one wife," it goes on to advise "or marry those women who have fallen in your possession" (namely, slave girls). Is that truly a recommendation for monogamous relationships?

In fact, later in the same *Surah*, the Quran even recognizes that it is not possible for the husband to do complete justice to all his wives, but it does not withdraw the permission to enter multiple marriages.[14] This was a perfect opportunity for the Quran to clarify that because a man cannot do justice to all, he must marry only one wife. But it did not.

The fact that men are permitted by the Quran to have multiple wives also, of course, reinforces the impression that women are inferior to men.

• *Prostitution*

We noted earlier that the Quran permits men sexual relations with slave girls, including married women taken as prisoners of war,[15] but can slave girls also be used towards prostitution? It seems unimaginable that the Quran would allow that. Consider the following verse, however:

> And do not force your slave girls into prostitution for your own worldly gains *when they themselves want to keep chaste*; and if any one forces them into it, after such a compulsion, Allah will be forgiving and merciful for them. (24:33)[16]

Does this mean that should the slave girls be willing—which perhaps they may, in order, for instance, to pay their way out of slavery—they could be used for prostitution?

The following verse, which prescribes punishment for indecency by slave girls, also throws some informative light on the issue:

> Whoever cannot afford to marry free Muslim women, should marry one of the Muslim slave-girls in your possession ... and give them their dowries so that they may live a decent life in wedlock and not in licentiousness nor may have secret illicit relations. *Then if they are guilty of indecency, after they have been fortified by wedlock, they shall be given half the punishment prescribed for free women.* (4:25)[17]

According to this verse, slave girls "guilty of indecency, after they have been fortified by wedlock" attract half the punishment prescribed for free women. What is notable is that no punishment is prescribed for slave girls who are still unmarried. Is there a suggestion in this as well that unmarried slave girls may be used for prostitution (with their consent) and hence no punishment is prescribed for their indecency?*

The other possibility, of course, is that these verses meant to prohibit slave girls (whether married or not, and regardless of consent) being used for prostitution but faltered when articulating this simple proposition.

- ### Dress code and the command to stay at home

Two noticeable features of all Islamic communities are that women dress conservatively, often covering their heads, and that the interaction between men and women outside the immediate family is generally restricted. It is instructive to trace the basis of this in the Quran. The first instruction in this respect was issued through the following verses:

> And O Prophet, enjoin the believing men to restrain their gaze and guard their private parts. This is a more righteous way for them: Allah has knowledge of what they do. *O Prophet enjoin the believing women to restrain their gaze and guard their private parts, and not to display their adornment except that which is displayed of itself and to draw their veils over their bosoms* and not to display their adornment except before their husbands, their fathers, the fathers of their husbands, their sons and the sons of their husbands (from other wives), their brothers, their brothers' sons, their sisters' sons, their female associates and those in their possession and male attendants incapable of sex desire and those boys who have not yet attained knowledge of sex matters concerning women; also forbid them to stamp their

---

It may also be noted that the question of indecency does not arise in respect to sexual relationship between the master and the slave girl, as that is expressly permitted by the Quran and cannot therefore be considered indecent, so when the Quran contemplates indecency by a slave girl, it can only be with respect to someone other than her master or husband.

feet on the ground lest their hidden ornaments should be displayed. (24:30–31)[18]

Believing men and believing women are both guided to restrain their gazes—which naturally curtails interaction between the two genders and encourages segregation. Additionally, the believing women are asked to "draw their veils over their bosoms"; however, they are not required to cover their faces.

These verses were then succeeded by the following verse, which imposes greater restrictions:

> O Prophet enjoin your wives and daughters and the women of the believers that they should let down over their faces a part of their outer garments; it is expected that they will thus be recognized and not molested. (33:59)[19]

Notably, this verse addresses not just the wives and daughters of the Prophet but also "the women of the believers." It therefore lays down the dress code for Muslim women generally.

According to Maududi's translation, the previous verses command women to cover their bosoms, whereas this verse takes it a step further and requires them to draw veils also over their faces. Yusuf Ali, however, holds a different interpretation.* According to him, there is no specific direction that the face be covered. This divergence of opinion explains the variation in recommendations made by different Islamic schools, some more restrictive than others.

There is no mention, though, in the above verses that women must stay at home. That is drawn from the following verses:

> *Wives of the Prophet, you are not like the other women.* If you are Godfearing, do not talk in a soft voice lest the man of the diseased heart should cherish false hopes from you, but speak in an unaffected manner. *Stay in your houses, and do not go about displaying your fineries as women used to do in the days of ignorance.* (33:32–33)[20]

---

* As follows:

> O Prophet! Tell thy wives and daughters, and the believing women, *that they should cast their outer garments over their persons* (when abroad): that is most convenient, that they should be known (as such) and not molested.

(Note: The last sentence evidences that women were quite emancipated in terms of dress before Islam.)

Even though the command is addressed specifically to the Prophet's wives, who are also cautioned "you are not like the other women," Maududi is of the view that the restriction applies to all Muslim women:

> The verses from here to the end of the paragraph are those with which the Commandments of *Purdah* were introduced in Islam. In these verses though the wives of the Holy Prophet only have been addressed, the intention is to enforce reforms in all the Muslim houses. ... Could Allah have intended only this that the holy wives alone should be free from uncleanliness and they alone should obey Allah and His Prophet and they alone should offer the *Salat* and pay the *Zakat*? If this could not be the intention, then how could the Command for them to stay in their houses and avoid displaying the fineries and abstain from talking to the other men in an alluring voice be meant particularly for them to the exclusion of all other Muslim women?[21]

Maududi has a point. Allah would not have instructed that the holy wives *alone* should stay away from uncleanliness, but the fact that verses 33:32–33 (unlike verse 33:59 quoted above) command only the wives of the Prophet (and not the other believing women) to "Stay in your houses, and do not go about displaying your fineries" can't be easily ignored either. To the skeptic, this is because Muhammad (unlike Allah) was less concerned about other women.[*]

---

[*] The following account (recorded by Ibn Ishaq in the words of a woman of B. Ghifar) also suggests that the Prophet may not always have applied the same standards to other women as he did to his own.

> She said, "I came to the apostle with some women of B. Ghifar and we told the apostle, as he was going to Khaybar, that we wanted to go with him where he went, to tend the wounded and to help the Muslims as far as we could. He told us to go with God's blessings, and so we went with him. I was a young girl and the apostle took me on the back of his saddle. When the apostle dismounted for morning prayer and I got off the back of his saddle, lo, some of my

The outcome at least of the Quranic verses quoted in this section is that there is marked gender segregation in most Islamic communities, not just in respect of physical space allowed to women (they are largely expected to stay at home) but also in terms of the roles they may fill. Muslim women have generally suffered as a result. And because these verses lend themselves to the construction that women must remain at home and must fully cover themselves on the odd occasion when they have to go out, those who do not follow these norms are often looked down upon, in certain segments at least. This mindset, which rests ultimately on the above-quoted verses, has prevented millions of women from participating in economic activities and leading fulfilling lives in Muslim societies. This has also thus prevented large-scale emancipation of women in Islam.

- ### *Women and paradise*

One striking feature of the Quran is that it does not mention any companions for women in paradise. Some scholars are of the view that a woman will join her husband (if married and if the husband qualifies as well). According to others, women will enjoy the company of other believing women, such as the Prophet's wives.

All this is speculation, as the Quran is silent on the matter. Not so in the case of men, though. They are promised the company of *houris*,[22] variously interpreted as gazelle-eyed women, fair-complexioned women, or women with swelling breasts. Men are also clearly promised young boys in paradise!

---

blood was on it. It was the first time that this had happened to me. I rushed to the camel in my shame. When the apostle saw my distress and the blood he guessed the reason and told me to cleanse myself; then to take water and put some salt in it, and then to wash the back of the saddle and go back to my mount." She added: "When the apostle conquered Khaybar he gave us a small part of the booty. He took this necklace which you see on my neck and gave it to me and hung it round my neck with his own hands, and by God it will never leave me." (Ibn Ishaq: *The Life of Muhammad*, p. 518)

One is entitled to doubt this account, however. The Prophet could not have asked an unrelated girl approaching puberty to accompany him on the saddle at night.

And there will go round to them young boys, exclusively appointed for their service, who will be as lovely as well-guarded pearls. (52:24)

They will be attended by brisk-moving boys who will forever remain boys. If you saw them, you would think they were pearls, scattered. (76:19)[23]

• *False allegations of indecency*

In one respect, the Quran does protect women—regarding accusations of indecency. For instance, if the husband accuses the wife of indecency but fails to produce a witness, the wife has the last say.[24]

In the same spirit, while prescribing that impure women are for impure men and pure women (who "are free from those scandals, which the slanderers utter")[25] are for pure men, the Quran (in recognition of the fact that false charges would eliminate the chances of a pure woman finding a pure partner) prescribes strict punishment for false accusations against chaste women:

As for those persons who charge chaste women with false accusations but do not produce four witnesses, flog them each with eighty stripes and never accept their evidence afterwards, for they themselves are transgressors, except those who repent and reform themselves; Allah is Forgiving and Merciful. (24:4–5)[26]

These verses were revealed after the slander incident described in Chapter 3 and formed the basis for punishing some who had participated in spreading slander against Aisha. In today's jurisprudence, it would be unjust for a person to be punished for conduct that was not an offense at the time it was committed, or to be awarded punishment stricter than what was applicable at the precise moment of the offense, but then, recognition of this rule was centuries away. In any case, and whatever the true motivation behind the above verses, they have provided much-needed protection to women against false allegations.

- ### Child brides

According to Ibn Ishaq, the earliest biographer of the Prophet (who is supported in this behalf by other Muslim historians as well), Muhammad "married Aisha in Mecca when she was a child of seven and lived with her in Medina when she was nine or ten."[27] The Prophet was fifty at the time of his marriage to Aisha (who outlived him by fifty-six years).* If this account were true, one would expect to find some corroboration in the Quran as well, perhaps in the form of endorsement of girls being married before puberty. Let us see if we can find traces in the following verse, which prescribes the waiting period a woman must observe after divorce before marrying again.

> And if you are in doubt about those of your women who have despaired of menstruation, (you should know that) their waiting period is three months, *and the same applies to those who have not menstruated as yet.* As far as pregnant women, their period ends when they deliver the burden. (65:4)[28]

What is the most notable feature is that the verse applies as much to "those who have not menstruated as yet," a point on which all translations find themselves in total agreement.† The Quran thus

---

* It also did not matter that she was his best friend's daughter. Subsequently, Muhammad would also marry Hafsa, who was Omar's daughter. Omar himself was twenty-odd years younger than the Prophet and would later marry Muhammad's granddaughter (Fatima's daughter) Umm Kulthum, who bore him two children (Rogerson: *The Heirs of the Prophet Muhammad*, p. 231; see also Reza Aslan *No God but God*, p. 123). Omar thus acquired the distinction of being Muhammad's father-in-law and also ultimately his grandson-in-law.

† The other translations follow:

  Such of your women as have passed the age of monthly courses, for them the prescribed period, if ye have any doubts, is three months, *and for those who have no courses (it is the same);* for those who carry (life within their wombs), their period is until they deliver their burdens. (Yusuf Ali)

  And those of your women as have passed the age of monthly courses, for them the *iddah* (prescribed period), if you have doubts (about their periods) is three months; *and for those who have no courses (i.e. they are still immature) their iddah (prescribed period) is three months likewise,* except in case of death. And for those who are pregnant

clearly recognizes marriages of underage girls. By not speaking up against the practice, it also endorses the custom—which of course is not surprising, considering Muhammad's own marriage to Aisha.

"Wife Beating" in Islam

How does one conclude from this entire discussion, much of it admittedly unfavorable to women, that "Allah honored wives by instating the punishment of beatings," as claimed by Sa'd Arafat? That is addressed by the following verse:

> As for those women whose defiance you have cause to fear, admonish them and keep them apart from your beds *and beat them*. Then, if they submit to you, do not look for excuses to punish them (4:34)[29]

Moderate Muslims are understandably embarrassed and try hard to soften the impact of this verse, as is apparent from Yusuf Ali's translation:

> As to those women on whose part ye fear disloyalty and ill-conduct, admonish them (first), (Next), refuse to share their beds, (And last) *beat them* (lightly); but if they return to obedience, seek not against them Means (of annoyance).

It is worth noting, however, that the words in parenthesis—first, Next, And last, lightly—are not part of the Quranic text but are inserted by Yusuf Ali on the pretext of the Prophet's sayings. Why the Quran did not make this clear is not addressed.

Yusuf Ali's additions, however, go against what the Quran intends. The Arabic word used in verse 4:34 is *wadribu*, which is also employed in verse 8:12 when instructing the believers to crush the disbelievers: "so smite their necks and *beat* every joint of

---

(whether they are divorced or their husbands are dead) their *Iddah* (prescribed period) is until they lay down their burden. (Hilali-Khan) And for such of your women as despair of menstruation, if ye doubt, their period (of waiting) shall be three months, *along with those who have it not*: for those who carry (life within their wombs), their period is until they deliver their burdens. (Pickthall)

their bodies."* That being so, why should this word mean "beat them (lightly)" in the context of verse 4:34 when it obviously has the opposite connotation in verse 8:12?†

The other issue is whether the beating can be inflicted only when the wife declines the husband's invitation to sex (as suggested by Sa'd Arafat). That may of course be one of the grounds. The following verse indicates that the wife would be ill advised to decline such invitation: "Your wives are your tilth; so you may go to your tilth as you please" (2:223).[30] There is absolutely nothing, however, in verse 4:34 that restricts the beating to only this kind of defiance.

In both respects, by proposing that the beating should be light and must be confined to the wife declining the husband's invitation to sex, Sa'd Arafat suggests a softer construction than may have been intended by verse 4:34.

*

---

* Yusuf Ali's translation is "smite ye above their necks and smite all their finger-tips off them."
† One unique interpretation of this verse is by Laleh Bakhtiar, an American woman who converted to Islam and who has also translated the Quran (*The Sublime Quran*). Leila Ahmad discusses this interpretation in *A Quiet Revolution*:

> Her research, Bakhtiar explains, led her to challenge conventional readings of a key word in this verse—the word *daraba*. Conventional readings understand the word as being derived from the root verb "to beat" or "to hit". ... Bakhtiar found that the root verb *daraba* had a number of possible root meanings besides "to beat" including "to go away". ... The verse thus basically instructs men, as Bakhtiar interprets it, to leave—divorce—women who persist in challenging or resisting them. (pp. 266–267)

What is interesting is that the entire thesis is based on the interpretation of "a key word in this verse—the word *daraba*," when in fact this word is not even used in verse 4:34. As noted above, the word used in the verse is *wadribu*, which is also used elsewhere in the Quran to mean "beat" or even "smite." Besides, if verse 4:34 was meant only to instruct men to divorce defiant wives, one wonders why the Quran did not use the word *talaq*, which is the word it otherwise uses to refer to divorce. Indeed, there is an entire *Surah* by that title. Also, if one agrees with Bakhtiar, this would mean that Allah chose a word that would be misinterpreted for fourteen centuries, until the true meaning was finally located.

We should now be able to answer the question who better represents the Quran on the status of women. Is it Sa'd Arafat or Benazir Bhutto? Perhaps neither. The fact is that the Quran simply fails to honor women as they ought to be honored!

THE SWORD VERSES

Then, when the months made unlawful for fighting expire, kill the mushriks wherever you find them, and seize them, and besiege them, and lie in wait for them at every place of ambush. But if they repent, and establish Salat *and pay the* Zakat *dues, then let them go their way: for Allah is Forgiving and Compassionate.* (9:5)

Fight with those from among the people of the Book, who do not believe in Allah nor in the Last Day; who do not make unlawful that which Allah and His Messenger have made unlawful, and do not adopt the Right way as their way. (Fight with them) until they pay Jizyah* *with their own hands and are humbled.* (9:29)[1]

Nothing troubles moderate Muslims quite as much as these "sword verses"—for good reason, too, as they violate the right to freely practice one's religion. Even the seemingly benevolent command that the polytheists should be spared if they "repent and establish *Salat* and pay the *Zakat*" is unacceptable, as it amounts effectively to forcing conversions.

The fact that these are amongst the last verses to be revealed is significant, too.[2] It means that verses more conciliatory to other religions,[3] which were revealed earlier when Islam was not

---

* poll tax

dominant, must give way to the Sword Verses, as the latter represent the last word on the subject.*

Equally noteworthy is the fact that the Sword Verses are placed in *Surah At–Taubah*, which is the only *Surah* in the Quran not to start "In the name of Allah, the Compassionate, the Merciful." It seems the Quran did not want the message to be diluted at all.

One is thus intrigued to discover the rationale behind such unadulterated intolerance towards the polytheists and the people of the Book. Before we find the true answer, it may help to eliminate certain possibilities.

WERE THE POLYTHEISTS AND THE PEOPLE OF THE BOOK IN BREACH OF TREATY OBLIGATIONS?

As recorded by Muslim historians, the polytheists had already been subjugated a year earlier, when the conquest of Mecca took place, and even prior to that had not launched an offensive against the believers since the Battle of Trench, which was about four years before these verses were revealed. Thus, even *Surah At–Taubah* refers to past breaches and transgressions going as far back as the banishment of the Prophet from Mecca, which was nearly a decade earlier: "Will you not fight such people who have

---

* As admitted by Hashmi:

> Most classical interpreters of the Quran and the vast majority of Western orientalists ... offer a "master narrative" that runs something like this: In Mecca, Muhammad's activity was confined to the non-violent propagation of his message. Here, because of his military weakness, he was restricted to an ethic of tolerance. ... Once relocated to Medina, the Prophet is transformed from religious preacher to warrior and statesman. Jihad now assumes a violent component as the Prophet first attacks his Meccan opponents and then eliminates the recalcitrant Jews of Medina, who had proved to be a threat both religious and military. ... The Quranic revelations of Medina reflect this steady progression toward an ethic of hostility and intolerance, leading to the two final injunctions on the subject, the "verse of the sword" (Q. 9:5) and the "verse on the poll-tax" (Q. 9:29). *Because these two verses were revealed shortly before the Prophet's death, they are held authoritative for the community henceforth.* ("The Quran and Tolerance: An Interpretive Essay on Verse 5:48" pp. 82–83)

been breaking their solemn pledges, *who conspired to banish the Messenger* and were the first to transgress against you?" (9:13).[4] That the polytheists were not guilty of any subsisting breaches is also indicated by the following verses of *Surah At-Taubah*: "Since *if they get power over you*, they will not respect ties of kindred with you *nor honor any treaty obligations*" (9:7–8).[5] Considering that the polytheists did not hold power over the believers (a fact evident from *Surah At-Taubah* itself), the hypothetical proposition that if they did, they would not honor any treaty obligations can only mean that the polytheists were not in actual breach of treaty obligations.*

Coming next to the people of the Book, the Quran does not accuse them either of treaty violations (as we shall see below).

SANCTITY OF TREATY OBLIGATIONS

Because the Quran does state that "if [the polytheists] get power over you, they will not respect ... any treaty obligations," it is pertinent to see what sanctity the Quran itself accords such obligations.

To begin with, it is surprising that the Prophet even entered treaties with the polytheists, considering that polytheism is declared by the Quran to be the only sin Allah shall never forgive.[6] One such treaty he forged was that of Hudaybiya, which was entered in 6 AH and was meant to declare peace with the Quraysh for a period of ten years. Ibn Ishaq describes the background to this treaty:

> The apostle ... went out on the little pilgrimage in Dhul-Qada [6 A.H.] with no intention of making war. He called together the Arabs and neighboring Bedouin to march with him, fearing that Quraysh would oppose him with arms or prevent him from visiting the temple, as they actually did. Many of the Arabs held back from him, and he went out with the emigrants and Ansar and such of the Arabs as stuck to him.[7]

---

* Such hypothetical and counterfactual arguments are unacceptable, however, as they may legitimize any act of aggression. The Quran's unique prowess to look into the hearts of the *mushriks* to see how they would behave "if they get power over you" cannot thus be adopted as a universal rule.

The Quraysh did oppose Muhammad's entry into Mecca, as was anticipated, but no fighting broke out. Instead, a peace treaty was negotiated, some important details of which are recorded below.

> Then the apostle summoned Ali and told him to write "In the name of Allah the Compassionate, the Merciful." Suhayl said "I do not recognize this; but write 'In the name of Allah'." The apostle told him to write the latter and he did so. Then he said: "Write 'This is what Muhammad, the apostle of God has agreed with Suhayl b. Amr'." Suhayl said, "If I witnessed that you were God's apostle I would not have fought you. Write your name and the name of your father." The apostle said "Write 'This is what Muhammad b. Abdullah has agreed with Suhayl b. Amr: they have agreed to lay aside war for ten years during which men can be safe and refrain from hostilities on the condition that *if anyone comes to Muhammad without the permission of the guardian he will return him to them; and if anyone of those with Muhammad comes to Quraysh they will not return him to him'.*"[8]

Muhammad agreed to go back to Medina and was allowed to visit Mecca the following year, which he did.

Soon after the treaty, some believing men escaped from Mecca and were returned to the Quraysh in accordance with the treaty, but when some believing women also found their way to Medina, they were not returned. The Quran intervened to block that:

> O you who have believed, when the believing women come to you as emigrants, examine and test (their faith), although Allah only knows best the truth of their faith. Then, when you find them to be true believers, do not return them to the disbelievers. Neither are they lawful for the disbelievers nor are the disbelievers lawful for them. Return to their disbelieving husbands the dowers that they had given them; and there is no blame on you if you marry them when you have paid them their dowers. ... And if you do not get back from the disbelievers a part of the dower of your disbelieving wives, and then your turn comes, pay to the people whose wives have been left on the other side an amount equivalent to the dowers given by them. (60:10–11)[9]

Ibn Ishaq also records this important event regarding the treaty:

The apostle made peace with Quraysh on the day of Al-Hudaybiya on the condition that he would return to them those who came without the permission of their guardians. But when women migrated to the apostle and to Islam God refused to allow them to be returned to the polytheists if they had been tested by the test of Islam, and they knew that they came only out of desire for Islam, and He ordered that their dowries should be returned to Quraysh if their women were withheld from them if they returned to the Muslims the dowries of the women they had withheld from them. ... *Had it not been for this judgment of God's the apostle would have returned the women as he returned the men.*[10]

This was a unilateral revision of the treaty, which would normally constitute a breach.* This, though, became merely an academic consideration when, a couple of years later, the Prophet even invaded and conquered Mecca, thereby renouncing the treaty altogether.†

The Treaty of Hudaybiya was thus no more at the time *Surah At-Taubah* was revealed, but there were other subsisting treaties with certain polytheists. *Surah At-Taubah* wasted no time in renouncing them, as well:

This is a declaration of immunity (from obligations) by Allah and His Messenger to those *mushriks* (polytheists) with whom you had made treaties: "You are free to move about in the land for four months more." ... This is a public proclamation from Allah and

---

* Had the Quran intervened at the time the treaty was being negotiated, to guide the Prophet to carve out an exception for believing women who might migrate to Medina, no such violation would have resulted.

† The excuse was a fight between two rival tribes, one allied to the Quraysh and the other to Muhammad. The Quraysh were accused of helping their allies and thus of violating the treaty of Hudaybiya. There is no allegation that the Quraysh broke peace with the believers directly. It is thus debatable whether, even if they did go to the aid of an ally, this entitled the believers to invade Mecca in return. The believers, too, were free to assist their ally in the conflict. The Quraysh were also not warned that if they continued supporting their ally, this would be considered a breach of the treaty— which shows that this may just have been a convenient excuse to invade Mecca. The Quraysh on their part did emphatically communicate to the Prophet that they were fully committed to the peace treaty, though that did not prevent the invasion. (See Ibn Ishaq: *The Life of Muhammad*, pp. 540–544.)

His Messenger for all the people on the Day of Great Haj: Allah
is free from the treaty obligations made with the mushriks and so
is His Messenger … excepting those with whom you made a
treaty at the Masjid-i-Haram: so long as they behave rightly with
you, you also should behave rightly with them, for Allah loves
the righteous people. (9:1–3, 7).[11]

The treaties that were preserved were those entered in the
precincts of Ka'ba after the conquest of Mecca. It must have
been felt that they were perhaps too fresh to be violated. All
other treaties with the polytheists were emphatically renounced. It
is thus ironic that the Quran should accuse the polytheists that
they would not honor treaty obligations if they got power over
the believers.

DID THE POLYTHEISTS OR THE PEOPLE OF THE BOOK POSE ANY REAL THREAT?

The answer to this, too, is in the negative. Certainly, *Surah At-Taubah* gives no indication of any real threat from either the
polytheists or the people of the Book.

It may be noted that at the time the Sword Verses were issued,
Mecca had already been conquered and the polytheists had been
totally defeated. Earlier, the Jews in and around Medina had also
been destroyed or subjugated. Islam thus was the new order in
Arabia, and there was absolutely no visible threat to it.

Incidentally, the Quran acknowledges that the polytheists
posed no threat. They would not have been extended immunity
for four months if they had. Also, by relying on the imaginary
situation "if they get power over you," the Quran concedes that
in actual fact, the polytheists were not in a position to challenge
the believers.

As for the people of the Book, they too posed no threat to the
believers. In fact, verse 9:29 (which is the one regarding the
people of the Book) was revealed in the context of an entirely
aggressive (nondefensive) expedition that was to take place
several hundred miles from Medina! There are also other verses
in *Surah At-Taubah*, to which we shall presently refer, which

support the conclusion that the Jews and the Christians did not pose any threat.

RATIONALE FOR THE SWORD VERSES

Now we discuss the real reason why the polytheists had to be eliminated and the people of the Book humbled.

Surah At-Taubah tells us regarding the polytheists that they had "bartered away Allah's revelations for paltry worldly gains."[12] It also tells us that they were "unclean":

> O Believers, the mushriks are unclean; therefore let them not come near the Masjid-i-Haram after this year (of their pilgrimage) (9:28)[13]

Why were they "unclean"? The polytheists' faith was the reason, for they had remained disbelievers even after the conquest of Mecca. Thus, if they would "repent and establish *Salat* and pay the *Zakat*," they would be spared; otherwise, they would be killed. This unmistakably establishes that it was ultimately only their belief that constituted the true cause for the pronouncement against them.

Moving on to the people of the Book, *Surah At-Taubah* (in verses that immediately follow the command "Fight with those from among the people of the Book ... until they pay *Jizyah* with their own hands and are humbled") explains their offense.

> The Jews say, "Ezra (`Uzair) is the son of Allah," and the Christians say, "The Messiah is the son of God." Such are the baseless things they utter with their tongues, following in the footsteps of the former unbelievers. May Allah afflict them with chastisement! Where from are they being perverted? They have made their scholars and monks as their Lords beside Allah, and likewise the Messiah, the son of Mary, although they were enjoined not to worship any other than the One Deity, besides Whom there is none worthy of worship. He is absolutely pure and free from what they associate with Him. *These people desire to extinguish the light of Allah with puffs from their mouths and Allah refuses (His consent to their desire) but wills to perfect His light, even though the disbelievers be*

much averse to it. He is Allah Who has sent His Messenger with Guidance and the Right way so that He may make it prevail over all other ways, even though the mushriks be much averse to it. (9:30–33)[14]

That the Jews do not believe that "Ezra is the son of Allah" is secondary.[*] What is more to the point for our purposes is that the only possible justification offered by *Surah At-Taubah*, why the Jews and the Christians were to be fought and humbled, is not because they violated a treaty, nor even because they posed a threat, but simply because they perverted the message of Allah by uttering "baseless things ... with their tongues, following in the footsteps of the former unbelievers." What is scary is that this reason applies even today!

It is worth noting again that the command against the people of the Book was revealed in relation to the Tabuk expedition, which was to take place hundreds of miles from Medina. It was thus quite unprovoked. Moreover, were there the slightest pretense to restrict these verses to defensive warfare (which, though, would have been incongruous with the occasion), the Quran should have addressed the counterparty not as the people of the Book but as "the aggressors" or as "those amongst the people of the Book who are the aggressors." It should have commanded the believers to fight "these aggressors" until they are humbled and forced to pay *Jizyah*. Instead, the Quran leaves no doubt that the people of the Book are to be fought only because they "utter baseless things ... with their tongues" and "desire to extinguish the light of Allah *with puffs from their mouths.*"

The saving grace, however, is that, unlike the *mushriks*, who are to be killed, the people of the Book are only to be humbled and forced to pay *Jizyah*. But that said:

---

[*] Though Maududi is understandably uncomfortable with this and explains: The Quran, however, does not assert that all the Jews were unanimous in declaring Ezra as "the son of God." What it intends to say is that the perversion in the articles of faith of the Jews concerning Allah had degenerated to such an extent that there were some amongst them who considered Ezra as the son of God. (Maududi: *The Meaning of the Qur'an*, Note 29 to *Surah At-Taubah*, Volume 2, pp. 190–191)

The only form of tolerance permitted to the People of the Book, according to the overwhelming majority of commentators, is that of the victor to the vanquished.[15]

SOME CRITICAL QUESTIONS

Some key questions may now be answered.

o ***Does the Quran order killings on a religious basis alone?***

The Quran does not, of course, command that the *mushriks* be killed right away. It extends them a certain immunity, during which they are not to be harmed. It also stipulates:

> [I]f any of the mushriks requests you for protection so that he may come to you (to hear the Word of Allah), give him protection till he hears the Word of Allah; then convey him to the place of his safety; this should be done because these people do not know the Truth."
> (9:6)[16]

After that, though, the *mushriks* are to be spared only if they convert; otherwise, they are to be killed. One would normally consider this to be a direction to kill on a religious basis alone.

o ***What about* mushriks *living outside Arabia?***

Though the primary focus may have been the Arab Bedouin tribes in the vicinity of Mecca and Medina, the command itself is more general: "Kill the *mushriks* wherever you find them." Besides, if *mushriks* in Arabia were to be eliminated for being unclean despite the peace treaties some of them had executed with Muhammad,* why should this not apply to those who do not even have the protection of such treaties?[17]

---

* It may be noted that even with respect to treaties executed in Masjid al-Haram, which were to be observed for the full term, the immunity lasted only that long and not beyond.

o *Are there territorial limits regarding the command against the people of the Book?*

Verses 9:30–33 amply clarify that it is the very faith of the people of the Book that is the cause of the grievance. It is difficult therefore to territorially confine verse 9:29.

o *What about other nonbelievers? How are they to be treated?*

The Quran deals with only two categories of nonbelievers: the *mushriks*, who are to be killed, and the people of the Book, who are to be humbled. It does not address the case of the other nonbelievers in these verses. This leaves their position a bit uncertain. It may, however, be that the Quran treats all other religions, except Christianity and Judaism, as forms of polytheism and their followers to be dealt with as polytheists.[*]

o *Does* Surah At-Taubah *promote religious wars?*

This includes nondefensive wars meant for no other object but to establish or promote a certain religion. In this perspective, the fact that the *mushriks* are to be killed unless they convert and the people of the Book are to be fought and humbled simply because of the faith they espouse makes it untenable to argue that *Surah At-Taubah* does not promote (nondefensive) religious wars.

---

[*] Hashmi, however, notes:

> As the Islamic empire expanded during the two centuries following the Prophet's death, all organized religious communities with which the Muslims came into contact were assimilated under Islamic law not on the basis of 9:5 but under the provisions of 9:29, the verse speaking directly to the condition of the People of the Book, which we shall discuss below. Thus, the scope of ayat al-sayf (the verse of the sword) was effectively limited to the intransigent and rebellious Arab Bedouin tribes who are clearly the focus of the series of verses leading up to Q. 9:5. ("The Quran and Tolerance: An Interpretive Essay on Verse 5:48," pp. 92–93)

Whether this is a concession necessarily intended by the Quran is open to question, though.

o **What does this mean for the world today?**

This, perhaps, is the most critical question. Because the Quran is believed to be a timeless command, there is no reason to suppose that the requirement to fight non-Muslims until they are destroyed or humbled ceases to apply in the present times. The rationale certainly is very much applicable still. (Recall that the only real rationale *Surah At-Taubah* offers is that polytheists are to be killed because they are "unclean" and the people of the Book humbled because "they utter baseless things with their tongues.") The *Surah* also emphasizes that Allah has sent "His Messenger with Guidance and the Right way," which is to "prevail over all other ways" (9:33). Is there any reason, then, for the Sword Verses to lose vitality in present times?

This, however, is problematic both for moderate Muslims who are understandably embarrassed to confront these verses, and for non-Muslims. To what extent should pluralism be extended to the adherents of a religion that commands destruction and humiliation for other faiths?*

RESPONSE BY MODERATE MUSLIMS

Moderate Muslims justifiably shy away from the Sword Verses. They realize that drawing attention to these verses will make it difficult to project the softer image of Islam. They therefore pretend mostly as if the Sword Verses do not exist. This is the more pragmatic approach to take, but what is interesting is that books have also been written (by acclaimed academics, at that) on how the concept of Jihad has been misunderstood by the

---

* Fortunately, a vast majority of Muslims are simply not aware of these verses. They are even perplexed by the approach of the militant Muslims and cannot understand how a message of absolute peace and harmony (as they see Islam) can be distorted by the jihadists. This large-scale ignorance of the Sword Verses is helpful in promoting peace and harmony, as is the fact that Islam is presently not in a strong enough position militarily to follow the Sword Verses' command.

militants and the West alike, without any discussion on the Sword Verses!*

Some moderates do, however, take the indefensible position that the verses against the polytheists were revealed in the context of a battle and should be confined accordingly.† A plain reading of the subject verses proves that this is simply incorrect. One may also ask, would the *mushriks* be extended immunity for four months in the midst of a battle?

It goes to Hashmi's credit that he opts for neither approach. He argues instead that when the message of the Quran is taken in its entirety, the Sword Verses are the exception, not the rule, and should not be interpreted to disturb the overall message, which he finds leans towards pluralism:

> [I]f the Qur'anic text is considered as a whole, the apparently belligerent verses emerge as limited in scope and application *while an ethic of pluralism (best expressed in Q. 5:48) is consistently upheld.*[18]

Notably, by "pluralism," Hashmi does not simply mean tolerance in the sense of "putting up" with another's view, but actual respect for the other person's belief "born out of acknowledgement of one's own limited knowledge of the truth and the possibility of the equal validity of different viewpoints."[19]

Hashmi finds this ethic of pluralism fully reflected in verse 5:48. He uses Yusuf Ali's translation:

> To you We sent the scripture in truth, confirming the scripture that came before it, and guarding it in safety; so judge between them by what God has revealed, and follow

---

* Khaled Abou El Fadl's work *The Great Theft* may fall in this category. He accuses militants of hijacking Islam and of misinterpreting the divine word, but no reference is made to the Sword Verses quoted above—which are the mainstay of the militants' argument—not even in the chapter entitled "Jihad, Warfare and Terrorism"!

† Benazir Bhutto, for instance, writes in respect of verse 9:5: "At first glance this verse seems to advocate violence against unbelievers. But its context is a specific battle in Medina occurring at the time of its revelation, a battle against idol worshippers, not people of the Book, not believers in monotheism. It commands that violence cease if the offenders repent." (*Reconciliation*, p. 24)

not their vain desires, diverging from the truth that has come to you. *To each among you have We prescribed a law and an open way. If God had so willed, He would have made you a single people, but [His plan is] to test you in what He has given you: so strive as in a race in all the virtues. The goal of you all is to God; it is He that will show you the truth of the matters in which you differ.*[20]

It is the emphasized words above that are reflective of pluralism to Hashmi. Regarding the opening lines, even he admits that they "seem to restrict narrowly the scope for tolerance envisioned by the Quran," as if "it is the standard of truth, seemingly to the exclusion of rival conceptions," but he feels that the verse then "takes a dramatic turn in the other direction, toward a far more inclusive vision of moral diversity," as reflected by the latter words. He thus concludes:

> The distinctions among religious communities are not simply the by products of human error; they are God's will. Unlike the case of the Arab polytheists, who as the immediate subjects of Q. 10:99 have chosen their own errant course, it is God in this verse who prescribes for each community a separate path (*shir'a*) and open road (*minhaj*).[21]

Is Hashmi's thesis well founded? If one focuses only on the emphasized words of verse 5:48, it is possible to read some level of pluralism in them (even if not as broad as Hashmi would like to think), but before concluding that this is what the Quran intended, too, one needs to consult the full context and background to verse 5:48.

The Quran claims to be a continuation of the Torah and the Bible but isn't always consistent with these earlier scriptures. The Jews exploited these discrepancies to establish that the Quran and their own scriptures could not therefore have emanated from the same source. They would also at times take their matters to Muhammad for decision, hoping that a verdict contrary to their scriptures would furnish proof that Muhammad was unknowledgeable about Divine Law. All this, incidentally, finds mention in the verses that precede 5:48, so we do not have to debate it.[22]

Such comparisons were embarrassing. The Quran therefore encouraged Muhammad not to judge the cases presented by the

Jews and, in any case, to always judge according to the law sent down to him and not the law prescribed for the Jews. It is in this precise context that verse 5:48 finds mention in the Quran. Verse 5:48 recognizes that there are differences between the Quran and the other scriptures—which was exactly the point agitated by the Jews, so there was no shying away from it. The verse then explains why this should be so even though the source was the same: "To each among you have We prescribed a law and an open way. If God had so willed, He would have made you a single people." Whether this is meant to reflect pluralism or is simply a defensive tactic to evade an embarrassing situation is at least open to debate.

Moreover, the discussion does not end there. The succeeding verses go on to stipulate:

> So, O Muhammad, judge between these people by the Law that has been sent down to you and do not follow their wishes: be on your guard lest these people should tempt you away, even in the least, from the Guidance that has been sent down to you by Allah. *If they turn away from it, then know that Allah wills to involve them in trouble in consequence of some of their sins. And the fact is that the majority of these people are transgressors.* (If they turn away from the Divine Law, then) do they desire to be judged by the laws of ignorance? Yet there is no better judge than Allah for those who believe in Him. *O Believers, do not take the Jews nor the Christians as your friends: they are one another's friends only. If anyone of you takes them as friends, surely he shall be counted among them; indeed Allah deprives the wrong-doers of His Guidance.* (5:49–51)[23]

These too are part of the same discussion and indeed provide the immediate context to verse 5:48, but do they reflect pluralism? That depends on what we understand by pluralism. If it means putting up with another's view though one may remain hostile towards that view, then perhaps yes. But if pluralism means respect for another's faith "born out of acknowledgement of one's own limited knowledge of the truth and the possibility of the equal validity of different viewpoints," which is what Hashmi desires to read into verse 5:48, then the above verses certainly do not lend themselves to such interpretation. They emphatically declare that "Allah wills to involve [the disbelievers who turn away from the Guidance sent down to Muhammad] in trouble in consequence of some of their sin." The disbelievers are also categorized as "transgressors." Such contempt for another's point of view can hardly be considered pluralism—it may even be the exact antithesis of pluralism. One can detect that it is the same disdain that finds reflection in the Sword Verses as well. The difference, of course, is that by the time the Sword Verses were revealed, the Prophet was powerful enough to also set the rules.

The above discussion is intended to show that it is not easy to trace pluralism in verse 5:48, but even if we could overcome that hurdle, the difficulty that would remain is that, like other conciliatory verses, this one too was revealed earlier, when the Prophet was not in a position to fully dictate terms, and it would therefore be considered abrogated by the Sword Verses, which were revealed later. This raises the important question of what room may fairly be allowed to the earlier conciliatory verses (of which verse 5:48 may perhaps form a part). The following discussion should provide the answer.

o *Abrogation as a deliberate tool employed by the Quran*

Hashmi argues that the Quran must be read as a whole and that abrogation of one part by another should be avoided as far as possible. This is admittedly the preferred rule of interpretation (though there would be circumstances in which abrogation cannot be avoided while interpreting a document), but what is absolutely unique about the Quran is that it actually celebrates abrogation as a deliberate tool, thereby diluting (if not excluding) the above rule:

> Allah abrogates whatever He pleases and keeps intact whatever He wills and He has the Original Book with Him. (13:39)[24]

> We bring a better verse or at least the like of it for whatever we abrogate or cause it to be forgotten. (2:106)[25]

Considering thus that abrogation is a calculated technique employed by the Quran, the principle that it should be avoided as a tool of interpretation naturally loses appeal in the context of the

Quran. It follows that if the natural meaning of the Sword Verses gives them an expanse that is inconsistent with the earlier conciliatory verses, then the Sword Verses must be the ones to prevail.

o *Contextual interpretation*

It is generally accepted that each text must be interpreted in its proper historical context, but when we look at the more conciliatory verses in the exact context in which they were revealed—at a time when the Quran could not but promote coexistence, whereas the moment it had a choice, it opted for the likes of the Sword Verses—the message that comes across is that the conciliatory verses are meant to guide the believers in circumstances where they are weak and unable to assert themselves (as when they are a minority) but the moment they gain ascendance, they must seek direction from the Sword Verses. When seen in this perspective, the conciliatory verses need not even be considered abrogated. They still have a role to play, though confined to circumstances in which the Muslims are weak.

o *Sword Verses not alone in delivering the message of belligerence*

It also turns out that the Sword Verses are not alone in conveying the message of belligerence towards other religions. There are other verses that reflect much the same message. In fact, when we look at the Quran in chronological order, it transpires that what started as a message of coexistence gradually changed tone as the Prophet grew in strength. This becomes visible long before the Sword Verses surface.

> How is it with you that there are two opinions among you concerning the hypocrites, whereas Allah has turned them back (to their former state) because of the evils they have earned?... They really wish that you should also become disbelievers, as they themselves are so that both may become alike. *So you should not take friends from among them unless they migrate in the way of Allah; and if they do not migrate, then seize them*

wherever you find them and slay them and do not take any of them as
friends and helpers. However, those hypocrites are excepted who
join a people who are allied to you by a treaty. Likewise, those
hypocrites are excepted who come to you and are averse to
fighting either against you or against their own people. (4:88–
90)[26]

These verses, which bear resemblance to the Sword Verses, are
directed against the hypocrites, whose only offense as disclosed
in the above verses is that "they really wish that you should also
become disbelievers, as they themselves are so that both may
become alike." This may have entitled the Quran to instruct its
followers not to take the hypocrites as friends "unless they
migrate in the way of Allah," but can this form the basis to
"seize them wherever you find them and slay them"? Can this
represent pluralism in any form?*

That the Quran never meant to promote pluralism is also
visible from other verses, such as "O Prophet, wage Jihad against
the disbelievers and the hypocrites, and be stern with them.
Their abode is Hell, and an evil abode it is!" (66:9).[27] The
discussion in Chapter 8 ("The Jews of Medina") is relevant, too.

It thus transpires that the Sword Verses are not the exception
but that there is a consistent progression towards intolerance,
which is discernible in other verses as well. Even if the Sword
Verses had stood alone, however, while an ethic of pluralism was
otherwise consistently upheld, could one have ignored these
verses altogether? Not quite! That is why even Hashmi is unable
to extend pluralism to the Arab polytheists, about whom he has
the following to say:

> By the time we reach the end of the Medinan period, the
> struggle between the Muslims and the Quraysh and other
> Arab tribes had surpassed the strictly religious dimension.

---

* Verses 4:88-90 do, of course, create an exception regarding hypocrites "who
join a people who are allied to you by a treaty," and those "who come to
you and are averse to fighting either against you or against their own
people," but this leaves many other "hypocrites" (a vague term at best)
vulnerable to attack, though they may not have intended to fight the
believers or shown any inclination in this regard. Why should even they have
been killed "wherever you find them," outside of actual warfare?

The conflict was now between two rival sociopolitical systems, each supported by its own ideology and identified by it. In this war, the general injunction to fight the polytheists found in Q. 9:5 was in fact not a change in tactics or strategy, not a call to rid the world of polytheism, but a command to conclude a 23–year struggle against an inveterate foe.[28]

The polytheists were to be killed "to conclude a 23–year struggle against an inveterate foe," which had a rival sociopolitical system with its own ideology. One is not sure whether to accept that hypothesis, considering that the struggle had already been concluded the year before, when Mecca was conquered without a fight and the polytheists were totally subjugated. But the point also is, can a conflict between "two rival sociopolitical systems, each supported by its own ideology" justify killing an inveterate foe outside actual warfare—particularly a foe that stands defeated and poses no threat? If yes, what if the same principle is applied by the powers of today against Islam—an inveterate foe with an ideology that instructs its followers to humble the Jews and Christians and to destroy the polytheists? One shudders to think of the consequences.

Regarding Hashmi's proposition that verse 9:5 is not a call to rid the world of polytheism, one may ask, Why did the Quran command "kill the *mushriks* wherever you find them"? And what about verse 9:29 regarding the people of the Book: how are we to find a restrictive interpretation to that? Recall that the command to fight and humble them was issued in the context of an expedition that was to take place several hundred miles from Medina and there is no indication in the Quran that there was any threat to the believers. To the contrary, the Quran clarifies in the immediately succeeding verses that the people of the Book are to be humbled not because they pose a danger but because they utter "baseless things ... with their tongues, following in the footsteps of the former unbelievers."

Yet, if one absolutely must find pluralism in the Quran, the question is: could the message at least have been expressed in clearer terms so we would not have to debate it? If yes, as must truthfully be the answer, is it plausible that a deficiently expressed word is from Allah?

CONCLUSION

Try as one may, it is not easy to curtail the scope of the Sword Verses, by any significant measure, at least. Such is their chronology and the confidence with which they express themselves. Any attempt to restrict their natural meaning also, of course, implies that Allah's word is deficient, that He did not mean to say what the Sword Verses so clearly spell out.

The dilemma of the moderate Muslims precisely is that they would like to believe in the Quran as the word of Allah but also to find tolerance reflected in it. It is difficult, however, to have it both ways. The non-moderates, in contrast, have no particular value for pluralism and are therefore less perplexed by these verses. To them, the message is clear: Muslims must struggle, and kill if necessary, until Islam is the only dominant religion. Other religions can be allowed to exist, but as subordinate to Islam, except polytheism, which has to be eliminated altogether. Until the believers are strong enough to achieve that, the Quran does guide them towards coexistence—but only until then!

Not for the non-moderates is the golden principle of pluralism, best depicted by words of Voltaire—and not by any of the verses contained in the Quran: "I may disagree with what you have to say, but I shall defend to the death your right to say it!"

THE JEWS OF MEDINA

*O Muhammad! We have sent you to be a real blessing for the people
of the world.*[1]

There was a sizeable Jewish community settled in Medina at the
time Muhammad migrated to the city. There would be virtually
none six years later. The three main tribes would all be banished,
killed, or enslaved. Because the Quran documents these events,
including the massacre and enslavement of an entire tribe, it is not
possible to deny the occurrence. Muslim scholars must therefore
find some other explanation for this happening. They conclude
that it was the treacherous behavior of the Jews that was
responsible. This chapter evaluates the claim.

We start the discussion with a brief overview of the interaction
between the Quran and the Jews, and how it evolved over time.

BRIEF OVERVIEW

The Quran's initial approach towards the people of the Book was not confrontational but was friendly and filled with hope. It must have been felt that there was a better chance of converting the Jews than the pagans, as Islam was a continuation of Judaism; thus, not only were conversions from amongst the Jews a cause for celebration,[2] but the Quran also extended them special recognition: "If you are in doubt regarding the Guidance We have sent down to you, you may inquire about this from those people who have been reading the Scriptures before you" (10:94).[3]

A conscious effort to find common ground with the Jews is also discernible during this period. The believers, for instance, were asked to pray facing Jerusalem, a place holy to the Jews. In much the same spirit, the Quran also tended to avoid confrontation.[4] This is reflected in certain Quranic verses of the time in which Isaac (from whom the Jews trace their descent) is mentioned while Abraham's other son, Ismail, (who is considered by the Jews to be the son of a concubine and therefore not worthy of equal respect) is ignored.[5] A noteworthy example is the story of Abraham's sacrifice.[6] The verses that narrate the story mention only Isaac.* The Quran informs us ultimately that it was Ismail (not Isaac) who constructed the Ka'ba with Abraham[7]—which makes his absence in these other verses all the more noticeable.

Despite such attempts, though, it must have become clear with time that the Jews were not going to accept Muhammad as the apostle of Allah. At this stage, the Quran ended the conciliatory period by commanding the believers to stop facing Jerusalem in prayers.[8] The new focal point, the Ka'ba (Masjid Haram), was still

---

*   Albeit not in clear enough terms for one to definitively conclude that it was Isaac who was offered for sacrifice. Some Muslim scholars do, however, conclude from these verses that it was he and not Ismail who was offered for sacrifice. This is, of course, consistent with the Jewish faith but not so much with the trend of Islamic thought, which is that it was Ismail who was offered for sacrifice. Maududi notes the authorities on both sides of the argument (Maududi: *The Meaning of the Qur'an*, Note 67 to *Surah As-Saaffat*, Volume 4 pp. 319-320).

home to idols, and it was therefore odd for the believers to face it in prayers, but it was more important to mark a clear departure from the earlier conciliatory approach towards the Jews.

Not long after this change, two of the three Jewish tribes were banished from Medina and the third butchered and enslaved. On the banishment of the first tribe, the Quran pronounced: "O Believers, do not take the Jews nor the Christians as your friends: they are one another's friends only. If anyone of you takes them as friends, surely he shall be counted among them; indeed Allah deprives the wrong-doers of His Guidance" (5:51).[9]

Muslim scholars recognize that the burden falls on them to justify the banishing, killing, and enslaving of the Jews who had lived in Medina since before the Prophet migrated there. They argue, however, that this was because the Jews were guilty of treacherous behavior. This assertion is based fundamentally on a certain treaty Muhammad is said to have entered with the Jews of Medina at the time he moved to the city. It is therefore relevant to take account of the document that lies at the heart of the justification offered by Muslim scholars. In doing so, we must not lose sight of the possibility that a document of this nature may not perhaps have existed and may only have been invented by Muslim scholars to find some justification for the treatment given to the Jews.

THE CHARTER OF MEDINA

Muslim historians state that soon after moving to Medina, the Prophet entered into a treaty[*] with the three Jewish tribes settled there for generations, namely Bani Qainuqa, Bani Nadir, and Bani Qurayzah.[†] The preamble to the treaty, as recorded by Muslim historians, is as follows:

---

[*] Meesaq-e-Medina

[†] Ibn Ishaq (the Prophet's earliest biographer), for instance, notes:
> The apostle wrote a document concerning the emigrants and the helpers in which he made a friendly agreement with the Jews and established them in their religion and their property, and stated the reciprocal obligations ... (*The Life of Muhammad*, p. 231)

In the name of God the Compassionate, the Merciful. This is a document from Muhammad the prophet [governing the relations] between the believers and Muslims of Quraysh and Yathrib, and those who followed them and joined them and labored with them. They are one community (umma) to the exclusion of all men.[10]

What instantly attracts attention is that the Jews are not listed as a party to the document—not in the preamble, at least.* It is also unlikely that they would have accepted the statement "Muhammad the prophet."

That the Jews may not have been signatories to the document is also supported by many of its terms that are relevant only to relations among the believers and other terms in which the Jews (though subjects of discussion) are referred to essentially as "outsiders" or third parties.† That notwithstanding, however, the document then takes an incongruous turn by imposing certain direct obligations on the Jews—which would be the case if they were indeed a party to the agreement:

> The Jews shall contribute to the cost of the war so long as they are fighting alongside the believers. The Jews of B. Auf are one community with the believers (the Jews have their religion and the Muslims have theirs), their freedmen and their persons except those who behave unjustly and sinfully, for they hurt but themselves and their families. ... The close friends of the Jews are as themselves. None of them shall go out to war save with the permission of Muhammad. ... The Jews must bear their expenses and the Muslims their expenses. Each must help the other against anyone who

---

* They would have been referred as the "people of the Book" or the "children of Israel," as the Quran mentions them, or as "the Jews," as the document itself refers to them in a later context.

† Ibn Ishaq records the following clause:

> *Believers are friends one to the other to the exclusion of outsiders.* To the Jew who follows us belong help and equality. He shall not be wronged nor shall his enemies be aided. The peace of the believers is indivisible. ... Whenever you differ about a matter it must be referred to God and to Muhammad. (*The Life of Muhammad*, p. 232)

The Jews seem to be referred to as outsiders. They would also not have agreed readily to refer disputes "to God and to Muhammad."

attacks the people of this document. They must seek mutual advice and consultation, and loyalty is a protection against treachery. ... The Jews must pay with the believers so long as the war lasts. Yathrib shall be a sanctuary for the people of this document. *If any dispute or controversy likely to cause trouble should arise it must be referred to God and to Muhammad the apostle of God. ... Quraysh and their helpers shall not be given protection.* The contracting parties are bound to help one another against any attack on Yathrib. ... Everyone shall have his portion from the side to which he belongs.[11]

The question is: Would the Jews have agreed to these terms? It seems doubtful. First, these terms are incongruous with the Preamble and certain other terms noted earlier, which depict the Jews as third parties. Second, the Jews of Medina had no quarrel with the Quraysh and may not therefore have agreed to treat them as a common enemy. Third, it does not appeal to reason that the Jews would acknowledge Muhammad as "the Apostle of God," even for purposes only of the treaty. Fourth, it also seems doubtful that the Jews would accept the Prophet as arbiter of disputes, considering that if there were any such disagreements, Muhammad would be an interested party.

If the above terms are unlikely to have been accepted by the Jews, could it even be that no such treaty was ever signed by them? Can the possibility be ruled out that Muslim scholars, who have felt under pressure to explain the treatment extended to the Jews of Medina, may have invented the treaty at a later stage or may have twisted the document that was essentially only amongst the believers to also include the Jews as a party, in order to create some justification for the harsh treatment given to them?

Before proceeding further, we must also take account of the view according to which the Quran itself evidences the existence of a treaty between Muhammad and the Jews. This view rests on the following verses.

Indeed the vilest creatures in the sight of Allah are those *people who denied the Truth,* and then would not believe in it. As regards those from among them *with whom you made treaties and who violate them* time after time and do not fear Allah in the least, if you encounter them in combat, make of them a fearsome example for others who would follow them so that they might be unnerved. It is expected that they will learn a lesson from the end of the treacherous people. And if you ever fear treachery from any people, throw their treaty openly before them; indeed Allah does not like the treacherous people. Let not those who deny the Truth delude themselves that they have won the game; indeed they are incapable of frustrating Us. (8:55–59)[12]

Muslim scholars believe that these verses refer to the Jews, even though they are not expressly named.*

Is this assessment well founded, though? It is noteworthy that these verses refer to "people who denied the Truth and then would not believe in it," which is not the style the Quran adopts when referring to the Jews. They are referred to instead as the "people of the Book" or the "children of Israel." It is also a fact that Muhammad entered treaties (such as the treaty of Hudaybiya) with the polytheists, who are even accused by the Quran of having violated these contracts—for instance, in the context of the Sword Verses. It therefore seems that in the above verses, too, the Quran (when it mentions "people who denied the Truth ... with whom you made treaties and who violate them") is referring to the polytheists and not the Jews.

It is fair thus to hold on to the possibility that the Charter of Medina may ultimately turn out to be a spurious document (at least so far as the Jews are concerned). With that observation, we

---

* Maududi, for instance, states:

"Those ... who violate the treaties ..." were the Jews. On his migration to Al-Madinah, they were the first people with whom the Holy Prophet had entered into an alliance to co-operate for mutual good. He did his very best to establish good relations with them, for he considered them to be nearer to Islam than the *mushriks*, and he preferred their way to those of the *mushriks*, whenever a choice had to be made between the two. But their scholars and rabbis did not at all like the pure doctrine of Tauhid, taught by him, and the high standard of morality presented by him, and the exertions put in by him for the establishment of the Right Way. Therefore, in spite of the treaties they were persistently trying to defeat the New Movement. (Maududi: *The Meaning of the Qur'an*, Note 41 to *Surah Al-Anfal*, Volume 2, p. 148)

move on to how the Jews of Medina were actually treated by the
Prophet.

BANISHMENT OF BANI QAINUQA AND BANI NADIR

Bani Qainuqa were the first Jewish tribe to be given the marching
orders from Medina. The story of their expulsion follows.

> The affair of the B. Qaynuqa arose thus: An Arab woman
> brought some goods and sold them in the market of the B.
> Qaynuqa. She sat down by a goldsmith, and the people tried
> to get her to uncover her face but she refused. The goldsmith
> took hold of the end of her skirt and fastened it to her back
> so when she got up she was immodestly exposed, and they
> laughed at her. She uttered a loud cry and one of the Muslims
> leapt upon the goldsmith and killed him. He was a Jew, and
> the Jews fell upon the Muslim and killed him, whereupon the
> Muslim's family called on the Muslims for help against the
> Jews. The Muslims were enraged, and bad feeling sprang up
> between the two parties.[13]

It is also reported:

> Casualties were thus equal and Muhammad was called in, in
> his official capacity as judge of disputes, to restore the peace.
> But the Jews refused to accept his arbitration, barricaded
> themselves in their fortresses and called upon their Arab allies
> to come to their aid.* ... They had taken a gamble, which had
> not come off because they had completely underestimated the
> power that Muhammad had acquired; ... They left the oasis
> apparently without protest knowing that they were lucky to
> have escaped with their lives.[14]

---

* Interestingly, if the issue ultimately turned on Bani Qainuqa's refusal to
accept Muhammad as the "judge of disputes," as this account suggests, it
throws doubt on the terms of the Charter of Medina as stated by Muslim
historians   particularly the term that records that Muhammad was to be the
arbiter of disputes, for in that case, the Jews may not have contested his
authority.

Bani Qainuqa were permitted, though, to take their belongings—as much as they could. One-fifth of what remained went to the Prophet.*

Bani Nadir were next to encounter the growing strength of the Prophet. They were accused of plotting against the life of Muhammad,† but Allah warned him in time before the design could be implemented.[15] Bani Nadir were resultantly expelled from Medina. The Quran tells us that this was "because they resisted Allah and His Messenger,"[16] but there is no mention that they were in breach of a treaty.

---

*   This is in light of verse 41 of *Surah Al-Anfal*, which had already been revealed.

†   Ibn Ishaq records:

    [T]he apostle went to B. al-Nadir to ask for help in paying the bloodwit for the two men of B. Amir whom Amr b. Umayya al-Damri had killed after he had given them a promise of security. There was a mutual alliance between B. al-Nadir and B. Amir. When the apostle came to them about the bloodwit they said that of course they would contribute in the way he wished; but they took counsel with one another apart, saying, "You will never get such a chance again. Who will go to the top of the house and drop a rock on him (T. so as to kill him) and rid us of him?" The apostle was sitting by the wall of one of their houses at the time. Amr b. Jihash b. Ka'b volunteered to do this and went up to throw down a rock. *As the apostle was with a number of his companions among whom were Abu Bakr, Umar and Ali, news came to him from heaven about what those people intended,* so he got up (T. and said to his companions "Don't go away until I come to you") and he went back to Medina. ... The apostle ordered them [his companions] to prepare for war and to march against them. ... The Jews took refuge in their forts and the apostle ordered that the palm-trees should be cut down and burnt. ... Now there was a number of B. Auf among whom were Abdullah b. Ubbay and Wadia and Malik ... who had sent to B al-Nadir saying, "Stand firm and protect yourselves, for we will not betray you. If you are attacked we will fight with you and if you are turned out, we will go with you." Accordingly they waited for help they had promised, but they did nothing and God cast terror into their hearts. They asked the apostle to deport them and to spare their lives on condition that they could retain all their properties which they could carry on camels, except their armour, and he agreed. So they loaded their camels with what they could carry. (*The Life of Muhammad*, p. 437)

Bani Nadir left substantial portions of their properties, which went entirely to the Prophet and "the kinsfolk and the orphans and the needy and the wayfarers."[17] It must have been felt that because the Jews had submitted without a fight, the believers who had participated in the siege against them were not entitled to any share in these circumstances.*

THE FATE OF BANI QURAYZAH

This brings us to Bani Qurayzah and how they were slaughtered and enslaved—an event truly so momentous that it deserves detailed consideration.

After the banishment of the other Jewish tribes, Bani Qurayzah were very largely at the mercy of the Prophet. What had worked in favor of Bani Qainuqa and, to a lesser extent, Bani Nadir was the possibility that the other Jewish tribes might come to their support, which caused softer terms to be offered, but this consideration no longer applied once Bani Qurayzah were left essentially by themselves in Medina. The Battle of Trench then exposed their precarious position.

• *The Battle of Trench*

This battle took place in the fifth year after the Prophet's migration to Medina (5 A.H.). According to Muslim historians:

> It was in fact a combined raid by many of the Arab tribes, who wanted to crush the power of Madinah. It had been instigated by the leaders of the Bani an-Nadir, who had settled in Khyber after their banishment from Madinah. They went round to the Quraysh and Ghatafan and Hudhail and many other tribes and induced them to gather all their forces together and attack Madinah jointly. Thus, in Shawwal, A.H. 5, an unprecedentedly large army of the Arab tribes marched against the small city of Madinah. ... Together they numbered from ten to twelve thousand men.[18]

---

* Why the same principle did not apply in the case of Bani Qainuqa is not entirely clear.

It is worth pausing to note that even Muslim historians do not accuse Bani Qurayzah of instigating this battle. The account, however, continues:

> But the Holy Prophet was not unaware of this in Madinah. Even before the enemy could reach his city, he got a trench dug out on the north-west of Madinah in six days, and having the Mount Salat at their back, took up a defensive position with 3,000 men in the protection of the Trench. To the south of Madinah there were many gardens (even now there are) so that it could not be attacked from that side. To the east there are lava rocks which are impassable for a large army. The same is the case with the south western side. The attack, therefore, could be made only from the eastern and western sides of the Uhud, which the Holy Prophet had secured by digging a trench. The disbelievers were not at all aware that they would have to counter the trench outside Madinah. This kind of a defensive stratagem was unknown to the Arabs. Thus, they had to lay a long siege in winter for which they had not come prepared.[19]

The Quraysh laid siege for a few days, but there was no direct engagement between the two armies and resultantly no mentionable casualties, certainly on the side of the believers. This is noted by the Quran and also by accounts recorded by Muslim historians.* The weather then turned hostile: "We sent against them a violent wind and the armies which you could not see."[20] The Quraysh decided to return to Mecca.

---

* Ibn Ishaq, for instance, records:

> *The siege continued without any actual fighting,* but some horsemen of *Quraysh* ... donned their armour and went forth on horseback. ... They galloped forward until they stopped at the trench. When they saw it they exclaimed, "This is a device which the Arabs have never employed!" Then they made for a narrow part of the trench and beat their horses so that they dashed through it and carried them into the swampy ground between the trench and Sal'. Ali with some Muslims came out to hold the gap through which they had forced a passage against (the rest of) them and the horsemen galloped to meet them. Now Amr b. Abdu Wudd ... challenged anyone to fight him. Ali accepted the challenge ... and they fought, the one circling the other. Ali killed him and their cavalry fled, bursting headlong in flight across the trench. (*The Life of Muhammad*, pp. 454–455)

While the Quraysh were camped across the trench, however, the believers were deeply apprehensive. Apart from having to face the Quraysh, who had come in huge numbers, the believers must also have feared the possibility of Bani Qurayzah joining forces with the enemy. We learn in this regard that many of them had sent their families for shelter towards the side of Bani Qurayzah.[21] The thought of Bani Qurayzah possibly supporting the Quraysh must therefore have been petrifying to the believers. These fears are vividly recorded in the Quran.[22]

The question, of course, is whether Bani Qurayzah did join hands with the Quraysh. Even Muslim historians concede that they were not so inclined in the beginning[23] and also that they desisted in the end. The very last encounter that Muslim historians report between the Jews and the Quraysh follows:

> On the night of Sabbath of Shawwal A.H. 5 it came about by God's action on behalf of his apostle that Abu Sufyan and the chiefs of Ghatafan sent Ikrama b. Abu Jahl to B. Qurayza with some of their number saying that they had no permanent camp, that the horses and camels were dying; therefore they must make ready for battle and make an end of Muhammad once and for all. They replied that this was the Sabbath, a day on which they did nothing, and it was well known what had happened to those of their people who had violated the Sabbath.[24]

The charge at best is that they waivered in between.[25] The Jews may have had their own story to tell on that, which we shall never know, but it is worth noting that even if the account recorded by Muslim historians is correct—that the Jews did at some point decide to join hands with the Quraysh before eventually desisting—this would not be blameworthy if ultimately they refrained.

The critical fact that Bani Qurayzah never joined the battle is, however, recorded in the Quran:

> Remember the time when the hypocrites and all those whose hearts were diseased were openly saying that the promises Allah and His Prophet had made with them were nothing but a delusion; when a party of them said, "O people of Yathrib, you have no chance to stay, so go back"; when *a section of them*

> *sought leave of the Prophet, saying "Our homes are insecure," whereas*
> *they were not insecure; in fact they wished to flee (the battle front). If the*
> *enemies had made entry from all sides of the city, and those people had*
> *been urged to treachery, they would have committed it, and would have*
> *little hesitated to become partners in it.* They had indeed already
> made a pledge with Allah that they would not show their
> backs; and the pledge made with Allah had to be questioned.
> (33:12–15)[26]

These verses note that there were some amongst the believers
who entertained doubts during the siege and wished to withdraw
on the ground that their homes were not secure. They are
categorized as "the hypocrites and all those whose hearts were
diseased." The Quran emphatically pronounces that, in fact, their
homes were not insecure. It further discloses that "if the enemies
had made entry from all sides of the city, and those people [i.e. the
hypocrites and those of diseased hearts] had been urged to
treachery, they would have committed it." This confirms that the
enemy did not in fact enter the city—which only goes to show
that Bani Qurayzah remained neutral in the fight. They not only
refrained from attacking the believers but also did not allow their
quarters to be used by the Quraysh to launch such an attack.[*] By
taunting the hypocrites that their homes were not insecure, the
Quran thus clearly documents that there was never any real threat
from Bani Qurayzah.[27]

• *The slaughter*

According to Muslim historians, as soon as the Quraysh
withdrew, the Prophet was guided by Allah to lay siege on Bani
Qurayzah. Ibn Ishaq records:

> The apostle besieged them for twenty-five nights until they
> were sore pressed and God cast terror into their hearts. In the
> morning they submitted to the apostle's judgment and al-Aus

---

[*] Even if the terms of the Charter of Medina as recorded by Muslim
historians are correct, the Bani Qurayzah thus seem to have been in total
compliance. Each party was required to defend "the side to which he
belongs," and the above verses establish that the Jewish quarters were not
used for any attack on the believers.

leapt up and said, "O Apostle, they are our allies." So when al-Aus spoke thus the apostle said: "Will you be satisfied, O Aus, if one of your own number pronounces judgment on them?" When they agreed he said that Sa'd b. Muadh was the man. Sa'd said, "Then I give judgment that the men should be killed, the property divided, and the women and children taken as captives." The apostle said to Sa'd, "You have given the judgment of Allah above the seven heavens."[28]

Ibn Ishaq's also then describes the execution:

They surrendered, and the apostle confined them in Medina in the quarter of d. al-Harith, a woman of B. al-Najjar. Then the apostle went out to the market of Medina (which is still its market today) and dug trenches in it. Then he sent for them and struck off their heads in those trenches as they were brought out to him in batches. Among them was the enemy of Allah Huyayy b. Akhtab and Ka'b b. Asad their chief. There were 600 or 700 in all, though some put the figure as high as 800 or 900. As they were being taken out in batches to the apostle they asked Ka'b what he thought would be done with them. He replied, "Will you never understand? Don't you see that the summoner never stops and those who are taken away do not return? By Allah it is death!" This went on until the apostle made an end of them.[29]

This may be one of the earliest documented instances of mass graves. It is blood-curdling. One would never accept that the Prophet of Allah could indulge in this kind of bloodletting. The Quran, however, confirms the account:

Allah turned back the disbelievers; they turned back in their rage without gaining any advantage, and Allah was sufficient to fight on behalf of the believers; Allah is All-Powerful, All-Mighty. *Allah brought down from their fortresses those of the people of the Book who had joined forces with the invaders and created such terror in their hearts that some of them you are slaying today and some taking as prisoners.* He made you heirs of their land and their dwellings and their wealth and gave you the land which you had never trodden before. Allah is All-Powerful. (33:25–27)[30]

These verses place several critical facts beyond dispute.

o The Quraysh "turned back without gaining any advantage." This confirms that the believers did not suffer any mentionable casualties in this battle.

o Regarding Bani Qurayzah, Allah "created such terror in their hearts" that they "came down from their fortresses." This confirms that the Jews surrendered without a fight.

o The Jews were killed and imprisoned. One may otherwise have disputed the massacre.

o At the time this happened, the Quraysh had already "turned back," which means that the Prophet was not acting under any clear and present danger.

o Quite needlessly perhaps, these verses also mention that Allah made the believers the "heirs of their [the Jews'] land and their dwellings and their wealth and gave you the land which you had never trodden before." One wonders if the desire to acquire their wealth had anything to do with the massacre of the Jews.

What is absolutely incredible, though, is that the above verses were revealed right in the midst of the slaughter: "some of them you are slaying today and some taking as prisoners."[31] The Quran felt no compulsion to intervene.

As soon as the task was accomplished, Muhammad had another onerous duty to perform—distributing the spoils. These spoils included women and children. Because Bani Qurayzah were killed with the active participation of the believers, the believers had earned their share of the spoils, too. The following account by Ibn Ishaq merits reiteration:

> Then the apostle divided the property, wives and children of B. Qurayza among the Muslims ... and took out the fifth. ... Then the apostle sent Sa'd b. Zayd with some of the captive women of B. Qurayza to Najd and he sold them for horses and weapons.

> The apostle had chosen one of their women for himself, Rayhana d. Amr, one of the women of B. Qurayza, and she remained with him until she died, in his power.[32]

- ### *The massacre justified*

Muslim scholars have taxed their analytical skills ever since the massacre to justify this dreadful event. After much deliberation, they put forward the following as possible justifications:

- The Jews were in breach of the Charter of Medina and rightly punished.
- Bani Qurayzah (or at least their allies) agreed to place their fate in the hands of Sad bin Muadh and were responsible if the decision was unjust.
- The Jews joined forces with the Quraysh and paid the price.

Although these do not even collectively provide enough justification for the mass execution of a tribe that had surrendered without a fight, let us also see whether any of the grounds are at all tenable.

Violation of the Charter of Medina

This assumes that there was such a treaty to begin with. All indications in the Quran are to the contrary, however. Even while recording the incident, the Quran accuses Bani Qurayzah of "joining forces" with the invaders (we shall see what the Quran may mean by that) but throws away the opportunity to tell us that they were guilty of a graver offense—that of breaching the treaty.

It is fair to hold that if the Jews were guilty of violating the treaty, the Quran would certainly have mentioned it. It does so regarding the polytheists in the Sword Verses (recall that even their past breaches are mentioned as justification for the command to kill them), so why not in the case of Bani Qurayzah? This was all the more necessary to make the point that not all "prisoners of war" were to be dealt with in this brutal fashion, but only those who had acted treacherously by breaching their treaty. That the Quran makes no mention of the treaty can mean only that either there was no treaty or that it was not breached by the Jews.

One may also ask: What did the treaty actually require? Even as recorded by Muslim historians, it prescribed that "everyone shall have his portion [to defend] from the side to which he belongs."

There is no suggestion that the Jews were remiss in this. All accounts are agreed that the Jews refrained from attacking the believers and that the Jewish quarters were not used by the invaders to launch an attack. At worst, the believers were understandably concerned about the possibility that such an attack may take place, but the fears never did materialize. The Quran itself testifies to that, as we saw earlier.*

Decision by Sad bin Muadh

One is not sure if the argument even deserves recognition, but to note it in the words of Maududi:

> Since the Bani Quraizah had surrendered on the condition that they would accept whatever decision Hadrat Sa'd bin Mu'adh would give in their regard, and he had decreed that all the males of the Quraizah should be killed, the Holy Prophet had them executed.[33]

If the decision was unjust—and will there ever be one if this wasn't?—how is it made good because Bani Qurayzah (or their allies) agreed to Sad bin Muadh as the arbiter? The consent, in any case, was given under extreme duress (the Quran itself records that there was terror in their hearts). The paramount assumption must also have been that they would be treated fairly and justly. So how does one absolve the Prophet of responsibility in these circumstances? Could he not have discarded Sad bin Muadh's decision if he thought it was unfair?

Remarkably, even the Quran did not intervene, though elsewhere it does condemn the one who "when he gets power he directs all his efforts towards spreading mischief in the land, destroying harvests and killing the human race whereas Allah (Whom he makes his witness) does not like mischief."[34] Despite such disapproval for the destruction of the human race, the

---

* Another question, though slightly legalistic, is that even if there were a treaty with the three Jewish tribes, would it have remained valid once two of the tribes were banished. Could Bani Qurayzah be held to the terms of the treaty despite such material change of circumstances? There is no suggestion that the Charter of Medina was renewed or restated after the banishment of Bani Qainuqa and Bani Nadir.

Quran did not feel the need to check the Prophet as he went about slaughtering an entire tribe.

Siding with the Quraysh

The final argument is that Bani Qurayzah joined forces with the Quraysh and therefore invited this punishment. Considering that no fighting took place at all (even the Quran records that the Quraysh left without any advantage and that there was no invasion of the city), what can it really mean to say that they "joined forces with the invaders"? Certainly not that they actually fought the believers!* The worst that can be said is that Bani Qurayzah sympathized with the invaders. This is not an unreasonable assumption (they were, after all, well aware of what had happened to the other Jewish tribes), but mere empathy without any positive assistance to the Quraysh cannot have deserved punishment, least of all wholesale massacre.

RECONSTRUCTION BASED ON THE QURAN

Because the massacre is such a critical event, let us reconstruct the various elements based only on Quranic verses.

o To begin with, the Quran does not provide any evidence of a treaty between the Prophet and the Jews. Whether regarding the banishment of Bani Qainuqa and Bani Nadir or even with respect to the slaughter and enslavement of Bani Qurayzah, the Quran is absolutely silent on any possible treaty violation.

o The Quran is not so silent, though, on whether Bani Qurayzah posed any genuine threat to the believers. Apart from affirming that they neither attacked the believers nor allowed their quarters to be used in this regard, the Quran, by taunting the hypocrites that their homes were not insecure, in fact concedes that Bani Qurayzah did not pose a genuine threat.

---

  * It is also noteworthy that the other translators translate this somewhat differently. Yusuf Ali translates this as "aided them," Hilali-Khan that they "backed" the invaders, and Pickthall that they "supported" them.

o The Quran also records that the Quraysh left without gaining any advantage, which means that the Prophet was not acting under the stress of a major defeat.

o That the Jews surrendered without a fight is also documented. The Quran informs us that this was because Allah created terror in the Jews' hearts.

o The Quran also clearly records the massacre: "some of them you are slaying today and some taking as prisoners." There cannot therefore be any debate that it took place.

o There is no mention that the massacre was committed because the Jews had violated the treaty or because they had agreed to leave their fate in the hands of Sad bin Muadh.

o The Quran confirms moreover that when the massacre was taking place, the Quraysh had already "turned back" without inflicting any damage. This means that the believers were not acting under any clear and present threat to their survival— which may otherwise have allowed them a certain license to act unjustly towards Bani Qurayzah.

o The Quran also records that Allah made the believers the "heirs of their land and their dwellings and their wealth and gave you the land which you had never trodden before." This leaves one wondering what role this incentive may have played!

These are facts recorded by the Quran and cannot therefore be disputed. Based on these, can there be any possible justification for what happened? We are told that even a bloodcurdling event such as this was not without a touch of mercy, though. As noted by Maududi:

> From among the prisoners of Bani Quraizah, the Holy Prophet forgave Zabir bin Bata and Amr bin Sa's (or Ibn Su'da), the former because he had given refuge to Hadrat Thabit bin Qais Ansari in the Battle of Bu'ath, in the pre-Islamic days of ignorance; therefore he handed him over to Hadrat Thabit that he may repay him for his favor. And he forgave Amr bin Sa'd because it was he who was exhorting his tribe not to be treacherous when the Bani Quraizah were committing breach of trust with the Holy Prophet.[35]

What Maududi omits to mention is that Zabir bin Bata actually declined the favor. Ibn Ishaq records:

> He said, "Then I ask you, Thabit, by my claim on you that you join me with my people, for life holds no joy now that they are dead, and I cannot bear to wait another moment to meet my loved ones." So Thabit went up to him and struck off his head.[36]

Having killed the menfolk, the Prophet could perhaps have considered handing over the women and children to other Jewish tribes. Rayhana, in fact, originally belonged to Bani Nadir but was married into the Bani Qurayzah. She and other women and children could have been handed back to Bani Nadir or to the other Jewish tribes. That would have enabled them to live among their own people. But the possibility did not perhaps occur to the Prophet. Even the Quran did not guide him in this direction. Instead, some of the captive women were even sold for horses and weapons.*

*

The question is: How should one look at the entire Jewish experience in Medina, particularly the slaughter of Bani Qurayzah? Karen Armstrong is perhaps correct to say, "Of course we are right to condemn it without reserve, but it was not as great a crime as it would be today."[37]

On relative scale, others in history have committed graver violations. Genghis Khan alone killed many more without mercy. He did not even have the justification that this was for a greater cause, to establish the message of Allah. And though he is regarded to be more progressive than others and to have abolished torture, granted universal religious freedom, and smashed the feudal system of aristocratic privileges,[38] Genghis Khan will just never be remembered as a blessing.

We sent thee not, but as a Mercy for all creatures.[39]

---

* Ibn Ishaq's account noted above records "some of the captive women of B. Qurayza ... [were] sold for horses and weapons"!

9

THE GLORIOUS QURAN

We have also bestowed on you ... the glorious Quran. (15:87)[1]

Muslims believe, inspired by the above verse, that the Quran is absolutely majestic. In order to prove the proposition, different claims are put forward—including the one we assessed in Chapter 4 that the Quran is a scientific miracle. This chapter analyzes three diverse claims stemming from the above verse, namely that the Quran is a masterpiece of literature, a discourse on reason far ahead of its time, and the architect of a just and efficient economic system.

MASTERPIECE OF LITERATURE

Muslims are unanimous that the Quran is literature par excellence.* This also happens to be part of their faith:

> And if you be in doubt whether the Book We have sent down to Our Servant is from Us or not, then produce, at least, one *Surah* like this. You may call all your associates to assist you and avail yourselves of the help of any one other than Allah. (2:23)[2]

What is surprising is that the Quran stops the detractors from seeking Allah's help in meeting the test. Does it consider that to be a possibility? Another mentionable feature is that only gradually did the Quran lower the challenge. At the start, the challenge was to bring a book[3] or an entire discourse[4] like the Quran, which was then reduced to ten *Surahs*,[5] and finally to just one. This is indicative perhaps of the confidence the Quran gained with time.†

The question, however, is: What does it mean to say "then produce at least one Surah like this"? Can any literature (good or bad) be replicated short of plagiarism? What the Quran probably means is that it is not possible to reach the literary heights set by it. The difficulty, however, is that unlike science or mathematics—on neither of which the Quran boasts an immaculate record—it is not possible to judge literature as black or white. Experts may legitimately disagree on what constitutes good literature. How, then, to assess the claim that the Quran is literature par excellence?

---

* Consider, for instance, the following passage:
  > Literature and poetry have been instruments of human expression and creativity, in all cultures. The world also witnessed an age when literature and poetry occupied pride of position, similar to that now enjoyed by science and technology. Even non-Muslim scholars agree that the Quran is Arabic literature par excellence—that it is the best Arabic literature on the face of the earth. (Naik: *The Quran and Modern Science: Compatible or Incompatible?* p. 4)

† In fact, the challenge to bring one *Surah* is noted in *Surah Al-Baqarah*, which was revealed in Medina. By this time, the Prophet had a number of steadfast followers, and it must have been felt that even if the challenge aroused a response, the believers would not be dissuaded.

The fact that the Quran deeply moves its followers (which, admittedly, it does) cannot be decisive, for they may just be so conditioned. After all, is it not a fact that the Quran fails to have the same impact on non-Muslims, who are moved by other literature that the Muslims find quite ordinary, just as one man's national anthem fails to touch another? The issue thus needs to be assessed more objectively. We shall therefore focus on the *ideas* the Quran embodies, the *expression* it employs, and the *clarity* with which it communicates with the readers.

One learns that good literature turns in no small measure on the *idea* it embodies—whether the thought it expresses is capable of good rendition. But this is perhaps where the Quran is at its weakest. Amongst the ideas it incorporates, innumerable are simply incapable of literary articulation. Take the mass execution of Bani Qurayzah that we just discussed. Can that be presented in an artistic manner? Take then the Sword Verses, or Muhammad's marriage to Zaynab, or the quarrel between Muhammad and his wives, or the inelegant distribution of inheritance shares, or the Prophet's entitlement to the spoils of war. One could go on, but the question would remain much the same: Are these capable of being described pleasingly?

Coming next to *expression,* one finds that the Quran fails, often enough, to express itself with the elegance that one normally associates with top-quality literature. Take *Surah Ar-Rahman,* which is about Allah's attribute as *Rahman,* or "merciful," and is widely regarded by Muslims to be the most poetic chapter of the Quran. The following passage is taken from it:

> O you burdens of the earth, We shall soon be free to call you to account. (Then We shall see) which of your Lord's favors you deny. O company of jinn and men! If you have the power to escape across the bounds of the earth and the heavens, then escape! You shall not escape, for it requires great power. So, O jinn and men, which of your Lord's powers will you deny? (If you try to escape) a flame of fire and smoke shall be let loose upon you, which you will not be able to withstand. O jinn and men, which of your Lord's powers will you deny? Then (how will it be) when the heaven will burst and redden like red leather? O jinn and men, which of your Lord's

powers will you (then) deny? On that Day no man and no
jinn will need be asked concerning his sin. Then (it will be
seen) which of your Lord's favors you deny. The culprits
there shall be recognized by their faces and they shall be
seized by their forelock and by their feet and dragged. (Then)
which of your Lord's powers will you deny? (At that time it
will be said:) "This is the same Hell which the culprits were
wont to deny." They will wander to and fro between the same
Hell and the hot boiling water. Then, which of your Lord's
powers will you deny? (55:31–45)[6]

Admittedly, a lot is often missed out in translations, but how
more elegant could the above passage sound in the original text?
Let us take another example.

And, O Muhammad, relate to them the story of the person
whom We had given the knowledge of Our Revelations, but he
turned away from their observance. ... Therefore he began to
behave like a dog: it lolls out its tongue if you chase it away
and it lolls out its tongue if you leave it alone. Such is the
likeness of those who treat Our Revelations as false. (7:175–
176)[7]

Again, can equating disbelievers with dogs be expressed
gracefully in any language?

Good literature must also be reasonably clear, which is a
standard adopted by the Quran as well: "This Book is a perfect
guidance for mankind and consists of clear teachings."[8] In some
respects, the Quran lives up to the promise. Consider, for
example, the pronouncement that married women taken as
prisoners of war may be used for sex, or that people of the Book
and the disbelievers are not to be taken as friends by the believers.
These verses do not suffer from lack of clarity.

This isn't always the case, however. Let us take prayer timings
as an example. It is believed that Muslims must pray five times a
day—before dawn (*fajr*), during the afternoon (*zuhar*), midway
between afternoon and sunset (*asr*), at sunset (*maghrib*), and then at
night (*isha*). The challenge is to find this in the following verses
that address the issue:

And listen! Establish Salat at the two ends of the day and in the early part of the night. (11:114)*

Establish Salat from the declining of the sun to the darkness of the night, and be particular about the recital of the Qur'an at the dawn of the morning, for the recital of the Qur'an at the dawn is witnessed. Besides this, offer Tahajjud Prayer at night: this is an additional prayer for you. (17:78–79)†

[A]nd glorify your Lord with His praise before the rising of the sun and before its setting, and glorify Him during the hours of the night and at the extremes of the day: perhaps you may feel satisfied. (20:130)‡

So, glorify Allah in the evening and in the morning: praise is due to Him alone in the heavens and the earth; and (glorify Him) in the afternoon and at the declining of the day. (30:17–18)§

Glorify your Lord with His praise when you rise up, and glorify Him in the night too, and also at the retreat of the stars. (52:48–49)**

Remember the name of your Lord morning and evening, prostrate yourself before Him in the night, and glorify Him during the long hours of night. (76:25–26)††,[9]

One can understand why reliance must ultimately be placed on the traditions of the Prophet to identify the exact prayer timings,

---

* This verse mentions only three prayers: *fajr, maghrib,* and *isha.*

† The words "from the declining of the sun to the darkness of the night" suggest *maghrib.* Recital of the Quran at dawn is perhaps a reference to *fajr.* These verses do not mention *zuhar, asr,* and *isha. Tahajjud,* which is to be performed in the middle of the night and is not mandatory, is, however, mentioned.

‡ This verse may refer to *fajr, asr, isha/tahajjud, fajr,* and *maghrib,* though other interpretations are also possible; however, *zuhar* is certainly left out, even though *fajr* is mentioned twice.

§ These verses seem to mention *maghrib, fajr, zuhar,* and *maghrib. Asr* and *isha* appear to be omitted.

** These verses seem to refer to *fajr, isha,* and then *fajr* again. And though *fajr* is repeated, there is no mention of the other three.

†† These seem to refer to *fajr, maghrib, isha,* and *tahajjud. Zuhar* and *asr* are omitted.

as the above verses are open to divergent interpretations. Indeed, based on these same verses, some followers of the Shiite faith offer prayers only three times a day![10]

Determined nonetheless to prove that the Quran is the finest literature ever produced, Muslim scholars argue that even the disbelievers of Mecca considered it so.

> Yet when he came to them with clear Signs, they said, *"This is plain magic."*(61:6)[11]

> Whenever Our clear Revelations are recited to them and the Truth comes before them, the disbelievers say, *"This is plain magic."* (46:7)[12]

The disbelievers of Mecca certainly understood the language and the context of the Quran better than us—though we may not hold their opinion to be decisive—but did they consider the Quran to be magical? Relying on the words "This is plain magic," Maududi informs us that they did:

> This means: When the Revelations of the Quran were recited before the disbelievers of Makkah, they realized that the Quran was far superior to human speech. The compositions of their greatest poets, orators and literary men were no match with the un-paralleled eloquence, enchanting oratory, sublime themes and heart-moving style of the Quran. Above all, even the Holy Prophet's own words and speech were not comparable with the discourses that were being sent down to him by God. ... This thing made the truth plain before them, but since they were bent upon denial, they would say: "This is plain magic," instead of acknowledging it as Divine Word after witnessing this manifest Sign.[13]

Closer scrutiny reveals that the disbelievers meant quite the opposite, as is apparent from the full context of the above-quoted verse.

> Whenever Our clear Revelations are recited to them and the Truth comes before them, *the disbelievers say, "This is plain magic." Do they mean to say that the Messenger himself has fabricated it?* Say to them, "If I have fabricated it myself, you will not be able to do anything to save me from Allah's punishment.

Allah knows full well whatever you utter. He is enough as a witness between me and you, and He is the All-Forgiving, the All-Merciful." (46:7–8)[14]

It turns out that what is presented by Maududi as "plain magic" means instead that the Quran is a fabrication—"Do they mean to say that the Messenger himself has fabricated it?" Moreover, the Arabic word used by the Quran is *sehr*, which also means "deception and fraud." This is even conceded by Maududi in the context of verse 61:7:

> *The word* sehr *here does not mean magic but deception and fraud, which is also a well-known meaning of this word in Arabic.* Thus, the verse means: "When the Prophet whose coming had been foretold by the Prophet Jesus came with the clear signs of his prophethood, the Israelites and the followers of Jesus, declared his claim to Prophet hood to be a deception and fraud."[15]

It is thus inaccurate to suggest that the disbelievers considered the Quran to be "plain magic"—as though they were impressed by its literary brilliance—when the fact is that they thought of it as plain fabrication in the name of Allah!

The fact that the disbelievers were dismissive of the Quran and believed that they too could come up with similar verses based on accounts they had heard from the Jews and Christians is documented in the Quran:

> When Our revelations were recited to them, they said, "Well, we have heard: if we will, we also can fabricate such things: for these are the same ancient tales which have already been told again and again by the former people." (8:31)[16]

The Quran also notes that the disbelievers thought of the Prophet as "a mad poet"[17] and the Quran as a "bundle of incoherent dreams."[18] *Surahs* such as the following may partly be responsible.

> By the (horses) who run with panting breath, then dash off sparks (with their hoofs), then charge suddenly in the morning, then raise up dust in doing so; then penetrate into a host in a body! Verily, man is ungrateful to his Lord, and he himself is a witness to it, and he loves the worldly wealth with all his heart. But, does he not know the time when all that lies

(buried) in the graves shall be brought out, and all that lies (hidden) in the breasts shall be divulged and examined? Surely, their Lord on that Day shall be well informed of them. (100:1–11)[19]

If one thought that with time, as more and more tribes converted to Islam, the Arabs would have revised their view on the Quran, the following verses revealed towards the end of the Prophet's life suggest that they didn't.

Whenever a new Surah is revealed, some of them ask the Muslims (in jest), "Say, whose Faith from among you has increased?" (The answer is that) most surely (every Surah) increases the Faith of those who have sincerely believed and they rejoice but it has added more filth to the existing filth of those whose hearts are suffering from the disease (of hypocrisy) and they shall remain disbelievers up to their death. (9:124–125)[20]

Such being the facts, it is difficult to concede that the Quran is exceptional literature. It lacks the fundamentals, and even the disbelievers of Mecca were far from impressed by its artistic qualities.*

THE QURAN AND REASON

Let us next consider the claim that the Quran is a discourse on reason far ahead of its time. The claim is perhaps based on the fact that the Quran makes numerous appeals to commonsense,[21] which gives the impression that it places paramount importance on reason. One learns, however, that the Quran's sense of reason is quite peculiar—anchored in the world of the *jinn*[22] and *satans*,[23] even black magic![24]

---

* An interesting exercise should be to present the believers with sayings of the Prophet intermixed with Quranic verses and recited the same way. The Prophet's sayings are not supposed to have the same "literary brilliance" as the Quran. One expects that if the Quran is truly unique, the believers should instantly be able to tell the sayings and verses apart. It would be instructive to find out.

*Surah Al-Falaq** corroborates that even Muhammad was once affected by black magic. Maududi notes:

> As far as the historical aspect is concerned, the incident of the Holy Prophet's being affected by magic is absolutely confirmed. ... It has been related ... through so many different and numerous channels that forgery is out of the question. ...After the peace treaty of Hudaibiyah when the Holy Prophet (upon whom be peace) returned to Madinah, a deputation of the Jews of Khaibar visited Madinah in Muharram, A.H. 7 and met a famous magician, Labid bin Asam, who belonged to the Ansar tribe of Bani Zurayq. They said to him: "You know how Muhammad (upon whom be Allah's peace and blessings) has treated us. We have tried our best to bewitch him but have not succeeded. Now we have come to you because you are a more skilled magician. Here are three gold coins, accept these and cast a powerful magic spell on Muhammad." In those days the Holy Prophet had a Jewish boy as his attendant. Through him they obtained a piece of the Holy Prophet's comb with some hair stuck to it. Magic was worked on the same hair and the teeth of the comb. ... The spell took one whole year to have effect upon the Holy Prophet (upon whom be peace). In the latter half of the year the Holy Prophet started feeling as if was unwell. The last forty days became hard on him, of which the last three days were even harder. But its maximum effect on him was that he was melting away from within. ... At last, one day when he was in the house of Hadrat Aishah, he prayed to Allah to be restored to full health. In the meantime he fell asleep or drowsed and on waking he said to Hadrat Aishah: "My Lord has told me

---

* *Surah Al-Falaq* verses 1–5:
    Say: "I seek refuge with the Lord of the dawn, from the evil of everything He has created. And from the evil of the darkness of night when it overspreads *and from the evil of the blowers (men or women) into knots*. And from the evil of an envious one when he envies." (113:1–5)
Yusuf Ali's translation:
    Say: I seek refuge with the Lord of the Dawn; From the mischief of created things; From the mischief of Darkness as it overspreads; *From the mischief of those who practice secret arts*; And from the mischief of the envious one as he practices envy.

what I had asked of Him." Hadrat Aishah asked what it was. He replied: "Two men (i.e. two angels in human guise) came to me. One sat near my head and the other near my feet. The first asked: what has happened to him? The other replied: Magic has been worked on him. The first asked: who has worked it? He replied: Labid bin Asam. He asked: In what is it contained? He replied: In the comb and hair covered in the spathe of a male date-tree. He asked: where is it? He replied: under a stone at the bottom of Dhi Arwan (or Dharwan), the well of Bani Zurayq. He asked: what should be done about it? He replied: the well should be emptied and it should be taken out from under the stone." The Holy Prophet then sent Hadrat Ali, Hadrat Ammar bin Yasir and Hadrat Zubair: They were also joined by Jubair bin Iyas az-Zurqi (two men from Bani Zurayq). Later the Holy Prophet also arrived at the well along with some Companions. The water was taken out and the spathe recovered. There they found that beside the comb and hair there was a cord with eleven knots on it and a wax image with needles pricked into it. Gabriel (peace be on him) came and told him to repeat the *Mu'awwidhatayn*. As he repeated verse after verse, a knot was loosened and a needle taken out every time, till on finishing the last words all the knots were loosened and all the needles removed, and he was entirely freed from the charm. After this he called Labid and questioned him. He confessed his guilt and the Holy Prophet let him go, for he never avenged himself on anyone for any harm done to his person.[25]

One does wonder whether this kind of superstitious belief structure can sit well with reason as we understand it in today's world.

The Quran's somewhat peculiar reason can also be gathered from the following circular argument, which it considers self-evident: "Allah Himself has testified to the fact that there is no deity save Him" (3:18).[26] The question of course is: how should the disbelievers have known that Allah has testified to this effect? Just because the Quran said so! But if they believed the Quran to be the word of Allah, would there be any debate in the first place?

It is also interesting that the Quran is not shy of blaming people for sins they have not committed:

When it is said to them, "Believe in that which Allah has sent down," they say, "We believe only in that which has been sent to us," and reject everything else, though it is the Truth and confirms what is with them. *Well, ask them, "If you sincerely believed in what was sent down to you, why did you kill the Messengers of Allah (who were sent to you from amongst yourselves)?"* Moses came to you with clear Signs, yet no sooner was he away from you than you transgressed and took the calf for worship. Recall also to mind the Covenant We made with you while We raised the Tur over you: "Follow strictly the precepts We are giving you and give ear to Our Commandments." Your forefathers replied, "We have heard but we will not obey." They were so prone to unbelief that they cherished the calf in their hearts. Tell them (O Muhammad). "If indeed you are believers, yours is a strange Faith that enjoins you to do such evil things." (2:91–93)[27]

The above verses are regarding the Jews of Medina, who are blamed for sins committed by their forefathers.[28] What is surprising is that elsewhere, the Quran tells us: "No bearer will bear the burden of another" (17:15).[29] Why the same principle should not have applied to the Jews, the Quran does not elaborate, however.

Such oddities must have invited mockery. The Quran's response was to instruct the believers to stay away from gatherings where its revelations were being ridiculed:

Allah has already sent down to you in this Book the Commandment: you should not sit in a company wherein you hear things of unbelief concerning the Revelations of Allah, *and wherein these are being ridiculed,* until those people are engaged in some other talk. Now if you remain here you shall be guilty like them. Rest assured that Allah is going to gather the hypocrites and the disbelievers all together in Hell. (4:140)[30]

This may represent the Quran's best chance to maintain its hold on the followers, but does it constitute faith in reason?

A JUST AND EFFICIENT ECONOMIC SYSTEM

The argument that the Quran is the architect of a just and efficient economic system is based on the prohibition against interest on loans. This is surprising, considering that interest is amongst the most useful of human inventions. Without a banking system based on interest, the industrial revolution may not have taken off, or it would at least have been much slower. Even today, there is no adequate replacement for interest; nor is there a reason to look for one!

Let us take a simple example to see how interest works—not for the benefit of only the lender but also the borrower—and how that translates ultimately at the macro level. Suppose one desires to pursue further studies or to set up a business venture but lacks the funds. The options one may have follow.

- o   *Charity.* A self-respecting individual may not be so inclined, however. The fact also is that charity is not freely available.

- o   *Interest-free loan.* Those who have spare funds may not, however, be inclined to part with their money on these terms, as this obviously does not entail any advantage for them. The borrower may also feel uncomfortable seeking such favor without offering a return.

- o   *Include other partner(s) in the project.* The difficulty here is that not everyone has the appetite to participate in a project on the basis of sharing the profit as well as the loss. Conversely, even the person seeking the funds may not be keen to associate another as a partner, as this would mean sharing the profits with that person. Also, this option does not lend itself to the scenario in which one seeks funds to finish studies.

- o   *Asset sale.* This is an option should one have a saleable asset, but it is not the most attractive if one also happens to value that asset.

- o   *Interest-based loan.* Finally, one could seek a loan on the promise that the money will be returned with interest. Those who are not inclined to extend interest-free loans may not perhaps be so averse to this proposition, considering that this option entails a benefit for them too.

Of all these possibilities, one may conclude in one's circumstances that the last is the best option—maybe even the only viable option. In most cases, one would make good use of borrowed money and would be able to return it with interest—which, of course, would represent a win-win solution for both sides. On the odd occasion that things would not work out as planned, one may need to sell the asset (one initially preserved) in order to repay the loan with interest or may have to pay additional interest for the time one is unable to repay the loan, but this at least is a calculated chance taken after weighing all other options.

At the macro level, interest works in the following way. There are people who have funds to spare and others who are in need. The banks offer interest to those who have spare funds, thereby inducing them to place the funds with the banks. These same funds the banks then lend against interest to those persons seeking financing for various reasons.

Interest thus lies at the heart of the banking system. It is the inducement for the depositor to deposit funds with the bank. It is also the incentive for the banks to lend the funds onwards to those who are in need. The borrower is, of course, free to explore other options. He avails himself of an interest-based loan not out of compulsion but only if it works best in his circumstances.

Such a banking system based on interest may indeed have been the engine of growth during the industrial revolution. It generated funds from depositors big and small, enabling entrepreneurs to access these funds through the banks and to use them towards projects that would not otherwise be possible. In the process, the entrepreneurs not only employed more people but also expanded the horizons of industrial development. As the size of the pie increased, the opportunities for the state to levy taxes did, as well. The money collected through taxation was then used to provide basic facilities, such as education and health, to citizens who would otherwise be deprived. This is how the welfare state took shape—interest being the stimulus and standing very much at center stage!

It is thus no coincidence that societies that lacked a structured banking system based on interest were left far behind. They were unable to generate funds (in a structured manner, at least) that could be borrowed by entrepreneurs to explore newer horizons.

One therefore wonders what could be so improper or unjust about interest! The borrower, after all, is not forced to borrow; he only avails himself of this option if he considers this to be in his best interest. The lender, too, could make alternative use of the money, and it is only fair that he be compensated for not doing so. Also, as noted above, at the macro level, interest provides the basis for growth, through the banking system, which benefits all.*

The Quran tells us, however, that there is something fundamentally wrong with interest:

> Those who spend their wealth secretly and openly by day and night, will have their reward with their Lord, and they have nothing to fear nor grieve. *But those who devour interest become like the one whom Satan has bewitched and maddened by his touch. They have been condemned to this condition because they say, "Trade is just like interest," whereas Allah has made trade lawful and interest unlawful. Henceforth, if one abstains from taking interest after receiving this admonition from his Lord, no legal action will be taken against him regarding the interest he had devoured before; his case shall ultimately go to Allah. But if one repeats the same crime after this, he shall go to Hell, where he shall abide forever. Allah deprives interest of all blessing and develops charity;* and Allah does not like an ungrateful, sinful person. As to those who believe and do good deeds, establish the Salat and pay the Zakat, they will most surely have their reward with their Lord and they will have nothing to fear nor to grieve. *O Believers, fear Allah and give up that interest which is still due to you, if you are true Believers; but if you do not do so, then you are warned of the declaration of war against you by Allah and His Messenger. If, however, you repent even now (and forego interest), you are entitled to your principal; do no wrong, and no wrong will be done to you.* If your debtor be in straitened circumstances, give him time till

---

*   Incidentally, the ups and downs one sees in the economy are not because of interest; they are for other reasons, such as speculation, which may make a thing more valuable than it really is. In fact, by adjusting interest, the government can, often enough, prevent economic fluctuations. It is certainly unthinkable to run the modern financial system without interest.

his monetary condition becomes better. But if you remit the debt by way of charity, it would be better for you, if you only knew it. Guard against the disgrace and misery of the day when you shall return to Allah: there everyone shall be paid in full, for the good or evil one has earned and none shall be wronged. (2:274–281)[31]

What is a bit ironic is that this was clearly meant as a favor to borrowers (so they don't have to pay interest on top of the principal), but it ends up depriving the very same people (those in need, who must borrow to bridge the gap between their immediate needs and resources) of the most viable option to overcome their difficulty. It is worth noting here that making interest illegal does not make the other alternatives (charity, interest-free loans, etc.) more accessible. The restriction thus seems counterproductive. Moreover, if the true rationale was to check exorbitant rates charged by moneylenders, the better way should have been through regulation and not prohibition. As it is, though, the prohibition ends up depriving people who need funds of the best chance to access these.* It thus leaves them worse off.

What is also interesting is that the Quran does not find any parallel between the charging of interest and trade. It declares trade to be lawful but considers interest immoral and illegal. Is the distinction meaningful? Take, for example, a student looking for a loan to buy books. He approaches A for an interest-based loan. Because A cannot lend on that basis (because of the Quranic command), he offers to buy the books himself and sell them to the student at a higher price, on the condition that the price can be paid at a later stage (say a year later, by which time it is expected that the student will have finished his studies and found a job). This is trade, pure and simple, buying at a lower price and selling at a higher; it is thus permissible in the eyes of the Quran.

---

* If the idea simply was that the state would step in and provide interest-free loans to all who are in need, then (1) the Quran makes no mention of it, (2) it is doubtful whether the state can ever accumulate the resources to fulfill all needs, and (3) there is, in any case, nothing stopping the state from providing interest-free loans to the extent it can. This does not have to come at the cost of barring interest-based loans by non-state lenders. Borrowers would only approach the latter once the resources of the state have been exhausted.

But how is this less exploitative (assuming interest is), considering that the interest element would be built into the trading profit?*

One outcome, certainly, of the prohibition against interest was that the development of any structured banking system was inhibited in Islamic communities—which is one significant reason the Islamic world, otherwise so well poised, was left far behind in the industrial race.

The prohibition against interest thus seems irrational. If the proof of the pudding is in the eating, one need only to look at how the industrial age has progressed. It would not have been possible to replicate this with a system that did not allow interest. It seems, therefore, that the Quran may not have realized how useful a device was being barred. The Quran may also not have appreciated that even in its worst form, interest does provide some breathing space to the borrower—to live and fight another day. It is, quite simply, illogical to ban interest.

*

We thus learn that the claims regarding the literary brilliance of the Quran, it being a discourse on reason far ahead of its time, and it providing the foundation of a just and efficient economic system, remain as unsubstantiated as the claim regarding its scientific attributes. One wonders if the Quran is truly so glorious!

---

* Millions of man-hours are spent every week as Muslim scholars find innovative techniques of replicating, through the "trade" mechanism, exactly what interest-based transactions would deliver. It is indeed remarkable that the Quran considers one good and the other bad.

10

THE "SATANIC" VERSES

And O Muhammad (it has always been so with) every Messenger and Prophet We sent before you that whenever he had a desire, Satan tried to interfere with his desire. But Allah eradicates the mischiefs worked by Satan and confirms His revelations, for Allah is All-knowing, All-Wise.[1]

"Satanic Verses" is a term authored by William Muir.[2] According to many of the Prophet's earliest biographers, Satan once appeared before Muhammad in the form of Gabriel and "revealed" verses that compromised the "Oneness" of Allah by permitting intercession by certain goddesses. Thinking the verses were from Allah, Muhammad disclosed them as part of the Quran. Gabriel then intervened to inform him that Satan had played a trick. These verses were thereupon stricken from the Quran, on the pretext that these were not from Allah but that Satan had managed to deceive the Prophet. They are hence labeled "Satanic Verses."

The incident, if true, would be devastating to the credibility of the Prophet and the Quran. Muslim scholars concede:

If the Prophet could confuse the words of Satan for those of
Gabriel on this occasion and on this fundamental point, then
why not on other, less significant points as well?[3]

The stakes, though, are decidedly higher. If the account were to
be true, if the Prophet confused the words of Satan for those of
Gabriel on this fundamental issue, not just "other less significant
points," the whole of the Quran would be suspect. Who is to say
that, having made a strategic concession to the Quraysh that he
later regretted, perhaps because it failed to create the desired
result, the Prophet did not invent the story to get out of the
situation and that Satan had no role except for providing a
convenient excuse? In such a case, could it also not be said that
the Quran is entirely Muhammad's own creation?

The matter hence deserves the closest scrutiny. We must strip
the myth from the facts. We begin with a look at Arab polytheism,
in which context the incident is stated to have taken place. This
should help place the subsequent discussion in perspective.

ARAB POLYTHEISM

Surprisingly, it wasn't Muhammad who introduced the Arabs (at
least those living in and around Mecca) to Allah. They already
believed in Him. Thus, even the cry "*Allah Akbar*" (God is Great)
predates Islam![4] The Ka'ba, too, was dedicated to Allah's worship,
and though it also had 360-odd idols, they were meant merely as
intercessors to Allah.

This important fact is substantiated by Muslim historians as
well as by the Quran.

• *Abrahah's attack on the Ka'ba*

That the polytheists of Mecca believed in Allah is stated for
instance in accounts handed down to Muslim historians regarding
Abrahah, the ruler of Yemen, who came to destroy the Ka'ba
some years prior to the advent of Islam. It is written that the
Quraysh vacated the city, imploring Allah to save the holy Ka'ba.
Responding to the prayers, Allah sent swarms of birds carrying

stones in their beaks and claws, which were showered on Abrahah's troops, causing them to withdraw in panic.*

The incident also finds mention in the Quran:

> Have you not seen how your Lord dealt with the people of the elephant? Did He not cause their plan to end in vain? And sent down on them swarms of birds, which pelted them with stones of baked clay. Then He rendered them like straw eaten up by cattle. (105:1–5)[5]

An interesting fact may be mentioned here, at the cost of slight digression. A few years after the death of the Prophet, the Ka'ba caught fire during infighting (as a result of events in Karbala, in which the Prophet's grandson was martyred). The fire destroyed the House of Allah[6] and also shattered the *hajre-aswad*† into many pieces.[7] What we see today is the pieces stitched together. Allah did not intervene on this occasion.

• *The Quran on the Arab belief in Allah*

The Quran, too, mentions that the Arabs believed in Allah:

> If you ask them, "Who has created the earth and the heavens and Who has subjected the moon and the sun?" *they will surely say, "Allah."* How are they then being deceived? … If you ask them, "Who sent down rainwater from the sky and thereby

---

* Maududi, for instance, collates (though this is a shortened account):
  There were at that time 360 idols in and around the Ka'bah, *but on that critical moment they forgot them and implored only Allah for help.* Next morning Abrahah prepared to enter Makkah, but his special elephant, Mahmud, which was in the forefront, knelt down. It was beaten with iron bars, goaded, even scarified, but it would not get up. In the meantime swarms of birds appeared carrying stones in their beaks and claws and showered these on the troops. Whoever was hit would start disintegrating. The same thing happened with Abrahah too. His flesh fell in pieces and there arose sores on his body emitting pus and blood. In confusion they withdrew and fled towards Yemen. (Maududi: *The Meaning of the Qur'an*, commentary on *Surah Al-Fil*, Volume 6, pp. 532–533)

† The black stone/meteorite revered by Muslims and believed to have been used by Abraham and Ismail to construct the Ka'ba.

raised the dead earth back to life?" *they will surely say, "Allah!"* (29:61–63)

If you ask them, "Who created the heavens and the earth?" they will say, "Allah." (39:38)[8]

The roles they ascribed to gods and goddesses were merely of intercessors to Allah, not more than that. This, too, is recorded in the Quran:

> These people worship besides Allah those which can neither harm nor benefit them, and say, *"These are our intercessors with Allah."* (10:18)[9]

> As for those who have taken other guardians besides Him (and justify their conduct, saying): *"We worship them only that they may bring us closer to Allah."* Allah will surely judge between them concerning all that in which they differ. (39:3)[10]

The Quran misunderstands the polytheists' faith, though. It accuses the Quraysh of holding partners with Allah,[11] whereas they worshipped the deities only as intercessors to Allah—not the same thing as holding partners.* The Quran's failure to appreciate this subtlety may partly be responsible for why it made no headway in the Prophet's initial years in Mecca. The Quraysh, at least, may not have viewed themselves as *mushrikin* (polytheists) or "disbelievers," as the Quran accused them of being. They may even have resisted the charge, as certain verses of the Quran seem to reflect.[12]

Amongst hundreds of deities considered by the Quraysh to be intercessors with Allah were three goddesses Al-Lat, Al-'Uzza, and Manat. They were not located in the Ka'ba but held prominence. The incident of the Satanic Verses relates to these goddesses.

---

* This is not much different, it would seem, from the belief many Muslims entertain all across the globe that certain saints, for instance, can intercede with Allah—hence the popularity of shrines dedicated to them!

THE INCIDENT OF THE SATANIC VERSES

Ibn Ishaq reports:

> When the apostle saw that his people turned their backs on
> him and he was pained by their estrangement from what he
> brought them from God *he longed that there should come to him
> from God a message that would reconcile his people to him.* Because of
> his love for his people and his anxiety over them it would
> delight him if the obstacle that made his task so difficult
> could be removed; so that he meditated on the project and
> longed for it and it was dear to him.[13]

It was out of this longing for a message as may reconcile him
with his people, that Muhammad is said to have made a
concession regarding the three goddesses (Al-Lat, Al-'Uzza, and
Manat) that they could intercede with Allah. Ibn Ishaq goes on to
record:

> When Quraysh heard that, they were delighted and greatly
> pleased at the way in which he spoke of their gods, and they
> listened to him; while the believers were holding that what
> their Prophet brought them from their Lord was true, not
> suspecting a mistake or a vain desire or a slip. ... The news
> reached the Prophet's companions who were in Abyssinia, it
> being reported that Quraysh had accepted Islam, so some
> men started to return while others remained behind. Then
> Gabriel came to the apostle and said, "What have you done,
> Muhammad? You have read to these people something I did
> not bring you from God and you have said what He did not
> say to you." The apostle was bitterly grieved and was greatly
> in fear of God. So God sent down (a revelation), for He was
> merciful to him, comforting him and making light of the
> affair and telling him that every prophet and apostle before
> him desired as he desired and wanted what he wanted and
> Satan interjected something into his desires as he had on his
> tongue. So God annulled what Satan had suggested and God
> established His verses i.e. you are just like the prophets and
> apostles. Then God sent down: "We have not sent a prophet
> or apostle before you but when he longed Satan cast
> suggestion into his longing. But God will annul what Satan

has suggested. Then God will establish his verses, God being knowing and wise." Thus God relieved his prophet's grief, and made him feel safe from his fears and annulled what Satan had suggested in the words used above about their gods by his revelation: "Are yours the males and his the females? That were indeed an unfair division" (i.e. most unjust); "they are nothing but names which your forefathers gave them" as far as the words "to whom he pleases and accepts," i.e. how can the intercession of their gods avail with Him?[14]

Some analysts are of the opinion that this account must be accepted as true simply because Muslim historians would not have invented a story so damaging to the Prophet. Maududi recognizes the merit in this argument.

> How is it that so many reporters of Traditions have related this story? Does it not show that there must have been some reality about it? So many reporters, who included many authentic and eminent scholars, could not have made such an heinous slander against the Quran and the Holy Prophet.[15]

But then Maududi dismisses the possibility that the Prophet could ever be misled by Satan on such a fundamental point.* Hashmi

---

* He notes:

> As regards a believer, he can never accept it, when he knows that it contradicts not only one verse but a large number of other verses of the Quran. He would rather believe, that the reporters of the Tradition might have been deluded by Satan and not the Holy Prophet. He would never believe that the Holy Prophet could interpolate even a single word in the Quran under the influence of a desire of his own: or that there could ever occur such a desire in his mind that he should make a compromise with the disbelievers by associating shirk with Tauhid: or that he could ever wish that Allah might not say anything to displease the disbelievers: or that the Revelation was made in such an unsafe and doubtful manner as to enable Satan to mix with it even a word in a manner as if it was also brought by Gabriel. Each of these things is contradictory to the clear Revelation of the Quran and the basic Articles of the Faith which we have learned from the Quran and the Holy Prophet. God forbid that we should accept any such Tradition that might lead to the above mentioned presumptions just because the Tradition seems to be "authentic" in every way. (Maududi: *The Meaning of the Qur'an*, note 101 to *Surah Al-Hajj* Volume 3, pp. 221–222)

too is satisfied that the story is not genuine, offering the following reasons:

> The story of the satanic verses is implausible because it is completely opposed to the entire Quran and to all other reports on the attitude and behavior of the Prophet during the Meccan period.[16]

It is worth inquiring, though, whether the story really is so opposed to the Quran and to the attitude of the Prophet, particularly during the period when the incident is stated to have taken place.

THE QURAN ON THE SATANIC VERSES

Let us first state the crux of the incident. It is as simple as this: Muhammad at one point accepted intercession by the three goddesses but then withdrew the concession on the ground that Satan had misled him.* Let us see if we can find this documented in the Quran.†

Before we come to the verses that are more directly implicated in the incident, it would help to consult some others that are also indicative of the incident.

• *The Prophet's inclination*

The Quran documents a certain despondent phase in Muhammad's life, resulting from the fact that despite preaching in Mecca for a number of years, he failed to make any appreciable impact. The message by and large was rejected. This caused the

---

* Some historians add that the concession regarding the three goddesses was made at the time *Surah An-Najm* was being recited by the Prophet, which caused all those present on the occasion (including some of the Quraysh) to prostrate. We are less interested in this detail (which some find implausible) and will focus on the more essential features of the incident.

† The exact reason why the Prophet may have withdrawn the concession— whether it was because he thought the better of it, or because it failed to create the desired effect with the Quraysh, or perhaps even that he was truly corrected by Gabriel—can be debated separately.

Quran to announce that if not men, the jinn, at least, had started to convert![17]

During the same despondent phase, the Quran also softened its position just a little regarding intercession: "And no intercession before Allah can avail anyone except for the one for whom Allah permits it" (34:23).[18] The absolute rule against intercession seems compromised here—and so, in the precise context of deities worshipped by the Arabs. Was this softening in preparation for something bigger?

Then comes another important disclosure:

> O Muhammad these people have left no stone unturned to tempt you away from that which We have revealed to you *so that you might fabricate something in Our name.* Had you done that, they would have made you their friend. *It was just possible that you might have inclined a little towards them, if We had not given you strength.* But if you had done so, We would have made you taste double chastisement in this world as well as in the Hereafter: then you would have found no helper against Us. (17:73–75)[19]

These verses unmistakably record that, had Allah not intervened, Muhammad "might have inclined a little" to "fabricate something in Our name." It seems unbelievable that the Prophet would develop any such inclination, but this is precisely what the Quran reveals.*

But if Muhammad was ever so inclined, did he perhaps yield at a later stage?

---

* This raises the question: Why did the Quran need to make such a damaging disclosure? The answer may lie in the fact, as depicted in the above verses, that there was an interactive engagement between the Quraysh and Muhammad. It is reasonable to infer that if the Prophet was inclining a little towards the Quraysh (which is documented by the Quran itself), this may have been revealed in his dialogs as well. The Quran may not thus have disclosed something that was hidden from the Quraysh or from the Prophet's companions who may have participated in such discussions.

• Surah Maryam *and the migration to Abyssinia*

This brings us to another important event, which too happened a little before the incident of the Satanic Verses is reported to have taken place. A contingent of the believers was instructed by the Prophet to migrate to the Christian kingdom of Abyssinia, to try to create an alternative base.* Muslim historians record that they presented themselves to the Christian king and recited verses 16–26 of *Surah Maryam*.[20] While reading these verses, it is interesting to ponder whether the Quran misunderstands the Christian faith regarding the contact between Mary and the spirit.

> And, O Muhammad, relate in this Book the story of Mary: how she had retired in seclusion from her people to the eastern side and had hung down a screen to hide herself from them. There *We sent to her Our Spirit ("an angel") and he appeared before her in the form of a perfect man.* Mary cried out involuntarily, "I seek God's refuge from you, if you are a pious man." He replied, *"I am a mere messenger from your Lord and have been sent to give you a pure son."* Mary said, "How can I bear a son, when no man has touched me, and I am not an unchaste woman?" The angel replied, "So shall it be. Your Lord says, 'This is an easy thing for Me to do, and We will do so in order to make that boy a Sign for the people and a blessing from Us, and this must happen'." Accordingly, Mary conceived the child, and with it she went away to a distant place. *Then the throes of childbirth urged her to take shelter under a date palm. There she began to cry, "Oh! would that I had died before this and sunk into oblivion."* (19:16–23)[21]

These verses avoid disputing the Christian faith, regarding Jesus as the son of God. They also raise the following questions.

- Why were the verses clearly rejecting the Christian faith not recited? These include certain later verses of *Surah Maryam* itself ["This is Jesus, the son of Mary, and this is the truth

---

* It is noted in Ibn Ishaq's account reproduced above that some of those who had migrated to Abyssinia, upon hearing the news of reconciliation between the Prophet and the Quraysh after the incident of the Satanic Verses, decided to return to Mecca. The incident of the Satanic Verses is thus dated a little after the migration to Abyssinia.

about him concerning which they are in doubt. It does not behoove God to beget a son for He is far above this. When He decrees a thing, He only says, 'Be,' and it does come into being." (19:34–35)].[22] These verses also do not sit well with the ones that were actually recited to the Christian king, and may perhaps have been revealed (and added to *Surah Maryam*) later.

- Why did God's spirit appear before Mary "in perfect human form," while she was in seclusion, so that she was even scared to see him?

- Why did the "perfect man" say "I have been sent to give you a pure son"? Why not simply the news of a son?*

- Why did Mary, while experiencing childbirth, express remorse: "Oh! would that I had died before this and sunk into oblivion"?

At the very least, these verses do seem tailored towards a Christian audience. It is not surprising, therefore, that the king of Abyssinia was touched and said, "Of a truth, this and what Jesus brought have come from the same niche."[23]

What is also the notable feature here is that this compromising spirit towards Christianity appeared just a little ahead of the incident of the Satanic Verses.

• **Surah An-Najm**

It is time now to consult the *Surah* most directly implicated in the incident. Before examining the relevant verses, it is woth noting that if the incident of the Satanic Verses did take place, one would expect certain other issues to arise in parallel. Some people would have accused Muhammad of going astray and of delusional behavior. To others, this may have established that the whole of the Quran was nothing but a concoction and that Gabriel never visited Muhammad. Yet others (including possibly some believers,

---

* Although Yusuf Ali's translation as well as Hilali and Khan's add the words "(to announce)," these are not part of the Quranic text. Pickthall agrees with Maududi and translates: "He said: I am only a messenger of thy Lord, *that I may bestow on thee a faultless son.*"

who may have welcomed the concession in favor of the three goddesses because of their own past association with them) would have demanded that Allah at least clarify in unambiguous terms that these goddesses did not have the authority to intercede with Allah. One would expect these issues to arise alongside the incident.

One striking feature of this *Surah* is that it addresses all three issues in the same breath:

> By the Star. When it set, *your companion is neither gone astray nor deluded.* He does not speak of his own desire; it is but a Revelation which is sent down to him. One mighty in power has taught him, who is endowed with great wisdom. He stood poised in front when he was on the uppermost horizon. Then he drew near and hung suspended above, two bow-lengths away or even closer. Then he revealed to the servant of Allah whatever he had to reveal. The heart belied not what he saw. *Do you then dispute with him concerning what he sees (with the eyes)?* And he saw him once again by the farthest lote-tree, nearby which is the Garden of Repose. At that time the lote-tree was covered with that which covered it. The sight was neither dazzled nor it exceeded the limit, and he saw of the greatest Signs of his Lord. "Now tell: Have you ever pondered over the reality of this Lat, and this 'Uzza, and another, the third goddess, Manat? Are the sons for you and the daughters for Allah? This would indeed be an unfair division! These are nothing but mere names which you and your forefathers have invented. Allah has sent down no authority for them." (53:1–23)[24]

The *Surah* starts with the assurance "your companion is neither gone astray nor deluded," which shows that questions must have been raised to this effect. That the issue should have arisen in the context exactly of the very verses implicated in the incident of the Satanic Verses is noteworthy.

Equally intriguing is the fact that the *Surah* then devotes so much space to how Muhammad interacted with Gabriel.* This suggests that doubts had arisen whether Gabriel at all visited

---

* According to Hilali-Khan this refers to "*Mi'raj* (Ascent of the Prophet over the seven heavens)," but the exact context is not so important.

Muhammad, which necessitated the explanation. That this should have been in the precise context of the verses that are so directly linked with the incident of the Satanic Verses is again informative.

Also, of hundreds of gods and goddesses all believed by the Arabs to have powers of intercession, the Quran somehow singled out just the three goddesses to tell the Arabs: "Allah had sent down no authority for them." They happened to be Lat, `Uzza, and Manat—the three at the heart of the debated incident. Why just these three? Why not say: "Allah has not sent down any authority for any of the idols worshipped by you"? Just excluding these three would normally mean that other gods and goddesses were not part of the exclusion—unless, of course, there was a special reason to mention only these three. And if there was such special reason, what could that be? It is at least fair to conclude that some incident regarding these goddesses must have taken place, as the Quran would not otherwise have any cause to separate them from the rest. And because Muslim historians do not record any other episode explaining why these three goddesses should have been mentioned in this *Surah*, the incident of the Satanic Verses is the only candidate in the field.

The fact, then, that all three issues that would naturally have arisen from the incident are discussed together is difficult to explain except in the context of the debated incident. *Surah An-Najm* thus provides fairly conclusive evidence that an incident of this nature did occur. Let us see if we can find further corroboration in the Quran, however.

- **Surah Al-Hajj**

This *Surah*, too, makes an important announcement:

> And O Muhammad (it has always been so with) every Messenger and Prophet We sent before you that whenever he had a desire, Satan tried to interfere with his desire. *But Allah eradicates the mischiefs worked by Satan and confirms His revelations*, for Allah is All-knowing, All-Wise. (He allows this) so that He may make Satan's obstacles a trial for those, whose hearts suffer from the disease (of hypocrisy) and whose hearts are false—the fact is that these unjust people have gone far away

in their enmity—and so that those who have knowledge may realize that this (Message) is the Truth from Allah and may believe in it, and their hearts may submit humbly to it. Most surely Allah always guides the Believers to the Straight Way. (22:52–54)[25]

The following critical disclosures are hard to miss.

- These verses record that "every Messenger and Prophet" had suffered some mischief at the hands of Satan. If Muhammad was an exception to this rule, the above verses fail to state that.

- They explain that this was so Allah could make a trial for those who were diseased.

- They further record that Allah "eradicates the mischief worked by Satan and confirms His revelations."

The question then is: What mischief had Muhammad suffered at the hands of Satan that needed to be eradicated through Allah confirming His revelations?

Ibn Ishaq informs us that these verses were revealed shortly after the incident of the Satanic Verses, when "the apostle was bitterly grieved and was greatly in fear of God," and were meant to console the Prophet.* The exact timing of these verses is not so relevant, however. They may have been issued immediately after the incident, to console Muhammad or even to resurrect his image, which must have taken a hit on account of the *volte-face* (his

---

* There is some debate on this, though. Maududi, for instance, disagrees with the timing and on that basis also disagrees with the object of these verses: "*This verse (52) in which the interpolation by Satan was abrogated* was sent down in the first year of Hijrah, i.e. about two years after the reproof (17:73). Can a person in his senses believe that the Holy Prophet was reproved for the interpolation after six years, and it was abrogated after nine years?" (Maududi: *The Meaning of the Qur'an*, note 101 to *Surah Al-Hajj* Volume 3, p. 220). Even Maududi, however, concedes that this verse does abrogate some interpolation by Satan. Hashmi, in contrast, though he challenges the incident of the Satanic Verses on other grounds, concedes, "Not all Quranic verses grouped into individual *suras* date from the same time, and it is possible that Q. 17:73–75 and 22:52–54 do indeed relate to 53:19–23, as held by some of the earliest traditionists" ("The Quran and Tolerance: An Interpretive Essay on Verse 5:48," p. 87).

followers needed to be reassured that other prophets, too, had been deceived in the past), or may perhaps have been revealed at a subsequent stage. What the verses do unmistakably establish, however, is that Satan did deceive Muhammad, at least once—to such an extent that Allah had to "eradicate the mischief" and "confirm His revelations."

That being the position stated by the Quran, unless one identifies another instance in which the Prophet was misled by Satan and in which Allah intervened to eradicate the mischief and to confirm His revelations, there is no choice but to accept the incident of the Satanic Verses as true. It is thus ironic that the only way for Muslim analysts to try to disprove the incident is to at least identify a similar occurrence! Short of that, there is no option but to accept that the incident of the Satanic Verses did take place.*

*

Bringing all this together, not only is the incident of the Satanic Verses reported by Muslim historians "who included many authentic and eminent scholars"26 and who would not lightly circulate a story so damaging to the Prophet, there is also evidence in the Quran that about the same period, the Prophet seemed willing to experiment with compromises. This is visible in the verse that softens the rule against intercession† as well as in the verses that tell us that Muhammad "might have inclined a little" to "fabricate something in Our name." The same compromising spirit is visible in certain verses of *Surah Maryam* as well. *Surah An-Najm* and *Surah Al-Hajj* then provide rather conclusive proof that Muhammad did in fact experiment with a contained compromise on intercession. It was a contained

---

*   Even if one finds another instance in which Satan misled the Prophet and Allah intervened to eradicate the mischief, however, this would still not dislocate the incident of the Satanic Verses, which also finds reflection in *Surah An-Najm*. It would only, at best, provide a different context to *Surah Al-Hajj*.

†   "And no intercession before Allah can avail anyone except for the one for whom Allah permits it." (34:23)

compromise in that he wasn't permitting intercession by all gods and goddesses, just by the three that happened to be located away from the Ka'ba. He backtracked, but he left enough traces in the Quran that are impossible to explain any other way.

Lastly, one may also note the following verse: "We bring a better verse or at least the like of it for whatever We abrogate *or cause it to be forgotten*" (2:106).[27] We encountered this in the context of the Sword Verses while discussing that abrogation is a deliberate tool employed by the Quran, but here it is the words "or cause it to be forgotten" that draw our attention. The abrogated verses clearly do not fit this description, as they are mentioned as a separate category from verses that are caused to be forgotten, and also remain part of the Quran even once superseded by other verses (so are not forgotten). Only a verse stricken from the Quran can qualify under the description "cause it to be forgotten." Which, then, are the "forgotten" verses that the Quran is referring to here? The Satanic Verses, perhaps?

*

If the incident of the Satanic Verses did happen—and the evidence is overwhelming that it did—is it possible that Satan may have deceived the Prophet on other occasions as well? Far more plausible is that Satan did not even interfere in the case of the Satanic Verses but is unjustly accused.

UNDISTRACTED BY RELIGION

*O Prophet, say to them, "Did you ever consider this: If this
Quran were really from Allah, And you went on denying it, who
could be more astray than the one who had gone far off in
antagonism towards it?"* (41:52)[1]

What if the Quran isn't really from Allah? Would one be less astray
for following it?

The proposition draws us back to the four possibilities we listed
in Chapter 3, why Muhammad may have presented the Quran as
Allah's word: (1) he may have thought that this was the best way to
influence thinking; (2) he may genuinely have seen visions of Gabriel
without any objective reality to it (many others report similar
experiences); (3) he may have acted out of self-interest; and (4) he
may truly be the Prophet of God.

Incidentally, the first three are not mutually exclusive, in that
Muhammad may honestly have thought of himself as a reformer,
may genuinely have had visions of Gabriel, and may also occasionally

have used Islam to promote self-interest (whether deliberately or subconsciously), all at the same time. The fourth stands by itself, but if the discussion in this book is anything to go by, it does seem the least likely of the possibilities!

Let's return, then, to the proposition that the Quran is not the word of Allah (but only, at best, Mohammad's interpretation of a vision). The fact is that persuading anyone to leave the religion of his or her birth is amongst the hardest tasks. Even Muhammad failed to make a clean break from his past. He chose the same Ka'ba to be the focal point of the new faith, adopted the same *hajj* rituals, and incorporated many of the same pagan notions and practices in Islam.*,2 The incident of the Satanic Verses too is perhaps reflective of the inner pull Muhammad felt towards his past, as is the fact that he continued to believe in the very same Allah as the pagans!

It would thus be presumptuous of this book to imagine anyone disavowing his or her religion.† Instead, it sets itself a far more modest goal—simply to inform Muslim readers why others justifiably take such a different view on Muhammad and on the Quran. The hope is that they may find such views more tolerable henceforth and may also perhaps lower their disdain for other religions—this through the realization that if they themselves are entitled to continue believing in Islam despite many flaws visible to others, why not also allow the same concession to followers of other religions that may hold many similar deficiencies visible to Muslims?

That said, though, Islam is not the only religion to invite this kind of attention. Most religions bitterly divide mankind, and a similar exercise regarding them should be equally beneficial. A bit of doubt in the minds and hearts of the adherents of all such religions

---

*   Such as the concept of the forbidden months in which fighting was prohibited:

> The fact is that the number of months ordained by Allah has been twelve since the time He created the heavens and the earth, and out *of these four are forbidden months*: this is the right code of reckoning: therefore do not wrong yourselves by violating these months. (9:36)
> O Believers, do not violate the emblems of God-worship. Do not make lawful for yourselves *any of the forbidden months*. (5:2)

†   Though it may be noted that relinquishing one's faith in religion does not have to be at the cost of discarding one's belief in God. One may continue to believe in a God who never sent any prophets!

regarding their faith cannot be harmful in promoting religious tolerance.

Despite its focus on the Quran, this book would like to be counted as part of the initiative that desires to promote understanding and inclusiveness amongst all religions (not just Islam) regarding differences in human belief systems and cultures. It is written in the belief that humanity has far greater potential than realized—once religious tolerance is universally accepted as the norm. It dreams of a world totally committed to fighting misery, hunger, and disease—a truly wonderful world, undistracted by religious divisions!

NOTES

Author's Note

1. Maududi, Syed Abul Ala: *Tafhim al-Qur'an—The Meaning of the Qur'an*, 5th Edition, 2005, Islamic Publications (Pvt) Limited, Lahore. Also available at englishtafsir.com.

2. This is acknowledged, for instance, by Khaled Abou El Fadl and Leila Ahmad (both of whom are of Arab origin and are affiliated with leading universities in the United States). See *The Great Theft* (Abou El Fadl) and *A Quiet Revolution* (Leila Ahmad).

3. Ali, Yusuf: *The Meanings of The Holy Qur'an*, Kindle edition. Also available at www.muslimaccess.com/quraan/translations/yusufali/yusuf_ali.htm

4. *The Meaning of the Holy Qur'an*, Eleventh Edition (1430 AH/2009 AC) Amana Corporation, Maryland, p. xi.

5. Pickthall, Mohammed Marmaduke: *The Koran*, thirteenth printing (US), 1992, Everyman's Library (Alfred A Knopf), New York.

6. Hilali-Khan, *Translation of the Meaning of the Noble Qur'an in the English Language*, 1426 AH, King Fahd Printing Complex, Madinah.

Chapter 1: The Quran Speaks

1. *Surah Al-Alaq* verses 1–2. Yusuf Ali's translation: "Proclaim! [or read!] in the name of thy Lord and Cherisher, Who created. Created man, out of a (mere) clot of congealed blood." The revised translation constructed on Yusuf Ali's interpretation is as follows: "Proclaim! [or read!] in the name of thy Lord and Cherisher, Who created. Created man, out of a (mere) *leech-like* clot of congealed blood." (*The Meaning of the Holy Qur'an*, Eleventh Edition (1430 AH/2009 AC) Amana Corporation, Maryland)

2. The Quran's various chapters, called *Surahs*, often include many themes intermingled in the same chapter and are arranged more or less so that the longer chapters are placed in the front and the shorter ones at the end—but this does not follow a hard and fast rule. Regarding these two verses, however, there is consensus that they are the first to be revealed to Muhammad. Maududi, for instance, states, "Muslim *Ummah* almost unanimously agreed that the earliest Revelation to the Holy Prophet (upon whom be peace) consisted of the first five verses of *Surah Al-Alaq*." (Maududi: *The Meaning of the Qur'an*, opening commentary to *Surah Al-Muddaththir*, Volume 6, pp. 113–114)

3. Is it possible that the Quran is referring to a slightly subsequent phase of an embryo's development, after blood has been formed? It would be odd for the Quran, though, to draw attention to a phase that is clearly not the starting point, when otherwise mentioning the very creation of man. Besides, the description seems inaccurate (even regarding a subsequent phase) as the embryo does not, during any phase of its development, involve "congealed blood" (i.e., coagulated or frozen or solidified blood). A miscarried embryo may possibly give the appearance of a clot of congealed blood (on account of the blood solidifying), if aborted during certain phases of the embryonic development, but not an embryo in the mother's womb.

4. E.g., *Surah Al-Hijr* verses 26–29 (15:26–29)

5. "Aristotle described sperm and ova and believed that the menstrual blood of viviparous organisms (those that give birth to living young) was the actual generative substance." (*Encyclopaedia Britannica*, Volume 14, p. 1072). For other *Encyclopaedia Britannica* editions, see under: The Biological Sciences/The history of biology/THE EARLY HERITAGE/The Greco-Roman world/Aristotelian concepts. Also: *Encyclopaedia Britannica Online* (www.britannica.com) (http:// www.britannica.com/EBchecked/topic/66054/biology/48830/The Greco Roman world) under "Aristotelian Concepts".

6   Respectively, *Surah Al Baqarah* verse 99 and *Surah Yusuf* verse 1. Yusuf Ali's translations: "We have sent down to thee Manifest Signs *[ayat]*; and none reject them but those who are perverse." "A.L.R. These are the symbols [or verses] of the perspicuous Book." Note: Perspicuous means "clearly expressed or presented; easy to understand; lucid."

7   Hilali-Khan: *Translation of the Meaning of the Noble Qur'an in the English Language*, p. 3

8   *Surah Al-Fajr* verses 1–5. Yusuf Ali's translation: "By the break of Day; By the Nights twice five; By the even and odd (contrasted); And by the Night when it passeth away; Is there (not) in these an adjuration (or evidence) for those who understand?"

9   Maududi: *The Meaning of the Qur'an*, note 1 to *Surah Al-Fajr*, Volume 6, p. 346

10   *Surah Al-Imran* verse 7. Yusuf Ali's translation: "He it is Who has sent down to thee the Book: In it are verses basic or fundamental (of established meaning); they are the foundation of the Book: others are allegorical. But those in whose hearts is perversity follow the part thereof that is allegorical, seeking discord, and searching for its hidden meanings, *but no one knows its hidden meanings except Allah.*"

11   Rogerson: *The Heirs of the Prophet Muhammad*, pp. 282–302. See also Aslan: *No God but God* pp. 130–131.

12   *Surah Al-Imran* verse 105. Yusuf Ali's translation: "Be not like those who are divided amongst themselves and fall into disputations *after receiving Clear Signs.*"

13   *Sura Al-Maidah* verse 51. Yusuf Ali's translation: "O ye who believe! take not the Jews and the Christians for your friends and protectors: They are but friends and protectors to each other. And he amongst you that turns to them (for friendship) is of them. Verily Allah guideth not a people unjust."

14   *Surah Al-Imran* verse 28. Yusuf Ali's translation: "Let not the believers Take for friends or helpers Unbelievers rather than believers: *if any do that, in nothing will there be help from Allah* except by way of precaution, that ye may Guard yourselves from them."

15   Rawls: *A Theory of Justice*

16   A person exceeds the limit if he chooses to murder or assault another, as that is not compatible with equal liberty for all, but stays well within the limit if his preference for homosexuality (say) is merely directed towards other consenting individuals in the privacy of the home.

17   *Surah An-Noor* verse 2. Yusuf Ali's translation: "The woman and the man guilty of adultery or fornication, flog each of them with a hundred stripes: Let not compassion move you in their case, in a matter prescribed by Allah, if ye believe in Allah and the Last Day: and let a party of the Believers witness their punishment."

18   E.g., *Surah At-Taubah* verse 33: "He is Allah Who has sent His Messenger with Guidance and the Right way so that He may make it prevail over all other ways." (9:33) (Maududi) Yusuf Ali's translation: "It is He Who hath sent His Messenger with guidance and the Religion of Truth, to proclaim it over all religion."

19   The Quran mentions that the Prophet was an orphan and was poor, but few things about his early life are otherwise recorded.

Chapter 2: The Contradictions Challenge

1   *Surah An-Nisa* verse 82. Yusuf Ali's translation appears later in the chapter.

2   *Surah As-Sajdah* verse 5. Yusuf Ali's translation: "He rules (all) affairs from the heavens to the earth: in the end will (all affairs) go up to Him, on a Day, the space whereof will be (as) a thousand years of your reckoning."

3   *Surah Al-Hajj* verse 47. Yusuf Ali's translation: "Yet they ask thee to hasten on the Punishment! But Allah will not fail in His Promise. Verily a Day in the sight of thy Lord is like a thousand years of your reckoning."

4   *Surah Al-Maarij* verses 1–5. Yusuf Ali's translation: "A questioner asked about a Penalty to befall the Unbelievers, the which there is none to ward off, (A Penalty) from Allah, Lord of the Ways of Ascent. The angels and the spirit ascend unto him in a Day the measure whereof is (as) fifty thousand years: Therefore do thou hold Patience, a Patience of beautiful (contentment)."

5   *Surah Al-Baqarah* verse 186. Yusuf Ali's translation: "When My servants ask thee concerning Me, I am indeed close (to them): I listen to the prayer of every suppliant when he calleth on Me."

6   *Surah Al-Anfal* verse 65. Yusuf Ali's translation: "O Messenger, rouse the Believers to the fight. If there are twenty amongst you, patient and persevering, they will vanquish two hundred: if a

hundred, they will vanquish a thousand of the Unbelievers: for these are a people without understanding."

7 *Surah Al-Anfal* verse 66. Yusuf Ali's translation: "For the present, Allah hath lightened your (task), for He knoweth that there is a weak spot in you: But (even so), if there are a hundred of you, patient and persevering, they will vanquish two hundred, and if a thousand, they will vanquish two thousand, with the leave of Allah. For Allah is with those who patiently persevere."

8 *Surah An-Nisa* verse 12. Yusuf Ali's translation: "… If the man or woman whose inheritance is in question, has left neither ascendants nor descendants, but has left a brother or a sister, each one of the two gets a sixth; but if more than two, they share in a third; after payment of legacies and debts; so that no loss is caused (to any one). Thus is it ordained by Allah and Allah is All-knowing, Most Forbearing."

9 Maududi: *The Meaning of the Qur'an*, note 23 to *Surah An-Nisa*, Volume 1, p. 316

10 *Surah An-Nisa* verse 176. Yusuf Ali's translation: "They ask thee for a legal decision. Say: Allah directs (thus) about those who leave no descendants or ascendants as heirs. *If it is a man that dies, leaving a sister but no child, she shall have half the inheritance: If (such a deceased was) a woman, who left no child, Her brother takes her inheritance: If there are two sisters, they shall have two-thirds of the inheritance (between them): if there are brothers and sisters, (they share), the male having twice the share of the female.* Thus doth Allah make clear to you (His law), lest ye err. And Allah hath knowledge of all things."

11 *Surah Al-Maidah* verse 101. Yusuf Ali's translation: "O ye who believe! Ask not questions about things which, if made plain to you, may cause you trouble. But if ye ask about things when the Qur'an is being revealed, they will be made plain to you …"

12 *Surah Al-Furqan* verses 32–33. Maududi's translation: "The disbelievers say, 'Why has not the entire Quran been sent down to this man all at once?' Well this has been done to impress it deeply on your mind and (for the same object) We have sent it down piecemeal by degrees. And (there is another wisdom in this): *whenever they brought to you an odd thing (or a strange question) We sent its right answer to you in time and explained it all in the best manner.*" (25:32–33) Yusuf Ali's translation: "Those who reject Faith say: 'Why is not the Qur'an revealed to him all at once?' Thus (is it revealed), that We may strengthen thy heart thereby, and We have rehearsed it to thee in slow, well-arranged stages, gradually. *And no question do they bring to thee but We reveal to thee the truth and the best explanation (thereof).*"

13 *Surah Ha-Mim As-Sajdah* verses 9–12. Yusuf Ali's translation: "Say: Is it that ye deny Him Who created the earth in two Days? And do ye join equals with Him? He is the Lord of (all) the Worlds. He set on the (earth), mountains standing firm, high above it, and bestowed blessings on the earth, and measure therein all things to give them nourishment in due proportion, in four Days, in accordance with (the needs of) those who seek (Sustenance). *Moreover He comprehended in His design the sky, and it had been (as) smoke.* He said to it and to the earth: 'Come ye together, willingly or unwillingly.' They said: 'We do come (together), in willing obedience.' *So He completed them as seven firmaments in two Days,* and He assigned to each heaven its duty and command. And We adorned the lower heaven with lights, and (provided it) with guard. Such is the Decree of (Him) the Exalted in Might, Full of Knowledge."

14 *Surah Al Baqarah* verse 29. Maududi's translation: "He it is Who created for you all that there is on the Earth; *He then turned to the sky and ordered it into seven heavens.*" Yusuf Ali's translation: "It is He Who hath created for you all things that are on earth; *Moreover His design comprehended the heavens, for He gave order and perfection to the seven firmaments.*" Interestingly, the revision to Yusuf Ali's translation reads as follows: "It is He Who hath created for you all things that are on earth; Then he turned to the heaven And made them into seven firmaments." (*The Meaning of the Holy Qur'an*, Eleventh Edition (1430 AH/2009 AC) Amana Corporation, Maryland). This recognizes (more clearly than the original translation) that according to this verse, the earth was created before the heavens.

15 *Surah Naziat* verses 27–33. Yusuf Ali's translation: "What! Are ye the more difficult to create or the heaven (above)? ((Allah)) hath constructed it: On high hath He raised its canopy, and He hath given it order and perfection. Its night doth He endow with darkness, and its splendour doth He bring out (with light). *And the earth, moreover, hath He extended (to a wide expanse);* He draweth out therefrom its moisture and its pasture; And the mountains hath He firmly fixed. For use and convenience to you and your cattle."

16 Maududi: *The Meaning of the Qur'an*, note 14 to *Surah Ha Mim As-Sajadah*, Volume 4, p. 482

17 *Surah Al-Hijr* verses 61–72. Yusuf Ali's translation: "At length when the messengers arrived among the adherents of Lut, He said: 'Ye appear to be uncommon folk.' They said: 'Yea, we have come to thee to accomplish that of which they doubt. We have brought to thee that which is inevitably due, and assuredly we tell the truth. Then travel by night with thy household, when a portion of the night (yet remains), and do thou bring up the rear: let no one amongst you look back, but pass on whither ye are ordered.' And We made known this decree to him, that the last remnants of those (sinners) should be cut off by the morning. The inhabitants of the city came in (mad) joy (at news of the young men). Lut said: 'These are my guests: disgrace me not: But fear Allah, and shame me not.' They said: 'Did we not forbid thee (to speak) for all and sundry?' He said: 'There are my daughters (to marry), if ye must act (so).' Verily, by thy life (O Prophet), in their wild intoxication, they wander in distraction, to and fro."

18 *Surah Hud* verses 77–83. Yusuf Ali's translation: "When Our messengers came to Lut, he was grieved on their account and felt himself powerless (to protect) them. He said: 'This is a distressful day.' And his people came rushing towards him, and they had been long in the habit of practicing abominations. He said: 'O my people! Here are my daughters: they are purer for you (if ye marry)! Now fear Allah, and cover me not with shame about my guests! Is there not among you a single right-minded man?' They said: 'Well dost thou know we have no need of thy daughters: indeed thou knowest quite well what we want!' He said: 'Would that I had power to suppress you or that I could betake myself to some powerful support.' *(The Messengers) said: 'O Lut! We are Messengers from thy Lord! By no means shall they reach thee! now travel with thy family while yet a part of the night remains, and let not any of you look back: but thy wife (will remain behind): To her will happen what happens to the people.* Morning is their time appointed: Is not the morning nigh?' When Our Decree issued, We turned (the cities) upside down, and rained down on them brimstones hard as baked clay, spread, layer on layer, Marked as from thy Lord: Nor are they ever far from those who do wrong!"

19 *Surah Al-Baqarah* verses 30–34. Yusuf Ali's translation: "Behold, thy Lord said *to the angels*: 'I will create a vicegerent on earth.' They said: 'Wilt Thou place therein one who will make mischief therein and shed blood whilst we do celebrate Thy praises and glorify Thy holy (name)?' He said: 'I know what ye know not.' And He taught Adam the nature of all things; then He placed them *before the angels*, and said: 'Tell me the nature of these if ye are right.' They said: 'Glory to Thee, of knowledge We have none, save what Thou Hast taught us: In truth it is Thou Who art perfect in knowledge and wisdom.' He said: 'O Adam! Tell them their natures.' When he had told them, Allah said: 'Did I not tell you that I know the secrets of heaven and earth, and I know what ye reveal and what ye conceal?' *And behold, We said to the angels: 'Bow down to Adam' and they bowed down. Not so Iblis: he refused and was haughty: He was of those who reject Faith.*"

20 Respectively, *Surah Bani Israil* verse 61 and *Surah Ta Ha* verse 116. Yusuf Ali's translations: "Behold! *We said to the angels*: 'Bow down unto Adam': *They bowed down except Iblis*. He said, 'Shall I bow down to one whom Thou didst create from clay?'"; "When *We said to the angels*, 'Prostrate yourselves to Adam', *they prostrated themselves, but not Iblis*: he refused."

21 *Surah Al-Hijr* verses 26–33. Yusuf Ali's translation: "We created man from sounding clay, from mud molded into shape; *And the Jinn race, We had created before, from the fire of a scorching wind*. Behold! *thy Lord said to the angels*: 'I am about to create man, from sounding clay from mud molded into shape; When I have fashioned him (in due proportion) and breathed into him of My spirit, fall ye down in obeisance unto him.' *So the angels prostrated themselves, all of them together: Not so Iblis*: he refused to be among those who prostrated themselves. ((Allah)) said: 'O Iblis! what is your reason for not being among those who prostrated themselves?' (Iblis) said: 'I am not one to prostrate myself to man, whom Thou didst create from sounding clay, from mud moulded into shape.'"

22 Respectively, *Surah Al-Aaraf* verses 11–12 and *Surah Saad*, verses 71–76. Yusuf Ali's translations: "It is We Who created you and gave you shape; then We bade the angels bow down to Adam, and they bowed down; not so Iblis; He refused to be of those who bow down. ((Allah)) said: 'What prevented thee from bowing down when I commanded thee?' *He said: 'I am better than he: Thou didst create me from fire, and him from clay.'* "; "So the angels prostrated themselves, all of them together: Not so Iblis: he was haughty, and became one of those who reject Faith. ((Allah)) said: 'O Iblis! What prevents thee from prostrating thyself to one whom I have created with my hands? Art thou haughty? Or art thou one of the high (and mighty) ones?' *(Iblis) said: 'I am better than he: thou createdst me from fire, and him thou createdst from clay.'*"

23   *Surah Al-Kahf* verse 50. Yusuf Ali's translation: "Behold! We said to the angels, 'Bow down to Adam': They bowed down except Iblis. *He was one of the Jinns,* and he broke the Command of his Lord."

24   *Surah An-Nisa* verses 11–12. Yusuf Ali's translation: "Allah (thus) directs you as regards your Children's (Inheritance): to the male, a portion equal to that of two females: if only daughters, two or more, their share is two-thirds of the inheritance; if only one, her share is a half. For parents, a sixth share of the inheritance to each, if the deceased left children; if no children, and the parents are the (only) heirs, the mother has a third; if the deceased left brothers (or sisters) the mother has a sixth. (The distribution in all cases) after the payment of legacies and debts. Ye know not whether your parents or your children are nearest to you in benefit. These are settled portions ordained by Allah. And Allah is All-knowing, All-wise. In what your wives leave, your share is a half, if they leave no child; but if they leave a child, ye get a fourth; after payment of legacies and debts. In what ye leave, their share is a fourth, if ye leave no child; but if ye leave a child, they get an eighth; after payment of legacies and debts. …"

25   *Surah Al Tariq* verses 5–7

26   Indeed, even the ovaries do not fall in this region—not that the verse is referring to them in any manner.

27   *The American Heritage Dictionary:* "**1.** The part of the body of a human or quadruped on either side of the backbone and between the ribs and hips. **2.** One of several cuts of meat, such as tenderloin, taken from this part of an animal's body, typically including the vertebrae of the segment from which it is taken. **3. Loins a.** The region of the hips, groin, and lower abdomen. **b.** The reproductive organs."

28   Maududi: *The Meaning of the Qur'an,* Appendix 1 to the commentary on *Surah Al-Tariq,* Volume 6, pp. 310, 313.

29   *Surah Al Qiyama* verses 36–40

30   *Surah Al-Mulk* verse 23. Strictly speaking, the verse may only refer to "the hearts," and the words "to think and understand" are an extrapolation.

31   *Surah Al-Muminoon* verse 78

32   *Surah Al Aaraf* verse 179

33   Reference may, for instance, be made to the following verses: 7:100–102; 26:10–17; 45:23; and 47:16–18.

34   Yusuf Ali translates verses 67:23 and 23:78 without reference to the heart:
> Say: "It is He Who has created you (and made you grow), and made for you the *faculties of hearing, seeing, feeling and understanding:* little thanks it is ye give." (67:23)
> It is He Who has created for you *(the faculties of) hearing, sight, feeling and understanding:* little thanks it is ye give! (23:78)

Hilali-Khan translate with reference to the heart:
> Say it is He Who has created you and endowed you with *hearing (ears) and seeing (eyes) and hearts.* Little thanks you give. (67:23)
> It is He Who has created for you (the sense of) *hearing (ears), eyes (sight) and hearts (understanding).* Little thanks you give. (23:78)

Pickthall follows the same pattern as Hilali-Khan:
> Say (unto them, O Muhammad): He it is who gave you being, and hath assigned unto you *ears and eyes and hearts.* Small thanks give ye! (67:23)
> He it is Who hath created for you *ears and eyes and hearts.* Small thanks give ye! (23:78)

What is common, of course, is that all three avoid any direct correlation between the heart and understanding, perhaps as that would make the Quran scientifically inaccurate. They however choose opposite routes. But when it comes to verse 7:179, there is no avoiding the issue:
> Many are the Jinns and men we have made for Hell: *They have hearts wherewith they understand not,* eyes wherewith they see not, and ears wherewith they hear not. They are like cattle, nay more misguided: for they are heedless (of warning). (Yusuf Ali)
> And surely, We have created many of the jinn and mankind for Hell. *They have hearts wherewith they understand not,* and they have eyes wherewith they see not, and they have ears wherewith they hear not (the truth). (Hilali-Khan)
> Already have We urged unto hell many of the jinn and humankind, *having hearts wherewith they understand not,* and having eyes wherewith they see not, and having ears wherewith they hear not. These are as the cattle—nay, but they are worse! These are the neglectful. (Pickthall)

35   Respectively, *Surah Ar-Ra'ad* verse 3, *Surah Ya Sin* verse *36*, and *Surah Adh-Dhariyat* verse 49.
     Yusuf Ali's translations: "And fruit of *every* kind He made in pairs, two and two: He draweth the
     night as a veil o'er the Day. Behold, verily in these things there are signs for those who
     consider!"; "Glory to Allah, Who created in pairs *all* things that the earth produces, as well as
     their own (human) kind and (other) things of which they have no knowledge."; "And of *every
     thing* We have created pairs: That ye may receive instruction."
36   *Encyclopaedia Britannica*, Volume 27, p. 233. For other *Encyclopaedia Britannica* editions, see under:
     Sex and Sexuality/Animals and plants/SEXUAL AND NOSEXUAL REPRODUCTION. Also:
     Encyclopaedia   Britannica   Online   (www.britannica.com)   (http://www.britannica.com/
     EBchecked/topic/536936/sex) under "Sexual and nonsexual reproduction".
37   *Encyclopaedia Britannica*, Volume 26, p. 616. For other *Encyclopaedia Britannica* editions, see under:
     Reproduction and Reproductive Systems/PLANT REPRODUCTION/Plant reproductive
     systems/GENERAL FEATURES OF SEXUAL SYSTEMS. Also: *Encyclopaedia Britannica Online*
     (www.britannica.com)   (http://www.britannica.com/EBchecked/topic/498651/plant-
     reproductive-system/76161/General-features-of-sexual-systems) under "General features of
     sexual systems".
38   *Encyclopaedia Britannica*, Volume 26, p. 617. For other *Encyclopaedia Britannica* editions, see under:
     Reproduction and Reproductive Systems/PLANT REPRODUCTION/Plant reproductive
     systems/GENERAL FEATURES OF SEXUAL SYSTEMS/The plant basis. Also: *Encyclopaedia
     Britannica   Online*   (www.britannica.com)   (http://www.britannica.com/
     EBchecked/topic/498651/plant-reproductive-system/76163/The-plant-basis) under the "The
     plant basis".
39   *Encyclopaedia Britannica*, Volume 26, p. 636. For other *Encyclopaedia Britannica* editions, see under:
     ANIMAL REPRODUCTION. Also: *Encyclopaedia Britannica Online* (www.britannica.com)
     (http://www.britannica.com/ EBchecked/topic/498613/animal-reproductive-system) under
     "Animal Reproductive System".
40   Millius: "Life Without Sex," p. 406
41   One such species on which quite a bit of research has been done is "Class Bdelloidea of the
     Phylum Rotifera [which] is the largest metazoan taxon in which males, hermaphrodites, and
     meiosis are unknown." Welch and Meselson: "Evidence for the Evolution of Bdelloid Rotifers
     Without Sexual Reproduction or Genetic Exchange," p. 1211

Chapter 3: Muhammad: The Last Prophet

1   *Surah Al-Ahzab* verses 50–52. These verses are quoted in full later in the chapter. Yusuf Ali's
     translation is deferred until then.
2   Michael Hart, for instance, places him at number 1. (Hart: *The 100—A Ranking of the Most
     Influential Persons in History*)
3   *Surah Al-Ankabut* verses 48–49. Maududi's translation: "(O Prophet) you did not read any book
     before this, nor did you write any with your hand. If it were so, the worshippers of falsehood
     could have been involved in doubt. These are in fact clear Signs in the hearts of those who have
     been given knowledge; and none deny Our revelations except the wicked." (29:48–49) Yusuf
     Ali's translation: "And thou wast not (able) to recite a Book before this (Book came), nor art
     thou (able) to transcribe it with thy right hand: In that case, indeed, would the talkers of vanities
     have doubted. Nay, here are Signs self-evident in the hearts of those endowed with knowledge:
     and none but the unjust reject Our Signs."
4   *Surah Az-Zukhruf* verses 31–32. Yusuf Ali's translation: "Also, they say: 'Why is not this Qur'an
     sent down to some leading man in either of the two (chief) cities?' Is it they who would portion
     out the Mercy of thy Lord?"
5   *Surah Al-Alaq* verses 9–10. Yusuf Ali's translation: "Seest thou one who forbids—A votary when
     he (turns) to pray?"
6   *Surah Al-Lahab* verses 1–4. Yusuf Ali's translation: "Perish the hands of the Father of Flame!
     Perish he! No profit to him from all his wealth, and all his gains! Burnt soon will he be in a Fire
     of Blazing Flame! His wife shall carry the (crackling) wood—As fuel!"
7   Maududi, for instance, notes:
         Before the proclamation of Prophet-hood, two of the Holy Prophet's daughters were
         married to two of Abu Lahab's sons, 'Utbah and 'Utaibah. After his call, when the Holy
         Prophet began to invite the people to Islam, Abu Lahab said to both his sons: "I would

forbid myself seeing and meeting you until you divorced the daughters of Muhammad" (upon whom be Allah's peace and blessings). So both of them divorced their wives. (Maududi: *The Meaning of the Qur'an*, introduction to *Surah Al-Lahab*, Volume 6, p. 612)

8   *Surah Al-Mutaffifin* verses 29–36. Yusuf Ali's translation: "Those in sin used to laugh at those who believed, And whenever they passed by them, used to wink at each other (in mockery); And when they returned to their own people, they would return jesting; And whenever they saw them, they would say, 'Behold! These are the people truly astray!' But they had not been sent as keepers over them! But on this Day the Believers will laugh at the Unbelievers: On Thrones (of Dignity) they will command (a sight) (of all things). Will not the Unbelievers have been paid back for what they did?"

9   Respectively, *Surah Bani Israil* verse 76 and *Surah Al-Tariq* verses 15–17. Yusuf Ali's translations: "Their purpose was to scare thee off the land, in order to expel thee; but in that case they would not have stayed (therein) after thee, except for a little while."; "As for them, they are but plotting a scheme, And I am planning a scheme. Therefore grant a delay to the Unbelievers: Give respite to them gently (for awhile)."

10   *Surah Az-Zukhruf* verses 79–80. Yusuf Ali's translation: "What! have they settled some plan (among themselves)? But it is We Who settle things. Or do they think that We hear not their secrets and their private counsels? *Indeed (We do), and Our messengers are by them, to record.*"

11   *Surah Al-Anfal* verse 30. Yusuf Ali's translation: "Remember how the Unbelievers *plotted* against thee, *to keep thee in bonds, or slay thee, or get thee out (of thy home).* They plot and plan, and Allah too plans; but the best of planners is Allah."

12   *Surah Al-Anfal* verse 26. Yusuf Ali's translation: "Call to mind *when ye were a small (band)*, despised through the land, *and afraid that men might despoil and kidnap you*, But He provided a safe asylum for you, strengthened you with His aid, and gave you Good things for sustenance. that ye might be grateful."

13   *Surah Al-Mumtahina* verse 1. Yusuf Ali's translation: "O ye who believe! Take not my enemies and yours as friends (or protectors), *offering them (your) love, even though they have rejected the Truth that has come to you, and have (on the contrary) driven out the Prophet and yourselves (from your homes), (simply) because ye believe in Allah your Lord! If ye have come out to strive in My Way and to seek My Good Pleasure, (take them not as friends), holding secret converse of love (and friendship) with them: for I know full well all that ye conceal and all that ye reveal.* And any of you that does this has strayed from the Straight Path."

14   *Surah Al-Mumtahina* verse 9. Yusuf Ali's translation: "Allah only forbids you, with regard to those who fight you for (your) Faith, and drive you out of your homes, and support (others) in driving you out, from turning to them (for friendship and protection). It is such as turn to them (in these circumstances), that do wrong."

15   Muslim scholars understandably attempt to downplay these verses. They assert that these verses are based on an isolated incident involving just one companion (Hatib bin Abi Balta'a), whose family was in Mecca as the final assault against the Quraysh was under preparation by the Prophet. Hatib wanted to gain the sympathy of the Quraysh so his family would not be harmed during the conflict, and he secretly sent a letter to the Quraysh to warn them of the attack. Allah informed the Prophet, however, and the letter was intercepted. According to some Muslim scholars, these verses were revealed after this incident and before the conquest of Mecca. It seems unlikely, though, that such a general and overpowering command would be issued on account of just one companion, unless there was a genuine fear that many more were either already on friendly terms with the Quraysh or were likely to follow suit.

16   The following verses (*Surah Al-Burooj* verses 2–10) may be noted, though. Maududi's translation: "Doomed *were* the people of the ditch, (of that ditch) which had the fire fed by the intensely blazing fuel, when they were sitting by the ditch and witnessing what they were doing with the believers. And their enmity against the believers was for no other reason that that they had believed in that Allah. Who is the All-Mighty, the Self-Praiseworthy, Who is the Owner of the Kingdom of the heavens and the earth; and Allah is watching over everything. For those who persecuted the believing men and women and did not repent of it, there is the torment of Hell and the punishment of burning." (85:2-10) Yusuf Ali's translation: "By the promised Day (of Judgment); By one that witnesses, and the subject of the witness; Woe to the makers of the pit (of fire), Fire supplied (abundantly) with fuel: Behold! they sat over against the (fire), And they witnessed (all) that they were doing against the Believers. And they ill-treated them for no other reason than that they believed in Allah, Exalted in Power, Worthy of all Praise! Him to Whom belongs the dominion of the heavens and the earth! And Allah is Witness to all things. Those

who persecute (or draw into temptation) the Believers, men and women, and do not turn in repentance, will have the Penalty of Hell: They will have the Penalty of the Burning Fire."

These verses were revealed during the Meccan period. They curse "people of the ditch" as though they are from the past: "Doomed *were* the people of the ditch." The mythical incident that is the subject matter of these verses is referred by Hilali-Khan as pertaining to earlier times. Ibn Ishaq, too, mentions no such incident in his biography of Muhammad. Rogerson also relates these verses to an incident that happened in AD 523, long before Muhammad was born (*The Prophet Muhammad*, p. 27). These verses do not therefore refer to an incident in Mecca.

17   Ibn Ishaq: *The Life of Muhammad*, p. 314

18   Respectively *Surah At-Taubah* verses 40 and 13. Yusuf Ali's translations: "If ye help not (your leader), (it is no matter): for Allah did indeed help him, *when the Unbelievers drove him out:* he had no more than one companion; they two were in the cave."; "Will ye not fight people who violated their oaths, *plotted to expel the Messenger,* and took the aggressive by being the first (to assault) you?"

19   Reference may also be made to *Surah Al Hajj* verse 39-40. Maududi's translation: "Permission (to fight) has been granted to those against whom war has been waged *because they have been treated unjustly,* and Allah is certainly able to help them. *These are the people who have been expelled unjustly from their homes,* only for the reason that they said, 'Our Lord is Allah.'" (22:39-40) Yusuf Ali's translation: "To those against whom war is made, permission is given (to fight), *because they are wronged;* and verily, Allah is most powerful for their aid; (They are) *those who have been expelled from their homes in defiance* of right, (for no cause) except that they say, 'our Lord is Allah.'"

This verse states that the believers were "treated unjustly" and "expelled unjustly from their homes." Because the Quran is unspecific, however, one needs to rely on other verses to understand how the believers were treated unjustly—and the only positive evidence one finds is of ridicule.

20   Ibn Ishaq: *The Life of Muhammad*, pp. 130–131

21   In fact, should one believe in Muhammad as the Prophet but waver slightly that he was the last, one is excluded from the faith by a vast majority of Muslims.

22   *Surah Al-Ahzab* verses 40. Yusuf Ali's translation: "Muhammad is not the father of any of your men, but (he is) the Messenger of Allah, and the Seal of the Prophets: and Allah has full knowledge of all things."

23   *Surah Al-Maidah* verse 19. Maududi's translation: "O People of the Book, this Messenger of Ours has come to you and is making clear to you the teachings of the Right Way after a long interval during which there had come no Messenger, lest you should say: 'No bearer of good news nor warner came to us.' Lo, now the bearer of the good news and warner has come. And Allah has power over everything." (5:19) Yusuf Ali's translation: "O People of the Book! Now hath come unto you, making (things) clear unto you, Our Messenger, after the break in (the series of) our apostles, lest ye should say: 'There came unto us no bringer of glad tidings and no warner (from evil)': But now hath come unto you a bringer of glad tidings and a warner (from evil). And Allah hath power over all things."

24   *Surah Ar-Ra'ad* verse 38. Maududi's translation: "We have sent many Messengers before you and … Every age had its book." (13:38) Yusuf Ali's translation: "We did send apostles before thee, … For each period is a Book (revealed)."

25   The other translations follow:
> Muhammad is not the father of any of your men, but (he is) the Messenger of Allah, *and the Seal of the Prophets:* and Allah has full knowledge of all things. (Yusuf Ali)
> Muhammad is not the father of any of your men, but he is the Messenger of Allah *and the last (end) of the Prophets.* And Allah is Ever All-Knower of everything. (Hilali-Khan)
> Muhammad is not the father of any man among you, but he is the messenger of Allah *and Seal of the Prophets;* and Allah is Aware of all things. (Pickthall)

26   *Surah Al-Anaam* verse 46. Yusuf Ali's translation: "Say: 'Think ye, if Allah took away your hearing and your sight, and *sealed* up your hearts …'"

27   *Surah Al-Maidah* verse 6. Maududi's translation: "O Believers, when you rise to offer the Salat, you must wash your faces and hands and arms up to the elbows and wipe your heads with wet hands and wash your feet up to the ankles; and if you have become unclean, cleanse yourselves with a full bath …" (5:6) Yusuf Ali's translation: "O ye who believe! when ye prepare for prayer, wash your faces, and your hands (and arms) to the elbows; Rub your heads (with water); and

(wash) your feet to the ankles. If ye are in a state of ceremonial impurity, bathe your whole body."

28 *Surah Ha-Mim As-Sajadah* verse 44. Yusuf Ali's translation: "Had We sent this as a Qur'an (in the language) other than Arabic, they would have said: 'Why are not its verses explained in detail? What! (a Book) not in Arabic and (a Messenger an Arab?'"

29 In much the same vein, *Surah Yunus* verse 47 suggests that the Quran may not have thought of Muhammad as the last prophet. Maududi's translation: "There is a Messenger for every ummat then, when its Messenger comes a just judgment is passed on its people and they are not wronged in the least." (10:47) Yusuf Ali's translation: "To every people (was sent) an apostle: when their apostle comes (before them), the matter will be judged between them with justice, and they will not be wronged."

Although the Quran also states (e.g., in *Surah Saba* verse 28) that Muhammad is a messenger for mankind, even this does not stipulate that other messengers would not follow. Moreover, the Quran's understanding of all of mankind can be gathered from verse 42:7, which treats Mecca as the "center of habitation" or "Mother of Cities" depending upon the translation. This shows that it had a very local perspective.

30 *Surah Al-Imran* verse 21. Yusuf Ali's translation: "As to *those who deny the Signs of Allah and in defiance of right, slay the prophets*, and slay those who teach just dealing with mankind, announce to them a grievous penalty."

31 Hilali-Khan: *Translation of the Meaning of the Noble Qur'an in the English Language*, Appendix II, p. 896.

32 *Surah Al-Anfal* verse 7 may be referred to. Maududi's translation: "Remember the occasion when Allah was holding out to you the promise that one of the two hosts would fall to you: *you wished the weaker host should fall to you.*" (8:7) Maududi clarifies: "That is, the trade caravan, or the army of the *Quraish*. That is, the trade caravan, that was accompanied by a guard band numbering between thirty and forty" (Maududi: *The Meaning of the Qur'an*, notes 5 &6 to *Surah Al-Anfal* Volume 2, p. 131). Yusuf Ali's translation of the above verse: "Behold! Allah promised you one of the two (enemy) parties, that it should be yours: *Ye wished that the one unarmed should be yours.*"

33 *Surah Al-Imran* verse13. Maududi's translation: "You have already had a Sign in the two hosts which met on the battle-field (at Badr). One of these hosts was fighting for the cause of Allah and the other was of the disbelievers: *the lookers-on saw with their own eyes that the host of the disbelievers, was twice as big as that of the believers,* but (the result of the Battle proved conclusively that) Allah strengthens with His succor whom He wills: there is truly a great lesson hidden in it for those who have eyes to discern." (3:13) Yusuf Ali's translation: "There has already been for you a Sign in the two armies that met (in combat): One was fighting in the cause of Allah, the other resisting Allah. *These saw with their own eyes Twice their number.* But Allah doth support with His aid whom He pleaseth. In this is a warning for such as have eyes to see."

There are also historical accounts that record that although the Quraysh were initially estimated to be about 1,000, once Abu Sufyan managed to remove the caravan from harm's way and to send a message to the Quraysh that there was no further need to fight, a number of them withdrew.

34 *Surah Al-Anfal* verse 41. Yusuf Ali's translation: "And know that out of all the booty that ye may acquire (in war), *a fifth share is assigned to Allah, and to the Messenger, and to near relatives, orphans, the needy, and the wayfarer.*"

35 *Surah Al-Hashr* verses 6–7. Maududi's translation: "And the properties that Allah took out from their possession and restored to His Messenger, are not such that you might have rushed your horses and camels upon them, but Allah gives His Messengers authority over whomever He wills, and Allah has power over everything. Whatever Allah restored to His Messenger from the people of the settlements, belongs to Allah and the Messenger and the kinsfolk and the orphans and the needy and the wayfarers." (59:6-7) Yusuf Ali's translation: "What Allah has bestowed on His Messenger (and taken away) from them—for this ye made no expedition with either cavalry or camelry: but Allah gives power to His apostles over any He pleases: and Allah has power over all things. What Allah has bestowed on His Messenger (and taken away) from the people of the townships, belongs to Allah, to His Messenger and to kindred and orphans, the needy and the wayfarer."

36 *Surah Al-Fath* verses 15. Yusuf Ali's translation: "Those who lagged behind (will say), *when ye (are free to) march and take booty (in war)*: 'Permit us to follow you.' They wish to change Allah's decree: Say: 'Not thus will ye follow us: Allah has already declared (this) beforehand.'"

37 Ibn Ishaq: *The Life of Muhammad*, p. 493

38 *Surah Al-Ahzab* verses 50–52. Yusuf Ali's translation: "O Prophet! We have made lawful to thee thy wives to whom thou hast paid their dowers; *and those whom thy right hand possesses out of the prisoners of war whom Allah has assigned to thee*; and daughters of thy paternal uncles and aunts, and daughters of thy maternal uncles and aunts, who migrated (from Makka) with thee; and any believing woman who dedicates her soul to the Prophet if the Prophet wishes to wed her; *this only for thee, and not for the Believers (at large); We know what We have appointed for them as to their wives and the captives whom their right hands possess; in order that there should be no difficulty for thee. And Allah is Oft-Forgiving, Most Merciful.* Thou mayest defer (the turn of) any of them that thou pleasest, and thou mayest receive any thou pleasest: and there is no blame on thee if thou invite one whose (turn) thou hadst set aside. This were nigher to the cooling of their eyes, the prevention of their grief, and their satisfaction—that of all of them—with that which thou hast to give them: and Allah knows (all) that is in your hearts: and Allah is All-Knowing, Most Forbearing. *It is not lawful for thee (to marry more) women after this, nor to change them for (other) wives, even though their beauty attract thee, except any thy right hand should possess (as handmaidens)*: and Allah doth watch over all things."

39 Ibn Ishaq: *The Life of Muhammad*, pp. 792–794:
> He married thirteen women: *Khadija* d. Khuwaylid, his first wife … He married *Aisha* in Mecca when she was a child of seven and lived with her in Medina when she was nine or ten. … *Sauda* d. Zama'a … He married *Zaynab* d. Jahsh. … She had been previously married to Zayd b. Haritha, the freed slave of the apostle … *Umm Salama* d. Abu Umayya … *Hafsa* d. Umar … *Umm Habiba* … *Juwayriya* who was among the captives of B. Mustaliq … He married *Safiya* d. Huyay whom he had captured at Khaybar. … He married *Maymuna* d. al-Harith. … He married *Zaynab* b. Khuzayma, who was called the "Mother of the Poor" because of her kindness to them and her pity for them. … The apostle consummated his marriage with eleven women, two of whom died before him, namely Khadija and Zaynab. He died leaving the nine we have mentioned. With two he had no marital relations, namely *Asma* d. al-Nauman, the Kindite woman, whom he married and found to be suffering from leprosy and so returned her to her people with a suitable gift; and *Amra* d. Yazid the Kilab woman who was recently an unbeliever. When she came to the apostle she said "I seek God's protection against you," and he replied that one who did that was inviolable so he sent her back to her people.

40 Ibn Ishaq: *The Life of Muhammad*, pp. 678–679

41 Rogerson: *The Heirs of the Prophet Muhammad*, p. 80

42 *Surah Al-Ahzab* verses 4–5. Yusuf Ali's translation: "Allah has not made for any man two hearts in his (one) body … *nor has He made your adopted sons your sons.* Such is (only) your (manner of) speech by your mouths. But Allah tells (you) the Truth, and He shows the (right) Way. *Call them by (the names of) their fathers: that is juster in the sight of Allah.*"

43 *Surah Al-Ahzab* verses 37–40. Yusuf Ali's translation: "*Behold! Thou didst say to one who had received the grace of Allah and thy favour: 'Retain thou (in wedlock) thy wife, and fear Allah.'* But thou didst hide in thy heart that which Allah was about to make manifest: thou didst fear the people, but it is more fitting that thou shouldst fear Allah. Then when Zaid had dissolved (his marriage) with her, with the necessary (formality), We joined her in marriage to thee: *in order that (in future) there may be no difficulty to the Believers in (the matter of) marriage with the wives of their adopted sons, when the latter have dissolved with the necessary (formality) (their marriage) with them. And Allah's command must be fulfilled. There can be no difficulty to the Prophet in what Allah has indicated to him as a duty.* It was the practice (approved) of Allah amongst those of old that have passed away. And the command of Allah is a decree determined. (It is the practice of those) who preach the Messages of Allah, and fear Him, and fear none but Allah. And enough is Allah to call (men) to account. Muhammad is not the father of any of your men, but (he is) the Messenger of Allah, and the Seal of the Prophets: and Allah has full knowledge of all things."

44 Armstrong: *Muhammad: A Biography of the Prophet*, p. 196

45 Maududi: *The Meaning of the Qur'an*, note 70 to *Surah Al-Ahzab*, Volume 4, p. 112

46 Maududi: *The Meaning of the Qur'an*, note 70 to *Surah Al-Ahzab*, Volume 4, pp. 112–113

47 Maududi: *The Meaning of the Qur'an*, note 94 to *Surah Al-Ahzab*, Volume 4, p. 131

48 Ibn Ishaq: *The Life of Muhammad*, pp. 515–517

49   *Surah An-Nisa* verse 24. Yusuf Ali's translation: "Also (prohibited are) women already married, *except those whom your right hands possess.*"

50   Respectively, *Surah Hujaraat* verses 2 and 4. Maududi's translations: "O you who have believed, do not raise your voices above the Prophet's voice, nor speak to him as loud as you speak loud to one another, lest all your works be rendered void, while you do not know." (49:2); "O Prophet, those who call out to you from outside the apartments, most of them have no sense. If only they had had patience until you came out to them, it would be better for them." (49:4) Yusuf Ali's translations: "O ye who believe! Raise not your voices above the voice of the Prophet, nor speak aloud to him in talk, as ye may speak aloud to one another, lest your deeds become vain and ye perceive not."; "Those who shout out to thee from without the inner apartments—most of them lack understanding."

51   *Surah An-Noor* verses 62–63. Maududi's translation: "True Believers are those who sincerely believe in Allah and His Messenger and who do not leave him without permission when they are with the Messenger for some common good; only those who ask your permission sincerely believe in Allah and His Messenger. ... *O Believers, do not consider the summoning by the Messenger like the summoning among you by one another.* Allah knows well those of you who steal away, concealing themselves behind others. Let those who disobey the order of the Messenger beware lest they should be involved in some affliction, or are visited by a woeful scourge." (24:62–63) Yusuf Ali's translation: "Only those are believers, who believe in Allah and His Messenger. when they are with him on a matter requiring collective action, they do not depart until they have asked for his leave; those who ask for thy leave are those who believe in Allah and His Messenger ... *Deem not the summons of the Messenger among yourselves like the summons of one of you to another.* Allah doth know those of you who slip away under shelter of some excuse: then let those beware who withstand the Messenger's order, lest some trial befall them, or a grievous penalty be inflicted on them."

52   *Surah Al-Imran* verses 31–32. Maududi's translation: "O Prophet, tell the people, 'If you sincerely love Allah follow me; then will Allah love you and forgive your sins, for He is Forgiving and Merciful.' Also say to them, 'Obey Allah and His Messenger.' And if, in spite of this, they do not accept your invitation, (warn them that) Allah does not love those who refuse to obey Him and His Messenger." (3:31–32) Yusuf Ali's translation: "Say: 'If ye do love Allah, Follow me: Allah will love you and forgive you your sins: For Allah is Oft-Forgiving, Most Merciful.' Say: 'Obey Allah and His Messenger.' But if they turn back, Allah loveth not those who reject Faith."

53   *Surah Al-Mujadilah* verses 8–10. Yusuf Ali's translation: "*Turnest thou not thy sight towards those who were forbidden secret counsels yet revert to that which they were forbidden (to do)? And they hold secret counsels among themselves for iniquity and hostility, and disobedience to the Messenger.* And when they come to thee, they salute thee, not as Allah salutes thee, (but in crooked ways): And they say to themselves, 'Why does not Allah punish us for our words?' Enough for them is Hell: In it will they burn, and evil is that destination! *O ye who believe! When ye hold secret counsel, do it not for iniquity and hostility, and disobedience to the Prophet; but do it for righteousness and self-restraint; and fear Allah, to Whom ye shall be brought back. Secret counsels are only (inspired) by the Evil One,* in order that he may cause grief to the Believers; but he cannot harm them in the least, except as Allah permits; and on Allah let the Believers put their trust."

54   *Surah Al-Hujaraat* verse 12. Yusuf Ali's translation: "And spy not on each other behind their backs. Would any of you like to eat the flesh of his dead brother? Nay, ye would abhor it."

55   *Surah Al-Imran* verses 139–140. Maududi's translation: "Be not faint hearted and be not sorrowful, you will surely gain the upper hand, if you be true believers. If you have received a blow now, your enemy also received a similar blow. These are the vicissitudes of time that We alternate among the people; this has been done so that Allah may test from among you who were believers and choose the righteous witnesses of the Truth." (3:139–140) Yusuf Ali's translation: "So lose not heart, nor fall into despair: For ye must gain mastery if ye are true in Faith. If a wound hath touched you, be sure a similar wound hath touched the others. Such days (of varying fortunes) We give to men and men by turns: that Allah may know those that believe, and that He may take to Himself from your ranks Martyr-witnesses (to Truth)."

56   *Surah Al-Imran* verses 124–127. Maududi's translation: "Remember when you said to the Believers, 'Does it not suffice you that Allah should help you by sending down three thousand angels?' Yes, if you show fortitude and fear Allah in whatever you do, Allah will help you with (not three thousand but) five thousand angels, known by certain marks, *in case of a sudden attack from the enemy.* ... (He will succor you) so that He may cut off a flank of the disbelievers or put them to rout with dishonor." (3:124–127) Yusuf Ali's translation: "Remember thou saidst to the

Faithful: 'Is it not enough for you that Allah should help you with three thousand angels (Specially) sent down?' Yea, if ye remain firm, and act aright, *even if the enemy should rush here on you in hot haste*, your Lord would help you with five thousand angels Making a terrific onslaught. ... That He might cut off a fringe of the Unbelievers or expose them to infamy, and they should then be turned back, frustrated of their purpose."

57   *Surah Al-Imran* verses 166–168 corroborate this. Maududi's translation: "It was by Allah's leave that you suffered the loss on the day the two armies met so that Allah might test the true believers and also the hypocrites. When these hypocrites were told to come and fight in the way of Allah or at least in the defence (of their city), they said, 'Had we known that the fighting would take place today, we would have certainly gone out with you.' At the time they were uttering these words, they were nearer to unbelief than to faith, for they utter with their tongues what is not in their hearts; but Allah knows well what they conceal in their hearts. These are the very people who, while they themselves stayed at home, said of their brethren, who had gone to the battle and had been slain, 'If they had obeyed us, they would not have been slain.'" (3:166–168) Yusuf Ali's translation: "What ye suffered on the day the two armies met, was with the leave of Allah, in order that He might test the believers, And the Hypocrites also. These were told: 'Come, fight in the way of Allah, or (at least) drive (The foe from your city).' They said: 'Had we known how to fight, we should certainly have followed you.' They were that day nearer to Unbelief than to Faith, saying with their lips what was not in their hearts but Allah hath full knowledge of all they conceal. (They are) the ones that say, (of their brethren slain), while they themselves sit (at ease): 'If only they had listened to us they would not have been slain.'"

58   *Surah Al-Imran* verses 152–153. Yusuf Ali's translation: "Allah did indeed fulfil His promise to you when ye with His permission Were about to annihilate your enemy, *until ye flinched and fell to disputing about the order, and disobeyed it after He brought you in sight (of the booty) which ye covet. Among you are some that hanker after this world and some that desire the Hereafter.* Then did He divert you from your foes in order to test you but He forgave you: For Allah is full of grace to those who believe. *Behold! ye were climbing up the high ground, without even casting a side glance at any one, and the Messenger in your rear was calling you back.* There did Allah give you one distress after another by way of requital, to teach you not to grieve for (the booty) that had escaped you and for (the ill) that had befallen you. For Allah is well aware of all that ye do."

59   *Surah Al-Imran* verse 161. Yusuf Ali's translation: "No prophet could (ever) be false to his trust."

60   Maududi: *The Meaning of the Qur'an*, note 114 to *Surah Al-Imran*, Volume 1, p. 283

61   Rogerson: *The Heirs of the Prophet Muhammad*, p. 241

62   *Surah Al-Imran* verse 154. Maududi's translation: "Now they ask, 'Have we also a say in the conduct of affairs?' Say, '(No one has share in this.) The authority over the affairs rests wholly with Allah.' *In fact they are not disclosing to you what they are concealing in their hearts: what they really mean is this: 'If we had a say (in the conduct of) the affairs, none of us would have been slain here.'*" (3:154) Yusuf Ali's translation: "They said: 'What affair is this of ours?' Say thou: 'Indeed, this affair is wholly Allah's.' *They hide in their minds what they dare not reveal to thee. They say (to themselves): 'If we had had anything to do with this affair, We should not have been in the slaughter here.'*"

63   *Surah At-Taubah* verse 38. Yusuf Ali's translation: "O ye who believe! what is the matter with you, that, when ye are asked to go forth in the cause of Allah, ye cling heavily to the earth? Do ye prefer the life of this world to the Hereafter?"

64   *Surah At-Taubah* verses 119–122. Maududi's translation: "O Believers, fear Allah and be with those who are Truthful. It did not behoove the people of Al-Madinah and the Bedouins, dwelling around, to abandon Allah's Messenger and stay at home in order to safeguard their own interests, in utter disregard of him. ... And it was not required that all *the believers* should leave their homes, but why did not some people from every habitation leave their homes in order to understand the Way of Islam and to warn their people when they returned to them, so that they should refrain from un-Islamic conduct?" (9:119–122) Yusuf Ali's translation: "O ye who believe! Fear Allah and be with those who are true (in word and deed). It was not fitting for the people of Medina and the Bedouin Arabs of the neighborhood, to refuse to follow Allah's Messenger, nor to prefer their own lives to his. ... Nor should *the Believers* all go forth together: if a contingent from every expedition remained behind, they could devote themselves to studies in religion, and admonish the people when they return to them, that thus they (may learn) to guard themselves (against evil)."

65   *Surah Al-Jumuah* verses 9–11. Yusuf Ali's translation: "O ye who believe! When the call is proclaimed to prayer on Friday (the Day of Assembly), hasten earnestly to the Remembrance of

Allah, and leave off business (and traffic): That is best for you if ye but knew! And when the Prayer is finished, then may ye disperse through the land, and seek of the Bounty of Allah and celebrate the Praises of Allah often (and without stint): that ye may prosper. *But when they see some bargain or some amusement, they disperse headlong to it, and leave thee standing.* Say: 'The (blessing) from the Presence of Allah is better than any amusement or bargain! and Allah is the Best to provide (for all needs).'"

66 Maududi: *The Meaning of the Qur'an*, note 19 to *Surah Al-Jumuah*, Volume 5, pp. 541–542

67 *Surah An-Nisa* verse 65. Yusuf Ali's translation: "But no, by the Lord, they can have no (real) Faith, until they make thee judge in all disputes between them, and find in their souls no resistance against Thy decisions, but accept them with the fullest conviction."

68 *Surah Al-Ahzab* verse 36. Yusuf Ali's translation: "*It is not fitting for a Believer, man or woman, when a matter has been decided by Allah and His Messenger to have any option about their decision*: if any one disobeys Allah and His Messenger, he is indeed on a clearly wrong Path."

69 *Surah Al-Mujadilah* verses 12–13. Maududi's translation: "O you who have believed, when you consult the Messenger in private, you should give something in charity before your consultation. This is better for you and purer. However, if you do not have the means to give charity, Allah is indeed All-Forgiving, All-Merciful. Are you afraid that before your consultation in private, you will have to give charity?" (58:12–13) Yusuf Ali's translation: "O ye who believe! When ye consult the Messenger in private, spend something in charity before your private consultation. That will be best for you, and most conducive to purity (of conduct). But if ye find not (the wherewithal), Allah is Oft-Forgiving, Most Merciful. Is it that ye are afraid of spending sums in charity before your private consultation (with him)?"

70 *Surah At-Taubah* verse 58. Yusuf Ali's translation: "And among them are men who slander thee in the matter of (the distribution of) the alms: if they are given part thereof, they are pleased, but if not, behold! they are *indignant!*"

71 Ibn Ishaq: *The Life of Muhammad*, pp. 494–497

72 Maududi: *The Meaning of the Qur'an*, opening commentary to *Surah An-Noor*, Volume 3, p. 281

73 *Surah An-Noor* verses 11–18. Yusuf Ali's translation: "*Those who brought forward the lie are a body among yourselves:* think it not to be an evil to you; On the contrary it is good for you: to every man among them (will come the punishment) of the sin that he earned, and to him who took on himself the lead among them, will be a penalty grievous. *Why did not the believers—men and women— when ye heard of the affair, put the best construction on it in their own minds and say, 'This (charge) is an obvious lie'?* Why did they not bring four witnesses to prove it? When they have not brought the witnesses, such men, in the sight of Allah, (stand forth) themselves as liars! Were it not for the grace and mercy of Allah on you, in this world and the Hereafter, a grievous penalty would have seized you in that ye rushed glibly into this affair. Behold, ye received it on your tongues, and said out of your mouths things of which ye had no knowledge; and ye thought it to be a light matter, while it was most serious in the sight of Allah. And why did ye not, when ye heard it, say? 'It is not right of us to speak of this: Glory to Allah.' This is a most serious slander! Allah doth admonish you, that ye may never repeat such (conduct), if ye are (true) Believers. And Allah makes the Signs plain to you: for Allah is full of knowledge and wisdom."

74 The Quran records this in verse 3:50.

75 Ibn Ishaq: *The Life of Muhammad*, p. 794

76 *Surah Al-Ahzab* verse 51. Yusuf Ali's translation: "Thou mayest defer (the turn of) any of them that thou pleasest, and thou mayest receive any thou pleasest: and there is no blame on thee if thou invite one whose (turn) thou hadst set aside."

77 Maududi: *The Meaning of the Qur'an*, note 8 to *Surah Muhammad*, Volume 5, p. 17

78 *Surah Al-Maidah* verses 33–34. Maududi's translation: "*The punishment of those who wage war against Allah and His Messenger* and run about to spread mischief in the land *is this: they should be put to death or crucified or their alternate hands and feet should be cut off, or they should be banished from the land.* This is the disgrace and ignominy for them in this world and there is in store for them a harsher torment in the Hereafter, except those, who repent before you have power over them for you should know that Allah is Forgiving and Compassionate." (5:33–34) Yusuf Ali's translation: "The punishment of those who wage war against Allah and His Messenger, and strive with might and main for mischief through the land is: execution, or crucifixion, or the cutting off of hands and feet from opposite sides, or exile from the land: that is their disgrace in this world, and a heavy punishment is theirs in the Hereafter; Except for those who repent before they fall into your power: in that case, know that Allah is Oft-forgiving, Most Merciful."

79   Maududi: *The Meaning of the Qur'an*, note 8 to *Surah Muhammad*, Volume 5, p. 13
80   Maududi: *The Meaning of the Qur'an*, note 44 to *Surah An-Nisa*, Volume 1, p. 324
81   *Surah Al-Baqarah* verse 234. Maududi's translation: "If those of you, who die, leave wives behind, they should abstain (from marriage) for four months and ten days. Then when their waiting term expires, they are free to do whatever they choose for themselves, provided that it is decent." (2:234) Yusuf Ali's translation: "If any of you die and leave widows behind, they shall wait concerning themselves four months and ten days: When they have fulfilled their term, there is no blame on you if they dispose of themselves in a just and reasonable manner."
82   Respectively, *Surah Al-Anaam* verses 37–38, *Surah Al-Anaam* verse 109, *Surah Yunus* verse 20, *Surah Ar-Ra'ad* verse 7, and *Surah Al-Ankabut* verses 50-51. Yusuf Ali's translations: "They say: 'Why is not a sign sent down to him from his Lord?' Say: '(Allah) hath certainly power to send down a sign: but most of them understand not. There is not an animal (that lives) on the earth, nor a being that flies on its wings, but (forms part of) communities like you.'"; "They swear their strongest oaths by Allah, that if a (special) sign came to them, by it they would believe. Say: 'Certainly (all) signs are in the power of Allah. But what will make you (Muslims) realise that (even) if (special) signs came, they will not believe'?"; "They say: 'Why is not a sign sent down to him from his Lord?' Say: 'The Unseen is only for Allah (to know), then wait ye: I too will wait with you.'"; "And the Unbelievers say: 'Why is not a sign sent down to him from his Lord?' But thou art truly a warner, and to every people a guide."; "Yet they say: 'Why are not Signs sent down to him from his Lord?' Say: 'The signs are indeed with Allah and I am indeed a clear Warner.' And is it not enough for them that we have sent down to thee the Book which is rehearsed to them?"
83   *Surah Al-Qamar* verses 1–3. Yusuf Ali's translation: "The Hour (of Judgment) is nigh, *and the moon is cleft asunder*. But if they see a Sign, they turn away, and say, 'This is (but) transient magic.' They reject (the warning) and follow their (own) lusts but every matter has its appointed time."
84   *Surah Al-Ala* verses 6–7. Maududi's translation: "We shall enable you to recite, then you shall not forget except what Allah wills. He knows what is open and also what is hidden." (87:6–7) Yusuf Ali's translation: "By degrees shall We teach thee to declare (the Message), so thou shalt not forget, Except as Allah wills: For He knoweth what is manifest and what is hidden." Verses 75:15–19 and 20:114 may also be referenced.
85   *Surah Al-Mu'min* verse 55. Maududi's translation: "O Prophet: Allah's promise is true. *Ask forgiveness of your errors*, and glorify your Lord morning and evening with His praise." (40:55) Yusuf Ali's translation: "Patiently, then, persevere: for the Promise of Allah is true: and ask forgiveness for thy fault, and celebrate the Praises of thy Lord in the evening and in the morning."
86   *Surah At-Tahrim* verses 1–5. Yusuf Ali's translation: "*O Prophet! Why holdest thou to be forbidden that which Allah has made lawful to thee?* Thou seekest to please thy consorts. But Allah is Oft-Forgiving, Most Merciful. *Allah has already ordained for you, (O men), the dissolution of your oaths (in some cases)*: and Allah is your Protector, and He is Full of Knowledge and Wisdom. *When the Prophet disclosed a matter in confidence to one of his consorts, and she then divulged it (to another), and Allah made it known to him, he confirmed part thereof and repudiated a part.* Then when he told her thereof, she said, 'Who told thee this?' He said, 'He told me Who knows and is well-acquainted (with all things).' If ye two turn in repentance to Him, your hearts are indeed so inclined; But if ye back up each other against him, truly Allah is his Protector, and Gabriel, and (every) righteous one among those who believe, and furthermore, the angels will back (him) up. *It may be, if he divorced you (all), that Allah will give him in exchange consorts better than you, who submit (their wills), who believe, who are devout, who turn to Allah in repentance, who worship (in humility), who travel (for Faith) and fast, previously married or virgins.*"
87   *Surah Al-Baqarah* verse 225 and *Surah Al-Maidah verse 89*. Maududi's translation of verse 5:89: "Allah does not take you to task for the inadvertent oaths you swear, but He will surely call you to account for the intentional and deliberate oaths you make. The expiation (of breaking such an oath) is to feed ten indigent persons with the normal food you serve in your own family, or to give them clothes, or to free one slave, and the one who cannot afford any of these let him fast three days. This is the expiation of breaking the solemn oaths you have taken; be mindful of your oaths. Thus Allah makes His Commandments plain to you so that you may show gratitude." Yusuf Ali's translation: "Allah will not call you to account for what is futile in your oaths, but He will call you to account for your deliberate oaths: for expiation, feed ten indigent persons, on a scale of the average for the food of your families; or clothe them; or give a slave his freedom. If that is beyond your means, fast for three days. That is the expiation for the oaths ye have sworn. But keep to your oaths. Thus doth Allah make clear to you His signs, that ye may be grateful."

88   Maududi: *The Meaning of the Qur'an*, note 2 to *Surah At-Tahrim*, Volume 5, pp. 643–644

Chapter 4: The Quran: A Scientific Miracle

1   *Surah Al-Hajj* verses 15–16. Yusuf Ali (supported by Hilali-Khan and Pickthall) translates:
> If any think that Allah will not help him (His Messenger) in this world and the Hereafter, let him stretch out a rope to the *ceiling* and cut (himself) off: then let him see whether his plan will remove that which enrages (him)! Thus have We sent down Clear Signs; and verily Allah doth guide whom He will!

Interestingly, the word used in the above verses is *samaa*, which means "the sky" (as conceded by the other three translators in respect of verse 6:35, for instance)! Maududi's translation is thus more accurate, even if it makes the Quran look scientifically inelegant.

2   Roberts: *The Pelican History of the World*, p. 88

3   Sagan: *Cosmos*, p. 205

4   *Encyclopaedia Britannica*, Volume 14, p. 1072. For other *Encyclopaedia Britannica* editions, see under: The Biological Sciences/The history of biology/THE EARLY HERITAGE/The Greco-Roman world/Theories about man and origin of life. Also: *Encyclopaedia Britannica Online* (www.britannica.com) (http://www.britannica.com/EBchecked/topic/66054/biology/48830/The-Greco-Roman-world) under "Theories about man and the origin of life".

5   Sagan: *Cosmos*, pp. 25–27

6   Naik: *The Quran and Modern Science: Compatible or Incompatible?* p. 34

7   *Encyclopaedia Britannica*, Volume 14, p. 1071. For other *Encyclopaedia Britannica* editions, see under: The Biological Sciences/The history of biology/THE EARLY HERITAGE/Earliest biological records/Biological practices among Assyrians and Babylonians. Also: *Encyclopaedia Britannica Online* (www.britannica.com) (http://www.britannica.com/EBchecked/topic/66054/biology/48827/Earliest-biological-records) under "Earliest biological records".

8   We will draw on the discussion contained in: http://www.speed-light.info/relativity_quran.htm, as indicative. The reasoning is convoluted, but we will try to focus on the main features.

9   http://www.speed-light.info/relativity_quran.htm

10   Naik: *The Quran and Modern Science: Compatible or Incompatible?* pp. 8–9

11   Naik: footnote 1 to *The Quran and Modern Science: Compatible or Incompatible?* p. 4. Dr. Naik may also discover that the ostrich egg, because of its huge size compared to other eggs, has only in recent times, after the shape of the earth has become common knowledge, acquired the description *dahaahaa*.

12   *Surah Al-Baqarah* verse 187. Yusuf Ali's translation: "and eat and drink, until the white thread of dawn appears to you distinct from its black thread; then complete your fast Till the night appears."

13   Naik: *The Quran and Modern Science: Compatible or Incompatible?* pp. 13–14. He does, though, note the following facts as well (in the above referenced work):
> For a long time European philosophers and scientists believed that the earth stood still in the center of the universe and every other body including the sun moved around it. In the West, this geocentric concept of universe was prevalent right from the time of Ptolemy in the second century BC. In 1512, Nicholas Copernicus put forward his Heliocentric Theory of Planetary Motion, which asserted that the sun is motionless at the center of the solar system with the planets revolving around it. (pp. 11–12)

Copernicus, of course, discovered that it is the earth that orbits the sun, though he mistakenly thought that the sun stood motionlessly at the center of the solar system. This error was corrected subsequently, but his discovery does constitute a watershed. It would be interesting to see on which side of the divide—the age before or after Copernicus—the Quran stands.

14   *Surah Ya Sin* verse 40. Yusuf Ali's translation: "It is not permitted to the Sun to catch up the Moon, nor can the Night outstrip the Day: *Each (just) swims along in (its own) orbit (according to Law).*"

15   *Surah Ya Sin* verses 37–40. Yusuf Ali's translation: "And a Sign for them is the Night: We withdraw therefrom the Day, and behold they are plunged in darkness; *And the sun runs his course for a period determined for him.* that is the decree of (Him), the Exalted in Might, the All-Knowing. And the Moon, We have measured for her mansions (to traverse) till she returns like the old (and

withered) lower part of a date-stalk. *It is not permitted to the Sun to catch up the Moon, nor can the Night outstrip the Day: Each (just) swims along in (its own) orbit (according to Law)."*

16 *Surah Al-Anbiyya* verses 32–33. Yusuf Ali's translation: "And We have made the heavens as a canopy well guarded: yet do they turn away from the Signs which these things (point to)! *It is He Who created the Night and the Day, and the sun and the moon: all (the celestial bodies) swim along, each in its rounded course."*

17 Naik seems to glorify even this error:

> The "fixed place" towards which the sun travels, carrying with it the solar system, has been located precisely by modern astronomy. It has been given a name, the Solar Apex. The solar system is indeed moving in space towards a point situated in the constellation of Hercules (alpha Lyrae) whose exact location is now firmly established. (*The Quran and Modern Science: Compatible or Incompatible?* p. 14)

In fact, it is inaccurate to describe the solar apex as a "place of rest" towards which the sun is moving, but in any case, what does that have to do with darkness and night? That is the context in which the Quran tells us that the sun is moving to its place of rest. It was of course considered at the time that the sun rested during the night—why else would it disappear? It wasn't widely known that the sun was always at work, showering the earth with its rays all the time. If the Quran meant to refer to the solar apex, it certainly chose the wrong context.

18 *Surah Al-Kahf* verses 83–90. Yusuf Ali's translation: "They ask thee concerning Zul-qarnain. Say, 'I will rehearse to you something of his story.' Verily We established his power on earth, and We gave him the ways and the means to all ends. One (such) way he followed, *Until, when he reached the setting of the sun,* he found it set in a spring of murky water: Near it he found a People … Then followed he (another) way, *Until, when he came to the rising of the sun,* he found it rising on a people for whom We had provided no covering protection against the sun."

19 Note 2430, *The Meaning of the Holy Qur'an,* Eleventh Edition (1430 AH/2009 AC) Amana Corporation, Maryland, p. 732

20 For instance, *Surah Al-Hijr* verses 26–27. Maududi's translation: "We created man from dried clay of rotten earth, and before that We had created jinn from the flame of heat." (15:26-27) Yusuf Ali's translation: "We created man from sounding clay, from mud moulded into shape; And the Jinn race, We had created before, from the fire of a scorching wind."

21 *Surah Al-Anbiyya* verse 30. Yusuf Ali's translation: "We made from water every living thing."

22 Respectively, *Surah As-Sajdah* verses 7–8 and *Surah An-Noor* verse 45. Yusuf Ali's translations: "He Who has made everything which He has created most good: He began the creation of man with (nothing more than) clay, And made his progeny from a quintessence of the nature of *a fluid despised.*"; "And Allah has created every animal from *water:* of them there are some that creep on their bellies; some that walk on two legs; and some that walk on four. Allah creates what He wills for verily Allah has power over all things."

23 www.miraclesofthequran.com

24 *Encyclopaedia Britannica,* Volume 14, p. 1072. For other *Encyclopaedia Britannica* editions, see under: The Biological Sciences/The history of biology/THE EARLY HERITAGE/The Greco-Roman world/Theories about man and origin of life. Also: *Encyclopaedia Britannica Online* (www.britannica.com) (http://www.britannica.com/ EBchecked/topic/66054/biology/48830/The-Greco-Roman-world) under "Theories about man and the origin of life".

25 *Surah Al-Kahf* verses 22–26. Yusuf Ali's translation: "(Some) say they were three, the dog being the fourth among them; (others) say they were five, the dog being the sixth, doubtfully guessing at the unknown; (yet others) say they were seven, the dog being the eighth. Say thou: 'My Lord knoweth best their number; It is but few that know their (real case).' Enter not, therefore, into controversies concerning them, except on a matter that is clear, nor consult any of them about (the affair of) the Sleepers. Nor say of anything, 'I shall be sure to do so and so tomorrow.' Without adding, 'So please Allah.' and call thy Lord to mind when thou forgettest, and say, 'I hope that my Lord will guide me ever closer (even) than this to the right road.' *So they stayed in their Cave three hundred years, and (some) add nine (more).* Say: '(Allah) knows best how long they stayed: with Him is (the knowledge of) the secrets of the heavens and the earth.'"

26 Maududi: *The Meaning of the Qur'an,* note 25 to *Surah Al-Kahf,* Volume 3, p. 24

27 *Surah Nuh* verses 15–16 and *Surah Al-Furqan* verse 61, for instance, are quoted in this behalf. Maududi's translations: "Do you not see how Allah has created seven heavens, one above the other and made *the moon a light* in them and *the sun a lamp?*" (71:15–16); "Highly blessed is He,

Who has made fortified spheres in the heavens and has set in it a 'lamp' and a shining moon." (25:61) Yusuf Ali's translations: "See ye not how Allah has created the seven heavens one above another, And made the moon a light in their midst, and made the sun as a (Glorious) Lamp?"; "Blessed is He Who made constellations in the skies, and placed therein a Lamp and a Moon giving light." Interestingly, some who wish to establish that the Quran knows the moon does not have its own light translate the latter verse as "Blessed is He Who made constellations in the skies, And placed therein a lamp (siraaj) *And a moon which has reflected light."*

28 Naik· *The Quran and Modern Science: Compatible or Incompatible?* pp. 10–11

29 *Surah An-Noor* verse 35. Yusuf Ali's translation: "Allah is the Light of the heavens and the earth. The Parable of His Light is as if there were a Niche and within it a Lamp: the Lamp enclosed in Glass: the glass as it were a brilliant star: Lit from a blessed Tree, an Olive, neither of the east nor of the west, whose oil is well-nigh luminous, though fire scarce touched it: Light upon Light! Allah doth guide whom He will to His Light"

30 *Surah Al-Ahzab* verses 45–46. Yusuf Ali's translation: "O Prophet! Truly We have sent thee as a Witness, a Bearer of Glad Tidings, and Warner, And as one who invites to Allah's (grace) by His leave, and as *a lamp spreading light."*

31 *Surah An-Naba* verses 6–7. Maududi's translation: "Is it not a fact that We have made the earth a bed and set the mountains as pegs." (78:6–7) Yusuf Ali's translation: "Have We not made the earth as a wide expanse, And the mountains as pegs?"

32 www.answering-christianity.com/mountains.htm. Naik, too, endorses the view:

> MOUNTAINS ARE LIKE TENT PEGS
>
> In geology, the phenomenon of "folding", is a recently discovered fact. Folding is responsible for the formation of mountain ranges. ... It is also known that the stability of the mountains is linked to the phenomenon of folding, for it was the folds that were to provide foundations for the reliefs that constitute mountains. ... The Quranic descriptions are in perfect agreement with modern geological data. (Naik: *The Quran and Modern Science: Compatible or Incompatible?* pp. 24–25)

33 *Encyclopaedia Britannica* may be consulted on the types of mountains that exist. That the Quran did not mean to accurately inform us about geological facts is evident from the following verses: *Surah Luqman* verse 10: "He created the heavens without pillars that you could see. He set mountains in the earth lest it should tilt away along with you." (31;10) (Maududi) "He created the heavens without any pillars that ye can see; He set on the earth mountains standing firm, lest it should shake with you." (Yusuf Ali). *Surah Al-Anbiyya* verse 31: "And We set mountains firmly in the earth lest it should tilt to one side along with them." (21:31) (Maududi) "And We have set on the earth mountains standing firm, lest it should shake with them." (Yusuf Ali)
"He set mountains in the earth" seems to suggest that mountains were added after the earth was formed, much as pegs may be driven into the earth. The fact, however, is that mountains result from activity within the earth; they are not added from the outside. Neither do they serve the purpose of preventing the earth from tilting—which phrasing gives the impression that the earth is flat like a seesaw and needs to be kept in balance by having weights placed on it. As for the suggestion that mountains are set "firmly in the earth lest it should tilt to one side along with them," it is worth mentioning that the processes through which mountains are created do cause the earth to shake, at times resulting in a tilt, so if there is any relationship between mountains and tilting of the earth, it is the reverse of what the Quran suggests.

34 *Surah An-Noor* verses 39–40. Yusuf Ali's translation: "But the Unbelievers, their deeds are like a mirage in sandy deserts, which the man parched with thirst mistakes for water; until when he comes up to it, he finds it to be nothing: But he finds Allah (ever) with him, and Allah will pay him his account: and Allah is swift in taking account. Or (the Unbelievers' state) is like the depths of darkness in a vast deep ocean, overwhelmed with billow topped by billow, topped by (dark) clouds: depths of darkness, one above another: if a man stretches out his hands, he can hardly see it! for any to whom Allah giveth not light, there is no light!"

35 Stated, for instance, as follows:

> the statement in Surat an-Nur 40 "... *like the darkness of a fathomless sea which is covered by waves above which are waves above which are clouds..."* draws our attention to another miracle of the Qur'an. Scientists have only recently discovered that there are sub-surface waves, which "occur on density interfaces between layers of different densities." These internal waves cover the deep waters of seas and oceans. ... Internal waves cannot be discerned by the human eye, but they can be detected by studying temperature or salinity changes

at a given location. *The statements in the Qur'an run parallel precisely the above explanation. Certainly, this fact, which scientists have discovered very recently, shows once again that the Qur'an is the word of Allah.* (www.miraclesofthequran.com)

36 This view is stated as follows:

Measurements made with today's technology have revealed that between 3 and 30 percent of the sunlight is reflected at the surface of the sea. Then, almost all of the seven colours of the light spectrum are absorbed, one after another, in the first 200 metres, except for blue light. Below a depth of 1,000 metres, there is no light at all. This scientific fact was pointed out in *Sura Nur* 40 in the Qur'an 1,400 years ago. In deep seas and oceans, the darkness is found at a depth of 200 meters and deeper. At this depth, there is almost no light, and below a depth of 1,000 meters there is no light at all. Human beings are not able to dive to a depth of more than 70 meters without the aid of special equipment. They cannot survive unaided in the dark depths of the oceans, such as at a depth of 200 meters. For these reasons, scientists have only recently been able to discover detailed information about the seas. However, that the depth of the sea is dark was revealed in the Qur'an 1,400 years ago. It is certainly one of the miracles of the Qur'an that such information was given at a time where no equipment to enable man to dive into the depths of the oceans was available. (www.miraclesofthequran.com)

37 *Surah Al-Furqan* verse 53. Yusuf Ali's translation: "It is He Who has let free the two bodies of flowing water: One palatable and sweet, and the other salt and bitter; yet has He made a barrier between them, a partition that is forbidden to be passed."

38 Pritchard: "What Is an Estuary: Physical Viewpoint," p. 3

39 Two other instances of the Quran using somewhat similar descriptions may also be noted.

The first is "And Who is it Who made the earth as a place of rest and caused in it rivers to flow, and set in it firm mountains and placed barriers between the two bodies of water?" (27:61). This, however, seems to refer to rivers separated by landmass.

The second instance is provided by the following verses: "He let loose the two seas that they may meet together. Yet there stands between them a barrier which they do not transgress" (55:19–20). One is not entirely sure what the Quran is referring to here. The following possibilities present themselves. The first is that it is referring to estuaries, as in the verse quoted earlier. (Both employ words to the effect "let loose the two seas ... and there stands a barrier between them." There is no mention in verses 55:19–20 of sweet and salty waters, as there is in verse 25:53, but that may be a detail the Quran chose to omit on this occasion.) If the reference is indeed to an estuary, the description is scientifically inaccurate, as we have already discussed above, for there is no barrier that the two waters do not transgress. A second possibility, along the lines of verse 27:61 noted above, is that these verses are referring to two rivers flowing in parallel, separated by a landmass until the point at which they meet. Yusuf Ali's translation gives the impression that that is what the Quran may have intended in these verses: "He has let free the two bodies of *flowing water*, meeting together: Between them is a Barrier which they do not transgress" (55:19–20). As in the case of an estuary, it is seen that even when two rivers meet and each brings with it water of different color and character, they may retain their distinctive character for a while, but there is no barrier between the two that they may not transgress. They do always mix downstream. A third possibility is that the Quran is referring to the meeting of two oceans or seas, as when the Atlantic meets the Pacific or the Red Sea meets the Arabian Sea; however, even in such cases, there is no barrier that the two waters cannot transgress. In fact, seas and oceans have different characteristics, such as temperature and salinity level, in different regions, but there is a gradual and not an abrupt transition as one moves from one area to the other or even from one sea or ocean to another.

Here is Yusuf Ali's translation of *Surah An-Naml* verse 61, quoted above: "Or, Who has made the earth firm to live in; made rivers in its midst; set thereon mountains immovable; and made a separating bar between the two bodies of flowing water?"

40 *Surah Al-Muddaththir* verses 27–31. Maududi's translation: "And what do you know what Hell is? It leaves nothing and it spares none. It scorches the skin. Nineteen keepers are appointed over it.'" (74:27–31) Yusuf Ali's translation: "And what will explain to thee what Hell-Fire is? Naught doth it permit to endure, and naught doth it leave alone! Darkening and changing the colour of man! Over it are Nineteen. And We have set none but angels as Guardians of the Fire."

41 www.miraclesofthequran.com

42 For instance, one may discover that the 19th word of a work is used 114 times, which would be 19 x 6, or that the 19th paragraph of the first chapter starts with a letter or possibly even the word that also appears at the start of the 19th paragraph from the end of the chapter or the book. And so on!

43 www.miraclesofthequran.com

44 *Surah An-Naml* verses 87–88. Yusuf Ali's translation: "And the Day that the Trumpet will be sounded—then will be smitten with terror those who are in the heavens, and those who are on earth, except such as Allah will please (to exempt); and all shall come to His (Presence) as beings conscious of their lowliness. *Thou seest the mountains and thinkest them firmly fixed: but they shall pass away as the clouds pass away.*"

45 These translations of *Surah Al-Anbiyaa* verse 30 and *Surah Adh-Dhariyat* verses 47–48 are taken from www.speed-light.info/expanding_universe.htm

46 For instance: "*Do you not know* that Allah has full power over everything? *Do you not know* that the sovereignty of the heavens and the earth belongs to Allah alone and that you have neither any protector nor helper beside Him?" (2:107) (Maududi) Yusuf Ali's translation of *Surah Al-Baqarah* verse 107 is "*Knowest thou not* that to Allah belongeth the dominion of the heavens and the earth? And besides Him ye have neither patron nor helper."

47 As, for instance, in *Surah Al-Hijr* verses 2–3: "The time is not far when the same people who have today refused to accept (the Message of Islam) will regret and say, 'we wish we had surrendered to it!' Leave them alone to eat, drink and be merry and to be deluded by false hopes. *They will soon realize it.*" (15:2-3) (Maududi) "Again and again will those who disbelieve, wish that they had bowed (to Allah's will) in Islam. Leave them alone, to enjoy (the good things of this life) and to please themselves: let (false) hope amuse them: *soon will knowledge (undeceive them).*" (Yusuf Ali)

48 *Surah Ha-Mim As-Sajdah* verses 9–12. Yusuf Ali's translation: "Say: Is it that ye deny Him *Who created the earth in two Days?* And do ye join equals with Him? He is the Lord of (all) the Worlds. He set on the (earth), mountains standing firm, high above it, and bestowed blessings on the earth, and measure therein all things to give them nourishment in due proportion, *in four Days, in accordance with (the needs of) those who seek (Sustenance).* Moreover He comprehended in His design the sky, and it had been (as) smoke. He said to it and to the earth: 'Come ye together, willingly or unwillingly.' They said: 'We do come (together), in willing obedience.' *So He completed them as seven firmaments in two Days,* and He assigned to each heaven its duty and command. *And We adorned the lower heaven with lights, and (provided it) with guard.* Such is the Decree of (Him) the Exalted in Might, Full of Knowledge."
Yusuf Ali uses the word "moreover" instead of "then"—in order, perhaps, to hide the shortcoming; however, even he cannot change the order in which the creation of the earth and the heavens is mentioned in the above verses. Moreover, his interpretation is not supported by the other translations we rely on this book, which follow: "Then He rose over (Istawa) towards the heaven when it was smoke, and said to it and the earth: 'Come both of you willingly or unwillingly.' They both said: 'We come willingly.' *Then* He completed and finished from their creation (as) seven heavens in two Days and He made in each heaven its affairs." (Hilali-Khan); "*Then* turned He to the heaven when it was smoke, and said unto it and unto the earth: Come both of you, willingly or loth. They said: We come, obedient. *Then* He ordained them seven heavens in two Days and inspired in each heaven its mandate." (Pickthall)

49 Elsewhere in the Quran, as discussed in Chapter 2, the order gets reversed, however.

50 As noted in *Surah As-Sajdah* verse 4 and *Surah Hud* verse 7. Maududi's translations: "Allah it is who created the heavens and the earth and all that is between them in *six days,* and then sat Himself upon the throne!" (32:4); "It is He who created the heavens and the earth in *six days—* whereas before this His Throne rested on water." (11:7) Yusuf Ali's translations: "It is Allah Who has created the heavens and the earth, and all between them, in six Days, and is firmly established on the Throne (of Authority)."; "He it is Who created the heavens and the earth in six Days—and His Throne was over the waters."

51 The error is not corrected even if we take each day to be the equivalent of 50,000 years, as explained elsewhere in the Quran.

52 Indeed, even if we add the time since the creation of the solar system (i.e., add another 4.6 billion years towards the creation of the earth), this would still come to less than half.

53 One is, of course, mindful of what the Quran says elsewhere:

When We desire to bring a thing into existence, We need only say, "Be," and it is there. (16:40)

He is the Creator of the heavens and the earth: when He decrees a thing, He merely says, "Be," and there it is. (2:117)

Going by this pronouncement, however, we see that it should not have taken even six days to create the universe!

Yusuf Ali's translation of these verses: "For to anything which We have willed, We but say the word, 'Be,' and it is."; "To Him is due the primal origin of the heavens and the earth: When He decreeth a matter, He saith to it: 'Be,' and it is."

54   Moore: "A Scientist's Interpretation of References to Embryology in the Quran" p. 15

55   He writes:
This is an appropriate description of the human embryo from days 7–24 when it clings to the endometrium of the uterus, in the same way that a leech clings to the skin. Just as the leech derives blood from the host, the human embryo derives blood from the decidua or pregnant endometrium. *It is remarkable how much the embryo of 23–24 days resembles a leech.* As there were no microscopes or lenses available in the 7th century, doctors would not have known that the human embryo had this leech-like appearance. *In the early part of the fourth week, the embryo is just visible to the unaided eye because it is smaller than a kernel of wheat.* (Moore: "A Scientist's Interpretation of References to Embryology in the Quran" pp. 15–16)

56   Zendani's is the translation Moore relies on in the article. He informs us:
The translations of the verses from the Quran which are interpreted in this paper were provided by Sheik Abdul Majid Zendani, a Professor of Islamic Studies in King Abdulaziz University in Jeddah, Saudi Arabia. (Moore: "A Scientist's Interpretation of References to Embryology in the Quran," p. 15)

57   In fact, the word that Zendani translates as "leech-like structure" is *alaqah*, which is also used in the first verses to be revealed in the Quran. Adopting the same meaning would make them read "Read in the name of your Lord Who created man from *a leach-like structure*," whereas we do know that the "leach-like structure" is at least not the starting point but at best only a subsequent phase of the embryo. Moreover, if the word *alaqah* means "a leech" (in addition to blood), then isn't that how it should be stated in the translation as well, as opposed to "a leech-like *structure*"? Finally, there is another word in Arabic for leech (i.e., *salatah*), and one wonders why the Quran did not use that if it did not mean to refer to blood.

58   Moore: "A Scientist's Interpretation of References to Embryology in the Quran," p. 16

59   Translated by Zendani as "Then We placed him as *a drop* in a place of rest." Other translations mention "sperm" or "sperm drop," though, perhaps to make it consistent with verse 76:2, Hilali and Khan translate it as "mixed drops of the male and female sexual discharge."

60   Moore: "A Scientist's Interpretation of References to Embryology in the Quran," p. 15

61   *Surah Az-Zumar* verse 6 (39:6). Yusuf Ali's translation: "He makes you, in the wombs of your mothers, in stages, one after another, in three veils of darkness."

62   Moore: "A Scientist's Interpretation of References to Embryology in the Quran," p. 15

63   *Surah Al Tariq* verses 5–7. Yusuf Ali's translation: "Now let man but think from what he is created! *He is created from a drop emitted—Proceeding from between the backbone and the ribs.*"

64   Naik, however, offers the following explanation:
In embryonic stages, the reproductive organs of the male and female, i.e. the testicles and the ovaries, begin their development near the kidney between the spinal column and the eleventh and twelfth ribs. Later they descend; the female gonads (ovaries) stop in the pelvis while the male gonads (testicles) continue their descent before birth to reach the scrotum through the inguinal canal. Even in adulthood after the descent of the reproductive organs, these organs receive their nerve supply and blood supply from the Abdominal Aorta, which is in the area between the backbone (spinal column) and the ribs. The lymphatic drainage and the venous return also go to the same area. (*The Quran and Modern Science: Compatible or Incompatible?* p. 50)

This concedes, as it must, that the referenced fluid (sperm) does not in fact issue forth from between the backbone and the breastbones. The argument Naik advances is that during the embryonic stage of a male child, long before the discharge of the fluid, it is this part of the embryo where development of the testes originally begins, and the testes then descend to the scrotum shortly before birth. While it is debatable whether even the point where the testes begin their formation falls in the area between the breastbone and the backbone, the question is what possible relevance that has. Even if one concedes this debatable point, does that mean that the sperm "issues forth from between the backbone and the breast bones"?

The other argument put forward by Naik, that even in adulthood, these organs receive their nerve and blood supply from the area between the backbone and the ribs, is not new. We confronted this in Chapter 2 as well but noted that if one yields to the argument, it might as well be said that the fluid issues forth from the brain or the heart, for both are involved in the larger scheme of things. We also noted that this argument, at best, addresses why the organs between the backbone and the breastbones (which otherwise have nothing to do with the process) are yet implicated but does not tell us why the testes have been excluded altogether.

65   Maududi: *The Meaning of the Qur'an*, note 6 to *Surah Al-Hajj*, Volume 3, p. 187

Chapter 5: The Quran and Justice

1   Rawls: *A Theory of Justice*, pp. 3-4
2   *Surah An-Nisa* verse 58. Yusuf Ali's translation: "Allah doth command you … when ye judge between man and man, that ye judge with justice."
3   Respectively, *Surah An-Nisa* verse 92, *Surah Al-Maidah* verse 89, and *Surah An-Noor* verse 33. Yusuf Ali's translations: "Never should a believer kill a believer; but (If it so happens) by mistake, (Compensation is due): If one (so) kills a believer, *it is ordained that he should free a believing slave.*"; "Allah will … call you to account for your deliberate oaths: for expiation … *give a slave his freedom.*"; "And if any of your slaves ask for a deed in writing (to enable them to earn their freedom for a certain sum), give them such a deed if ye know any good in them." There are also other verses in the Quran that express the same thought.
4   Respectively, *Surah Al-Muminoon* verses 1–6 and *Surah Al-Maarij* verses 22–30. Yusuf Ali's translations: "The believers must (eventually) win through … Who abstain from sex, Except with those joined to them in the marriage bond, *or (the captives) whom their right hands possess*, for (in their case) they are free from blame."; "Not so those devoted to Prayer; … And those who guard their chastity, Except with their wives *and the (captives) whom their right hands possess*, for (then) they are not to be blamed."
5   *Surah Al-Ahzab* verse 55. Yusuf Ali's translation: "There is no blame (on these ladies if they appear) before their fathers or their sons, their brothers, or their brother's sons, or their sisters' sons, or their women, *or the (slaves) whom their right hands possess.*"
6   That the Prophet's household had slaves is also substantiated by historical accounts—for instance, the incident of slander in which Aisha's slave girl was asked to testify regarding Aisha's character—but clear acknowledgment in the Quran itself puts the issue entirely beyond dispute.
7   *Surah Al-Ahzab* verses 50–52. Yusuf Ali's translation: "O Prophet! We have made lawful to thee … those whom thy right hand possesses out of the prisoners of war whom Allah has assigned to thee. … [and] any thy right hand should possess (as handmaidens)."
8   *Surah Al-Maidah* verses 33–34. Yusuf Ali's translation: "The punishment of those who wage war against Allah and His Messenger, and strive with might and main for mischief through the land is: execution, or crucifixion, or the cutting off of hands and feet from opposite sides, or exile from the land: that is their disgrace in this world, and a heavy punishment is theirs in the Hereafter. Except for those who repent before they fall into your power: in that case, know that Allah is Oft-forgiving, Most Merciful."
9   As reported by Ibn Ishaq (*The Life of Muhammad*, pp. 367-369):

> The apostle said, "Who will rid me of Ibnu'l Ashraf?" Muhammad b. Maslama said, "I will deal with him for you, O apostle of God, I will kill him." He said, "Do so if you can." So Muhammad b. Maslama returned and waited for three days without food or drink, apart from what was absolutely necessary. When the apostle was told of this he summoned him and asked him why he had given up eating and drinking. He said that he had given him an undertaking and he did not know whether he could fulfill it. The apostle said, "All that is incumbent upon you is that you should try." He said, "O apostle of God, we shall have to tell lies." He answered, "Say what you would like, for you are free in the matter."

Muhammad b. Maslma thereupon sent Ka'b's own foster brother (Silkan b. Salama), who, to gain Ka'b's sympathy, posed as if he were disgruntled with the Prophet.

Then he said, "O Ibn Ashraf, ... the coming of this man is a great trial to us. It has provoked the hostilities of the Arabs, and they are all in league against us. The roads have become impassable so that our families are in want and privation, and we and our families are in great distress." Ka'b answered, "By God, I kept telling you, O Ibn Salama, that the things I warned you of would happen." Silkan said to him, "I want you to sell us food ... I have friends who share my opinion and I want to bring them to you so that you may sell to them and act generously and we will give you enough weapons for a good pledge." Silkan's object was that he should not take alarm at the sight of weapons when they brought them. Ka'b answered, "Weapons are a good pledge." Thereupon Silkan returned to his companions, told them what had happened, and ordered them to take their arms. Then they went away and assembled with him and met the apostle.

It is reported that the Prophet sent them off with his blessings and they stealthily killed Ka'b. Ibn Ishaq also then reports on the authority of Muhammad b. Masalma: "Our attack upon God's enemy cast terror among the Jews, and there was no Jew in Medina who did not fear for his life." Ka'b b. Malik said:

> Of them Ka'b was left prostrate there
> (After his fall al-Nadir were brought low).
> *Sword in hand we cut him down*
> *By Muhammad's order when he sent secretly by night*
> *Ka'b's brother to go to Ka'b.*
> He beguiled him and brought him down with guile
> Mahmud was trustworthy, bold

10 Ibn Ishaq reports:

al-Huwayrith b. Nuqaydh, one of those who used to insult him in Mecca [*and was killed by Ali*] ... And Sara, freed slave of one of the B. Abdul Muttalib ... Sara had insulted him in Mecca. (*The Life of Muhammad*, p. 551)

11 Ibn Ishaq: *The Life of Muhammad*, p. 676

12 Ibn Ishaq: *The Life of Muhammad*, pp. 550–551. Ibn Ishaq notes that "As for Ibn Khatal's two singing girls, one was killed and the other ran away until the apostle, asked for immunity, gave it her."

13 Rawls: *A Theory of Justice*

14 There are laws even in non-Muslim countries that make blasphemy an offense—though not punishable with death. These must be reviewed as well.

15 *Surah An-Nisa* verses 15–16. Yusuf Ali's translation: "If any of your women are guilty of lewdness, Take the evidence of four (Reliable) witnesses from amongst you against them; and if they testify, confine them to houses until death do claim them, or Allah ordain for them some (other) way. If two men among you are guilty of lewdness, punish them both. If they repent and amend, Leave them alone; for Allah is Oft-returning, Most Merciful."

16 *Surah An-Noor* verses 2–3. Yusuf Ali's translation: "*The woman and the man guilty of adultery or fornication, flog each of them with a hundred stripes.* Let not compassion move you in their case, in a matter prescribed by Allah, if ye believe in Allah and the Last Day: and let a party of the Believers witness their punishment. Let no man guilty of adultery or fornication marry and but a woman similarly guilty, or an Unbeliever: nor let any but such a man or an Unbeliever marry such a woman: to the Believers such a thing is forbidden."

17 *Surah An-Nisa* verse 25. Yusuf Ali's translation: "If any of you have not the means wherewith to wed free believing women, they may wed believing girls from among those whom your right hands possess: ... when they are taken in wedlock, if they fall into shame, their punishment is half that for free women."

18 *Surah Al-Ahzab* verse 30. Yusuf Ali's translation: "O Consorts of the Prophet! If any of you were guilty of evident unseemly conduct, the Punishment would be doubled to her."

19 *Surah Al-Baqarah* verse 178 (A.J. Arberry: *The Koran Interpreted*)

20 Ibn Ishaq: *The Life of Muhammad*, pp. 291–292:

The cause of the war between Quraysh and B. Bakr ... was 'Amir b. Lu'ayy. He had gone out seeking a lost camel. ... He passed by Amir b. Yazid, he being the chief of B. Bakr at that time. When he saw him he liked him and asked who he was. When he told him, and had gone away, he called his tribesmen, and asked them if there was any blood outstanding with Quraysh, and when they said there was, he said, "Any man who kills this youngster in revenge for one of his tribe will have exacted the blood due to him." So one of them followed him and killed him in revenge for the blood Quraysh had shed. When Quraysh discussed the matter, Amir b. Yazid said, "You owed us blood so what do you want? If you wish pay us what you owe us, and we will pay what we owe. If you want only blood, man for man, then ignore your claims and we will ignore ours"; and since this youth was of no great importance to this clan of Quraysh, they said, "All right, man for man", and ignored his death and sought no compensation.

71 Hilali and Khan include "(or the relatives, etc.)" while interpreting the verse, but this is not part of the Quranic text.

22 *Surah Al-Qasas* verses 15–16. Maududi's translation: "[Moses] saw two men fighting, the one of his own people, the other of his enemies. The one belonging to his own people asked his help against the one belonging to the enemy. Moses gave him a blow and killed him. (On seeing what had happened) Moses said, 'This is the work of Satan: he is a deadly enemy (of man) and an open misleader.' Then he said, 'O my Lord, I have sinned against myself, so forgive me.' So, Allah forgave him: He is the All-Forgiving, the All-Merciful." (28:15–16) Yusuf Ali's translation: "And he found there two men fighting, one of his own religion, and the other, of his foes [sic]. Now the man of his own religion appealed to him against his foe, and Moses struck him with his fist and made an end of him. He said: 'This is a work of Evil (Satan): for he is an enemy that manifestly misleads!' He prayed: 'O my Lord! I have indeed wronged my soul! Do Thou then forgive me!' So ((Allah)) forgave him: for He is the Oft-Forgiving, Most Merciful."

23 *Surah Al-Kahf* verses 65–82. Yusuf Ali's translation: "So they found one of Our servants, on whom We had bestowed Mercy from Ourselves and whom We had taught knowledge from Our own Presence. Moses said to him: 'May I follow thee, on the footing that thou teach me something of the (Higher) Truth which thou hast been taught?' (The other) said: 'Verily thou wilt not be able to have patience with me! And how canst thou have patience about things about which thy understanding is not complete?' Moses said: 'Thou wilt find me, if Allah so will, (truly) patient: nor shall I disobey thee in aught.' The other said: 'If then thou wouldst follow me, ask me no questions about anything until I myself speak to thee concerning it.' So they both proceeded: until, when they were in the boat, he scuttled it. Said Moses: 'Hast thou scuttled it in order to drown those in it? Truly a strange thing hast thou done!' He answered: 'Did I not tell thee that thou canst have no patience with me?' Moses said: 'Rebuke me not for forgetting, nor grieve me by raising difficulties in my case.' *Then they proceeded: until, when they met a young man, he slew him. Moses said: 'Hast thou slain an innocent person who had slain none? Truly a foul (unheard of) thing hast thou done!'* He answered: 'Did I not tell thee that thou canst have no patience with me?' (Moses) said: 'If ever I ask thee about anything after this, keep me not in thy company: then wouldst thou have received (full) excuse from my side.' Then they proceeded: until, when they came to the inhabitants of a town, they asked them for food, but they refused them hospitality. They found there a wall on the point of falling down, but he set it up straight. (Moses) said: 'If thou hadst wished, surely thou couldst have exacted some recompense for it!' He answered: 'This is the parting between me and thee: now will I tell thee the interpretation of (those things) over which thou wast unable to hold patience. As for the boat, it belonged to certain men in dire want: they plied on the water: I but wished to render it unserviceable, for there was after them a certain king who seized on every boat by force. *As for the youth, his parents were people of Faith, and we feared that he would grieve them by obstinate rebellion and ingratitude (to Allah and man). So we desired that their Lord would give them in exchange (a son) better in purity (of conduct) and closer in affection.* As for the wall, it belonged to two youths, orphans, in the Town; there was, beneath it, a buried treasure, to which they were entitled: their father had been a righteous man: So thy Lord desired that they should attain their age of full strength and get out their treasure—a mercy (and favour) from thy Lord. I did it not of my own accord. Such is the interpretation of (those things) over which thou wast unable to hold patience.'"

24 Maududi: *The Meaning of the Qur'an*, note 60 to *Surah Al-Kahf*, Volume 3, pp. 41–42

25 *Surah Al-Maidah* verse 45. Maududi's translation: "We had prescribed this decree in the Torah for the Jews: 'Life for life, eye for eye, nose for nose, ear for ear, tooth for tooth, and for all wounds equal retaliation.' However, whoever forgoes retaliation as charity, it shall be expiation for him: those, who do not judge by the Law which Allah has sent down, are indeed the unjust people." (5.45) Yusuf Ali's translation: "We ordained therein for them 'Life for life, eye for eye, nose for nose, ear for ear, tooth for tooth, and wounds equal for equal.' But if any one remits the

retaliation by way of charity, it is an act of atonement for himself. And if any fail to judge by (the light of) what Allah hath revealed, they are (No better than) wrong-doers."

26 *Surah Al-Maidah* verse 38. Yusuf Ali's translation: "As to the thief, Male or female, cut off his or her hands: a punishment by way of example, from Allah, for their crime: and Allah is Exalted in power."

27 Ibn Ishaq: *The Life of Muhammad*, p. 84:
> Quraysh decided to rebuild the Ka'ba when the apostle was thirty five years of age. ... They wanted to raise it and roof it because men had stolen part of the treasure for the Ka'ba which used to be in a well in the middle of it. The treasure was found with Duwayk a freedman of B. Mulayh. *Quraysh cut his hand off.*

28 *De Ira* (On Anger), Book I, Chapter XVIII. The above passage is taken from Wikipedia.

Chapter 6: The Quran and Women

1 Benazir Bhutto: *Reconciliation*, p. 18
2 Al-Nas TV aired the discussion on 4 February 2010.
3 Couch: "Women in Early Roman Law," pp. 39–50
4 Rogerson: *The Prophet Muhammad*, p. 73: "Khadijah was a beautiful, intelligent, wealthy woman who, through the death of her two previous husbands, now commanded a considerable fortune."
5 The Quran gives an indication of this in *Surah Al-Takwir* verse 4, though there is also indication in *Surah Bani Israil* verse 31 that this practice was not just confined to girls: "Do not kill your off springs for fear of want: for it is We Who provide them and you as well. Indeed their killing is a heinous crime." (17:31) (Maududi) Yusuf Ali's translation: "Kill not your children for fear of want: We shall provide sustenance for them as well as for you. Verily the killing of them is a great sin."
6 *Sura An-Nahl* verse 72. Maududi's translation: "And He alone bestowed upon you sons and grandsons from those wives, and provided you with good things to eat. What, do they then (even after seeing and knowing all this) believe in falsehood, and deny Allah's favors?" (16:72) Yusuf Ali's translation: "... and made for you, out of them, sons and daughters and grandchildren, and provided for you sustenance of the best: will they then believe in vain things, and be ungrateful for Allah's favors?" Yusuf Ali translates the verse to include daughters and granddaughters; however, both Hilali-Khan and Pickthall clearly disagree with him, as can be seen in the appendix.
7 *Surah An Najam* verses 21–22. Yusuf Ali's translation: "'What! for you the male sex, and for Him, the female? Behold, such would be indeed a division most unfair!"
The additional verses, along the same lines, follow (respectively, *Surah An-Nahl* verse 57, *Surah Bani Israel* verse 40, *Surah As-Saaffat* verse 149, *Surah At-Tur* verse 39). Maududi's translations: "They assign daughters to Allah. ... What an evil judgment they have about Allah!" (16:57); "'What! has your Lord favored you with sons and adopted angels as daughters for Himself?" (17:40); "Just ask the people (whether it appeals to them) that their Lord should have daughters and they should have sons!" (37:149); "Is Allah to have daughters and you sons?" (52:39) Yusuf Ali's translations: "And they assign daughters for Allah. Glory be to Him! and for themselves (sons, the issue) they desire!"; "Has then your Lord (O Pagans!) preferred for you sons, and taken for Himself daughters among the angels?"; "Now ask them their opinion: Is it that thy Lord has (only) daughters, and they have sons?"; "Or has He only daughters and ye have sons?"
8 *Surah Al-Baqarah* verse 228 and *Surah An-Nisa* verse 34. Maududi's translations: "Wives have the same rights as the husbands have on them in accordance with the generally known principles. *Of course, men are a degree above them in status,* and above all is Allah, the All-Mighty, the All-Wise." (2:228); "*Men are the managers of the affairs of women because Allah has made the one superior to the other* and because men spend of their wealth on women." (4:34) Yusuf Ali's translations: "And women shall have rights similar to the rights against them, according to what is equitable; *but men have a degree (of advantage) over them.* And Allah is Exalted in Power, Wise."; "*Men are the protectors and maintainers of women, because Allah has given the one more (strength) than the other,* and because they support them from their means."
9 *Surah An-Nisa* verse 24. Maududi's translation: "With the exception of the above, all have been made lawful for you to seek in marriage with your wealth any other woman provided that you keep them in wedlock and not in licentiousness. *Then you should pay them their dowries as an obligation*

for enjoyment of conjugal relations with them. However, there is no harm if a compromise is made in the dower by mutual consent after an agreement about it; Allah is All-Knowing, All-Wise." (4:24) Yusuf Ali's translation: "Except for these, all others are lawful, provided ye seek (them in marriage) with gifts from your property, desiring chastity, not lust, seeing that ye derive benefit from them, *give them their dowers (at least) as prescribed;* but if, after a dower is prescribed, agree Mutually (to vary it), there is no blame on you, and Allah is All-knowing, All-wise."

10   *Surah Al-Mumtahina* verse 10. Maududi's translation: "O you who have believed, when the believing women come to you as emigrants, ... do not return them to the disbelievers. ... *Return to their disbelieving husbands the dowers that they had given them.*" (60:10) Yusuf Ali's translation: "O ye who believe! When there come to you believing women refugees ... then send them not back to the Unbelievers. ... *But pay the Unbelievers what they have spent (on their dower).*"

11   *Surah Al-Baqarah* verse 282. Yusuf Ali's translation: "O ye who believe! When ye deal with each other, in transactions involving future obligations in a fixed period of time, reduce them to writing ... and get two witnesses, out of your own men, *and if there are not two men, then a man and two women, such as ye choose, for witnesses, so that if one of them errs, the other can remind her.*"

12   *Surah Al-Maidah* verse 106. Maududi's translation: "O Believers, when the time of death approaches anyone of you, and he is going to make his will, *the principle of evidence is that two just men from among you should act as witnesses.* Or, if you are on a journey and the calamity of death befalls you there, the two witnesses may be taken from among the non Muslims." (5:106) Yusuf Ali's translation: "O ye who believe! When death approaches any of you, *(take) witnesses among yourselves when making bequests, two just men of your own (brotherhood)* or others from outside if ye are journeying through the earth, and the chance of death befalls you (thus)."

13   *Surah An-Nisa* verse 3. Yusuf Ali's translation: "Marry women of your choice, Two or three or four; but if ye fear that ye shall not be able to deal justly (with them), then only one, or (a captive) that your right hands possess, that will be more suitable, to prevent you from doing injustice."

14   *Surah An-Nisa* verse 129. Maududi's translation: "It is not within your power to be perfectly equitable in your treatment with all your wives, even if you wish to be so; therefore (in order to satisfy the dictates of Divine Law) do not lean wholly towards one wife so as to leave the other in a state of suspense." (4:129) Yusuf Ali's translation: "Ye are never able to be fair and just as between women, even if it is your ardent desire: But turn not away (from a woman) altogether, so as to leave her (as it were) hanging (in the air)."

15   Chapter 5, "Quran and Justice," may be referred to for further discussion.

16   *Surah An-Noor* verse 33. Yusuf Ali's translation: "But force not your maids to prostitution *when they desire chastity,* in order that ye may make a gain in the goods of this life. But if anyone compels them, yet, after such compulsion, is Allah, Oft-Forgiving, Most Merciful (to them)."

17   *Surah An-Nisa* verse 25. Yusuf Ali's translation: "If any of you have not the means wherewith to wed free believing women, they may wed believing girls from among those whom your right hands possess ... and give them their dowers, according to what is reasonable: They should be chaste, not lustful, nor taking paramours: *when they are taken in wedlock, if they fall into shame, their punishment is half that for free women.*"

18   *Surah An-Noor* verses 30–31. Yusuf Ali's translation: "Say to the believing men that they should lower their gaze and guard their modesty: that will make for greater purity for them: And Allah is well acquainted with all that they do. *And say to the believing women that they should lower their gaze and guard their modesty; that they should not display their beauty and ornaments except what (must ordinarily) appear thereof; that they should draw their veils over their bosoms* and not display their beauty except to their husbands, their fathers, their husbands' fathers, their sons, their husbands' sons, their brothers or their brothers' sons, or their sisters' sons, or their women, or the slaves whom their right hands possess, or male servants free of physical needs, or small children who have no sense of the shame of sex; and that they should not strike their feet in order to draw attention to their hidden ornaments."

19   *Surah Al-Ahzab* verse 59. Yusuf Ali's translation may be found later in the text.

20   *Surah Al-Ahzab* verses 32–33. Yusuf Ali's translation: "*O Consorts of the Prophet! Ye are not like any of the (other) women:* if ye do fear ((Allah)), be not too complacent of speech, lest one in whose heart is a disease should be moved with desire: but speak ye a speech (that is) just. *And stay quietly in your houses, and make not a dazzling display, like that of the former Times of Ignorance.*"

21   Maududi: *The Meaning of the Qur'an,* note 46 to *Surah Al-Ahzab,* Volume 4, p. 98.

22 Respectively, *Surah Al-Waqia* verses 22–23, *Surah At-Tur* verse 20, and *Surah Ad-Dukhan* verse 54. Maududi's translations: "And for them there shall be beautiful-eyed *houris*, as lovely as well-guarded pearls." (56:22–23); "And We shall wed them to *houris* with beautiful eyes." (52:20); "And We shall wed to them fair-complexioned, gazelle-eyed women." (44:54) Yusuf Ali's translations: "And (there will be) Companions with beautiful, big, and lustrous eyes, Like unto Pearls well-guarded."; "And We shall join them to Companions, with beautiful big and lustrous eyes."; "And We shall join them to Companions with beautiful, big, and lustrous eyes."

23 Respectively, *Surah At-Tur* verse 24 and *Surah Ad-Dahr* verse 19. Yusuf Ali's translations: "Round about them will serve, (devoted) to them. Youths (handsome) as Pearls well-guarded."; "And round about them will (serve) youths of perpetual (freshness): If thou seest them, thou wouldst think them scattered Pearls."

24 *Surah An-Noor*, verses 6–9. Maududi's translation: "As for those who accuse their own wives but have no witness except themselves, the evidence of one of them is that he shall swear four times by Allah and declare that he is true (in his charge). Then the fifth time he shall declare that Allah's curse be upon him if he be false (in his charge). (As for the woman), *it shall avert the punishment from her if she swears four times by Allah that the man is false (in his charge) and the fifth time she invokes Allah's wrath upon herself, if he be true (in his charge)."* (24:6–9) Yusuf Ali's translation: "And for those who launch a charge against their spouses, and have (in support) no evidence but their own, their solitary evidence (can be received) if they bear witness four times (with an oath) by Allah that they are solemnly telling the truth; And the fifth (oath) (should be) that they solemnly invoke the curse of Allah on themselves if they tell a lie. *But it would avert the punishment from the wife, if she bears witness four times (with an oath) By Allah, that (her husband) is telling a lie; And the fifth (oath) should be that she solemnly invokes the wrath of Allah on herself if (her accuser) is telling the truth."*

25 *Surah An-Noor* verse 26. Maududi's translation: "Impure women are for impure men and impure men for impure women, and pure women are for pure men and pure men for pure women. *They are free from those scandals, which the slanderers utter.* There is forgiveness for them and honorable provision." (24:26) Yusuf Ali's translation: "Women impure are for men impure, and men impure for women impure and women of purity are for men of purity, and men of purity are for women of purity: *these are not affected by what people say:* for them there is forgiveness, and a provision honorable."

26 *Surah An-Noor* verses 4–5. Yusuf Ali's translation: "And those who launch a charge against chaste women, and produce not four witnesses (to support their allegations), flog them with eighty stripes; and reject their evidence ever after: for such men are wicked transgressors; Unless they repent thereafter and mend (their conduct); for Allah is Oft- Forgiving, Most Merciful."

27 Ibn Ishaq: *The Life of Muhammad,* p. 792

28 *Surah At Talaq* verse 4. Yusuf Ali's translation is provided further in the text.

29 *Surah An-Nisa* verse 34. Yusuf Ali's translation is provided further in the text.

30 *Surah Al-Baqarah* verse 223. Yusuf Ali's translation: "Your wives are as a tilth unto you; so approach your tilth when or how ye will."

Chapter 7: The Sword Verses

1 *Surah At-Taubah* verses 5 and 29. Yusuf Ali's translations: "But when the forbidden months are past, then fight and slay the Pagans wherever ye find them, and seize them, beleaguer them, and lie in wait for them in every stratagem (of war); but if they repent, and establish regular prayers and practise regular charity, then open the way for them: for Allah is Oft-forgiving, Most Merciful."; "Fight those who believe not in Allah nor the Last Day, nor hold that forbidden which hath been forbidden by Allah and His Messenger, nor acknowledge the religion of Truth, (even if they are) of the People of the Book, until they pay the *Jizya* with willing submission, and feel themselves subdued."

2 *Surah At-Taubah* verse 5 (9:5) was revealed at the time of *Hajj* in 9 AH, as can be gathered from the preceding verse: "This is a public proclamation from Allah and His Messenger for all the people on the Day of Great Hajj." This helps date it with absolute precision. *Surah At-Taubah* verse 29 (9:29), too, was issued the same year, at the time of the Tabuk expedition against the people of the Book.

3 These include *Surah Al-Baqarah* verse 114, *Surah Al-Baqarah* verse 190, *Surah Al-Baqarah* verse 256, *Surah Al-Maidah* verse 2, *Surah Al-Maidah* verse 69, *Surah Al-Anaam* verse 108, *Surah An-Nahl* verse 126, and *Surah Al-Kafirun* verse 6. Maududi's translations: "And who could be a

greater wrongdoer than the one who forbids the mention of Allah's name in places of worship and strives for their ruin?" (2:114); "And fight in the way of Allah with those who fight against you but do not commit aggression because Allah does not like aggressors." (2:190); "There is no compulsion and coercion in regard to religion." (2:256); "Let not your resentment against those, who have barred you from visiting the Ka'ba, incite you so much as to transgress the prescribed limits." (5:2); "Whoever from among the Muslims or the Jews or the Sabaeans or the Christians believes in Allah and the Last Day and does good deeds will have no cause of fear or grief or sorrow." (5:69); "And (O Believers), do not revile those whom they invoke besides Allah lest they should, in their ignorance, revile Allah (besides committing shirk)." (6:108); "And if you retaliate, let your retaliation be to the extent that you were wronged, but if you endure it with patience, it is indeed best for those who endure with patience." (16:126); "For you is your religion and for me is mine." (109:6). Yusuf Ali's translations: "And who is more unjust than he who forbids that in places for the worship of Allah, Allah's name should be celebrated? Whose zeal is (in fact) to ruin them?"; "Fight in the cause of Allah those who fight you, but do not transgress limits; for Allah loveth not transgressors."; "Let there be no compulsion in religion."; "And let not the hatred of some people in (once) shutting you out of the Sacred Mosque lead you to transgression (and hostility on your part)."; "Those who believe (in the Qur'an), those who follow the Jewish (scriptures), and the Sabians and the Christians, any who believe in Allah and the Last Day, and work righteousness, on them shall be no fear, nor shall they grieve."; "Revile not ye those whom they call upon besides Allah, lest they out of spite revile Allah in their ignorance."; "And if ye do catch them out, catch them out no worse than they catch you out: But if ye show patience, that is indeed the best (course) for those who are patient."; "To you be your Way, and to me mine."

4   *Surah At-Taubah* verse 13. Yusuf Ali's translation: "Will ye not fight people who violated their oaths, *plotted to expel the Messenger*, and took the aggressive by being the first (to assault) you?"

5   *Surah At-Taubah* verses 7-8. Yusuf Ali's translation: "How (can there be such a league), seeing that *if they get an advantage over you, they respect not in you the ties either of kinship or of covenant?*"

6   *Surah An-Nisa* verse 48. Maududi's translation: "Shirk is the only sin that Allah does not forgive, and He forgives whomsoever He pleases, other sins than this, for whosoever associates any other partner with Allah, does indeed forge a big lie and commit the most heinous sin" (4:48). Yusuf Ali's translation: "Allah forgiveth not that partners should be set up with Him; but He forgiveth anything else, to whom He pleaseth; to set up partners with Allah is to devise a sin Most heinous indeed."

7   Ibn Ishaq: *The Life of Muhammad*, p. 499

8   Ibn Ishaq: *The Life of Muhammad*, p. 504

9   *Surah Al-Mumtahina* verses 10–11. Yusuf Ali's translation: "O ye who believe! When there come to you believing women refugees, examine (and test) them: Allah knows best as to their Faith: if ye ascertain that they are Believers, then send them not back to the Unbelievers. They are not lawful (wives) for the Unbelievers, nor are the (Unbelievers) lawful (husbands) for them. But pay the Unbelievers what they have spent (on their dower), and there will be no blame on you if ye marry them on payment of their dower to them. ... And if any of your wives deserts you to the Unbelievers, and ye have an accession (by the coming over of a woman from the other side), then pay to those whose wives have deserted the equivalent of what they had spent (on their dower)."

10   Ibn Ishaq: *The Life of Muhammad*, p. 509

11   *Surah At-Taubah* verses 1-3, 7. Yusuf Ali's translation: "A (declaration) of immunity from Allah and His Messenger, to those of the Pagans with whom ye have contracted mutual alliances. Go ye, then, for four months, backwards and forwards, (as ye will), throughout the land. ... And an announcement from Allah and His Messenger, to the people (assembled) on the day of the Great Pilgrimage, that Allah and His Messenger dissolve (treaty) obligations with the Pagans ... except those with whom ye made a treaty near the sacred Mosque? As long as these stand true to you, stand ye true to them: for Allah doth love the righteous."

12   *Surah At-Taubah* verse 9. Yusuf Ali's translation is "The Signs of Allah have they sold for a miserable price, and (many) have they hindered from His way."

13   *Surah At-Taubah* verse 28. Yusuf Ali's translation: "O ye who believe! Truly the Pagans are unclean; so let them not, after this year of theirs, approach the Sacred Mosque."

14   *Surah At-Taubah* verses 30–33. Yusuf Ali's translation: "The Jews call 'Uzair a son of Allah, and the Christians call Christ the son of Allah. That is a saying from their mouth; (in this) they but

imitate what the unbelievers of old used to say. Allah's curse be on them: how they are deluded away from the Truth! They take their priests and their anchorites to be their lords in derogation of Allah, and (they take as their Lord) Christ the son of Mary; yet they were commanded to worship but One Allah. There is no god but He. Praise and glory to Him: (Far is He) from having the partners they associate (with Him). *Fain would they extinguish Allah's light with their mouths, but Allah will not allow but that His light should be perfected, even though the Unbelievers may detest (it). It is He Who hath sent His Messenger with guidance and the Religion of Truth, to proclaim it over all religion, even though the Pagans may detest (it)."*

15 Hashmi: "The Quran and Tolerance: An Interpretive Essay on Verse 5:48," p. 95. *Hashmi notes the consensus but himself disagrees with it.*

16 *Surah At-Taubah* verse 6. Yusuf Ali's translation: "If one amongst the Pagans ask thee for asylum, grant it to him, so that he may hear the word of Allah, and then escort him to where he can be secure. That is because they are men without knowledge."

17 If we accept the argument that the Quran never imagined that its message would one day be carried beyond Arab lands, however, that may help contain the impact of the verse to Arab polytheists only. For that, though, we would have to discard the claim that the Quran is the word of Allah meant for the entirety of mankind.

18 Hashmi: "The Quran and Tolerance: An Interpretive Essay on Verse 5:48," p. 81

19 Hashmi: "The Quran and Tolerance: An Interpretive Essay on Verse 5:48," p. 82

20 *Surah Al-Maidah* verse 48. Maududi's translation: "Then, O Muhammad, We sent this Book to you which has brought the Truth: it confirms whatever has remained intact from the Book at the time of its revelation and safeguards and protects it. Therefore you should judge between the people by the Law sent down by Allah and do not follow their desires by turning aside from the Truth that has come to you. *We prescribed a law and a way of life for each of you, though your Lord could have made all of you a single community, if He had so willed. But (He willed otherwise) in order to test you in what He has bestowed upon each of you: therefore try to excel one another in good deeds. Ultimately, you shall all return to Him; then He will let you know the truth about that in which you have been differing."*

21 Hashmi: "The Quran and Tolerance: An Interpretive Essay on Verse 5:48," p. 99

22 *Surah Al-Maidah* verses 41–43. Maududi's translation: "O Messenger, let not those who are striving hard in the way of disbelief, grieve you, whether they be from among those who say with their mouths, 'We believe,' but their hearts do not believe, or from among those who have become Jews; for the latter eagerly listen to lies. *They spy for other people who have never had any chance of coming to you: they twist the words of Allah's Book out of their context in order to distort their proper meaning: they say to the people, 'If you are enjoined to observe such and such teaching, accept it; if it is other than this, reject it.'* ... If, therefore, they come to you (with their cases), you may judge between them or refuse to do so. ... Yet, how is it that they make you their judge, when they themselves possess the Torah, in which there is Allah's judgment, and even then they are turning away from it?'" (5:41–43) Yusuf Ali's translation: "O Messenger, let not those grieve thee, who race each other into unbelief: (whether it be) among those who say 'We believe' with their lips but whose hearts have no faith; *or it be among the Jews, men who will listen to any lie, will listen even to others who have never so much as come to thee. They change the words from their (right) times and places: they say, 'If ye are given this, take it, but if not, beware!'* ... If they do come to thee, either judge between them, or decline to interfere.. ... But why do they come to thee for decision, when they have (their own) law before them? Therein is the (plain) command of Allah. Yet even after that, they would turn away."

23 *Surah At-Taubah* verses 49–51. Yusuf Ali's translation: "And this (He commands): Judge thou between them by what Allah hath revealed, and follow not their vain desires, but beware of them lest they beguile thee from any of that (teaching) which Allah hath sent down to thee. *And if they turn away, be assured that for some of their crime it is Allah's purpose to punish them. And truly most men are rebellious.* Do they then seek after a judgment of (the days of) ignorance? But who, for a people whose faith is assured, can give better judgment than Allah. *O ye who believe! take not the Jews and the Christians for your friends and protectors: They are but friends and protectors to each other. And he amongst you that turns to them (for friendship) is of them. Verily Allah guideth not a people unjust."*

24 *Surah Ar-Ra'ad* verse 39. Yusuf Ali's translation: "Allah doth blot out or confirm what He pleaseth: with Him is the Mother of the Book."

25 *Surah Al-Baqarah* verse 106. Yusuf Ali's translation: "None of Our revelations do We abrogate or cause to be forgotten, but We substitute something better or similar."

26 *Surah An-Nisa* verses 88–90. Yusuf Ali's translation: "Why should ye be divided into two parties about the Hypocrites? Allah hath upset them for their (evil) deeds. ... They but wish that ye

should reject Faith, as they do, and thus be on the same footing (as they): *But take not friends from their ranks until they flee in the way of Allah (From what is forbidden). But if they turn renegades, seize them and slay them wherever ye find them; and (in any case) take no friends or helpers from their ranks;* Except those who join a group between whom and you there is a treaty (of peace), or those who approach you with hearts restraining them from fighting you as well as fighting their own people."

27 *Surah At-Tahrim* verse 9. Yusuf Ali's translation: "O Prophet! Strive hard against the Unbelievers and the Hypocrites, and be firm against them. Their abode is Hell, an evil refuge (indeed)."

29 Hashmi. "The Quran and Tolerance: An Interpretive Essay on Verse 5:48," p. 97

Chapter 8: The Jews of Medina

1 *Rehmat-ulil-Alimeen*! (*Surah Al-Anbiyaa* verse 107). Yusuf Ali's translation: "We sent thee not, but as a Mercy for all creatures."

2 *Surah Al-Imran* verse 199, *Surah Bani Israil* verse 107, *Surah Ash Shuaraa* verse 197, and *Surah Al-Qasas* verse 52. Maududi's translations: "And there are some even among the people of the Book, who believe in Allah and in the Book which has been sent down to you and in the Scripture which was sent down to themselves before this." (3:199); "O Muhammad, say to these people, 'Whether you believe in it or not, those who were given the knowledge before this, fall prostrate on their faces when it is recited to them.'" (17:107); "Is it not a Sign for the people (of Makkah) that the learned men of the Children of Israel know it?" (26:197). "The people whom We gave the Book before this, believe in this (Qur'an)." (28:52) Yusuf Ali's translations: "And there are, certainly, among the People of the Book, those who believe in Allah, in the revelation to you, and in the revelation to them, bowing in humility to Allah.", "Say. 'Whether ye believe in it or not, it is true that those who were given knowledge beforehand, when it is recited to them, fall down on their faces in humble prostration.'"; "Is it not a Sign to them that the Learned of the Children of Israel knew it (as true)?"; "Those to whom We sent the Book before this, they do believe in this (revelation)."

3 *Surah Yunus* verse 94. Yusuf Ali's translation: "If thou wert in doubt as to what We have revealed unto thee, then ask those who have been reading the Book from before thee:"

4 As noted, for instance, in *Surah Al-Ankabut* verse 46. Maududi's translation: "And do not dispute with the people of the Book except in the best manner, save with those who are wicked among them and say to them, 'We have believed in that which has been sent down to us as well as in that which had been sent down to you. Our God and your God is One, and to Him we have surrendered (as Muslims). (O Prophet,)'." (29:46) Yusuf Ali's translation: "And dispute ye not with the People of the Book, except with means better (than mere disputation), unless it be with those of them who inflict wrong (and injury): but say, 'We believe in the revelation which has come down to us and in that which came down to you; Our Allah and your Allah is one; and it is to Him we bow (in Islam)'."

5 For instance, *Surah Al-Ankabut* verse 27. Maududi's translation: "And We bestowed on him (children like) Isaac and Jacob, and placed in his progeny the Prophethood and the Book, and give him his reward in, this world, and in the Hereafter he will surely be among the righteous." (29:27) Yusuf Ali's translation: "And We gave (Abraham) Isaac and Jacob, and ordained among his progeny Prophethood and Revelation, and We granted him his reward in this life; and he was in the Hereafter (of the company) of the Righteous."
Ismail's omission can also be noted in verses 19:49–50 and 38:45–46.

6 *Surah As-Saaffat* verses 99–113

7 *Surah Al-Baqarah* verse 125 may be referred to.

8 *Surah Al-Baqarah* verse 144. Maududi's translation: "We have seen you (O Muhammad), turning your face over and over again towards Heaven. Now, therefore, We turn you towards the qiblah that you like best: so turn your face towards the Masjid Haram. Henceforth, wheresoever you may be, turn your face at prayer towards it." (2:144) Yusuf Ali's translation: "We see the turning of thy face (for guidance to the heavens: now Shall We turn thee to a Qibla that shall please thee. Turn then Thy face in the direction of the sacred Mosque: Wherever ye are, turn your faces in that direction."

9 *Surah Al-Maidah* verse 51. Yusuf Ali's translation: "O ye who believe! take not the Jews and the Christians for your friends and protectors: They are but friends and protectors to each other. And he amongst you that turns to them (for friendship) is of them. Verily Allah guideth not a

people unjust." That this was revealed on the occasion of banishment of Bani Qaynuqa is noted, for instance, by Ibn Ishaq (see *The Life of Muhammad*, p. 363).

10 Ibn Ishaq: *The Life of Muhammad*, pp. 231–232

11 Ibn Ishaq: *The Life of Muhammad*, pp. 232–233

12 *Surah Al-Anfal* verses 55–59. Yusuf Ali's translation: "For the worst of beasts in the sight of Allah are *those who reject Him*. They will not believe. They are *those with whom thou didst make a covenant, but they break their covenant* every time, and they have not the fear (of Allah). If ye gain the mastery over them in war, disperse, with them, those who follow them, that they may remember. If thou fearest treachery from any group, throw back (their covenant) to them, (so as to be) on equal terms: for Allah loveth not the treacherous. Let not the unbelievers think that they can get the better (of the godly): they will never frustrate (them)."

13 Ibn Ishaq: *The Life of Muhammad*, p. 751

14 Armstrong: *Muhammad: A Biography of the Prophet*, pp. 184–185

15 This is corroborated by *Surah Al-Maidah* verse 11. Maududi's translation: "O Believers, recall to mind the favor which Allah has (recently) shown to you: when some people intended to do harm to you, Allah restrained their hands from you. Fear Allah in whatever you do for the Believers should put their trust in Allah alone." (5:11) Yusuf Ali's translation: "O ye who believe! Call in remembrance the favour of Allah unto you when certain men formed the design to stretch out their hands against you, but ((Allah)) held back their hands from you: so fear Allah. And on Allah let believers put (all) their trust."

16 *Surah Al-Hashr* verses 2–4. Maududi's translation: "He it is Who drove the disbelievers from among the people of the Book out of their houses at the very first assault. ... *All this happened because they resisted Allah and His Messenger*, and whoever resists Allah (should know that) Allah is stern in inflicting punishment." (59:2–4) Yusuf Ali's translation: "It is He Who got out the Unbelievers among the People of the Book from their homes at the first gathering (of the forces). ... *That is because they resisted Allah and His Messenger* and if any one resists Allah, verily Allah is severe in Punishment."

17 *Surah Al-Hashr* verses 6–7. Maududi's translation: "And the properties that Allah took out from their possession and restored to His Messenger, are not such that you might have rushed your horses and camels upon them, but Allah gives His Messengers authority over whomever He wills, and Allah has power over everything. Whatever Allah restored to His Messenger from the people of the settlements, belongs to Allah and the Messenger and the kinsfolk and the orphans and the needy and the wayfarers." (59:6–7) Yusuf Ali's translation is noted in Chapter 3.

18 Maududi: *The Meaning of the Qur'an*, opening commentary to *Surah Al-Ahzab*, Volume 4, p. 63. This account is somewhat shortened.

19 Maududi: *The Meaning of the Qur'an*, opening commentary to *Surah Al-Ahzab*, Volume 4, pp. 63–64. This account is somewhat shortened.

20 *Surah Al-Ahzab* verse 9. Maududi's translation: "O people who have believed! Remember the bounty of Allah, which He has (just now) shown you. When the hosts came down on you, We sent against them a violent wind and the armies which you could not see. Allah was watching all that you were doing." (33:9) Yusuf Ali's translation: "O ye who believe! Remember the Grace of Allah, (bestowed) on you, when there came down on you hosts (to overwhelm you): But We sent against them a hurricane and forces that ye saw not: but Allah sees (clearly) all that ye do."

21 As noted by Maududi:

> After this, only one alternative remained with the disbelievers: to incite the Jewish tribe of *Bani Quraizah*, who inhabited the south eastern part of the city, to rebellion. As the Muslims had entered a treaty with them that in case of an attack on Madinah they would defend the city along with them, *the Muslims had made no defensive arrangement there and had even sent their families to take shelter in the forts situated on that side.* (*The Meaning of the Qur'an*, opening commentary to *Surah Al-Ahzab*, Volume 4, p. 64)

22 *Surah Al-Ahzab* verses 10–11. Maududi's translation: "When the enemies came upon you from above and from below you? When eyes were petrified due to fear and the hearts leapt up to the throats, and you began to entertain all sorts of doubts about Allah, the believers then were thoroughly tested and severely shaken." (33:10–11) Yusuf Ali's translation: "Behold! they came on you from above you and from below you, and behold, the eyes became dim and the hearts gaped up to the throats, and ye imagined various (vain) thoughts about Allah. In that situation were the Believers tried: they were shaken as by a tremendous shaking."

23 Ibn Ishaq records:

The enemy of God Huyayy b. Akhtab al-Nadri went out to Ka'b b. Asad al-Qurazi who had made a treaty with the apostle. When Ka'b heard of Huyayy's coming he shut the door of this fort in his face, and when he asked permission to enter he refused to see him, saying he was a man of ill omen and that he himself was in treaty with Muhammad and did not intend to go back on his word because he had always found him loyal and faithful. Then Huyayy accused him of shutting him out because he was unwilling to let him eat his corn. This so enraged him that he opened his door. He said, "Good heavens, Ka'b, I have brought you immortal fame and great army. I have come with Quraysh with their leaders and chiefs ... and Ghatafan with their leaders and chiefs. ... They have made a firm commitment and promised me that they will not depart until we have made an end of Muhammad and his men." Ka'b said: "By God, you have brought me immortal shame and an empty cloud which has shed its water while it thunders and lightens with nothing in it. Woe to you Huyayy leave me (T. and Muhammad) as I am, for I have always found him loyal and faithful." (*The Life of Muhammad*, p. 453)

24 Ibn Ishaq: *The Life of Muhammad*, p. 459. The full account leading up to this:

As God has described, the apostle and his companions remained in fear and difficulty when the enemy came on them from above and below. Then Nu'aym b. Masu'd came to the apostle saying that he had become a Muslim though his own people did not know of it, and let him give him what orders he would. The apostle said: "You are only one man among us, so go and awake distrust among the enemy to draw them off us, for war is deceit". Thereupon Nu'aym went off to B. Qurayza with whom he had been a boon companion in heathen days, and reminded them of his affection for them and of the special tie between them. When they admitted that they did not suspect him he said: "Quraysh and Ghatafan are not like you: the land is your land, your property, your wives and your children are in it; you cannot leave it and go somewhere else. Now Quraysh and Ghatafan have come to fight Muhammad and his companions and you have aided them against him, but their land, their property, and their wives are not here, so they are not like you. If they see an opportunity they will make the most of it; but if things go badly they will go back on their own and leave you to face the man in your country and you will not be able to do so if you are left alone. So do not fight along with these people until you take hostages from their chiefs who will remain in your hands as security that they will fight Muhammad with you until you make an end of him". The Jews said that this was an excellent advice. (Ibn Ishaq: *The Life of Muhammad*, pp. 458–459)

25 Ibn Ishaq reports:

Huyayy kept on wheeling Ka'b until at last he gave way in giving him a solemn promise that if Quraysh and Ghatafan left without having killed Muhammad he would enter his fort with him and await his fate. Thus Ka'b broke his promise and cut loose from the bond that was between him and the apostle. ... When the apostle and the Muslims heard of this ... the situation became serious and fear was everywhere. ... It reached such a point that Aus b. Qayzi said to the apostle, "Our houses are exposed to the enemy"—this he said before a large gathering of his people—"so let us go and return to our home, for it is outside Medina." The apostle and the polytheists remained twenty days and more, nearly a month, without fighting except for some shooting with arrows, and the siege. (*The Life of Muhammad*, pp. 453–454)

26 *Surah Al-Ahzab* verses 12–15. Yusuf Ali's translation: "And behold! The Hypocrites and those in whose hearts is a disease (even) say: '(Allah) and His Messenger promised us nothing but delusion!' Behold! A party among them said: 'Ye men of Yathrib! ye cannot stand (the attack)! therefore go back!' *And a band of them ask for leave of the Prophet, saying, 'Truly our houses are bare and exposed,' though they were not exposed they intended nothing but to run away. And if an entry had been effected to them from the sides of the (city), and they had been incited to sedition, they would certainly have brought it to pass, with none but a brief delay!* And yet they had already covenanted with Allah not to turn their backs, and a covenant with Allah must (surely) be answered for."

27 One incident recorded by Muslim historians may be mentioned, though:

Safiya d. Abdul Muttalib was in Fari, the fort of Hassan b. Thabit. She said: "Hassan was with us there with the women and children, when a Jew came along and began to go round the fort. ... I told Hassan that he could see this Jew going round the fort and I feared that he would discover our weakness and inform the Jews who were in our rear while the apostle and his companions were too occupied to help us, so he must go down and kill him. 'God forgive you', he said, 'You know quite well that I am not the man to do that.' When he said that and I saw that no help was to be expected from him I girded myself [fastened my veil] and took a club, and went down to him from the fort above and hit him with the club until I killed him. This done I went back to the fort and told Hassan to go down and strip him: I could not do it myself because he was a man. He said, 'I have no need to strip him, Bint Abdul-Muttalib.'" (Ibn Ishaq: *The Life of Muhammad*, p. 458)

It is open to debate whether the Jewish man was there to spy on the believers (these were Jewish quarters, after all, and his presence there was quite natural). Moreover, it is noteworthy that despite such provocation on the part of the believers, there is no suggestion that the Jews reciprocated by fighting alongside the enemy. The latter point is not only conceded by Muslim historians but also fully corroborated by the Quran, as noted above.

28   Ibn Ishaq: *The Life of Muhammad*, pp. 461–464. A fuller version follows:
      At the time of noon prayers Gabriel came to the apostle wearing an embroidered turban and riding on a mule with a saddle covered with a piece of brocade. He asked the apostle if he had abandoned fighting, and when he said that he had he said that the angels had not yet laid aside their arms and that he had just come from pursuing the enemy. "God commands you, Muhammad, to go to B. Qurayza. I am about to go to them to shake their stronghold." The prophet ordered it to be announced that none should perform the afternoon prayer until after he reached B. Qurayza. ... When the apostle approached their forts he said, "You brothers of monkeys, has God disgraced you and brought His vengeance upon you?" They replied, "O Abul-Qasim, you are not a barbarous person." ... The apostle besieged them for twenty-five nights until they were sore pressed and God cast terror into their hearts. ... Then they sent to the apostle saying, "Send us Abu Lababa that we may consult him." So the apostle sent him to them ... They said, "Oh Abu Lababa, do you think that we should submit to Muhammad's judgment?" He said, "Yes", and pointed with his hand to his throat, signifying slaughter. ... In the morning they submitted to the apostle's judgment and al-Aus leapt up and said, "O Apostle, they are our allies, not allies of Khazraj, and you know how you recently treated the allies of our brethren." ... So when al-Aus spoke thus the apostle said: "Will you be satisfied, O Aus, if one of your own number pronounces judgment on them?" When they agreed he said that Sa'd b. Muadh was the man. ... When Sa'd reached the apostle and the Muslims the apostle told them to get up to greet their leader. ... Sa'd asked, "Do you covenant by Allah that you accept the judgment I pronounce on them?" They said Yes, and he said, "And is it incumbent on the one who is here?" (looking) in the direction of the apostle not mentioning him out of respect, and the apostle answered Yes. Sa'd said, "Then I give judgment that the men should be killed, the property divided, and the women and children taken as captives." ... The apostle said to Sa'd, "You have given the judgment of Allah above the seven heavens."

29   Ibn Ishaq: *The Life of Muhammad*, p. 464

30   *Surah Al-Ahzab* verses 25–27. Yusuf Ali's translation: "And Allah turned back the Unbelievers for (all) their fury: no advantage did they gain; and enough is Allah for the believers in their fight. And Allah is full of Strength, able to enforce His Will. *And those of the People of the Book who aided them—Allah did take them down from their strongholds and cast terror into their hearts. (So that) some ye slew, and some ye made prisoners.* And He made you heirs of their lands, their houses, and their goods, and of a land which ye had not frequented (before). And Allah has power over all things."

31   This is according to Maududi's translation, at least.

32   Ibn Ishaq: *The Life of Muhammad*, p. 466

33   Maududi: *The Meaning of the Qur'an*, note 8 to *Surah Muhammad*, Volume 5, p. 13

34   *Surah Al-Baqarah* verses 204-205. Yusuf Ali's translation: "Yet is he the most contentious of enemies. When he turns his back, His aim everywhere is to spread mischief through the earth and destroy crops and cattle. But Allah loveth not mischief."

35   Maududi: *The Meaning of the Qur'an*, note 8 to *Surah Muhammad*, Volume 5, p. 17

36   Ibn Ishaq: *The Life of Muhammad*, p. 465

37   Armstrong: *Muhammad: A Biography of the Prophet*, p. 208

38   Weatherford: *Genghis Khan and the Making of the Modern World*

39 *Surah Al-Anbiyaa* verse 107, Yusuf Ali's translation

Chapter 9: The Glorious Quran

1 *Surah Al-Hijr* verse 87. Yusuf Ali's translation: "And We have bestowed upon thee ... the Grand Quran."

2 *Surah Al-Baqarah* verse 23. Yusuf Ali's translation: "And if ye are in doubt as to what We have revealed from time to time to Our servant, then produce a Sura like thereunto; and call your witnesses or helpers (If there are any) besides Allah, if your (doubts) are true." The same challenge is also contained in *Surah Yusuf* verse 38.

3 *Surah Bani Israel* verse 88. Maududi's translation: "Declare this, 'Even if human beings and jinns should cooperate with one another *to bring forth a book like the Qur'an*, they will never be able to bring anything like it, even though all of them help one another'." (17:88) Yusuf Ali's translation: "Say: 'If the whole of mankind and Jinns were to gather together *to produce the like of this Quran*, they could not produce the like thereof, even if they backed up each other with help and support'."

4 *Surah At-Tur* verses 33–34. Maududi's translation: "Do they say, 'This man himself has forged this Qur'an'. The fact is that they do not want to believe. Let them then produce *a discourse like it*, if they are true in what they say." (52:33–34) Yusuf Ali's translation: "Or do they say, 'He fabricated the (Message)'? Nay, they have no faith! Let them then produce *a recital like unto it*, If (it be) they speak the truth!"

5 *Surah Hud* verse 13. Maududi's translation: "Do they say, 'He has invented the Book himself?' Say to them 'Very well, if it is so, bring *ten fabricated Surahs like this*'." (11:13) Yusuf Ali's translation: "Or they may say, 'He forged it,' Say, 'Bring ye then *ten suras forged, like unto it*'."

6 *Surah Ar-Rahman* verses 31–45. Yusuf Ali's translation: "Soon shall We settle your affairs, O both ye worlds! Then which of the favours of your Lord will ye deny? O ye assembly of Jinns and men! If it be ye can pass beyond the zones of the heavens and the earth, pass ye! not without authority shall ye be able to pass! Then which of the favours of your Lord will ye deny? On you will be sent (O ye evil ones twain!) a flame of fire (to burn) and a smoke (to choke): no defence will ye have: Then which of the favours of your Lord will ye deny? When the sky is rent asunder, and it becomes red like ointment: Then which of the favours of your Lord will ye deny? On that Day no question will be asked of man or Jinn as to his sin. Then which of the favours of your Lord will ye deny? (For) the sinners will be known by their marks: and they will be seized by their forelocks and their feet. Then which of the favours of your Lord will ye deny? This is the Hell which the Sinners deny: In its midst and in the midst of boiling hot water will they wander round! Then which of the favours of your Lord will ye deny?"

7 *Surah Al-Aaraf* verses 175–176. Yusuf Ali's translation: "Relate to them the story of the man to whom We sent Our signs, but he passed them by: ... His similitude is that of a dog: if you attack him, he lolls out his tongue, or if you leave him alone, he (still) lolls out his tongue. That is the similitude of those who reject Our signs; So relate the story; perchance they may reflect."

8 *Surah Al-Baqarah* verse 185. Maududi's translation: "... *this Book is a perfect guidance for mankind and consists of clear teachings* which show the right way and are a criterion of Truth and falsehood." (2:185) Yusuf Ali's translation: "... *the Qur'an, as a guide to mankind, also clear (Signs)* for guidance and judgment (Between right and wrong)."

9 Respectively, *Surah Hud* verse 114, *Surah Bani Israel* verses 78–79, *Surah Ta Ha* verse 130, *Surah Ar-Rum* verses 17–18, *Surah At-Tur* verses 48–49, and *Surah Al-Insan* verses 25–26. Yusuf Ali's translations: "And establish regular prayers at the two ends of the day and at the approaches of the night."; "Establish regular prayers—at the sun's decline till the darkness of the night, and the morning prayer and reading: for the prayer and reading in the morning carry their testimony. And pray in the small watches of the morning: (it would be) an additional prayer (or spiritual profit) for thee: soon will thy Lord raise thee to a Station of Praise and Glory!"; "Therefore be patient with what they say, and celebrate (constantly) the praises of thy Lord, before the rising of the sun, and before its setting; yea, celebrate them for part of the hours of the night, and at the sides of the day: that thou mayest have (spiritual) joy."; "So (give) glory to Allah, when ye reach eventide and when ye rise in the morning; Yea, to Him be praise, in the heavens and on earth; and in the late afternoon and when the day begins to decline."; "Now await in patience the command of thy Lord: for verily thou art in Our eyes: and celebrate the praises of thy Lord the

while thou standest forth, And for part of the night also praise thou Him,—and at the retreat of the stars!"; "And celebrate the name of thy Lord morning and evening, And part of the night, prostrate thyself to Him; and glorify Him a long night through."

10   Abou El Fadl: *The Great Theft*, pp. 117–118: "Muslims are required to perform five formal ritual prayers a day. Shi'I Muslims perform the same five prayers, but instead of doing them five separate times, they perform them three separate times during the day."

11   *Surah As-Saff* verse 6. Yusuf Ali's translation: "But when he came to them with Clear Signs, they said, *'this is evident sorcery!'*"

12   *Surah Al-Ahqaf* verse 7. Yusuf Ali's translation: "When Our Clear Signs are rehearsed to them, the Unbelievers say, of the Truth when it comes to them: *'This is evident sorcery!'*"

13   Maududi: *The Meaning of the Qur'an*, note 8 to *Surah Al-Ahqaf*, Volume 4, p. 655

14   *Surah Al-Ahqaf* verses 7–8. Yusuf Ali's translation: "When Our Clear Signs are rehearsed to them, the Unbelievers say, of the Truth when it comes to them: *'This is evident sorcery!'* Or do they say, *'He has forged it'?* Say: 'Had I forged it, then can ye obtain no single (blessing) for me from Allah. He knows best of that whereof ye talk (so glibly)! Enough is He for a witness between me and you! And he is Oft-Forgiving, Most Merciful.'"

15   Maududi: *The Meaning of the Qur'an*, note 9 to *Surah As-Saff*, Volume 5, p. 511

16   *Surah Al-Anfal* verse 31. Also relevant are *Surah An-Nahl* verse 24 and *Surah Al-Anaam* verse 93. Maududi's translations: "And when they are asked, 'What is it that your Lord has sent down?' they say these are mere fairy tales of the ancients." (16:24); "And who could be more wicked than the one who invents a falsehood about Allah or says, 'A Revelation has come to me,' whereas no Revelation has come to him, *or says, 'I will also send down the like of what God has sent down?'*" (6:93). Yusuf Ali's translations: "When Our Signs are rehearsed to them, they say: 'We have heard this (before): if we wished, we could say (words) like these: these are nothing but tales of the ancients.'"; "When it is said to them, 'What is it that your Lord has revealed?' they say, 'Tales of the ancients!'"; "Who can be more wicked than one who inventeth a lie against Allah, or saith, 'I have received inspiration,' when he hath received none, *or (again) who saith, 'I can reveal the like of what Allah hath revealed'?*"

17   *Surah As-Saaffat* verses 34–37, for instance. Maududi's translation: "These were the people that when it was said to them, 'There is no god but Allah,' they were puffed up with pride and would say, 'Should we give up our gods for the sake of a *mad poet?*' Whereas he had come with the Truth and had confirmed the Messengers." (37:34–37) Yusuf Ali's translation: "Verily that is how We shall deal with Sinners. For they, when they were told that there is no god except Allah, would puff themselves up with Pride, And say: 'What! shall we give up our gods for the sake of a *Poet possessed?*' Nay! he has come with the (very) Truth, and he confirms (the Message of) the apostles (before him)."

18   *Surah Al-Anbiyaa* verse 5. Maududi's translation: "Then, they say, 'It is a bundle of incoherent dreams: nay, he himself has invented it: nay, he is a poet'." (21:5) Yusuf Ali's translation: "'Nay,' they say, '(these are) medleys of dream!—Nay, He forged it!—Nay, He is (but) a poet!'"

19   *Surah Al-Adiyat* verses 1–11. Yusuf Ali's translation: "By the (Steeds) that run, with panting (breath), And strike sparks of fire, And push home the charge in the morning, And raise the dust in clouds the while, And penetrate forthwith into the midst (of the foe) en masse; Truly man is, to his Lord, ungrateful; And to that (fact) he bears witness (by his deeds); And violent is he in his love of wealth. Does he not know, when that which is in the graves is scattered abroad. And that which is (locked up) in (human) breasts is made manifest. That their Lord had been Well-acquainted with them, (even to) that Day?"

20   *Surah At-Taubah* verses 124–125. Yusuf Ali's translation: "Whenever there cometh down a sura, some of them say: 'Which of you has had His faith increased by it?' Yea, those who believe, their faith is increased and they do rejoice. But those in whose hearts is a disease, it will add doubt to their doubt, and they will die in a state of Unbelief."

21   *Surah Al-Anfal* verses 20–22. Maududi's translation: "O Believers ... do not be like those who said, 'We have heard,' but have not listened to it, for the vilest beasts in Allah's sight are those deaf, dumb people *who do not use commonsense.*" (8:20–22) Yusuf Ali's translation: "O ye who believe! ... Nor be like those who say, 'We hear,' but listen not: For the worst of beasts in the sight of Allah are the deaf and the dumb, *those who understand not.*" Some other instances of the Quran's appeal to common sense can be noted in *Surah Yunus* verses 16 and 100 and *Surah An-Noor* verse 61.

22   *Surah Al-Jinn* verses 1–9. Maududi's translation: "O Prophet, say: It has been revealed to me that a company of the jinn listened, then (returning to their folks) they said, 'We have indeed heard a wonderful Qur'an which guides to the right way, so we have believed in it, and now we shall never associate anyone with our Lord.' … And that: 'We searched the heavens and found it filled with guards and shooting-stars.' And that: 'Before this we used to find a seat in heaven for eavesdropping, but now if some one tries to eavesdrop, he finds a shooting-star lying in ambush for him.'" (72:1–9) Yusuf Ali's translation: "Say: It has been revealed to me that a company of Jinns listened (to the Qur'an). They said, 'We have really heard a wonderful Recital! It gives guidance to the Right, and we have believed therein: we shall not join (in worship) any (gods) with our Lord. … And we pried into the secrets of heaven; but we found it filled with stern guards and flaming fires. We used, indeed, to sit there in (hidden) stations, to (steal) a hearing; but any who listen now will find a flaming fire watching him in ambush'."

23   *Surah As-Saaffat* verses 6–10. Maududi's translation: "We have adorned the lower heaven with the adornment of the stars and have secured it against every rebel satan. These satans cannot hear the words of the exalted ones; they are darted at and driven off from every side, and for them there is a perpetual torment. However, if some one snatches away something, a flashing flame follows him." (37:6–10) Yusuf Ali's translation: "We have indeed decked the lower heaven with beauty (in) the stars, (For beauty) and for guard against all obstinate rebellious evil spirits, (So) they should not strain their ears in the direction of the Exalted Assembly but be cast away from every side, Repulsed, for they are under a perpetual penalty, Except such as snatch away something by stealth, and they are pursued by a flaming fire, of piercing brightness."

24   *Surah Al-Baqarah* verses 101–103. Maududi's translation: "And whenever a Messenger came to them from Allah, confirming that Scripture which they already possessed, some from among the people of the Book threw the Book of Allah behind their backs as though they knew nothing about it. (Instead of this,) they began to follow that (magic) to which the devils falsely attributed (the greatness of) the kingdom of Solomon. In fact Solomon was never involved in any practice of disbelief, but the satans, who taught magic to the people were themselves guilty of disbelief. They were after that thing which was sent to Harut and Marut, the two angels at Babylon. Whenever these two angels taught black art to anyone, they would always give a clear warning beforehand, saying, 'We are merely a trial for you; so you should not commit blasphemy.' But in spite of this warning, those people used to learn from the angels the art which caused division between husband and wife. Although it was obvious that they could not do any harm to anyone by means of this magic without Allah's permission, yet they learnt that art which could not be profitable even for them but was actually harmful. Moreover, they knew it full well that anyone, who purchased that art, would have no share in the Hereafter." (2:101–103) Yusuf Ali's translation: "And when there came to them an apostle from Allah, confirming what was with them, a party of the people of the Book threw away the Book of Allah behind their backs, as if (it had been something) they did not know! They followed what the evil ones gave out (falsely) against the power of Solomon: the blasphemers Were, not Solomon, but the evil ones, teaching men Magic, and such things as came down at babylon to the angels Harut and Marut. But neither of these taught anyone (Such things) without saying: 'We are only for trial; so do not blaspheme.' They learned from them the means to sow discord between man and wife. But they could not thus harm anyone except by Allah's permission. And they learned what harmed them, not what profited them. And they knew that the buyers of (magic) would have no share in the happiness of the Hereafter. And vile was the price for which they did sell their souls, if they but knew! If they had kept their Faith and guarded themselves from evil, far better had been the reward from their Lord, if they but knew!"

25   Maududi: *The Meaning of the Qur'an*, commentary to *Surah Al-Falaq*, Volume 6, pp. 650–652

26   *Surah Al-Imran* verse 18. Yusuf Ali's translation: "There is no god but He: That is the witness of Allah …"

27   *Surah Al-Baqarah* verses 91–93. Yusuf Ali's translation: "When it is said to them, 'Believe in what Allah Hath sent down,' they say, 'We believe in what was sent down to us:' yet they reject all besides, even if it be Truth confirming what is with them. *Say: 'Why then have ye slain the prophets of Allah in times gone by, if ye did indeed believe?'* There came to you Moses with clear (Signs); yet ye worshipped the calf (Even) after that, and ye did behave wrongfully. And remember We took your covenant and We raised above you (the towering height) of Mount (Sinai): (Saying): 'Hold firmly to what We have given you, and hearken (to the Law)'. They said: 'We hear, and we

disobey:' And they had to drink into their hearts (of the taint) of the calf because of their Faithlessness. Say: 'Vile indeed are the behests of your Faith if ye have any faith!'"

28   It seems that they were not alone in being blamed for sins they did not commit. Consider *Surah Al-Maidah* verse 14 (Maududi's translation): "Likewise We bound by a covenant those people, who said, 'We are Nasara.' But they too, forgot much of what had been taught to them. *So We sowed among them seeds of discord, enmity and hatred that shall last up to the Day of Resurrection*, and surely the time will come when Allah will tell them of what they had been contriving in the world." (5:14) Why should subsequent generations have been made to suffer for sins committed by those ahead of them? Yusuf Ali's translation: "From those, too, who call themselves Christians, We did take a covenant, but they forgot a good part of the message that was sent them: *so we estranged them, with enmity and hatred between the one and the other, to the day of judgment*. And soon will Allah show them what it is they have done."

29   *Surah Bani Israel* verse 15. Yusuf Ali's translation: "No bearer of burdens can bear the burden of another."

30   *Surah An-Nisa* verse 140. Yusuf Ali's translation: "Already has He sent you Word in the Book, that when ye hear the *signs of Allah held in defiance and ridicule*, ye are not to sit with them unless they turn to a different theme: if ye did, ye would be like them. For Allah will collect the hypocrites and those who defy faith—all in Hell."

31   *Surah Al-Baqarah* verses 274–281. Yusuf Ali's translation: "Those who (in charity) spend of their goods by night and by day, in secret and in public, have their reward with their Lord: on them shall be no fear, nor shall they grieve. *Those who devour usury will not stand except as stand one whom the Evil one by his touch Hath driven to madness. That is because they say: 'Trade is like usury,' but Allah hath permitted trade and forbidden usury. Those who after receiving direction from their Lord, desist, shall be pardoned for the past; their case is for Allah (to judge); but those who repeat (The offence) are companions of the Fire: They will abide therein (for ever). Allah will deprive usury of all blessing, but will give increase for deeds of charity.* For He loveth not creatures ungrateful and wicked. Those who believe, and do deeds of righteousness, and establish regular prayers and regular charity, will have their reward with their Lord: on them shall be no fear, nor shall they grieve. *O ye who believe! Fear Allah, and give up what remains of your demand for usury, if ye are indeed believers. If ye do it not, Take notice of war from Allah and His Messenger. But if ye turn back, ye shall have your capital sums: Deal not unjustly, and ye shall not be dealt with unjustly.* If the debtor is in a difficulty, grant him time Till it is easy for him to repay. But if ye remit it by way of charity, that is best for you if ye only knew. And fear the Day when ye shall be brought back to Allah. Then shall every soul be paid what it earned, and none shall be dealt with unjustly."

Chapter 10: The "Satanic" Verses

1   *Surah Al-Hajj*, verse 52. Yusuf Ali's translation appears later in the chapter.

2   Esposito: *The Oxford Dictionary of Islam*, p. 563

3   Hashmi: "The Quran and Tolerance: An Interpretive Essay on Verse 5:48," p. 87

4   Ibn Ishaq: *The Life of Muhammad*, p. 62

5   *Surah Al-Fil* verses 1–5. Yusuf Ali's translation: "Seest thou not how thy Lord dealt with the Companions of the Elephant? Did He not make their treacherous plan go astray? And He sent against them Flights of Birds, Striking them with stones of baked clay. Then did He make them like an empty field of stalks and straw, (of which the corn) has been eaten up."

6   Reza Aslan: *No God but God*, p. 178

7   According to other accounts, however, it was struck and broken into pieces by a stone fired from a catapult at the time of the Umayyad siege of Mecca in 756, and according to yet other accounts, this happened after the stone was stolen in 930 by a Bahraini tribe.

8   Respectively, *Surah Al-Ankabut* verses 61–63 and *Surah Az-Zumar* verse 38. Yusuf Ali's translations: "If indeed thou ask them who has created the heavens and the earth and subjected the sun and the moon (to his Law), *they will certainly reply, '(Allah)'*. How are they then deluded away (from the truth)? ... And if indeed thou ask them who it is that sends down rain from the sky, and gives life therewith to the earth after its death, *they will certainly reply, '(Allah)!'*"; "If indeed thou ask them who it is that created the heavens and the earth, they would be sure to say, '(Allah)'." The same message is also expressed in *Surah Yunus* verse 31 (10:31) and *Surah Al-Muminoon* verses 86-92 (23:86-92).

9   *Surah Yunus* verse 18. Yusuf Ali's translation: "They serve, besides Allah, things that hurt them not nor profit them, and they say: *'These are our intercessors with Allah'*."

10   *Surah Az-Zumar* verse 3. Yusuf Ali's translation: "But those who take for protectors other than Allah (say): *'We only serve them in order that they may bring us nearer to Allah.'* Truly Allah will judge between them in that wherein they differ."

11   As in *Surah Al-Imran* verse 151. Maududi's translation: "The time is coming when We will cast awe into the hearts of the rejecters of the Truth: *this is because they have set up with Allah partners*, for whom He has sent no authority." (3:151) Yusuf Ali's translation: "Soon shall We cast terror into the hearts of the Unbelievers, *for that they joined companions with Allah*, for which He had sent no authority."

12   That they did not concede the charge is demonstrated by *Surah Al-Anaam* verses 22–24. Maududi's translation: "On the Day, when We muster them all together, We shall ask the *mushrikin*, 'Where are now your associates whom you had taken for your deities?' Then they shall not be able to play any other trick (than make this false statement): *'We swear by You, our Lord, we were not at all*_mushrikin.' Behold, how they will invent a lie against themselves and how all the false gods, they had forged, will forsake them!" (6:22–24). Also *Surah An Nahl* verse 28-29: "Yes, this is for those *disbelievers*, who, while they are still engaged in wronging themselves, shall surrender themselves when seized by the angels, saying, *'We were doing nothing wrong at all.'* The angels will retort, 'What, dare you deny this! Allah is fully aware of what you were doing. Now, go and enter the gates of Hell, where you shall abide for ever.' The fact is that a very miserable abode it is for the haughty ones.'" (16:28–29) Yusuf Ali's translations: "One day shall We gather them all together: We shall say to those who ascribed partners (to Us): 'Where are the partners whom ye (invented and) talked about?' There will then be (left) no subterfuge for them but to say: *'By Allah our Lord, we were not those who joined gods with Allah.'* Behold! how they lie against their own souls! But the (lie) which they invented will leave them in the lurch."; "(Namely) those whose lives the angels take in a state of wrong-doing to their own souls. Then would they offer submission (with the pretence), *'We did no evil (knowingly).'* (The angels will reply), 'Nay, but verily Allah knoweth all that ye did; 'So enter the gates of Hell, to dwell therein. Thus evil indeed is the abode of the arrogant.'"

13   Ibn Ishaq: *The Life of Muhammad*, p. 165

14   Ibn Ishaq: *The Life of Muhammad*, p. 166

15   Maududi: *The Meaning of the Qur'an*, note 101 to *Surah Al-Hajj*, Volume 3, p. 222

16   Hashmi: "The Quran and Tolerance: An Interpretive Essay on Verse 5:48," p. 87

17   *Surah Al-Jinn* verses 1–2. Maududi's translation: "O Prophet, say: It has been revealed to me that a company of the jinn listened, then (returning to their folks) they said, 'We have indeed heard a wonderful Quran which guides to the right way, so we have believed in it, and now we shall never associate anyone with our Lord'." (72:1–2) Yusuf Ali's translation: "Say: It has been revealed to me that a company of Jinns listened (to the Qur'an). They said, 'We have really heard a wonderful Recital! It gives guidance to the Right, and we have believed therein: we shall not join (in worship) any (gods) with our Lord.'" The same theme is then repeated in *Surah Al-Ahqaf* verses 39–42 (46:39–42).

18   *Surah Saba* verses 22–23. Maududi's translation: "(O Prophet) say (to the Mushriks), 'Call those whom you worship as deities instead of Allah. They neither own an atom's weight of anything in the heavens nor in the earth, nor have they anything to share in either, nor is any of them a helper of Allah. *And no intercession before Allah can avail anyone except for the one for whom Allah permits it'.*" (34:22–23) Yusuf Ali's translation: "Say: 'Call upon other (gods) whom ye fancy, besides Allah. They have no power, not the weight of an atom, in the heavens or on earth: No (sort of) share have they therein, nor is any of them a helper to Allah. *No intercession can avail in His Presence, except for those for whom He has granted permission'*."

19   *Surah Bani Israel* verses 73–75. Yusuf Ali's translation: "And their purpose was to tempt thee away from that which We had revealed unto thee, *to substitute in our name something quite different;* (in that case), behold! they would certainly have made thee (their) friend! *And had We not given thee strength, thou wouldst nearly have inclined to them a little.* In that case We should have made thee taste an equal portion (of punishment) in this life, and an equal portion in death: and moreover thou wouldst have found none to help thee against Us!"

20   Rogerson: *The Prophet Muhammad*, p. 106

21   *Surah Maryam* verses 16–23. Yusuf Ali's translation: "Relate in the Book (the story of) Mary, when she withdrew from her family to a place in the East. She placed a screen (to screen herself)

from them; *then We sent her our angel, and he appeared before her as a man in all respects.* She said: 'I seek refuge from thee to ((Allah)) Most Gracious: (come not near) if thou dost fear Allah.' He said: *'Nay, I am only a messenger from thy Lord, (to announce) to thee the gift of a holy son.* She said: 'How shall I have a son, seeing that no man has touched me, and I am not unchaste?' He said: 'So (it will be): Thy Lord saith, "that is easy for Me: and (We wish) to appoint him as a Sign unto men and a Mercy from Us": It is a matter (so) decreed.' So she conceived him, and she retired with him to a remote place. *And the pains of childbirth drove her to the trunk of a palm-tree: She cried (in her anguish): 'Ah! would that I had died before this! would that I had been a thing forgotten and out of sight!'"*

22   Yusuf Ali's translation: "Such (was) Jesus the son Of Mary: (it is) a statement Of truth, about which They (vainly) dispute. It is not befitting To (the majesty of) God That He should beget A son. Glory be to Him! When He determines A matter, He only says To it, 'Be', and it is."

23   Ibn Ishaq: *The Life of Muhammad,* p. 152

24   *Surah An-Najm* verses 1–23. Yusuf Ali's translation: "By the Star when it goes down, *Your Companion is neither astray nor being misled.* Nor does he say (aught) of (his own) Desire. It is no less than inspiration sent down to him: He was taught by one Mighty in Power, Endued with Wisdom: for he appeared (in stately form); While he was in the highest part of the horizon: Then he approached and came closer, And was at a distance of but two bow-lengths or (even) nearer; So did ((Allah)) convey the inspiration to His Servant (conveyed) what He (meant) to convey. The (Prophet's) (mind and) heart in no way falsified that which he saw. *Will ye then dispute with him concerning what he saw?* For indeed he saw him at a second descent, Near the Lote-tree beyond which none may pass: Near it is the Garden of Abode. Behold, the Lote-tree was shrouded (in mystery unspeakable!) (His) sight never swerved, nor did it go wrong! For truly did he see, of the Signs of his Lord, the Greatest! 'Have ye seen Lat and 'Uzza, And another, the third (goddess), Manat? What! for you the male sex, and for Him, the female? Behold, such would be indeed a division most unfair! These are nothing but names which ye have devised, ye and your fathers, for which Allah has sent down no authority (whatever).'"

25   *Surah Al-Hajj* verses 52–54. Yusuf Ali's translation: "Never did We send an apostle or a prophet before thee, but, when he framed a desire, Satan threw some (vanity) into his desire: *but Allah will cancel anything (vain) that Satan throws in, and Allah will confirm (and establish) His Signs:* for Allah is full of Knowledge and Wisdom: That He may make the suggestions thrown in by Satan, but a trial for those in whose hearts is a disease and who are hardened of heart: verily the wrong-doers are in a schism far (from the Truth): And that those on whom knowledge has been bestowed may learn that the (Qur'an) is the Truth from thy Lord, and that they may believe therein, and their hearts may be made humbly (open) to it: for verily Allah is the Guide of those who believe, to the Straight Way."

26   Maududi (as quoted above)

27   *Surah Al-Baqarah* verse 106. Yusuf Ali's translation: "None of Our revelations do We abrogate *or cause to be forgotten,* but We substitute something better or similar."

Chapter 11: Undistracted by Religion

1   *Surah Ha Mim As Sajdah* verse 52. Yusuf Ali's translation: "Say: 'See ye if the (Revelation) is (really) from Allah, and yet do ye reject it? Who is more astray than one who is in a schism far (from any purpose)?'"

2   Respectively, *Surah At-Taubah* verse 36 and *Surah Al-Maidah* verse 2. Yusuf Ali's translations: "The number of months in the sight of Allah is twelve (in a year) so ordained by Him the day He created the heavens and the earth; *of them four are sacred:* that is the straight usage. So wrong not yourselves therein."; "O ye who believe! Violate not the sanctity of the symbols of Allah, *nor of the sacred month."*

APPENDIX

Following are translations by Hilali-Khan (**HK**) and Pickthall (**P**) of all the verses quoted in the book (except those already included in the main discussion)—in the same order as they appear in the book.

Chapter 1: The Quran Speaks

96:1–2 Read! In the Name of your Lord, Who has created (all that exists), Has created man from a clot (a piece of thick coagulated blood). (**HK**) Read: In the name of thy Lord Who createth, Createth man from a clot. (**P**)

2:99 And indeed We have sent down to you manifest *Ayat* (these Verses of the Qur'an which inform in detail about the news of the Jews and their secret intentions, etc.), and none disbelieve in them but *Fasiqun* (those who rebel against Allah's Command). (**HK**) Verily We have revealed unto thee clear tokens, and only miscreants will disbelieve in them. (**P**)

12:1 *Alif-Lam-Ra.* [These letters are one of the miracles of the Qur'an, and none but Allah (Alone) knows their meanings]. These are the Verses of the Clear Book (the Qur'an that makes clear the legal and illegal things, legal laws, a guidance and a blessing). (**HK**) Alif. Lam. Ra. These are verses of the Scripture that maketh plain. (**P**)

89:1–5 By the dawn; By the ten nights (i.e. the first ten days of the month of Dhul-Hijjah), And by the even and the odd (of all the creations of Allah). And by the night when it departs. There is indeed in them (the above oaths) sufficient proofs for men of understanding (and that, they should avoid all kinds of sins and disbeliefs, etc.)! (**HK**) By the Dawn And ten nights, And the Even and the Odd, And the night when it departeth, There surely is an oath for thinking man. (**P**)

3:7 It is He Who has sent down to you (Muhammad) the Book (this Qur'an). In it are Verses that are entirely clear, they are the foundations of the Book [and those are the Verses of *Al-Ahkam* (commandments, etc.), *Al-Fara'id* (obligatory duties) and *Al-Hudud* (legal laws for the punishment of thieves, adulterers, etc.)]; and others not entirely clear. So as for those in whose hearts there is a deviation (from the truth) they follow that which is not entirely clear thereof, seeking *Al-Fitnah* (polytheism and trials, etc.), and seeking for its hidden meanings, *but none knows its hidden meanings save Allah.* (**HK**) He it is Who hath revealed unto thee (Muhammad) the Scripture wherein are clear revelations—they are the substance of the Book—and others (which are) allegorical. But those in whose hearts is doubt pursue, forsooth, that which is allegorical seeking (to cause) dissension by seeking to explain it. *None knoweth its explanation save Allah.* (**P**)

3:105 And be not as those who divided and differed among themselves *after the clear proofs had come to them.* (**HK**) And be ye not as those who separated and disputed *after the clear proofs had come unto them.* (**P**)

5:51 O you who believe! Take not the Jews and the Christians as *Auliya'* (friends, protectors, helpers, etc.), they are but *Auliya'* to one another. And if any amongst you takes them as *Auliya'*, then surely he is one of them. Verily, Allah guides not those people who are the *Zalimun* (polytheists and wrong-doers and unjust). (**HK**) O ye who believe! Take not the Jews and the Christians for friends. They are friends one to another. He among you who taketh them for friends is (one) of them. Lo! Allah guideth not wrongdoing folk. (**P**)

3:28 Let not the believers take the disbelievers as *Auliya* (supporters, helpers, etc.) instead of the believers, and whoever does that will never be helped by Allah in any way, except if you indeed fear a danger from them. (**HK**) Let not the believers take disbelievers for their friends in preference to believers. Whoso doeth that hath no connection with Allah unless (it be) that ye but guard yourselves against them, taking (as it were) security. (**P**)

24:2 The woman and the man guilty of illegal sexual intercourse, flog each of them with a hundred stripes. Let not pity withhold you in their case, in a punishment prescribed by Allah, if you believe in Allah and the Last Day. And let a party of the believers witness their punishment. (This punishment is for unmarried persons guilty of the above crime but if married persons commit it, the punishment is to stone them to death, according to Allah's Law). (**HK**) The adulterer and the adulteress, scourge ye each one of them (with) a hundred stripes. And let not pity for the twain withhold you from obedience to Allah, if ye believe in Allah and the Last Day. And let a party of believers witness their punishment. (**P**)

9:33 It is He Who has sent His Messenger (Muhammad) with guidance and the religion of truth (Islam), to make it superior over all religions … (**HK**) He it is Who hath sent His messenger with the guidance and the Religion of Truth, that He may cause it to prevail over all religion… (**P**)

Chapter 2: The Contradictions Challenge

4:82 Do they not then consider the Qur'an carefully? Had it been from other than Allah, they would surely have found therein much contradictions. (**HK**) Will they not then ponder on the Qur'an? If it had been from other than Allah they would have found therein much incongruity. (**P**)

32:5 He arranges (every) affair from the heavens to the earth, then it (affair) will go up to Him, in one Day, the space whereof is a thousand years of your reckoning (i.e. reckoning of our present world's time). (**HK**) He directeth the ordinance from the heaven unto the earth; then it ascendeth unto Him in a Day, whereof the measure is a thousand years of that ye reckon. (**P**)

22:47 And they ask you to hasten on the torment! And Allah fails not His Promise. And verily, a day with your Lord is as a thousand years of what you reckon. (**HK**) And they will bid thee hasten on the Doom, and Allah faileth not His promise, but lo! a Day with Allah is as a thousand years of what ye reckon. (**P**)

70:1–5 A questioner asked concerning a torment about to befall Upon the disbelievers, which none can avert, From Allah, the Lord of the ways of ascent. The angels and the *Ruh* [Jibrael (Gabriel)] ascend to Him in a Day the measure whereof is fifty thousand years, So be patient (O Muhammad), with a good patience. (**HK**) A questioner questioned concerning the doom about to fall. Upon the disbelievers, which none can repel, From Allah, Lord of the Ascending Stairways. (Whereby) the angels and the Spirit ascend unto Him in a Day whereof the span is fifty thousand years. But be patient (O Muhammad) with a patience fair to see. (**P**)

2:186 And when My slaves ask you (O Muhammad) concerning Me, then (answer them), I am indeed near (to them by My Knowledge). I respond to the invocations of the supplicant when he calls on Me (without any mediator or intercessor). (**HK**) And when My servants question thee concerning Me, then surely I am nigh. I answer the prayer of the suppliant when he crieth unto Me. (**P**)

8:65 O Prophet (Muhammad)! Urge the believers to fight. If there are twenty steadfast persons amongst you, they will overcome two hundred, and if there be a hundred steadfast persons they will overcome a thousand of those who disbelieve, because they (the disbelievers) are people who do not understand. (**HK**) O Prophet! Exhort the believers to fight. If there be of you twenty steadfast they shall overcome two hundred, and if there be of you a hundred (steadfast) they shall overcome a thousand of those who disbelieve, because they (the disbelievers) are a folk without intelligence. (**P**)

8:66 Now Allah has lightened your (task), for He knows that there is weakness in you. So if there are of you a hundred steadfast persons, they shall overcome two hundred, and if there are a thousand of you, they shall overcome two thousand with the Leave of Allah. And Allah is with *As-Sabirin* (the patient ones, etc.). (**HK**) Now hath Allah lightened your burden, for He knoweth that there is weakness in you. So if there be of you a steadfast hundred they shall overcome two hundred, and if there be of you a thousand (steadfast) they shall overcome two thousand by permission of Allah. Allah is with the steadfast. (**P**)

4:12 ... If the man or woman whose inheritance is in question has left neither ascendants nor descendants, but has left a brother or a sister, each one of the two gets a sixth; but if more than two, they share in a third; after payment of legacies he (or she) may have bequeathed or debts, so that no loss is caused (to anyone). This is a Commandment from Allah; and Allah is Ever All-Knowing, Most-Forbearing. (**HK**) ... And if a man or a woman have a distant heir (having left neither parent nor child), and he (or she) have a brother or a sister (only on the mother's side) then to each of them twain (the brother and the sister) the sixth, and if they be more than two, then they shall be sharers in the third, after any legacy that may have been bequeathed or debt (contracted) not injuring (the heirs by willing away more than a third of the heritage) hath been. These are the limits (imposed by) Allah. (**P**)

4:176 They ask you for a legal verdict. Say: "Allah directs (thus) about *Al-Kalalah* (those who leave neither descendants nor ascendants as heirs). *If it is a man that dies, leaving a sister, but no child, she shall have half the inheritance. If (such a deceased was) a woman, who left no child, her brother takes her inheritance. If there are two sisters, they shall have two-thirds of the inheritance; if there are brothers and sisters, the male will have twice the share of the female.* (Thus) does Allah make clear to you (His Law) lest you go astray. And Allah is the All-Knower of everything." (**HK**) They ask thee for a pronouncement. Say: Allah hath pronounced for you concerning distant kindred. *If a man die childless and he have a sister, hers is half the heritage, and he would have inherited from her had she died childless. And if there be two sisters, then theirs are two-thirds of the heritage, and if they be brethren, men and women, unto the male is the equivalent of the share of two females.* Allah expoundeth unto you, so that ye err not. Allah is Knower of all things. (**P**)

5:101 O you who believe! Ask not about things which, if made plain to you, may cause you trouble. But if you ask about them while the Qur'an is being revealed, they will be made plain to you. (**HK**) O ye who believe! Ask not of things which, if they were made unto you, would trouble you; but if ye ask of them when the Qur'an is being revealed, they will be made known unto you. (**P**)

25:32–33 And those who disbelieve say: "Why is not the Qur'an revealed to him all at once?" Thus (it is sent down in parts), that We may strengthen your heart thereby. And We have revealed it to you gradually, in stages. (It was revealed to the Prophet in 23 years). *And no example or similitude do they bring (to oppose or to find fault in you or in this Qur'an), but We reveal to you the truth (against that similitude or example), and the better explanation thereof.* (**HK**) And those who disbelieve say: Why is the Qur'an not revealed unto him all at once? (It is revealed) thus that We may strengthen thy heart therewith; and We have arranged it in right order. *And they* *bring thee no similitude but We bring thee the Truth (as against it), and better (than their similitude) as argument.* (**P**)

41:9–12 Say (O Muhammad): "Do you verily disbelieve in Him Who created the earth in two Days and you set up rivals (in worship) with Him? That is the Lord of the *'Alamin* (mankind, jinns and all that exists). He placed therein (i.e. the earth) firm mountains from above it, and He blessed it, and measured therein its sustenance (for its dwellers) in four Days equal (i.e. all these four 'days' were equal in the length of time), for all those who ask (about its creation). *Then He Istawa (rose over) towards the heaven when it was smoke,* and said to it and to the earth: 'Come both of you willingly or unwillingly.' They both said: 'We come, willingly.' *Then He completed and finished from their creation (as) seven heavens in two Days* and He made in each heaven its affair. And We adorned the nearest (lowest) heaven with lamps (stars) to be an adornment as well as to guard (from the devils by using them as missiles against the devils). Such is the Decree of Him the All-Mighty, the All-Knower." (**HK**) Say (O Muhammad, unto the idolaters): Disbelieve ye verily in Him Who created the earth in two Days, and ascribe ye unto Him rivals? He (and none else) is the Lord of the Worlds. He placed therein firm hills rising above it, and blessed it and measured therein its sustenance in four Days, alike for (all) who ask; *Then turned He to the heaven when it was smoke,* and said unto it and unto the earth: Come both of you, willingly or loth. They said: We come, obedient. *Then He ordained them seven heavens in two Days* and inspired in each heaven its mandate; and We decked the nether heaven with lamps, and rendered it inviolable. That is the measuring of the Mighty, the Knower. (**P**)

2:29 He it is Who created for you all that is on earth. *Then He Istawa (rose over) towards the heaven and made them seven heavens ...* (**HK**) He it is Who created for you all that is in the earth. *Then turned He to the heaven, and fashioned it as seven heavens.* (**P**)

79:27–33 Are you more difficult to create, or is the heaven that He constructed? He raised its height, and He has equally ordered it, Its night He covers with darkness, and its forenoon He brings out (with light). *And after that He spread the earth;* And brought forth therefrom its water and its pasture; And the mountains He has fixed firmly; (To be) a provision and benefit for you and your cattle. (**HK**) Are ye the harder to create, or is the heaven that He built? He raised the height thereof and ordered it; And He made dark the night thereof, and He brought forth the morn thereof. *And after that He spread the earth,* And produced therefrom the water thereof and the pasture thereof, And He made fast the hills, A provision for you and for your cattle. (**P**)

15:61–72 Then, when the Messengers (the angels) came unto the family of Lout (Lot). He said. "Verily! You are people unknown to me." They said: "Nay, we have come to you with that (torment) which they have been doubting. And we have brought to you the truth (the news of the destruction of your nation) and certainly, we tell the truth. Then travel in a part of the night with your family, and you go behind them in the rear, and let no one amongst you look back, but go on to where you are ordered." And We made known this decree to him, that the root of these (sinners) was to be cut off in the early morning. And the inhabitants of the city came rejoicing (at the news of the young men's arrival). [Lout (Lot)] said: "Verily! these are my guests, so shame me not And fear Allah and disgrace me not." They (people of the city) said: "Did we not forbid you to entertain (or protect) any of the *'Alamin* (people, foreigners, strangers, etc. from us)?" [Lout (Lot)] said: "These (the girls of the nation) are my daughters (to marry lawfully), if you must act (so)." Verily, by your life (O Muhammad), in their wild intoxication, they were wandering blindly. (**HK**) And when the messengers came unto the family of Lot, He said: Lo! ye are folk unknown (to me). They said: Nay, but we bring thee that concerning which they keep disputing, And bring thee the Truth, and lo! we are truth-tellers. So travel with thy household in a portion of the night, and follow thou their backs. Let none of you turn round, but go whither ye are commanded. And We made plain the case to him, that the root of them (who did wrong) was to be cut at early morn. And the people of the city came, rejoicing at the news (of new arrivals). He said: Lo! they are my guests. Affront me not! And keep your duty to Allah, and shame me not! They said: Have we not forbidden you from (entertaining) anyone? He said: Here are my daughters, if ye must be doing (so). By thy life (O Muhammad) they moved blindly in the frenzy of approaching death. (**P**)

11:77–83 And when Our Messengers came to Lout (Lot), he was grieved on their account and felt himself straitened for them (lest the town people should approach them to commit sodomy with them). He said: "This is a distressful day." And his people came rushing towards him, and since aforetime they used to commit crimes (sodomy, etc.), he said: "O my people! Here are my daughters (i.e. the daughters of my nation), they are purer for you (if you marry them lawfully). So fear Allah and degrade me not as regards my guests! Is there not among you a single right-minded man?" They said: "Surely you know that we have neither any desire nor in need of your daughters, and indeed you know well what we want!" He said: "Would that I had strength (men) to overpower you, or that I could betake myself to some powerful support (to resist you)." *They (Messengers) said: "O Lout (Lot)! Verily, we are the Messengers from your Lord! They shall not reach you! So travel with your family in a part of the night, and let not any of you look back, but your wife (will remain behind), verily, the punishment which will afflict them, will afflict her.* Indeed, morning is their appointed time. Is not the morning near?" So when Our Commandment came, We turned (the towns of Sodom in Palestine) upside down, and rained on them stones of baked clay, piled up; Marked from your Lord, and they are not ever far from the *Zalimun* (polytheists, evil-doers, etc.). (**HK**) And when Our messengers came unto Lot, he was distressed and knew not how to protect them. He said: This is a distressful day. And his people came unto him, running towards him—and before then they used to commit abominations—He said: O my people! Here are my daughters! They are purer for you. Beware of Allah, and degrade me not in (the person of) my guests. Is there not among you any upright man? They said: Well thou knowest that we have no right to thy daughters, and well thou knowest what we want. He said: Would that I had strength to resist you or had some strong support (among you)! *(The messengers) said: O Lot! Lo! we are messengers of thy Lord; they shall not reach thee. So travel with thy people in a part of the night, and let not one of you turn round—(all) save thy wife. Lo! that which smiteth them will smite her (also).* Lo! their tryst is (for) the morning. Is not the morning nigh? So when Our commandment came to pass We overthrew (that township) and rained upon it stones of clay, one after another, Marked with fire in the providence of thy Lord (for the destruction of the wicked). And they are never far from the wrong-doers. (**P**)

2:30–34 And (remember) when your Lord said *to the angels*: "Verily, I am going to place (mankind) generations after generations on earth." They said: "Will You place therein those who will make mischief therein and shed blood,—while we glorify You with praises and thanks (Exalted be You above all that they associate with You as partners) and sanctify You." He (Allah) said: "I know that which you do not know." And He taught Adam all the names (of everything), then He showed them *to the angels* and said, "Tell Me the names of these if you are truthful." They (angels) said: "Glory be to You, we have no knowledge except what you have taught us. Verily, it is You, the All-Knower, the All-Wise." He said: "O Adam! Inform them of their names," and when he had informed them of their names, He said: "Did I not tell you that I know the *Ghaib* (unseen) in the heavens and the earth, and I know what you reveal and what you have been concealing?" *And (remember) when We said to the angels: "Prostrate yourselves before Adam." And they prostrated except Iblis (Satan), he refused and was proud and was one of the disbelievers (disobedient to Allah).* (**HK**) And when thy Lord said *unto the angels*: Lo! I am about to place a viceroy in the earth, they said: Wilt thou place therein one who will do harm therein and will shed blood, while we, we hymn Thy praise and sanctify Thee? He said: Surely I know that which ye know not. And He taught Adam all the names, then showed them *to the angels*, saying: Inform Me of the names of these, if ye are truthful. They said: Be glorified! We have no knowledge saving that which Thou hast taught us. Lo! Thou, only Thou, art the Knower, the Wise. He said: O Adam! Inform them of their names, and when he had informed them of their names, He said: Did I not tell you that I know the secret of the heavens and the earth? And I know that which ye disclose and which ye hide. *And when We said unto the angels: Prostrate yourselves before Adam, they fell prostrate, all save Iblis. He demurred through pride, and so became a disbeliever.* (**P**)

17:61 And (remember) when *We said to the angels*: "Prostrate unto Adam." *They prostrated except Iblis (Satan).* He said: "Shall I prostrate to one whom You created from clay?" (**HK**) And when *We said unto the angels*: Fall down prostrate before Adam *and they fell prostrate all save Iblis*, he said: Shall I fall prostrate before that which Thou hast created of clay? (**P**)

20:116 And (remember) when *We said to the angels*: "Prostrate yourselves to Adam." *They prostrated (all) except Iblis (Satan),* who refused. (**HK**) And *when We said unto the angels*: Fall prostrate before Adam, *they fell prostrate (all) save Iblis*; he refused. (**P**)

15:26–33 And indeed, We created man from sounding clay of altered black smooth mud. *And the jinn, We created aforetime from the smokeless flame of fire.* And (remember) *when your Lord said to the angels*: "I am going to create a man (Adam) from sounding clay of altered black smooth mud. So, when I have fashioned him completely and breathed into him (Adam) the soul which I created for him, then fall (you) down prostrating yourselves unto him." *So, the angels prostrated themselves, all of them together.* Except Iblis (Satan),—he refused to be among the prostrators. (Allah) said: "O Iblis (Satan)! What is your reason for not being among the prostrators?" [*Iblis* (Satan)] said: "I am not the one to prostrate myself to a human being, whom You created from sounding clay of altered black smooth mud." (**HK**) Verily We created man of potter's clay of black mud altered, *And the jinn did We create aforetime of essential fire.* And (remember) *when thy Lord said unto the angels*: Lo! I am creating a mortal out of potter's clay of black mud altered, So, when I have made him and have breathed into him of My Spirit, do ye fall down, prostrating yourselves unto him. *So the angels fell prostrate, all of them together. Save Iblis.* He refused to be among the prostrate. He said: O Iblis! What aileth thee that thou art not among the prostrate? He said: I am not one to prostrate myself unto a mortal whom Thou hast created out of potter's clay of black mud altered! (**P**)

7:11–12 And surely, We created you (your father Adam) and then gave you shape (the noble shape of a human being), then We told the angels, "Prostrate to Adam", and they prostrated, except *Iblis* (Satan), he refused to be of those who prostrate. (Allah) said: "What prevented you (O *Iblis*) that you did not prostrate, when I commanded you?" *Iblis said: "I am better than him (Adam), You created me from fire, and him You created from clay."* (**HK**) And We created you, then fashioned you, then told the angels: Fall ye prostrate before Adam! And they fell prostrate, all save Iblis, who was not of those who make prostration. He said: What hindered thee that thou didst not fall prostrate when I bade thee ? *(Iblis) said: I am better than him. Thou createdst me of fire while him Thou didst create of mud.* (**P**)

38:71–76 (Remember) when your Lord said to the angels: "Truly, I am going to create man from clay". So when I have fashioned him and breathed into him (his) soul created by Me, then you fall down prostrate to him." So the angels prostrated themselves, all of them: Except *Iblis* (Satan) he was proud and was one of the disbelievers. (Allah) said: "O *Iblis* (Satan)! What prevents you from prostrating yourself to one whom I have created with Both My Hands. Are you too proud (to fall prostrate to Adam) or are you one of the high exalted?" *[Iblis (Satan)] said: "I am better than he, You created me from fire, and You created him from clay."* (**HK**) When thy Lord said unto the angels: Lo! I am about to create a mortal out of mire, And when I have fashioned him and breathed into him of My Spirit, then fall down before him prostrate, The angels fell down prostrate, every one, Saving Iblis; he was scornful and became one of the disbelievers. He said: O Iblis! What hindereth thee from falling prostrate before that which I have created with both My hands? Art thou too proud or art thou of the high exalted? *He said: I am better than him. Thou createdst me of fire, whilst him Thou didst create of clay.* (**P**)

18:50 And (remember) when We said to the angels; "Prostrate to Adam." So they prostrated except *Iblis* (Satan). *He was one of the jinns;* he disobeyed the Command of his Lord. (**HK**) And (remember) when We said unto the angels: Fall prostrate before Adam, and they fell prostrate, all save Iblis. *He was of the jinn*, so he rebelled against his Lord's command. (**P**)

4:11–12 Allah commands you as regards your children's (inheritance); to the male, a portion equal to that of two females; if (there are) only daughters, two or more, their share is two thirds of the inheritance; if only one, her share is half. For parents, a sixth share of inheritance to each if the deceased left children; if no children, and the parents are the (only) heirs, the mother has a third; if the deceased left brothers or (sisters), the mother has a sixth. (The distribution in all cases is) after the payment of legacies he may have bequeathed or debts. You know not which of them, whether your parents or your children, are nearest to you in benefit, (these fixed shares) are ordained by Allah. And Allah is Ever All-Knower, All-Wise. In that which your wives leave, your share is a half if they have no child; but if they leave a child, you get a fourth of that which they leave after payment of legacies that they may have bequeathed or debts. In that which you leave, their (your wives) share is a fourth if you leave no child; but if you leave a child, they get an eighth of that which you leave after payment of legacies that you may have bequeathed or debts. ... (**HK**) Allah chargeth you concerning (the provision for) your children: to the male the equivalent of the portion of two females, and if there be women more than two, then theirs is two-thirds of the inheritance, and if there be one (only) then the half. And to each of his parents a sixth of the inheritance, if he have a son; and if he have no son and his parents are his heirs, then to his mother appertaineth the third; and if he have brethren, then to his mother appertaineth the sixth, after any legacy he may have bequeathed, or debt (hath been paid). Your parents and your children: Ye know not which of them is nearer unto you in usefulness. It is an injunction from Allah. Lo! Allah is Knower, Wise. And unto you belongeth a half of that which your wives leave, if they have no child; but if they have a child then unto you the fourth of that which they leave, after any legacy they may have bequeathed, or debt (they may have contracted, hath been paid). And unto them belongeth the fourth of that which ye leave if ye have no child, but if ye have a child then the eighth of that which ye leave, after any legacy ye may have bequeathed, or debt (ye may have contracted, hath been paid). ... (**P**)

75:36–40 Does man think that he will be left *Suda* [neglected without being punished or rewarded for the obligatory duties enjoined by his Lord (Allah) on him]? Was he not a *Nutfah* (mixed male and female discharge of semen) poured forth? Then he became an *'Alaqa* (a clot); then (Allah) shaped and fashioned (him) in due proportion. *And made him in two sexes, male and female.* Is not He (Allah Who does that), Able to give life to the dead? (Yes! He is Able to do all things). (**HK**) Thinketh man that he is to be left aimless? Was he not a drop of fluid which gushed forth? Then he became a clot; then (Allah) shaped and fashioned *And made of him a pair, the male and female.* Is not He (Who doeth so) Able to bring the dead to life? (**P**)

13:3 And of *every* kind of fruits He made *Zawjain Ithnain* (two in pairs—may mean two kinds or it may mean: of two sorts, e.g. black and white, sweet and sour, small and big, etc.) He brings the night as a cover over the day. Verily, in these things, there are *Ayat* (proofs, evidences, lessons, signs, etc.) for people who reflect. (**HK**) And of *all* fruits He placed therein two spouses (male and female). He covereth the night with the day. Lo! herein verily are portents for people who take thought. (**P**)

36:36 Glory be to Him, Who has created *all* the pairs of that which the earth produces, as well as of their own (human) kind (male and female), and of that which they know not. (**HK**) Glory be to Him Who created *all* the sexual pairs, of that which the earth groweth, and of themselves, and of that which they know not! (**P**)

51:49 And of *everything* We have created pairs, that you may remember (the Grace of Allah). (**HK**) And *all things* We have created by pairs, that haply ye may reflect. (**P**)

Chapter 3: Muhammad: The Last Prophet

29:48–49 Neither did you (O Muhammad) read any book before it (this Qur'an), nor did you write any book (whatsoever) with your right hand. In that case, indeed, the followers of falsehood might have doubted. Nay, but they, the clear *Ayat* [i.e the description and the qualities of Prophet Muhammad written like verses in the Taurat (Torah) and the Injeel (Gospel)] are preserved in the breasts of those who have been given knowledge (from the people of the Scriptures). And none but the *Zalimun* (polytheists and wrongdoers, etc.) deny Our *Ayat* (proofs, evidences, verses, lessons, signs, revelations, etc.). (**HK**) And thou (O Muhammad) wast not a reader of any scripture before it, nor didst thou write it with thy right hand, for then might those have doubted, who follow falsehood. But it is clear revelations in the hearts of those who have been given knowledge, and none deny Our revelations save wrong-doers. (**P**)

43:31–32 And they say: "Why is not this Qur'an sent down to some great man of the two towns (Makkah and Ta'if)?" Is it they who would portion out the Mercy of your Lord? (**HK**) And they say: If only this Qur'an had been revealed to some great man of the two towns? Is it they who apportion thy Lord's mercy? (**P**)

96:9–10 Have you (O Muhammad) seen him (i.e. Abu Jahl) who prevents, A slave (Muhammad) when he prays? (**HK**) Hast thou seen him who dissuadeth A slave when he prayeth? (**P**)

111:1–4 Perish the two hands of Abu Lahab (an uncle of the Prophet), and perish he! His wealth and his children (etc.) will not benefit him! He will be burnt in a Fire of blazing flames! And his wife too, who carries wood (thorns of *Sadan* which she used to put on the way of the Prophet, *or use to slander him*). (**HK**) The power of Abu Lahab will perish, and he will perish. His wealth and gains will not exempt him. He will be plunged in flaming Fire, And his wife, the wood-carrier. (**P**)

83:29–36 Verily! (During the worldly life) those who committed crimes used to laugh at those who believed. And whenever they passed by them, used to wink one to another (in mockery); And when they returned to their own people, they would return jesting; And when they saw them, they said: "Verily! These have indeed gone astray!" But they (disbelievers, sinners) had not been sent as watchers over them (the believers). But this Day (the Day of Resurrection) those who believe will laugh at the disbelievers. On (high) thrones, looking (at all things). Are not the disbelievers paid (fully) for what they used to do? (**HK**) Lo! the guilty used to laugh at those who believed, And wink one to another when they passed them; And when they returned to their own folk, they returned jesting; And when they saw them they said: Lo! these have gone astray. Yet they were not sent as guardians over them. This day it is those who believe who have the laugh of disbelievers, On high couches, gazing. Are not the disbelievers paid for what they used to do? (**P**)

17:76 And Verily, they were about to frighten you so much as to drive you out from the land. But in that case they would not have stayed (therein) after you, except for a little while. (**HK**) And they indeed wished to scare thee from the land that they might drive thee forth from thence, and then they would have stayed (there) but a little after thee. (**P**)

86:15–17 Verily, they are but plotting a plot (against you O Muhammad). And I (too) am planning a plan. So give a respite to the disbelievers. Deal you gently with them for a while. (**HK**) Lo! they plot a plot (against thee, O Muhammad) And I plot a plot (against them). So give a respite to the disbelievers. Deal thou gently with them for a while. (**P**)

43:79–80 Or have they plotted some plan? Then We too are planning. Or do they think that We hear not their secrets and their private counsel? *(Yes We do) and Our Messengers (appointed angels in charge of mankind) are by them, to record.* (**HK**) Or do they determine any thing (against the Prophet)? Lo! We (also) are determining. Or deem they that We cannot hear their secret thoughts and private confidences? *Nay, but Our envoys, present with them, do record.* (**P**)

8:30 And (remember) when the disbelievers *plotted* against you (O Muhammad) *to imprison you, or to kill you, or to get you out (from your home, i.e. Makkah)*; they were plotting and Allah too was planning, and Allah is the Best of the planners. (**HK**) And when those who disbelieve *plot* against thee (O Muhammad) *to wound thee fatally, or to kill thee or to drive thee forth*; they plot, but Allah (also) plotteth; and Allah is the best of plotters. (**P**)

8:26 And remember *when you were few* and were reckoned weak in the land, *and were afraid that men might kidnap you*, but He provided a safe place for you, strengthened you with His Help, and provided you with good things so that you might be grateful. (**HK**) And remember, *when ye were few* and reckoned feeble in the land, *and were in fear lest men should extirpate you*, how He gave you refuge, and strengthened you with His help, and made provision of good things for you, that haply ye might be thankful. (**P**)

60:1 O you who believe! Take not My enemies and your enemies (i.e. disbelievers and polytheists, etc.) as friends, *showing affection towards them, while they have disbelieved in what has come to you of the truth (i.e. Islamic Monotheism, this Qur'an, and Muhammad), and have driven out the Messenger (Muhammad) and yourselves (from your homeland) because you believe in Allah your Lord! If you have come forth to strive in My Cause and to seek My Good Pleasure, (then take not these disbelievers and polytheists, etc., as your friends).* You show friendship to them in secret, while I am All-Aware of what you conceal and what you reveal. And whosoever of you (Muslims) does that, then indeed he has gone (far) astray, (away) from the Straight Path. (**HK**) O ye who believe! Choose not My enemy and your enemy for allies. *Do ye give them friendship when they disbelieve in that truth which hath come unto you, driving out the messenger and you because ye believe in Allah, your Lord? If ye have come forth to strive in My way and seeking My good pleasure, (show them not friendship). Do ye show friendship unto them in secret, when I am Best Aware of what ye hide and what ye proclaim?* And whosoever doeth it among you, he verily hath strayed from the right way. (**P**)

60:9 It is only as regards those who fought against you on account of religion, and have driven you out of your homes, and helped to drive you out, that Allah forbids you to befriend them. And whosoever will befriend them, then such are the *Zalimun* (wrong-doers those who disobey Allah). (**HK**) Allah forbiddeth you only those who warred against you on account of religion and have driven you out from your homes and helped to drive you out, that ye make friends of them. Whosoever maketh friends of them—(All) such are wrong-doers. (**P**)

85:2–10 And by the Promised Day (i.e. the Day of Resurrection); And by the witnessing day (i.e. Friday), and by the witnessed day [i.e. the day of 'Arafat (*Hajj*) the ninth of Dhul-Hijjah]; Cursed were the people of the ditch (the story of the Boy and the King). Fire supplied (abundantly) with fuel, When they sat by it (fire), And they witnessed what they were doing against the believers (i.e. burning them). They had nothing against them, except that they believed in Allah, the All-Mighty, Worthy of all Praise! Who, to Whom belongs the dominion of the heavens and the earth! And Allah is Witness over everything. Verily, those who put into trial the believing men and believing women (by torturing them and burning them), and then do not turn in repentance, (to Allah), will have the torment of Hell, and they will have the punishment of the burning Fire. (**HK**) And by the Promised Day. And by the witness and that whereunto he beareth testimony, (Self) destroyed were the owners of the ditch Of the fuel-fed fire, When they sat by it, And were themselves the witnesses of what they did to the believers. They had naught against them save that they believed in Allah, the Mighty, the Owner of Praise, Him unto Whom belongeth the Sovereignty of the heavens and the earth; and Allah is of all things the Witness. Lo! they who persecute believing men and believing women and repent not, theirs verily will be the doom of hell, and theirs the doom of burning. **(P)**

9:40 If you help him (Muhammad) not (it does not matter), for Allah did indeed help him *when the disbelievers drove him out*, the second of two, when they (Muhammad and Abu Bakr) were in the cave **(HK)** If ye help him not, still Allah helped him *when those who disbelieve drove him forth*, the second of two; when they two were in the cave, when he said unto his comrade... **(P)**

9:13 Will you not fight a people who have violated their oaths (pagans of Makkah) *and intended to expel the Messenger*, while they did attack you first? **(HK)** Will ye not fight a folk who broke their solemn pledges, *and purposed to drive out the messenger* and did attack you first? **(P)**

22:39-40 Permission to fight is given to those (i.e. believers against disbelievers), who are fighting them, (and) *because they (believers) have been wronged*, and surely, Allah is Able to give them (believers) victory. *Those who have been expelled from their homes unjustly* only because they said: "Our Lord is Allah." **(HK)** Sanction is given unto those who fight *because they have been wronged*; and Allah is indeed Able to give them victory; *Those who have been driven from their homes unjustly* only because they said: Our Lord is Allah **(P)**

33:40 Muhammad is not the father of any man among you, but he is the Messenger of Allah and the last (end) of the Prophets. And Allah is Ever All-Aware of everything. **(HK)** Muhammad is not the father of any man among you, but he is the messenger of Allah and the Seal of the Prophets; and Allah is ever Aware of all things. **(P)**

33:37–40 And (remember) when you said to him (Zaid bin Harithah; the freed-slave of the Prophet) on whom Allah has bestowed Grace (by guiding him to Islam) and you (O Muhammad too) have done favour (by manumitting him) "Keep your wife to yourself, and fear Allah." But you did hide in yourself (i.e. what Allah has already made known to you that He will give her to you in marriage) that which Allah will make manifest, you did fear the people (i.e. Muhammad married the divorced wife of his manumitted slave) whereas Allah had a better right that you should fear Him. So when Zaid had accomplished his desire from her (i.e. divorced her), We gave her to you in marriage, so that (in future) there may be no difficulty to the believers in respect of (the marriage of) the wives of their adopted sons when the latter have no desire to keep them (i.e. they have divorced them). And Allah's Command must be fulfilled. There is no blame on the Prophet in that which Allah has made legal for him. That has been Allah's Way with those who have passed away of (the Prophets of) old. And the Command of Allah is a decree determined. Those who convey the Message of Allah and fear Him, and fear none save Allah. And Sufficient is Allah as a Reckoner. Muhammad is not the father of any man among you, but he is the Messenger of Allah and the last (end) of the Prophets. And Allah is Ever All-Aware of everything. **(HK)** And when thou saidst unto him on whom Allah hath conferred favour and thou hast conferred favour: Keep thy wife to thyself, and fear Allah. And thou didst hide in thy mind that which Allah was to bring to light, and thou didst fear mankind whereas Allah hath a better right that thou shouldst fear Him. So when Zeyd had performed that necessary formality (of divorce) from her, We gave her unto thee in marriage, so that (henceforth) there may be no sin for believers in respect of wives of their adopted sons, when the latter have performed the necessary formality (of release) from them. The commandment of Allah must be fulfilled. There is no reproach for the Prophet in that which Allah maketh his due. That was Allah's way with those who passed away of old—and the commandment of Allah is certain destiny. Who delivered the messages of Allah and feared Him, and feared none save Allah. Allah keepeth good account. Muhammad is not the father of any man among you, but he is the messenger of Allah and the Seal of the Prophets; and Allah is ever Aware of all things. **(P)**

5:19 O people of the Scripture (Jews and Christians)! Now has come to you Our Messenger (Muhammad) making (things) clear unto you, after a break in (the series of) Messengers, lest you say: "There came unto us no bringer of glad tidings and no warner." But now has come unto you a bringer of glad tidings and a warner. And Allah is Able to do all things. **(HK)** O People of the Scripture! Now hath Our messenger come unto you to make things plain unto you after an interval (of cessation) of the messengers, lest ye should say: There came not unto us a messenger of cheer nor any warner. Now hath a messenger of cheer and a warner come unto you. Allah is Able to do all things. **(P)**

13:38 And indeed We sent Messengers before you (O Muhammad), ... (For) each and every matter there is a Decree (from Allah). **(HK)** And verily We sent messengers (to mankind) before thee ... For everything there is a time prescribed. **(P)**

6:46 Say (to the disbelievers): "Tell me, if Allah took away your hearing and your sight, and sealed up your hearts ... **(HK)** Say: Have ye imagined, if Allah should take away your hearing and your sight and seal your hearts ... **(P)**

5:6 O you who believe! When you intend to offer *As-Salat* (the prayer), wash your faces and your hands (forearms) up to the elbows, rub (by passing wet hands over) your heads, and (wash) your feet up to ankles. If you are in a state of *Janaba* (i.e. had a sexual discharge), purify yourself (bathe your whole body). **(HK)** O ye who believe! When ye rise up for prayer, wash your faces, and your hands up to the elbows, and lightly rub your heads and (wash) your feet up to the ankles. And if ye are unclean, purify yourselves. **(P)**

12:2 Verily, We have sent it down as an Arabic Qur'an in order that you may understand. **(HK)** Lo! We have revealed it, a Lecture in Arabic, that ye may understand. (**P**)

13:37 And thus have We sent it (the Qur'an) down to be a judgement of authority in Arabic. (**HK**) Thus have We revealed it, a decisive utterance in Arabic; (**P**)

20:113 And thus We have sent it down as a Qur'an in Arabic, and have explained therein in detail the warnings, in order that they may fear Allah, or that it may cause them to have a lesson from it (or to have the honour for believing and acting on its teachings). (**HK**) Thus we have revealed it as a Lecture in Arabic, and have displayed therein certain threats, that peradventure they may keep from evil or that it may cause them to take heed. (**P**)

41:44 And if We had sent this as a Qur'an in a foreign language other than Arabic, they would have said: "Why are not its Verses explained in detail (in our language)? What! (A Book) not in Arabic and (the Messenger) an Arab?" (**HK**) And if We had appointed it a Lecture in a foreign tongue they would assuredly have said: If only its verses were expounded (so that we might understand)? What! A foreign tongue and an Arab? (**P**)

10:47 And for every *Ummah* (a community or a nation), there is a Messenger; when their Messenger comes, the matter will be judged between them with justice, and they will not be wronged. (**HK**) And for every nation there is a messenger. And when their messenger cometh (on the Day of Judgment) it will be judged between them fairly, and they will not be wronged. (**P**)

3:21 Verily! *Those who disbelieve in the Ayat (proofs, evidences, verses, lessons, signs, revelations, etc.) of Allah and kill the Prophets without right*, and kill those men who order just dealings, ... announce to them a painful torment. (**HK**) Lo! *those who disbelieve the revelations of Allah, and slay the prophets wrongfully*, and slay those of mankind who enjoin equity: ... Promise them a painful doom. (**P**)

8:7 And (remember) when Allah promised you (Muslims) one of the two parties (of the enemy i.e. either the army or the caravan) that it should be yours, you wished that the one not armed (the caravan) should be yours ... (**HK**) And when Allah promised you one of the two bands (of the enemy) that it should be yours, and ye longed that other than the armed one might be yours. (**P**)

3:13 There has already been a sign for you (O Jews) in the two armies that met (in combat i.e. the battle of Badr): One was fighting in the Cause of Allah, and as for the other (they) were disbelievers. They (the believers) saw them (the disbelievers) with their own eyes twice their number (although they were thrice their number). And Allah supports with His Victory whom He pleases. Verily, in this is a lesson for those who understand. (See Verse 8:44). (*Tafsir At-Tabari*) (**HK**) There was a token for you in two hosts which met: one army fighting in the way of Allah, and another disbelieving, whom they saw as twice their number, clearly, with their very eyes. Thus Allah strengtheneth with His succour whom He will. Lo! herein verily is a lesson for those who have eyes. (**P**)

8:1 They ask you (O Muhammad) about the spoils of war. Say: "The spoils are for Allah and the Messenger." So fear Allah and adjust all matters of difference among you, and obey Allah and His Messenger (Muhammad), if you are believers. (**HK**) They ask thee (O Muhammad) of the spoils of war. Say: The spoils of war belong to Allah and the messenger, so keep your duty to Allah, and adjust the matter of your difference, and obey Allah and His messenger, if ye are (true) believers. (**P**)

8:41 And know that whatever of war-booty that you may gain, *verily one-fifth (1 / 5th) of it is assigned to Allah, and to the Messenger, and to the near relatives [of the Messenger (Muhammad)], (and also) the orphans, Al-Masakin (the poor) and the wayfarer* ... (**HK**) And know that whatever ye take as spoils of war, lo! *a fifth thereof is for Allah, and for the messenger and for the kinsman (who hath need) and orphans and the needy and the wayfarer* ... (**P**)

59:6–7 And what Allah gave as booty (*Fai'*) to His Messenger (Muhammad) from them, for which you made no expedition with either cavalry or camelry. But Allah gives power to His Messengers over whomsoever He wills. And Allah is Able to do all things. What Allah gave as booty (*Fai'*) to His Messenger (Muhammad) from the people of the townships,—it is for Allah, His Messenger (Muhammad), the kindred (of Messenger Muhammad), the orphans, *Al-Masakin* (the poor), and the wayfarer ... (**HK**) And that which Allah gave as spoil unto His messenger from them, ye urged not any horse or riding-camel for the sake thereof, but Allah giveth His messenger lordship over whom He will. Allah is Able to do all things. That which Allah giveth as spoil unto His messenger from the people of the townships, it is for Allah and His messenger and for the near of kin and the orphans and the needy and the wayfarer, ... (**P**)

48:15 Those who lagged behind will say, *when you set forth to take the spoils*, "Allow us to follow you," They want to change Allah's Words. Say: "You shall not follow us; thus Allah has said beforehand." (**HK**) Those who were left behind will say, *when ye set forth to capture booty:* Let us go with you. They fain would change the verdict of Allah. Say (unto them, O Muhammad): Ye shall not go with us. Thus hath Allah said beforehand. (**P**)

33:50–52 O Prophet (Muhammad)! Verily, We have made lawful to you your wives, to whom you have paid their *Mahr* (bridal money given by the husband to his wife at the time of marriage), *and those (captives or slaves) whom your right hand possesses—whom Allah has given to you,* and the daughters of your *'Amm* (paternal uncles) and the daughters of your *'Ammah* (paternal aunts) and the daughters of your *Khal* (maternal uncles) and the daughters of your *Khalah* (maternal aunts) who migrated (from Makkah) with you, and a believing woman if she offers herself to the Prophet, and the Prophet wishes to marry her; *a privilege for you only, not for the (rest of) the believers. Indeed We know what We have enjoined upon them about their wives and those (captives or slaves) whom their right hands possess,—in order that there should be no difficulty on you. And Allah is Ever Oft-Forgiving, Most Merciful.* You

(O Muhammad) can postpone (the turn of) whom you will of them (your wives), and you may receive whom you will. And whomsoever you desire of those whom you have set aside (her turn temporarily), it is no sin on you (to receive her again), that is better; that they may be comforted and not grieved, and may all be pleased with what you give them. Allah knows what is in your hearts. And Allah is Ever All-Knowing, Most Forbearing. *It is not lawful for you (to marry other) women after this, nor to change them for other wives even though their beauty attracts you, except those (captives or slaves) whom your right hand possesses.* And Allah is Ever a Watcher over all things. (**HK**) O Prophet! Lo! We have made lawful unto thee thy wives unto whom thou hast paid their dowries, *and those whom thy right hand possesseth of those whom Allah hath given thee as spoils of war*, and the daughters of thine uncle on the father's side and the daughters of thine aunts on the father's side, and the daughters of thine uncle on the mother's side and the daughters of thine aunts on the mother's side who emigrated with thee, and a believing woman if she give herself unto the Prophet and the Prophet desire to ask her in marriage—*a privilege for thee only, not for the (rest of) believers—We are Aware of that which We enjoined upon them concerning their wives and those whom their right hands possess—that thou mayst be free from blame, for Allah is ever Forgiving, Merciful.* Thou canst defer whom thou wilt of them and receive unto thee whom thou wilt, and whomsoever thou desirest of those whom thou hast set aside (temporarily), it is no sin for thee (to receive her again); that is better; that they may be comforted and not grieve, and may all be pleased with what thou givest them. Allah knoweth what is in your hearts (O men), and Allah is ever Forgiving, Clement. *It is not allowed thee to take (other) women henceforth, nor that thou shouldst change them for other wives even though their beauty pleased thee, save those whom thy right hand possesseth.* And Allah is ever Watcher over all things. (**P**)

33:4–5 Allah has not put for any man two hearts inside his body ... *nor has He made your adopted sons your real sons.* That is but your saying with your mouths. But Allah says the truth, and He guides to the (Right) Way. *Call them (adopted sons) by (the names of) their fathers, that is more just with Allah.* (**HK**) Allah hath not assigned unto any man two hearts within his body ... *nor hath He made those whom ye claim (to be your sons) your sons.* This is but a saying of your mouths. But Allah saith the truth and He showeth the way. *Proclaim their real parentage. That will be more equitable in the sight of Allah.* (**P**)

33:37–40 *And (remember) when you said to him (Zaid bin Harithah; the freed-slave of the Prophet) on whom Allah has bestowed Grace (by guiding him to Islam) and you (O Muhammad too) have done favour (by manumitting him) "Keep your wife to yourself, and fear Allah." But you did hide in yourself (i.e. what Allah has already made known to you that He will give her to you in marriage) that which Allah will make manifest, you did fear the people (i.e., Muhammad married the divorced wife of his manumitted slave) whereas Allah had a better right that you should fear Him.* So when Zaid had accomplished his desire from her (i.e. divorced her), We gave her to you in marriage, *so that (in future) there may be no difficulty to the believers in respect of (the marriage of) the wives of their adopted sons when the latter have no desire to keep them (i.e. they have divorced them). And Allah's Command must be fulfilled. There is no blame on the Prophet in that which Allah has made legal for him.* That has been Allah's Way with those who have passed away of (the Prophets of) old. And the Command of Allah is a decree determined. Those who convey the Message of Allah and fear Him, and fear none save Allah. And Sufficient is Allah as a Reckoner. Muhammad is not the father of any man among you, but he is the Messenger of Allah and the last (end) of the Prophets. And Allah is Ever All-Aware of everything. (**HK**) *And when thou saidst unto him on whom Allah hath conferred favour and thou hast conferred favour: Keep thy wife to thyself, and fear Allah. And thou didst hide in thy mind that which Allah was to bring to light, and thou didst fear mankind whereas Allah hath a better right that thou shouldst fear Him.* So when Zeyd had performed that necessary formality (of divorce) from her, We gave her unto thee in marriage, *so that (henceforth) there may be no sin for believers in respect of wives of their adopted sons, when the latter have performed the necessary formality (of release) from them. The commandment of Allah must be fulfilled. There is no reproach for the Prophet in that which Allah maketh his due.* That was Allah's way with those who passed away of old—and the commandment of Allah is certain destiny. Who delivered the messages of Allah and feared Him, and feared none save Allah. Allah keepeth good account. Muhammad is not the father of any man among you, but he is the messenger of Allah and the Seal of the Prophets; and Allah is ever Aware of all things. (**P**)

4:24 Also (forbidden are) women already married, *except those (captives and slaves) whom your right hands possess.* (**HK**) And all married women (are forbidden unto you) *save those (captives) whom your right hands possess.* (**P**)

49:2 O you who believe! Raise not your voices above the voice of the Prophet, nor speak aloud to him in talk as you speak aloud to one another, lest your deeds may be rendered fruitless while you perceive not. (**HK**) O ye who believe! Lift not up your voices above the voice of the Prophet, nor shout when speaking to him as ye shout one to another, lest your works be rendered vain while ye perceive not. (**P**)

49:4 Verily! Those who call you from behind the dwellings, most of them have no sense. (**HK**) Lo! those who call thee from behind the private apartments, most of them have no sense. (**P**)

24:62–63 The true believers are only those, who believe in (the Oneness of) Allah and His Messenger (Muhammad), and when they are with him on some common matter, they go not away until they have asked his permission. Verily! Those who ask your permission, those are they who (really) believe in Allah and His Messenger. ... *Make not the calling of the Messenger (Muhammad) among you as your calling of one another.* Allah knows those of you who slip away under shelter (of some excuse without taking the permission to leave, from the Messenger). And let those who oppose the Messenger's (Muhammad) commandment (i.e. his *Sunnah* legal ways, orders, acts of worship, statements, etc.) (among the sects) beware, lest some *Fitnah* (disbelief, trials, afflictions, earthquakes, killing, overpowered by a tyrant, etc.) befall them or a painful torment be inflicted on them.

(**HK**) They only are the true believers who believe in Allah and His messenger and, when they are with him on some common errand, go not away until they have asked leave of him. Lo! those who ask leave of thee, those are they who believe in Allah and His messenger. … *Make not the calling of the messenger among you as your calling one of another.* Allah knoweth those of you who steal away, hiding themselves. And let those who conspire to evade orders beware lest grief or painful punishment befall them. (**P**)

3:31–32 Say (O Muhammad to mankind): "If you (really) love Allah then follow me (i.e. accept Islamic Monotheism, follow the Qur'an and the *Sunnah*), Allah will love you and forgive you of your sins. And Allah is Oft-Forgiving, Most Merciful." Say (O Muhammad): "Obey Allah and the Messenger (Muhammad)." But if they turn away, then Allah does not like the disbelievers. (**HK**) Say, (O Muhammad, to mankind): If ye love Allah, follow me; Allah will love you and forgive you your sins. Allah is Forgiving, Merciful. Say: Obey Allah and the messenger. But if they turn away, lo! Allah loveth not the disbelievers (in His guidance). (**P**)

58:8–10 *Have you not seen those who were forbidden to hold secret counsels, and afterwards returned to that which they had been forbidden, and conspired together for sin and wrong doing and disobedience to the Messenger (Muhammad).* And when they come to you, they greet you with a greeting wherewith Allah greets you not, and say within themselves: "Why should Allah punish us not for what we say?" Hell will be sufficient for them, they will burn therein, and worst indeed is that destination! *O you who believe! When you hold secret counsel, do it not for sin and wrong-doing, and disobedience towards the Messenger (Muhammad) but do it for Al-Birr (righteousness) and Taqwa (virtues and piety); and fear Allah unto Whom you shall be gathered. Secret counsels (conspiracies) are only from Shaitan (Satan),* in order that he may cause grief to the believers. But he cannot harm them in the least, except as Allah permits, and in Allah let the believers put their trust. (**HK**) *Hast thou not observed those who were forbidden conspiracy and afterward returned to that which they had been forbidden, and (now) conspire together for crime and wrongdoing and disobedience toward the messenger?* And when they come unto thee they greet thee with a greeting wherewith Allah greeteth thee not, and say within themselves: Why should Allah punish us for what we say? Hell will suffice them; they will feel the heat thereof—a hapless journey's end! *O ye who believe! When ye conspire together, conspire not together for crime and wrongdoing and disobedience toward the messenger, but conspire together for righteousness and piety, and keep your duty toward Allah, unto whom ye will be gathered. Lo! Conspiracy is only of the devil,* that he may vex those who believe; but he can harm them not at all unless by Allah's leave. In Allah let believers put their trust. (**P**)

49:12 And spy not, neither backbite one another. Would one of you like to eat the flesh of his dead brother? (**HK**) And spy not, neither backbite one another. Would one of you love to eat the flesh of his dead brother? (**P**)

3:139–140 So do not become weak (against your enemy), nor be sad, and you will be superior (in victory) if you are indeed (true) believers. If a wound (and killing) has touched you, be sure a similar wound (and killing) has touched the others. And so are the days (good and not so good), We give to men by turns, that Allah may test those who believe, and that He may take martyrs from among you. (**HK**) Faint not nor grieve, for ye will overcome them if ye are (indeed) believers. If ye have received a blow, the (disbelieving) people have received a blow the like thereof. These are (only) the vicissitudes which We cause to follow one another for mankind, to the end that Allah may know those who believe and may choose witnesses from among you; (**P**)

3:124–127 (Remember) when you (Muhammad) said to the believers, "Is it not enough for you that your Lord (Allah) should help you with three thousand angels; sent down?" "Yes, if you hold on to patience and piety, *and the enemy comes rushing at you,* your Lord will help you with five thousand angels having marks (of distinction)." … That He might cut off a part of those who disbelieve, or expose them to infamy, so that they retire frustrated. (**HK**) When thou didst say unto the believers: Is it not sufficient for you that your Lord should support you with three thousand angels sent down (to your help)? Nay, but if ye persevere, and keep from evil, *and (the enemy) attack you suddenly,* your Lord will help you with five thousand angels sweeping on. … That He may cut off a part of those who disbelieve, or overwhelm them so that they retire, frustrated. (**P**)

3:166–168 And what you suffered (of the disaster) on the day (of the battle of Uhud when) the two armies met, was by the leave of Allah, in order that He might test the believers. And that He might test the hypocrites, it was said to them: "Come, fight in the Way of Allah or (at least) defend yourselves." They said: "Had we known that fighting will take place, we would certainly have followed you." They were that day, nearer to disbelief than to Faith, saying with their mouths what was not in their hearts. And Allah has full knowledge of what they conceal. (They are) the ones who said about their killed brethren while they themselves sat (at home): "If only they had listened to us, they would not have been killed." (**HK**) That which befell you, on the day when the two armies met, was by permission of Allah; that He might know the true believers; And that He might know the hypocrites, unto whom it was said: Come, fight in the way of Allah, or defend yourselves. They answered: If we knew aught of fighting we would follow you. On that day they were nearer disbelief than faith. They utter with their mouths a thing which is not in their hearts. Allah is Best Aware of what they hide. Those who, while they sat at home, said of their brethren (who were fighting for the cause of Allah): If they had been guided by us they would not have been slain. (**P**)

3:152–153 And Allah did indeed fulfil His Promise to you when you were killing them (your enemy) with His Permission; *until (the moment) you lost your courage and fell to disputing about the order, and disobeyed after He showed you (of the booty) which you love. Among you are some that desire this world and some that desire the Hereafter.* Then He made you flee from them (your enemy), that He might test you. But surely, He forgave you, and Allah is Most Gracious to the believers. *(And remember) when you ran away (dreadfully) without even casting a side glance at anyone,* *and the Messenger (Muhammad) was in your rear calling you back.* There did Allah give you one distress after another by way of requital to teach you not to grieve for that which had escaped you, nor for that which had befallen you. And Allah is Well-Aware of all that you do. (**HK**) Allah verily made good His promise unto you when ye routed them by His leave, *until (the moment) when your courage failed you, and ye disagreed about the order and ye disobeyed, after He had shown you that for which ye long. Some of you desired the world, and some of you desired the Hereafter.* Therefore He made you flee from them, that He might try you. Yet now He hath forgiven you. Allah is a Lord of Kindness to believers. *When ye climbed (the hill) and paid no heed to anyone, while the messenger, in your rear, was calling you (to fight).* Therefor He rewarded you grief for (his) grief, that (He might teach) you not to sorrow either for that which ye missed or for that which befell you. Allah is Informed of what ye do. (**P**)

3:161 It is not for any Prophet to take illegally a part of booty (*Ghulul*), …. (**HK**) It is not for any prophet to embezzle. (**P**)

3:154 They said, "Have we any part in the affair?" Say you (O Muhammad): "Indeed the affair belongs wholly to Allah." *They hide within themselves what they dare not reveal to you, saying: "If we had anything to do with the affair, none of us would have been killed here."* (**HK**) They said: Have we any part in the cause? Say (O Muhammad): The cause belongeth wholly to Allah. *They hide within themselves (a thought) which they reveal not unto thee, saying: Had we had any part in the cause we should not have been slain here.* (**P**)

9:38 *O you who believe!* What is the matter with you, that when you are asked to march forth in the Cause of Allah (i.e. *Jihad*) you cling heavily to the earth? Are you pleased with the life of this world rather than the Hereafter? (**HK**) *O ye who believe!* What aileth you that when it is said unto you: Go forth in the way of Allah, ye are bowed down to the ground with heaviness. Take ye pleasure in the life of the world rather than in the Hereafter? (**P**)

9:119–122 *O you who believe!* Be afraid of Allah, and be with those who are true (in words and deeds). It was not becoming of the people of Al-Madinah and the bedouins of the neighbourhood to remain behind Allah's Messenger (Muhammad when fighting in Allah's Cause) and (it was not becoming of them) to prefer their own lives to his life. … And it is not (proper) for *the believers* to go out to fight (*Jihad*) all together. Of every troop of them, a party only should go forth, that they (who are left behind) may get instructions in (Islamic) religion, and that they may warn their people when they return to them, so that they may beware (of evil). (**HK**) *O ye who believe!* Be careful of your duty to Allah, and be with the truthful. It is not for the townsfolk of Al-Madinah and for those around them of the wandering Arabs to stay behind the messenger of Allah and prefer their lives to his life. … And *the believers* should not all go out to fight. Of every troop of them, a party only should go forth, that they (who are left behind) may gain sound knowledge in religion, and that they may warn their folk when they return to them, so that they may beware. (**P**)

62:9–11 O you who believe (Muslims)! When the call is proclaimed for the *Salat* (prayer) on the day of Friday (*Jumu'ah* prayer), come to the remembrance of Allah [*Jumu'ah* religious talk (*Khutbah*) and *Salat* (prayer)] and leave off business (and every other thing), that is better for you if you did but know! Then when the (*Jumu'ah*) *Salat* (prayer) is finished, you may disperse through the land, and seek the Bounty of Allah (by working, etc.), and remember Allah much, that you may be successful. *And when they see some merchandise or some amusement (beating of Tambur (drum) etc.) they disperse headlong to it, and leave you (Muhammad) standing (while delivering Jumu'ah's religious talk (Khutbah)).* Say "That which Allah has is better than any amusement or merchandise! And Allah is the Best of providers." (**HK**) O ye who believe! When the call is heard for the prayer of the day of congregation, haste unto remembrance of Allah and leave your trading. That is better for you if ye did but know. And when the prayer is ended, then disperse in the land and seek of Allah's bounty, and remember Allah much, that ye may be successful. *But when they spy some merchandise or pastime they break away to it and leave thee standing.* Say: That which Allah hath is better than pastime and than merchandise, and Allah is the Best of providers. (**P**)

4:65 But no, by your Lord, they can have no Faith, until they make you (O Muhammad) judge in all disputes between them, and find in themselves no resistance against your decisions, and accept (them) with full submission. (**HK**) But nay, by thy Lord, they will not believe (in truth) until they make thee judge of what is in dispute between them and find within themselves no dislike of that which thou decidest, and submit with full submission. (**P**)

33:36 *It is not for a believer, man or woman, when Allah and His Messenger have decreed a matter that they should have any option in their decision.* And whoever disobeys Allah and His Messenger, he has indeed strayed in a plain error. (**HK**) *And it becometh not a believing man or a believing woman, when Allah and His messenger have decided an affair (for them), that they should (after that) claim any say in their affair;* and whoso is rebellious to Allah and His messenger, he verily goeth astray in error manifest. (**P**)

58:12–13 O you who believe! When you (want to) consult the Messenger (Muhammad) in private, spend something in charity before your private consultation. That will be better and purer for you. But if you find not (the means for it), then verily, Allah is Oft-Forgiving, Most Merciful. Are you afraid of spending in charity before your private consultation (with him)? (**HK**) O ye who believe! When ye hold conference with the messenger, offer an alms before your conference. That is better and purer for you. But if ye cannot find (the wherewithal) then lo! Allah is Forgiving, Merciful. Fear ye to offer alms before your conference? (**P**)

9:58 And of them are some who accuse you (O Muhammad) in the matter of (the distribution of) the alms. If they are given part thereof, they are pleased, but if they are not given thereof, behold! They are *enraged.* (**HK**) And of them is he who defameth thee in the matter of the alms. If they are given thereof they are content, and if they are not given thereof, behold! they are *enraged.* (P)

24:11–18 *Verily! Those who brought forth the slander (against 'Aishah (may Allah be pleased with her) the wife of the Prophet) are a group among you.* Consider it not a bad thing for you. Nay, it is good for you. Unto every man among them will be paid that which he had earned of the sin, and as for him among them who had the greater share therein, his will be a great torment. *Why then, did not the believers, men and women, when you heard it (the slander) think good of their own people and say: "This (charge) is an obvious lie?"* Why did they not produce four witnesses? Since they (the slanderers) have not produced witnesses! Then with Allah they are the liars. Had it not been for the Grace of Allah and His Mercy unto you in this world and in the Hereafter, a great torment would have touched you for that whereof you had spoken. When you were propagating it with your tongues, and uttering with your mouths that whereof you had no knowledge, you counted it a little thing, while with Allah it was very great. And why did you not, when you heard it, say? "It is not right for us to speak of this. Glory be to You (O Allah) this is a great lie." Allah forbids you from it and warns you not to repeat the like of it forever, if you are believers. And Allah makes the *Ayat* (proofs, evidences, verses, lessons, signs, revelations, etc.) plain to you, and Allah is All-Knowing, All-Wise. (**HK**) *Lo! they who spread the slander are a gang among you.* Deem it not a bad thing for you; nay, it is good for you. Unto every man of them (will be paid) that which he hath earned of the sin; and as for him among them who had the greater share therein, his will be an awful doom. *Why did not the believers, men and women, when ye heard it, think good of their own own folk, and say: It is a manifest untruth?* Why did they not produce four witnesses ? Since they produce not witnesses, they verily are liars in the sight of Allah. Had it not been for the grace of Allah and His mercy unto you in the world and the Hereafter an awful doom had overtaken you for that whereof ye murmured. When ye welcomed it with your tongues, and uttered with your mouths that whereof ye had no knowledge, ye counted it a trifle. In the sight of Allah it is very great. Wherefor, when ye heard it, said ye not: It is not for us to speak of this. Glory be to Thee (O Allah)! This is awful calumny. Allah admonisheth you that ye repeat not the like thereof ever, if ye are (in truth) believers. And He expoundeth unto you the revelations. Allah is Knower, Wise. (P)

33:51 You (O Muhammad) can postpone (the turn of) whom you will of them (your wives), and you may receive whom you will. And whomsoever you desire of those whom you have set aside (her turn temporarily), it is no sin on you (to receive her again), (**HK**) Thou canst defer whom thou wilt of them and receive unto thee whom thou wilt, and whomsoever thou desirest of those whom thou hast set aside (temporarily), it is no sin for thee (to receive her again); that is better; that they may be comforted and not grieve, and may all be pleased with what thou givest them. Allah knoweth what is in your hearts (O men), and Allah is ever Forgiving, Clement. (P)

5:33–34 The recompense of those who wage war against Allah and His Messenger and do mischief in the land is only that they shall be killed or crucified or their hands and their feet be cut off on the opposite sides, or be exiled from the land. That is their disgrace in this world, and a great torment is theirs in the Hereafter. Except for those who (having fled away and then) came back (as Muslims) with repentance before they fall into your power; in that case, know that Allah is Oft-Forgiving, Most Merciful. (**HK**) The only reward of those who make war upon Allah and His messenger and strive after corruption in the land will be that they will be killed or crucified, or have their hands and feet on alternate sides cut off, or will be expelled out of the land. Such will be their degradation in the world, and in the Hereafter theirs will be an awful doom; Save those who repent before ye overpower them. For know that Allah is Forgiving, Merciful. (P)

2:234 And those of you who die and leave wives behind them, they (the wives) shall wait (as regards their marriage) for four months and ten days, then when they have fulfilled their term, there is no sin on you if they (the wives) dispose of themselves in a just and honourable manner (i.e. they can marry). (**HK**) Such of you as die and leave behind them wives, they (the wives) shall wait, keeping themselves apart, four months and ten days. And when they reach the term (prescribed for them) then there is no sin for you in aught that they may do with themselves in decency. (P)

6:37–38 And they said: "Why is not a sign sent down to him from his Lord?" Say: "Allah is certainly Able to send down a sign, but most of them know not." There is not a moving (living) creature on earth, nor a bird that flies with its two wings, but are communities like you. (**HK**) They say: Why hath no portent been sent down upon him from his Lord ? Say: Lo! Allah is Able to send down a portent. But most of them know not. There is not an animal in the earth, nor a flying creature flying on two wings, but they are peoples like unto you. (P)

6:109 And they swear their strongest oaths by Allah, that if there came to them a sign, they would surely believe therein. Say: "Signs are but with Allah and what will make you (Muslims) perceive that (even) if it (the sign) came, they will not believe?" (**HK**) And they swear a solemn oath by Allah that if there come unto them a portent they will believe therein. Say: Portents are with Allah and (so is) that which telleth you that if such came unto them they would not believe. (P)

10:20 And they say: "How is it that not a sign is sent down on him from his Lord?" Say: "The unseen belongs to Allah Alone, so wait you, verily I am with you among those who wait (for Allah's Judgment)." (**HK**) And they will say: If only a portent were sent down upon him from his Lord! Then say, (O Muhammad): The Unseen belongeth to Allah. So wait! Lo! I am waiting with you. (P)

13:7 And the disbelievers say: "Why is not a sign sent down to him from his Lord?" You are only a warner, and to every people there is a guide. (**HK**) Those who disbelieve say? If only some portent were sent down upon him from his Lord! Thou art a warner only, and for every folk a guide. (**P**)

29:50-51 And they say: "Why are not signs sent down to him from his Lord?" Say: "The signs are only with Allah, and I am only a plain warner." Is it not sufficient for them that We have sent down to you the Book (the Qur'an) which is recited to them? (**HK**) And they say: Why are not portents sent down upon him from his Lord? Say: Portents are with Allah only, and I am but a plain warner. Is it not enough for them that We have sent down unto thee the Scripture which is read unto them?(**P**)

54:1-3 The Hour has drawn near, *and the moon has been cleft asunder* (the people of Makkah requested Prophet Muhammad to show them a miracle, so he showed them the splitting of the moon). And if they see a sign, they turn away, and say: "This is continuous magic." They belied [the Verses of Allah, this Qur'an), and followed their own lusts. And every matter will be settled [according to the kind of deeds (for the doer of good deeds, his deeds will take him to Paradise, and similarly evil deeds will take their doers to Hell)]. (**HK**) The hour drew nigh *and the moon was rent in twain.* And if they behold a portent they turn away and say: Prolonged illusion. They denied (the Truth) and followed their own lusts. Yet everything will come to a decision. (**P**)

87:6-7 We shall make you to recite (the Qur'an), so you (O Muhammad) shall not forget (it), Except what Allah, may will, He knows what is apparent and what is hidden. (**HK**) We shall make thee read (O Muhammad) so that thou shalt not forget Save that which Allah willeth. Lo! He knoweth the disclosed and that which still is hidden… (**P**)

40:55 So be patient (O Muhammad). Verily, the Promise of Allah is true, and ask forgiveness for your fault, and glorify the praises of your Lord in the *Ashi* (i.e. the time period after the midnoon till sunset) and in the *Ibkar* (i.e. the time period from early morning or sunrise till before midnoon) [it is said that, that means the five compulsory congregational *Salat* (prayers) or the *'Asr* and *Fajr* prayers]. (**HK**) Then have patience (O Muhammad). Lo! the promise of Allah is true. And ask forgiveness of thy sin, and hymn the praise of thy Lord at fall of night and in the early hours. (**P**)

66:1-5 *O Prophet! Why do you ban (for yourself) that which Allah has made lawful to you,* seeking to please your wives? And Allah is Oft-Forgiving, Most Merciful. *Allah has already ordained for you (O men), the dissolution of your oaths.* And Allah is your *Maula* (Lord, or Master, or Protector, etc.) and He is the All-Knower, the All-Wise. *And (remember) when the Prophet disclosed a matter in confidence to one of his wives* (Hafsah), *so when she told it (to another i.e. 'Aishah), and Allah made it known to him, he informed part thereof and left a part.* Then when he told her (Hafsah) thereof, she said: "Who told you this?" He said: "The All-Knower, the All-Aware (Allah) has told me". If you two (wives of the Prophet, namely 'Aishah and Hafsah) turn in repentance to Allah, (it will be better for you), your hearts are indeed so inclined (to oppose what the Prophet likes), but if you help one another against him (Muhammad), then verily, Allah is his *Maula* (Lord, or Master, or Protector, etc.), and Jibrael (Gabriel), and the righteous among the believers, and furthermore, the angels are his helpers. *It may be if he divorced you (all) that his Lord will give him instead of you, wives better than you, Muslims (who submit to Allah), believers, obedient to Allah, turning to Allah in repentance, worshipping Allah sincerely, fasting or emigrants (for Allah's sake), previously married and virgins.* (**HK**) O Prophet! Why bannest thou that which Allah hath made lawful for thee, seeking to please thy wives? And Allah is Forgiving, Merciful. *Allah hath made lawful for you (Muslims) absolution from your oaths (of such a kind),* and Allah is your Protector. He is the Knower, the Wise. *When the Prophet confided a fact unto one of his wives and when she afterward divulged it and Allah apprised him thereof, he made known (to her) part thereof and passed over part.* And when he told it her she said: Who hath told thee? He said: The Knower, the Aware hath told me. If ye twain turn unto Allah repentant, (ye have cause to do so) for your hearts desired (the ban); and if ye aid one another against him (Muhammad) then lo! Allah, even He, is his Protecting Friend, and Gabriel and the righteous among the believers; and furthermore the angels are his helpers. *It may happen that his Lord, if he divorce you, will give him in your stead wives better than you, submissive (to Allah), believing, pious, penitent, devout, inclined to fasting, widows and maids.* (**P**)

5:89 Allah will not punish you for what is unintentional in your oaths, but He will punish you for your deliberate oaths; for its expiation (a deliberate oath) feed ten *Masakin* (poor persons), on a scale of the average of that with which you feed your own families; or clothe them; or manumit a slave. But whosoever cannot afford (that), then he should fast for three days. That is the expiation for the oaths which you have sworn. And protect your oaths (i.e. do not swear much). Thus Allah make clear to you His *Ayat* (proofs, evidences, verses, lessons, signs, revelations, etc.) that you may be grateful. (**HK**) Allah will not take you to task for that which is unintentional in your oaths, but He will take you to task for the oaths which ye swear in earnest. The expiation thereof is the feeding of ten of the needy with the average of that wherewith ye feed your own folk, or the clothing of them, or the liberation of a slave, and for him who findeth not (the wherewithal to do so) then a three days' fast. This is the expiation of your oaths when ye have sworn; and keep your oaths. Thus Allah expoundeth unto you His revelations in order that ye may give thanks. (**P**)

Chapter 4: The Quran: A Scientific Miracle

22:15-16 Whoever thinks that Allah will not help him (Muhammad) in this world and in the Hereafter, let him stretch out a rope to the ceiling and let him strangle himself. Then let him see whether his plan will remove that whereat he rages! Thus have We sent it (this Qur'an) down (to Muhammad) as clear signs, evidences and proofs, and surely, Allah guides whom He wills. (**HK**) Whoso is wont to think (through envy) that Allah will not give him (Muhammad) victory in the world and the Hereafter (and is enraged at the thought of his victory), let him stretch a rope up to the roof (of his dwelling), and let him hang himself. Then let him see whether his strategy dispelleth that whereat he rageth!. Thus We reveal it as plain revelations, and verily Allah guideth whom He will. (P)

2:187 [A]nd eat and drink until the white thread (light) of dawn appears to you distinct from the black thread (darkness of night), then complete your *Saum* (fast) till the nightfall. (**HK**) [A]nd eat and drink until the white thread becometh distinct to you from the black thread of the dawn. Then strictly observe the fast till nightfall. (P)

36:37–40 And a sign for them is the night, We withdraw therefrom the day, and behold, they are in darkness. *And the sun runs on its fixed course for a term (appointed).* That is the Decree of the All-Mighty, the All-Knowing. And the moon, We have measured for it mansions (to traverse) till it returns like the old dried curved date stalk. *It is not for the sun to overtake the moon, nor does the night outstrip the day. They all float, each in an orbit.* (**HK**) A token unto them is night. We strip it of the day, and lo! they are in darkness. *And the sun runneth on unto a resting-place for him.* That is the measuring of the Mighty, the Wise. And for the moon We have appointed mansions till she return like an old shrivelled palm-leaf. *It is not for the sun to overtake the moon, nor doth the night outstrip the day. They float each in an orbit.* (P)

21:32–33 And We have made the heaven a roof, safe and well guarded. Yet they turn away from its signs (i.e. sun, moon, winds, clouds, etc.). *And He it is Who has created the night and the day, and the sun and the moon, each in an orbit floating.* (**HK**) And we have made the sky a roof withheld (from them). Yet they turn away from its portents. *And He it is Who created the night and the day, and the sun and the moon. They float, each in an orbit.* (P)

18:83–90 And they ask you about Dhul-Qarnain. Say: "I shall recite to you something of his story." Verily, We established him in the earth, and We gave him the means of everything. So he followed a way. *Until, when he reached the setting place of the sun,* he found it setting in a spring of black muddy (or hot) water. And he found near it a people. ... Then he followed another way, *Until, when he came to the rising place of the sun,* he found it rising on a people for whom We (Allah) had provided no shelter against the sun. (**HK**) They will ask thee of Dhu'l-Qarneyn. Say: I shall recite unto you a remembrance of him. Lo! We made him strong in the land and gave him unto every thing a road. And he followed a road *Till, when he reached the setting-place of the sun,* he found it setting in a muddy spring, and found a people thereabout. ... Then he followed a road *Till, when he reached the rising-place of the sun,* he found it rising on a people for whom We had appointed no shelter therefrom. (P)

15:26–27 And indeed, We created man from sounding clay of altered black smooth mud. And the jinn, We created aforetime from the smokeless flame of fire. (**HK**) Verily We created man of potter's clay of black mud altered, And the jinn did We create aforetime of essential fire. (P)

21:30 And We have made from water every living thing. (**HK**) [A]nd we made every living thing of water. (P)

32:7–8 Who made everything He has created good, and He began the creation of man from clay. Then He made his offspring from *semen of worthless water (male and female sexual discharge).* (**HK**) Who made all things good which He created, and He began the creation of man from clay; Then He made his seed from a *draught of despised fluid* ... (P)

24:45 Allah has created every moving (living) creature from *water.* Of them there are some that creep on their bellies, some that walk on two legs, and some that walk on four. Allah creates what He wills. Verily! Allah is Able to do all things. (**HK**) Allah hath created every animal of *water.* Of them is (a kind) that goeth upon its belly and (a kind) that goeth upon two legs and (a kind) that goeth upon four. Allah createth what He will. Lo! Allah is Able to do all things. (P)

18:22–26 (Some) say they were three, the dog being the fourth among them; (others) say they were five, the dog being the sixth, guessing at the unseen; (yet others) say they were seven, the dog being the eighth. Say (O Muhammad): "My Lord knows best their number; none knows them but a few." So debate not (about their number, etc.) except with the clear proof (which We have revealed to you). And consult not any of them (people of the Scripture, Jews and Christians) about (the affair of) the people of the Cave. And never say of anything, "I shall do such and such thing tomorrow." Except (with the saying), "If Allah will!" And remember your Lord when you forget and say: "It may be that my Lord guides me unto a nearer way of truth than this." *And they stayed in their Cave three hundred (solar) years, and add nine (for lunar years).* Say: "Allah knows best how long they stayed. With Him is (the knowledge of) the unseen of the heavens and the earth. ...." (**HK**) (Some) will say: They were three, their dog the fourth, and (some) say: Five, their dog the sixth, guessing at random; and (some) say: Seven, and their dog the eighth. Say (O Muhammad): My Lord is Best Aware of their number. None knoweth them save a few. So contend not concerning them except with an outward contending, and ask not any of them to pronounce concerning them. And say not of anything: Lo! I shall do that tomorrow, Except if Allah will. And remember thy Lord when thou forgettest, and say: It may be that my Lord guideth me unto a nearer way of truth than this. *And (it is said) they tarried in their Cave three hundred years and add nine.* Say: Allah is Best Aware how long they tarried. His is the Invisible of the heavens and the earth. (P)

71:15–16 See you not how Allah has created the seven heavens one above another, And has made the moon a light therein, and made the sun a lamp? (**HK**) See ye not how Allah hath created seven heavens in harmony, And hath made the moon a light therein, and made the sun a lamp? (P)

25:61 Blessed be He Who has placed in the heaven big stars, and has placed therein a great lamp (sun), and a moon giving light. (**HK**) Blessed be He Who hath placed in the heaven mansions of the stars, and hath placed therein a great lamp and a moon giving light! (**P**)

24:35 Allah is the Light of the heavens and the earth. The parable of His Light is as (if there were) a niche and within it a lamp, the lamp is in glass, the glass as it were a brilliant star, lit from a blessed tree, an olive, neither of the east (i.e. neither it gets sun-rays only in the morning) nor of the west (i.e. nor it gets sun-rays only in the afternoon, but it is exposed to the sun all day long), whose oil would almost glow forth (of itself), though no fire touched it. Light upon Light! Allah guides to His Light whom He wills. (**HK**) Allah is the Light of the heavens and the earth. The similitude of His light is as a niche wherein is a lamp. The lamp is in a glass. The glass is as it were a shining star. (This lamp is) kindled from a blessed tree, an olive neither of the East nor of the West, whose oil would almost glow forth (of itself) though no fire touched it. Light upon light. Allah guideth unto His light whom He will. (**P**)

33:45–46 O Prophet (Muhammad)! Verily, We have sent you as witness, and a bearer of glad tidings, and a warner, And as one who invites to Allah [Islamic Monotheism, i.e. to worship none but Allah (Alone)] by His Leave, and as *a lamp spreading light* (through your instructions from the Qur'an and the *Sunnah the legal ways of the Prophet*). (**HK**) O Prophet! Lo! We have sent thee as a witness and a bringer of good tidings and a warner. And as a summoner unto Allah by His permission, and as *a lamp that giveth light*. (**P**)

78:6–7 Have We not made the earth as a bed, And the mountains as pegs? (**HK**) Have We not made the earth an expanse, And the high hills bulwarks? (**P**)

31:10 He has created the heavens without any pillars, that you see and has set on the earth firm mountains, lest it should shake with you. (**HK**) He hath created the heavens without supports that ye can see, and hath cast into the earth firm hills, so that it quake not with you. (**P**)

21:31 And We have placed on the earth firm mountains, lest it should shake with them. (**HK**) And We have placed in the earth firm hills lest it quake with them. (**P**)

24:39–40 As for those who disbelieve, their deeds are like a mirage in a desert. The thirsty one thinks it to be water, until he comes up to it, he finds it to be nothing, but he finds Allah with him, Who will pay him his due (Hell). And Allah is Swift in taking account. Or [the state of a disbeliever] is like the darkness in a vast deep sea, overwhelmed with a great wave topped by a great wave, topped by dark clouds, darkness, one above another, if a man stretches out his hand, he can hardly see it! And he for whom Allah has not appointed light, for him there is no light. (**HK**) As for those who disbelieve, their deeds are as a mirage in a desert. The thirsty one supposeth it to be water till he cometh unto it and findeth it naught, and findeth, in the place thereof, Allah Who payeth him his due; and Allah is swift at reckoning. Or as darkness on a vast, abysmal sea. There covereth him a wave, above which is a wave, above which is a cloud. Layer upon layer of darkness. When he holdeth out his hand he scarce can see it. And he for whom Allah hath not appointed light, for him there is no light. (**P**)

25:53 And it is He Who has let free the two seas (kinds of water), one palatable and sweet, and the other salt and bitter, and He has set a barrier and a complete partition between them. (**HK**) And He it is Who hath given independence to the two seas (though they meet); one palatable, sweet, and the other saltish, bitter; and hath set a bar and a forbidding ban between them. (**P**)

27:61 Is not He (better than your gods) Who has made the earth as a fixed abode, and has placed rivers in its midst, and has placed firm mountains therein, and has set a barrier between the two seas (of salt and sweet water). (**HK**) Is not He (best) Who made the earth a fixed abode, and placed rivers in the folds thereof, and placed firm hills therein, and hath set a barrier between the two seas? (**P**)

55:19–20 He has let loose the two seas (the salt water and the sweet) meeting together. Between them is a barrier which none of them can transgress. (**HK**) He hath loosed the two seas. They meet. There is a barrier between them. They encroach not (one upon the other). (**P**)

74:27–31 And what will make you know exactly what Hell-fire is? It spares not (any sinner), nor does it leave (anything unburnt)! Burning the skins! Over it are nineteen (angels as guardians and keepers of Hell). (**HK**) Ah, what will convey unto thee what that burning is!—It leaveth naught; it spareth naught. It shrivelleth the man. Above it are nineteen. We have appointed only angels to be wardens of the Fire (**P**)

27:87–88 And (remember) the Day on which the Trumpet will be blown and all who are in the heavens and all who are on the earth, will be terrified except him whom Allah will (exempt). And all shall come to Him humbled. *And you will see the mountains and think them solid, but they shall pass away as the passing away of the clouds.* (**HK**) And (remind them of) the Day when the Trumpet will be blown, and all who are in the heavens and the earth will start in fear, save him whom Allah willeth. And all come unto Him, humbled. *And thou seest the hills thou deemest solid flying with the flight of clouds …* (**P**)

2:107 Know you not that it is Allah to Whom belongs the dominion of the heavens and the earth? And besides Allah you have neither any *Wali* (protector or guardian) nor any helper. (**HK**) Knowest thou not that it is Allah unto Whom belongeth the Sovereignty of the heavens and the earth; and ye have not, beside Allah, any guardian or helper? (**P**)

15:2–3 Perhaps (often) will those who disbelieve wish that they were Muslims [those who have submitted themselves to Allah's Will in Islamic Monotheism, this will be on the Day of Resurrection when they will see the disbelievers going to Hell and the Muslims going to Paradise] Leave them to eat and enjoy, and let them be preoccupied with (false) hope. *They will come to know!* (**HK**) It may be that those who disbelieve wish ardently that they were Muslims. Let them eat and enjoy life, and let (false) hope beguile them. *They will come* *to know!* (P)

41:9-12 Say (O Muhammad): "Do you verily disbelieve in Him Who created the earth in two Days and you set up rivals (in worship) with Him? That is the Lord of the *'Alamin* (mankind, jinns and all that exists). He placed therein (i.e. the earth) firm mountains from above it, and He blessed it, and measured therein its sustenance (for its dwellers) in four Days equal (i.e. all these four 'days' were equal in the length of time), for all those who ask (about its creation). *Then* He *Istawa* (rose over) towards the heaven when it was smoke, and said to it and to the earth: "Come both of you willingly or unwillingly." They both said: "We come, willingly." Then He completed and finished from their creation (as) seven heavens in two Days and He made in each heaven its affair. And We adorned the nearest (lowest) heaven with lamps (stars) to be an adornment as well as to guard (from the devils by using them as missiles against the devils). Such is the Decree of Him the All-Mighty, the All-Knower. (**HK**) Say (O Muhammad, unto the idolaters): Disbelieve ye verily in Him Who created the earth in two Days, and ascribe ye unto Him rivals ? He (and none else) is the Lord of the Worlds. He placed therein firm hills rising above it, and blessed it and measured therein its sustenance in four Days, alike for (all) who ask; *Then* turned He to the heaven when it was smoke, and said unto it and unto the earth: Come both of you, willingly or loth. They said: We come, obedient. Then He ordained them seven heavens in two Days and inspired in each heaven its mandate; and We decked the nether heaven with lamps, and rendered it inviolable. That is the measuring of the Mighty, the Knower. (**P**)

32:4 Allah it is He Who has created the heavens and the earth, and all that is between them in six Days. Then He *Istawa* (rose over) the Throne (in a manner that suits His Majesty). (**HK**) Allah it is Who created the heavens and the earth, and that which is between them, in six Days. Then He mounted the Throne. (**P**)

11:7 And He it is Who has created the heavens and the earth in six Days and His Throne was on the water... (**HK**) And He it is Who created the heavens and the earth in six Days—and His Throne was upon the water. (**P**)

16:40 Verily! Our Word unto a thing when We intend it, is only that We say unto it: "Be!" and it is. (**HK**) And Our word unto a thing, when We intend it, is only that We say unto it: Be! and it is. (**P**)

2:117 The Originator of the heavens and the earth. When He decrees a matter, He only says to it: "Be!"— and it is. (**HK**) The Originator of the heavens and the earth! When He decreeth a thing, He saith unto it only: Be! and it is. (**P**)

13:2 Allah is He Who raised the heavens without any pillars that you can see. Then, He *Istawa* (rose above) the Throne (really in a manner that suits His Majesty). (**HK**) Allah it is Who raised up the heavens without visible supports, then mounted the Throne. (**P**)

31:10 He has created the heavens without any pillars, that you see ... (**HK**) He hath created the heavens without supports that ye can see ... (**P**)

30:25 And among His Signs is *that the heaven and the earth stand by His Command* ... (**HK**) And of His signs is this: *The heavens and the earth stand fast by His command* ... (**P**)

52:38 Or have they a stairway (to heaven), by means of which they listen (to the talks of the angels)? Then let their listener produce some manifest proof. (**HK**) Or have they any stairway (unto heaven) by means of which they overhear (decrees). Then let their listener produce some warrant manifest! (**P**)

23:14 Then We made the *Nutfah* into a clot (a piece of thick coagulated blood), then We made the clot into a little lump of flesh, then We made out of that little lump of flesh bones, then We clothed the bones with flesh, and then We brought it forth as another creation. (**HK**) Then fashioned We the drop a clot, then fashioned We the clot a little lump, then fashioned We the little lump bones, then clothed the bones with flesh, and then produced it as another creation. (**P**)

39:6 He creates you in the wombs of your mothers, creation after creation in three veils of darkness. (**HK**) He created you in the wombs of your mothers, creation after creation, in a threefold gloom. (**P**)

86:5–7 So let man see from what he is created! *He is created from a water gushing forth Proceeding from between the back-bone and the ribs.* (**HK**) So let man consider from what he is created. *He is created from a gushing fluid That issued from between the loins and ribs.* (**P**)

Chapter 5: The Quran and Justice

4:58 Verily! Allah commands that ... when you judge between men, you judge with justice. (**HK**) Lo! Allah commandeth you that ... if ye judge between mankind, that ye judge justly. (**P**)

4:92 and whosoever kills a believer by mistake, (it is ordained that) *he must set free a believing slave* ... (**HK**) He who hath killed a believer by mistake *must set free a believing slave* ... (**P**)

5:89 [F]or its expiation (a deliberate oath) ... *manumit a slave.* (**HK**) The expiation thereof is ... *liberation of a slave.* (**P**)

24:33 And such of your slaves as seek a writing (of emancipation), give them such writing, if you know that they are good and trustworthy. (**HK**) And such of your slaves as seek a writing (of emancipation), write it for them if ye are aware of aught of good in them. (**P**)

23:1–6 Successful indeed are the believers. Those who ... guard their chastity (i.e. private parts, from illegal sexual acts) Except from their wives *or (the captives and slaves) that their right hands possess,* for then, they are free from blame ... (**HK**) Successful indeed are the believers Who ... guard their modesty—Save from their wives or the (slaves) that their right hands possess, for then they are not blameworthy ... (**P**)

70:22–30 Except those devoted to *Salat* (prayers) … And those who guard their chastity (i.e. private parts from illegal sexual acts). *Except with their wives and the (women slaves and captives) whom their right hands possess,* for (then) they are not to be blamed. (**HK**) Save worshippers. …And those who preserve their chastity Save with their wives *and those whom their right hands possess,* for thus they are not blameworthy. (**P**)

33:55 It is no sin on them (the Prophet's wives, if they appear unveiled) before their fathers, or their sons, or their brothers, or their brother's sons, or the sons of their sisters, or their own (believing) women, *or their (female) slaves.* (**HK**) It is no sin for them (thy wives) to converse freely) with their fathers, or their sons, or their brothers, or their brothers' sons, or the sons of their sisters or of their own women, *or their slaves.* (**P**)

33:50–52 O Prophet (Muhammad)! Verily, We have made lawful to you … those (captives or slaves) whom your right hand possesses. … those (captives or slaves) whom your right hand possesses … (**HK**) O Prophet! Lo! We have made lawful unto thee … those whom thy right hand possesseth of those whom Allah hath given thee as spoils of war. … those whom thy right hand possesseth. And Allah is ever Watcher over all things. (**P**)

5:33–34 The recompense of those who wage war against Allah and His Messenger and do mischief in the land is only that they shall be killed or crucified or their hands and their feet be cut off on the opposite sides, or be exiled from the land. That is their disgrace in this world, and a great torment is theirs in the Hereafter. Except for those who (having fled away and then) came back (as Muslims) with repentance before they fall into your power; in that case, know that Allah is Oft-Forgiving, Most Merciful. (**HK**) The only reward of those who make war upon Allah and His messenger and strive after corruption in the land will be that they will be killed or crucified, or have their hands and feet on alternate sides cut off, or will be expelled out of the land. Such will be their degradation in the world, and in the Hereafter theirs will be an awful doom; Save those who repent before ye overpower them. For know that Allah is Forgiving, Merciful. (**P**)

4:15–16 And those of your women who commit illegal sexual intercourse, take the evidence of four witnesses from amongst you against them; and if they testify, confine them (i.e. women) to houses until death comes to them or Allah ordains for them some (other) way. And the two persons (man and woman) among you who commit illegal sexual intercourse, punish them both. And if they repent (promise Allah that they will never repeat, i.e. commit illegal sexual intercourse and other similar sins) and do righteous good deeds, leave them alone. Surely, Allah is Ever the One Who accepts repentance, (and He is) Most Merciful. (**HK**) As for those of your women who are guilty of lewdness, call to witness four of you against them. And if they testify (to the truth of the allegation) then confine them to the houses until death take them or (until) Allah appoint for them a way (through new legislation). And as for the two of you who are guilty thereof, punish them both. And if they repent and improve, then let them be. Lo! Allah is ever relenting, Merciful. (**P**)

24:2–3 *The woman and the man guilty of illegal sexual intercourse, flog each of them with a hundred stripes.* Let not pity withhold you in their case, in a punishment prescribed by Allah, if you believe in Allah and the Last Day. And let a party of the believers witness their punishment. (This punishment is for unmarried persons guilty of the above crime but if married persons commit it, the punishment is to stone them to death, according to Allah's Law). The adulterer marries not but an adulteress or a *Mushrikah* [and that means that the man who agrees to marry (have a sexual relation with) a *Mushrikah* (female polytheist, pagan or idolatress) or a prostitute, then surely he is either an adulterer, or a *Mushrik* (polytheist, pagan or idolater, etc.) And the woman who agrees to marry (have a sexual relation with) a *Mushrik* (polytheist, pagan or idolater) or an adulterer, then she is either a prostitute or a *Mushrikah* (female polytheist, pagan, or idolatress, etc.)]. Such a thing is forbidden to the believers (of Islamic Monotheism). (**HK**) *The adulterer and the adulteress, scourge ye each one of them (with) a hundred stripes.* And let not pity for the twain withhold you from obedience to Allah, if ye believe in Allah and the Last Day. And let a party of believers witness their punishment. The adulterer shall not marry save an adulteress or an idolatress, and the adulteress none shall marry save an adulterer or an idolater. All that is forbidden unto believers. (**P**)

4:25 And whoever of you have not the means wherewith to wed free, believing women, they may wed believing girls from among those (captives and slaves) whom your right hands possess. … And after they have been taken in wedlock, if they commit illegal sexual intercourse, their punishment is half that for free (unmarried) women. (**HK**) And whoso is not able to afford to marry free, believing women, let them marry from the believing maids whom your right hands possess. … And if when they are honourably married they commit lewdness they shall incur the half of the punishment (prescribed) for free women (in that case). (**P**)

33:30 O wives of the Prophet! Whoever of you commits an open illegal sexual intercourse, the torment for her will be doubled … (**HK**) O ye wives of the Prophet! Whosoever of you committeth manifest lewdness, the punishment for her will be doubled … (**P**)

2:178 O you who believe! *Al-Qisas* (the Law of Equality in punishment) is prescribed for you in case of murder: *the free for the free, the slave for the slave, and the female for the female.* But if the killer is forgiven by the brother (or the relatives, etc.) of the killed against blood money, then adhering to it with fairness and payment of the blood money, to the heir should be made in fairness. This is an alleviation and a mercy from your Lord. So after this whoever transgresses the limits (i.e. kills the killer after taking the blood money), he shall have a painful torment. (**HK**) O ye who believe! Retaliation is prescribed for you in the matter of the murdered; *the freeman for the freeman, and the slave for the slave, and the female for the female.* And for him who is forgiven somewhat by his (injured) brother, prosecution according to usage and payment unto him in kindness. This is an alleviation and a mercy from your Lord. He who transgresseth after this will have a painful doom. (**P**)

28:15–16 And he entered the city at a time of unawareness of its people, and he found there two men fighting,—one of his party (his religion—from the Children of Israel), and the other of his foes. The man of his (own) party asked him for help against his foe, so Musa (Moses) struck him with his fist and killed him. He said: "This is of *Shaitan*'s (Satan) doing, verily, he is a plain misleading enemy." He said: "My Lord! Verily, I have wronged myself, so forgive me." Then He forgave him. Verily, He is the Oft-Forgiving, the Most Merciful. (**HK**) And he entered the city at a time of carelessness of its folk, and he found therein two men fighting, one of his own caste, and the other of his enemies; and he who was of his caste asked him for help against him who was of his enemies. So Moses struck him with his fist and killed him. He said: This is of the devil's doing. Lo! he is an enemy, a mere misleader. He said: My Lord! Lo! I have wronged my soul, so forgive me. Then He forgave him. Lo! He is the Forgiving, the Merciful. (**P**)

18:65–82 Then they found one of Our slaves, unto whom We had bestowed mercy from Us, and whom We had taught knowledge from Us. Musa (Moses) said to him (Khidr) "May I follow you so that you teach me something of that knowledge (guidance and true path) which you have been taught (by Allah)?" He (Khidr) said: "Verily! You will not be able to have patience with me! And how can you have patience about a thing which you know not?" Musa (Moses) said: "If Allah will, you will find me patient, and I will not disobey you in aught." He (Khidr) said: "Then, if you follow me, ask me not about anything till I myself mention it to you." So they both proceeded, till, when they embarked the ship, he (Khidr) scuttled it. Musa (Moses) said: "Have you scuttled it in order to drown its people? Verily, you have committed a thing *'Imra'* (a *Munkar*— evil, bad, dreadful thing)." He (Khidr) said: "Did I not tell you, that you would not be able to have patience with me?" [Musa (Moses)] said: "Call me not to account for what I forgot, and be not hard upon me for my affair (with you)." *Then they both proceeded, till they met a boy, he (Khidr) killed him. Musa (Moses) said: "Have you killed an innocent person who had killed none? Verily, you have committed a thing 'Nukra' (a great Munkar—prohibited, evil, dreadful thing)!"* (Khidr) said: "Did I not tell you that you can have no patience with me?" [Musa (Moses)] said: "If I ask you anything after this, keep me not in your company, you have received an excuse from me." Then they both proceeded, till, when they came to the people of a town, they asked them for food, but they refused to entertain them. Then they found therein a wall about to collapse and he (Khidr) set it up straight. [Musa (Moses)] said: "If you had wished, surely, you could have taken wages for it!" (Khidr) said: "This is the parting between me and you, I will tell you the interpretation of (those) things over which you were unable to hold patience. As for the ship, it belonged to *Masakin* (poor people) working in the sea. So I wished to make a defective damage in it, as there was a king after them who seized every ship by force. *And as for the boy, his parents were believers, and we feared lest he should oppress them by rebellion and disbelief. So we intended that their Lord should change him for them for one better in righteousness and near to mercy.* And as for the wall, it belonged to two orphan boys in the town; and there was under it a treasure belonging to them; and their father was a righteous man, and your Lord intended that they should attain their age of full strength and take out their treasure as a mercy from your Lord. And I did it not of my own accord. That is the interpretation of those (things) over which you could not hold patience." (**HK**) Then found they one of Our slaves, unto whom We had given mercy from Us, and had taught him knowledge from Our presence. Moses said unto him: May I follow thee, to the end that thou mayst teach me right conduct of that which thou hast been taught? He said: Lo! thou canst not bear with me. How canst thou bear with that whereof thou canst not compass any knowledge? He said: Allah willing, thou shalt find me patient and I shall not in aught gainsay thee. He said: Well, if thou go with me, ask me not concerning aught till I myself make mention of it unto thee. So they twain set out till, when they were in the ship, he made a hole therein. (Moses) said: Hast thou made a hole therein to drown the folk thereof? Thou verily hast done a dreadful thing. He said: Did I not tell thee that thou couldst not bear with me? (Moses) said: Be not wroth with me that I forgot, and be not hard upon me for my fault. *So they twain journeyed on till, when they met a lad, he slew him. (Moses) said: What! Hast thou slain an innocent soul who hath slain no man? Verily thou hast done a horrid thing.* He said: Did I not tell thee that thou couldst not bear with me? (Moses) said: If I ask thee after this concerning aught, keep not company with me. Thou hast received an excuse from me. So they twain journeyed on till, when they came unto the folk of a certain township, they asked its folk for food, but they refused to make them guests. And they found therein a wall upon the point of falling into ruin, and he repaired it. (Moses) said: If thou hadst wished, thou couldst have taken payment for it. He said: This is the parting between thee and me! I will announce unto thee the interpretation of that thou couldst not bear with patience. As for the ship, it belonged to poor people working on the river, and I wished to mar it, for there was a king behind them who is taking every ship by force. *And as for the lad, his parents were believers and we feared lest he should oppress them by rebellion and disbelief. And we intended that their Lord should change him for them for one better in purity and nearer to mercy.* And as for the wall, it belonged to two orphan boys in the city, and there was beneath it a treasure belonging to them, and their father had been righteous, and thy Lord intended that they should come to their full strength and should bring forth their treasure as a mercy from their Lord; and I did it not upon my own command. Such is the interpretation of that wherewith thou couldst not bear. (**P**)

5:45 And We ordained therein for them: "Life for life, eye for eye, nose for nose, ear for ear, tooth for tooth, and wounds equal for equal." But if anyone remits the retaliation by way of charity, it shall be for him an expiation. And whosoever does not judge by that which Allah has revealed, such are the *Zalimun* (polytheists and wrong-doers—of a lesser degree). (**HK**) And We prescribed for them therein: The life for the life, and the eye for the eye, and the nose for the nose, and the ear for the ear, and the tooth for the tooth, and for wounds retaliation. But whoso forgoeth it (in the way of charity) it shall be expiation for him. Whoso judgeth not by that which Allah hath revealed: such are wrong-doers. (**P**)

5:38 Cut off (from the wrist joint) the (right) hand of the thief, male or female, as a recompense for that which they committed, a punishment by way of example from Allah. And Allah is All-Powerful, All-Wise. (**HK**) As for the thief, both male and female, cut off their hands. It is the reward of their own deeds, an exemplary punishment from Allah. Allah is Mighty, Wise. (**P**)

Chapter 6: The Quran and Women

17:31 And kill not your children for fear of poverty. We provide for them and for you. Surely, the killing of them is a great sin. (**HK**) Slay not your children, fearing a fall to poverty, We shall provide for them and for you. Lo! the slaying of them is great sin. (**P**)

16:72 And Allah has made for you wives of your own kind, and has made for you, from your wives, sons and grandsons, and has bestowed on you good provision. Do they then believe in false deities and deny the Favour of Allah (by not worshipping Allah Alone). (**HK**) And Allah hath given you wives of your own kind, and hath given you, from your wives, sons and grandsons, and hath made provision of good things for you. Is it then in vanity that they believe and in the grace of Allah that they disbelieve? (**P**)

53:21–22 Is it for you the males and for Him the females? That indeed is a division most unfair! (**HK**) Are yours the males and His the females? That indeed were an unfair division! (**P**)

16:57 And they assign daughters unto Allah! Glorified (and Exalted) be He above all that they associate with Him! And unto themselves what they desire … (**HK**) And they assign unto Allah daughters—Be He Glorified!—and unto themselves what they desire … (**P**)

17:40 Has then your Lord (O pagans of Makkah) preferred for you sons, and taken for Himself from among the angels daughters. (**HK**) Hath your Lord then distinguished you (O men of Makka) by giving you sons, and hath chosen for Himself females from among the angels? (**P**)

37:149 Now ask them (O Muhammad): "Are there (only) daughters for your Lord and sons for them?" (**HK**) Now ask them (O Muhammad): Hath thy Lord daughters whereas they have sons? (**P**)

52:39 Or has He (Allah) only daughters and you have sons? (**HK**) Or hath He daughters whereas ye have sons? (**P**)

2:228 And they (women) have rights (over their husbands as regards living expenses, etc.) similar (to those of their husbands) over them (as regards obedience and respect, etc.) to what is reasonable, *but men have a degree (of responsibility) over them.* And Allah is All-Mighty, All-Wise. (**HK**) And they (women) have rights similar to those (of men) over them in kindness, *and men are a degree above them.* Allah is Mighty, Wise. (**P**)

4:34 Men are the protectors and maintainers of women, *because Allah has made one of them to excel the other,* and because they spend (to support them) from their means. (**HK**) Men are in charge of women, *because Allah hath made the one of them to excel the other,* and because they spend of their property (for the support of women). (**P**)

4:24 All others are lawful, provided you seek (them in marriage) with *Mahr* (bridal money given by the husband to his wife at the time of marriage) from your property, desiring chastity, not committing illegal sexual intercourse, so with those of whom you have enjoyed sexual relations, *give them their Mahr as prescribed;* but if after a *Mahr* is prescribed, you agree mutually (to give more), there is no sin on you. Surely, Allah is Ever All-Knowing, All-Wise. (**HK**) Lawful unto you are all beyond those mentioned, so that ye seek them with your wealth in honest wedlock, not debauchery. And those of whom ye seek content (by marrying them), *give unto them their portions as a duty.* And there is no sin for you in what ye do by mutual agreement after the duty (hath been done). Lo! Allah is ever Knower, Wise. (**P**)

60:10 O you who believe! When believing women come to you as emigrants … send them not back to the disbelievers. … *But give the disbelievers that (amount of money) which they have spent [as their Mahr] to them.* (**HK**) O ye who believe! When believing women come unto you as fugitives … send them not back unto the disbelievers. … *And give the disbelievers that which they have spent (upon them).* (**P**)

2:282 O you who believe! When you contract a debt for a fixed period, write it down. … And get two witnesses out of your own men. *And if there are not two men (available), then a man and two women, such as you agree for witnesses, so that if one of them (two women) errs, the other can remind her.* (**HK**) O ye who believe! When ye contract a debt for a fixed term, record it in writing. … And call to witness, from among your men, two witnesses. *And if two men be not (at hand) then a man and two women, of such as ye approve as witnesses, so that if the one erreth (through forgetfulness) the other will remember.* (**P**)

5:106 O you who believe! When death approaches any of you, and you make a bequest, *then take the testimony of two just men of your own folk* or two others from outside, if you are travelling through the land and the calamity of death befalls you. (**HK**) O ye who believe! Let there be witnesses between you when death draweth nigh unto one of you, at the time of bequest—*two witnesses, just men from among you,* or two others from another tribe, in case ye are campaigning in the land and the calamity of death befall you. (**P**)

4:3 … then marry (other) women of your choice, two or three, or four but if you fear that you shall not be able to deal justly (with them), then only one or (the captives and the slaves) that your right hands possess. That is nearer to prevent you from doing injustice. (**HK**) … marry of the women, who seem good to you, two or three or four; and if ye fear that ye cannot do justice (to so many) then one (only) or (the captives) that your right hands possess. Thus it is more likely that ye will not do injustice. (**P**)

4:129 You will never be able to do perfect justice between wives even if it is your ardent desire, so do not incline too much to one of them (by giving her more of your time and provision) so as to leave the other hanging (i.e. neither divorced nor married). (**HK**) Ye will not be able to deal equally between (your) wives, however much ye wish (to do so). But turn not altogether away (from one), leaving her as in suspense. (**P**)

24:33 And force not your maids to prostitution, *if they desire chastity*, in order that you may make a gain in the (perishable) goods of this worldly life. But if anyone compels them (to prostitution), then after such compulsion, Allah is Oft-Forgiving, Most Merciful (to those women, i.e. He will forgive them because they have been forced to do this evil action unwillingly). (**HK**) Force not your slave-girls to whoredom that ye may seek enjoyment of the life of the world, *if they would preserve their chastity*. And if one force them, then (unto them), after their compulsion, lo! Allah will be Forgiving, Merciful. (**P**)

4:25 And whoever of you have not the means wherewith to wed free, believing women, they may wed believing girls from among those (captives and slaves) whom your right hands possess, ... and give them their *Mahr* according to what is reasonable; they (the above said captive and slave-girls) should be chaste, not adulterous, nor taking boy-friends. *And after they have been taken in wedlock, if they commit illegal sexual intercourse, their punishment is half that for free (unmarried) women.* (**HK**) And whoso is not able to afford to marry free, believing women, let them marry from the believing maids whom your right hands possess. ... [A]nd give unto them their portions in kindness, they being honest, not debauched nor of loose conduct. *And if when they are honourably married they commit lewdness they shall incur the half of the punishment (prescribed) for free women (in that case).* (**P**)

24:30–31 Tell the believing men to lower their gaze (from looking at forbidden things), and protect their private parts (from illegal sexual acts, etc.). That is purer for them. Verily, Allah is All-Aware of what they do. *And tell the believing women to lower their gaze (from looking at forbidden things), and protect their private parts (from illegal sexual acts, etc.) and not to show off their adornment except only that which is apparent (like palms of hands or one eye or both eyes for necessity to see the way, or outer dress like veil, gloves, head-cover, apron, etc.), and to draw their veils all over Juyubihinna (i.e. their bodies, faces, necks and bosoms, etc.)* and not to reveal their adornment except to their husbands, their fathers, their husband's fathers, their sons, their husband's sons, their brothers or their brother's sons, or their sister's sons, or their (Muslim) women (i.e. their sisters in Islam), or the (female) slaves whom their right hands possess, or old male servants who lack vigour, or small children who have no sense of the shame of sex. And let them not stamp their feet so as to reveal what they hide of their adornment. (**HK**) Tell the believing men to lower their gaze and be modest. That is purer for them. Lo! Allah is aware of what they do. *And tell the believing women to lower their gaze and be modest, and to display of their adornment only that which is apparent, and to draw their veils over their bosoms,* and not to reveal their adornment save to their own husbands or fathers or husbands' fathers, or their sons or their husbands' sons, or their brothers or their brothers' sons or sisters' sons, or their women, or their slaves, or male attendants who lack vigour, or children who know naught of women's nakedness. And let them not stamp their feet so as to reveal what they hide of their adornment. (**P**)

33:59 O Prophet! Tell your wives and your daughters and the women of the believers to draw their cloaks (veils) all over their bodies (i.e. screen themselves completely except the eyes or one eye to see the way). That will be better, that they should be known (as free respectable women) so as not to be annoyed. (**HK**) O Prophet! Tell thy wives and thy daughters and the women of the believers to draw their cloaks close round them (when they go abroad). That will be better, so that they may be recognised and not annoyed. (**P**)

33:32–33 *O wives of the Prophet! You are not like any other women.* If you keep your duty (to Allah), then be not soft in speech, lest he in whose heart is a disease (of hypocrisy, or evil desire for adultery, etc.) should be moved with desire, but speak in an honourable manner. *And stay in your houses, and do not display yourselves like that of the times of ignorance ...* (**HK**) *O ye wives of the Prophet! Ye are not like any other women.* If ye keep your duty (to Allah), then be not soft of speech, lest he in whose heart is a disease aspire (to you), but utter customary speech. *And stay in your houses. Bedizen not yourselves with the bedizenment of the Time of Ignorance.* (**P**)

56:22–23 And (there will be) *Houris* (fair females) with wide, lovely eyes (as wives for the pious), Like unto preserved pearls. (**HK**) And (there are) fair ones with wide, lovely eyes, Like unto hidden pearls. (**P**)

52:20 And We shall marry them to *Houris* (female, fair ones) with wide lovely eyes. (**HK**) And we wed them unto fair ones with wide, lovely eyes. (**P**)

44:54 So (it will be), and We shall marry them to *Houris* (female fair ones) with wide, lovely eyes. (**HK**) Even so (it will be). And We shall wed them unto fair ones with wide, lovely eyes. (**P**)

52:24 And there will go round boy-servants of theirs, to serve them as if they were preserved pearls. (**HK**) And there go round, waiting on them menservants of their own, as they were hidden pearls. (**P**)

76:19 And round about them will (serve) boys of everlasting youth. If you see them, you would think them scattered pearls. (**HK**) There wait on them immortal youths, whom, when thou seest, thou wouldst take for scattered pearls. (**P**)

24:6–9 And for those who accuse their wives, but have no witnesses except themselves, let the testimony of one of them be four testimonies (i.e. testifies four times) by Allah that he is one of those who speak the truth. And the fifth (testimony) (should be) the invoking of the Curse of Allah on him if he be of those who tell a lie (against her). *But it shall avert the punishment (of stoning to death) from her, if she bears witness four times by*

Allah, that he (her husband) is telling a lie. And the fifth (testimony) should be that the Wrath of Allah be upon her if he (her husband) speaks the truth. (**HK**) As for those who accuse their wives but have no witnesses except themselves; let the testimony of one of them be four testimonies, (swearing) by Allah that he is of those who speak the truth; And yet a fifth, invoking the curse of Allah on him if he is of those who lie. *And it shall avert the punishment from her if she bear witness before Allah four times that the thing he saith is indeed false, And a fifth (time) that the wrath of Allah be upon her if he speaketh truth.* (**P**)

24:26 Bad statements are for bad people (or bad women for bad men) and bad people for bad statements (or bad men for bad women). Good statements are for good people (or good women for good men) and good people for good statements (or good men for good women), *such (good people) are innocent of (each and every) bad statement which they say*, for them is Forgiveness, and *Rizqun Karim* (generous provision i.e. Paradise). (**HK**) Vile women are for vile men, and vile men for vile women. Good women are for good men, and good men for good women; *such are innocent of that which people say.* For them is pardon and a bountiful provision. (**P**)

24:4–5 And those who accuse chaste women, and produce not four witnesses, flog them with eighty stripes, and reject their testimony forever, they indeed are the *Fasiqun* (liars, rebellious, disobedient to Allah). Except those who repent thereafter and do righteous deeds, (for such) verily, Allah is Oft-Forgiving, Most Merciful. (**HK**) And those who accuse honourable women but bring not four witnesses, scourge them (with) eighty stripes and never (afterward) accept their testimony—They indeed are evil-doers—Save those who afterward repent and make amends. (For such) lo! Allah is Forgiving, Merciful. (**P**)

4:34 As to those women on whose part you see ill-conduct, admonish them (first), (next), refuse to share their beds, (and last) *beat them* (lightly, if it is useful), but if they return to obedience, seek not against them means (of annoyance). (**HK**) As for those from whom ye fear rebellion, admonish them and banish them to beds apart, *and scourge them.* Then if they obey you, seek not a way against them. (**P**)

8:12 (Remember) when your Lord inspired the angels, "Verily, I am with you, so keep firm those who have believed. I will cast terror into the hearts of those who have disbelieved, so strike them over the necks, and smite over all their fingers and toes." (**HK**) When thy Lord inspired the angels, (saying): I am with you. So make those who believe stand firm. I will throw fear into the hearts of those who disbelieve. Then smite the necks and smite of them each finger. (**P**)

2:223 Your wives are a tilth for you, so go to your tilth (have sexual relations with your wives in any manner as long as it is in the vagina and not in the anus), when or how you will … (**HK**) Your women are a tilth for you (to cultivate) so go to your tilth as ye will … (**P**)

Chapter 7: The Sword Verses

9:5 Then when the Sacred Months (the 1st, 7th, 11th, and 12th months of the Islamic calendar) have passed, then kill the *Mushrikun* (see V.2:105) wherever you find them, and capture them and besiege them, and prepare for them each and every ambush. But if they repent and perform *As-Salat* (*Iqamat-as-Salat*), and give *Zakat*, then leave their way free. Verily, Allah is Oft-Forgiving, Most Merciful. (**HK**) Then, when the sacred months have passed, slay the idolaters wherever ye find them, and take them (captive), and besiege them, and prepare for them each ambush. But if they repent and establish worship and pay the poor-due, then leave their way free. Lo! Allah is Forgiving, Merciful. (**P**)

9:29 Fight against those who (1) believe not in Allah, (2) nor in the Last Day, (3) nor forbid that which has been forbidden by Allah and His Messenger (4) and those who acknowledge not the religion of truth (i.e. Islam) among the people of the Scripture (Jews and Christians), until they pay the *Jizyah* with willing submission, and feel themselves subdued. (**HK**) Fight against such of those who have been given the Scripture as believe not in Allah nor the Last Day, and forbid not that which Allah hath forbidden by His messenger, and follow not the Religion of Truth, until they pay the tribute readily, being brought low. (**P**)

2:114 And who is more unjust than those who forbid that Allah's Name be glorified and mentioned much (i.e. prayers and invocations, etc.) in Allah's Mosques and strive for their ruin? (**HK**) And who doth greater wrong than he who forbiddeth the approach to the sanctuaries of Allah lest His name should be mentioned therein, and striveth for their ruin. (**P**)

2:190 And fight not with them at *Al-Masjid-al-Haram* (the sanctuary at Makkah), unless they (first) fight you there. (**HK**) Fight in the way of Allah against those who fight against you, but begin not hostilities. (**P**)

2:256 There is no compulsion in religion. (**HK**) There is no compulsion in religion. (**P**)

5:2 [A]nd let not the hatred of some people in (once) stopping you from *Al-Masjid-al-Haram* (at Makkah) lead you to transgression (and hostility on your part). (**HK**) And let not your hatred of a folk who (once) stopped your going to the inviolable place of worship seduce you to transgress. (**P**)

5:69 Surely, those who believe (in the Oneness of Allah, in His Messenger Muhammad and all that was revealed to him from Allah), those who are the Jews and the Sabians and the Christians,—whosoever believed in Allah and the Last Day, and worked righteousness, on them shall be no fear, nor shall they grieve. (**HK**) Lo! those who believe, and those who are Jews, and Sabaeans, and Christians—Whosoever believeth in Allah and the Last Day and doeth right—there shall no fear come upon them neither shall they grieve. (**P**)

6:108 And insult not those whom they (disbelievers) worship besides Allah, lest they insult Allah wrongfully without knowledge. (**HK**) Revile not those unto whom they pray beside Allah lest they wrongfully revile

Allah through ignorance. (**P**)

16:126 And if you punish (your enemy, O you believers in the Oneness of Allah), then punish them with the like of that with which you were afflicted. But if you endure patiently, verily, it is better for *As-Sabirin* (the patient ones, etc.). (**HK**) If ye punish, then punish with the like of that wherewith ye were afflicted. But if ye endure patiently, verily it is better for the patient. (**P**)

109:6 "To you be your religion, and to me my religion (Islamic Monotheism)." (**HK**) Unto you your religion, and unto me my religion. (**P**)

9:13 Will you not fight a people who have violated their oaths (pagans of Makkah) *and intended to expel the Messenger*, while they did attack you first? Do you fear them? (**HK**) Will ye not fight a folk who broke their solemn pledges, *and purposed to drive out the messenger* and did attack you first? What! Fear ye them? (**P**)

9:7–8 How (can there be such a covenant with them) that *when you are overpowered by them, they regard not the ties, either of kinship or of covenant with you?* (**HK**) How (can there be any treaty for the others) when, *if they have the upper hand of you, they regard not pact nor honour in respect of you?* (**P**)

4:48 Verily, Allah forgives not that partners should be set up with him in worship, but He forgives except that (anything else) to whom He pleases, and whoever sets up partners with Allah in worship, he has indeed invented a tremendous sin. (**HK**) Lo! Allah forgiveth not that a partner should be ascribed unto Him. He forgiveth (all) save that to whom He will. Whoso ascribeth partners to Allah, he hath indeed invented a tremendous sin. (**P**)

60:10–11 O you who believe! When believing women come to you as emigrants, examine them, Allah knows best as to their Faith, then if you ascertain that they are true believers, send them not back to the disbelievers, they are not lawful (wives) for the disbelievers nor are the disbelievers lawful (husbands) for them. But give the disbelievers that (amount of money) which they have spent [as their *Mahr*] to them. ... [A]nd ask for (the return of) that which you have spent (as *Mahr*) and let them (the disbelievers, etc.) ask back for that which they have spent. (**HK**) O ye who believe! When believing women come unto you as fugitives, examine them. Allah is Best Aware of their faith. Then, if ye know them for true believers, send them not back unto the disbelievers. They are not lawful for them (the disbelievers), nor are they (the disbelievers) lawful for them. And give them (the disbelievers) that which they have spent (upon them). ... [A]nd ask for (the return of) that which ye have spent; and let them (the disbelievers) ask for that which they have spent. (**P**)

9:1–3, 7 Freedom from (all) obligations (is declared) from Allah and His Messenger to those of the *Mushrikun* (polytheists, pagans, idolaters, disbelievers in the Oneness of Allah), with whom you made a treaty. So travel freely (O *Mushrikun*—see V.2:105) for four months (as you will) throughout the land. ... And a declaration from Allah and His Messenger to mankind on the greatest day (the 10th of Dhul-Hijjah—the 12th month of Islamic calendar) that Allah is free from (all) obligations to the *Mushrikun* (see V.2:105) and so is His Messenger. ... except those with whom you made a covenant near *Al-Masjid-al-Haram* (at Makkah)? So long, as they are true to you, stand you true to them. (**HK**) Freedom from obligation (is proclaimed) from Allah and His messenger toward those of the idolaters with whom ye made a treaty. Travel freely in the land four months. ... And a proclamation from Allah and His messenger to all men on the day of the Greater Pilgrimage that Allah is free from obligation to the idolaters, and (so is) His messenger ... save those with whom ye made a treaty at the Inviolable Place of Worship? So long as they are true to you, be true to them. (**P**)

9:9 They have purchased with the *Ayat* (proofs, evidences, verses, lessons, signs, revelations, etc.) of Allah a little gain ... (**HK**) They have purchased with the revelations of Allah a little gain ... (**P**)

9:28 O you who believe (in Allah's Oneness and in His Messenger (Muhammad)! *Verily, the Mushrikun (polytheists, pagans, idolaters, disbelievers in the Oneness of Allah, and in the Message of Muhammad) are Najasun (impure).* So let them not come near *Al-Masjid-al-Haram* (at Makkah) after this year ... (**HK**) *O ye who believe! The idolaters only are unclean.* So let them not come near the Inviolable Place of Worship after this their year. (**P**)

9:30–33 And the Jews say: 'Uzair (Ezra) is the son of Allah, and the Christians say: Messiah is the son of Allah. That is a saying from their mouths. They imitate the saying of the disbelievers of old. Allah's Curse be on them, how they are deluded away from the truth! They (Jews and Christians) took their rabbis and their monks to be their lords besides Allah (by obeying them in things which they made lawful or unlawful according to their own desires without being ordered by Allah), and (they also took as their Lord) Messiah, son of Maryam (Mary), while they (Jews and Christians) were commanded [in the Taurat (Torah) and the Injeel (Gospel)] to worship none but One *Ilah* (God—Allah) *La ilaha illa Huwa* (none has the right to be worshipped but He). Praise and glory be to Him, (far above is He) from having the partners they associate (with Him). *They (the disbelievers, the Jews and the Christians) want to extinguish Allah's Light (with which Muhammad has been sent—Islamic Monotheism) with their mouths, but Allah will not allow except that His Light should be perfected even though the Kafirun (disbelievers) hate (it). It is He Who has sent His Messenger (Muhammad) with guidance and the religion of truth (Islam), to make it superior over all religions even though the Mushrikun (polytheists, pagans, idolaters, disbelievers in the Oneness of Allah) hate (it).* (**HK**) And the Jews say: Ezra is the son of Allah, and the Christians say: The Messiah is the son of Allah. That is their saying with their mouths. They imitate the saying of those who disbelieved of old. Allah (Himself) fighteth against them. How perverse are they! They have taken as lords beside Allah their rabbis and their monks and the Messiah son of Mary, when they were bidden to worship only One God. There is no God save Him. Be He Glorified from all that they ascribe as partner (unto Him)! *Fain would they put out the light of Allah with their mouths, but Allah disdaineth (aught) save that He shall perfect*

His light, however much the disbelievers are averse. He it is Who hath sent His messenger with the guidance and the Religion of Truth, that He may cause it to prevail over all religion, however much the idolaters may be averse. (**P**)

9:6 And if anyone of the *Mushrikun* (polytheists, idolaters, pagans, disbelievers in the Oneness of Allah) seeks your protection then grant him protection, so that he may hear the Word of Allah (the Qur'an), and then escort him to where he can be secure, that is because they are men who know not. (**HK**) And if anyone of the idolaters seeketh thy protection (O Muhammad), then protect him so that he may hear the Word of Allah, and afterward convey him to his place of safety. That is because they are a folk who know not. (**P**)

5:48 And We have sent down to you (O Muhammad) the Book (this Qur'an) in truth, confirming the Scripture that came before it and *Mohayminan* (trustworthy in highness and a witness) over it (old Scriptures). So judge between them by what Allah has revealed, and follow not their vain desires, diverging away from the truth that has come to you. *To each among you, We have prescribed a law and a clear way. If Allah willed, He would have made you one nation, but that (He) may test you in what He has given you; so strive as in a race in good deeds. The return of you (all) is to Allah; then He will inform you about that in which you used to differ.* (**HK**) And unto thee have We revealed the Scripture with the truth, confirming whatever Scripture was before it, and a watcher over it. So judge between them by that which Allah hath revealed, and follow not their desires away from the truth which hath come unto thee. *For each We have appointed a divine law and a traced-out way. Had Allah willed He could have made you one community. But that He may try you by that which He hath given you (He hath made you as ye are). So vie one with another in good works. Unto Allah ye will all return, and He will then inform you of that wherein ye differ.* (**P**)

5:41–43 O Messenger (Muhammad)! Let not those who hurry to fall into disbelief grieve you, of such who say: "We believe" with their mouths but their hearts have no faith. *And of the Jews are men who listen much and eagerly to lies—listen to others who have not come to you. They change the words from their places; they say, "If you are given this, take it, but if you are not given this, then beware!'* ... So if they come to you (O Muhammad), either judge between them, or turn away from them. ... But how do they come to you for decision while they have the Taurat (Torah), in which is the (plain) Decision of Allah; yet even after that, they turn away. (**HK**) O Messenger! Let not them grieve thee who vie one with another in the race to disbelief, of such as say with their mouths: "We believe," but their hearts believe not, *and of the Jews: listeners for the sake of falsehood, listeners on behalf of other folk who come not unto thee, changing words from their context and saying: If this be given unto you, receive it, but if this be not given unto you, then beware!* ... If then they have recourse unto thee (Muhammad) judge between them or disclaim jurisdiction. ... How come they unto thee for judgment when they have the Torah, wherein Allah hath delivered judgment (for them)? Yet even after that they turn away. Such (folk) are not believers. (**P**)

5:49–51 And so judge (you O Muhammad) between them by what Allah has revealed and follow not their vain desires, but beware of them lest they turn you (O Muhammad) far away from some of that which Allah has sent down to you. *And if they turn away, then know that Allah's Will is to punish them for some sins of theirs. And truly, most of men are Fasiqun (rebellious and disobedient to Allah).* Do they then seek the judgement of (the Days of) Ignorance? And who is better in judgement than Allah for a people who have firm Faith. *O you who believe! Take not the Jews and the Christians as Auliya' (friends, protectors, helpers, etc.), they are but Auliya' to one another. And if any amongst you takes them as Auliya', then surely he is one of them. Verily, Allah guides not those people who are the Zalimun (polytheists and wrong-doers and unjust).* (**HK**) So judge between them by that which Allah hath revealed, and follow not their desires, but beware of them lest they seduce thee from some part of that which Allah hath revealed unto thee. *And if they turn away, then know that Allah's Will is to smite them for some sin of theirs. Lo! many of mankind are evil-livers.* Is it a judgment of the time of (pagan) ignorance that they are seeking? Who is better than Allah for judgment to a people who have certainty (in their belief)? *O ye who believe! Take not the Jews and the Christians for friends. They are friends one to another. He among you who taketh them for friends is (one) of them. Lo! Allah guideth not wrongdoing folk.* (**P**)

13:39 Allah blots out what He wills and confirms (what He wills). And with Him is the Mother of the Book (*Al-Lauh Al-Mahfuz*). (**HK**) Allah effaceth what He will, and establisheth (what He will), and with Him is the source of ordinance. (**P**)

2:106 Whatever a Verse (revelation) do We abrogate or cause to be forgotten, We bring a better one or similar to it. (**HK**) Nothing of our revelation (even a single verse) do we abrogate or cause be forgotten, but we bring (in place) one better or the like thereof. (**P**)

4:88–90 Then what is the matter with you that you are divided into two parties about the hypocrites? Allah has cast them back (to disbelief) because of what they have earned. ... They wish that you reject Faith, as they have rejected (Faith), and thus that you all become equal (like one another). *So take not Auliya' (protectors or friends) from them, till they emigrate in the Way of Allah (to Muhammad). But if they turn back (from Islam), take (hold) of them and kill them wherever you find them, and take neither Auliya' (protectors or friends) nor helpers from them.* Except those who join a group, between you and whom there is a treaty (of peace), or those who approach you with their breasts restraining from fighting you as well as fighting their own people. (**HK**) What aileth you that ye are become two parties regarding the hypocrites, when Allah cast them back (to disbelief) because of what they earned? ... They long that ye should disbelieve even as they disbelieve, that ye may be upon a level (with them), *So choose not friends from them till they forsake their homes in the way of Allah; if they turn back (to enmity) then take them and kill them wherever ye find them, and choose no friend nor helper from among them,* Except those who seek refuge with a people between whom and you there is a covenant, or (those who) come unto you because their hearts forbid them to make war on you or make war on their own folk. (**P**)

66:9 O Prophet (Muhammad)! Strive hard against the disbelievers and the hypocrites, and be severe against them, their abode will be Hell, and worst indeed is that destination. (**HK**) O Prophet! Strive against the disbelievers and the hypocrites, and be stern with them. Hell will be their home, a hapless journey's end. (**P**)

Chapter 8: The Jews of Medina

21:107 And We have sent you (O Muhammad) not but as a mercy for the *'Alamin* (mankind, jinns and all that exists). (**HK**) We sent thee not save as a mercy for the peoples. (**P**)

3:199 And there are, certainly, among the people of the Scripture (Jews and Christians), those who believe in Allah and in that which has been revealed to you, and in that which has been revealed to them. (**HK**) And lo! of the People of the Scripture there are some who believe in Allah and that which is revealed unto you and that which was revealed unto them. (**P**)

17:107 Say (O Muhammad to them): "Believe in it (the Qur'an) or do not believe (in it). Verily! Those who were given knowledge before it (the Jews and the Christians like 'Abdullah bin Salam and Salman Al-Farisi), when it is recited to them, fall down on their faces in humble prostration." (**HK**) Say: Believe therein or believe not, lo! those who were given knowledge before it, when it is read unto them, fall down prostrate on their faces, adoring. (**P**)

26:197 Is it not a sign to them that the learned scholars (like 'Abdullah bin Salam who embraced Islam) of the Children of Israel knew it (as true)? (**HK**) Is it not a token for them that the doctors of the Children of Israel know it? (**P**)

28:52 Those to whom We gave the Scripture [i.e. the Taurat (Torah) and the Injeel (Gospel), etc.] before it,—they believe in it (the Qur'an). (**HK**) Those unto whom We gave the Scripture before it, they believe in it (**P**)

10:94 So if you (O Muhammad) are in doubt concerning that which We have revealed unto you, [i.e. that your name is written in the Taurat (Torah) and the Injeel (Gospel)] then ask those who are reading the Book [the Taurat (Torah) and the Injeel (Gospel)] before you. (**HK**) And if thou (Muhammad) art in doubt concerning that which We reveal unto thee, then question those who read the Scripture (that was) before thee. (**P**)

29:46 And argue not with the people of the Scripture (Jews and Christians), unless it be in (a way) that is better (with good words and in good manner, inviting them to Islamic Monotheism with His Verses), except with such of them as do wrong, and say (to them): "We believe in that which has been revealed to us and revealed to you; our *Ilah* (God) and your *Ilah* (God) is One (i.e. Allah), and to Him we have submitted (as Muslims)." (**HK**) And argue not with the People of the Scripture unless it be in (a way) that is better, save with such of them as do wrong; and say: We believe in that which hath been revealed unto us and revealed unto you; our God and your God is One, and unto Him we surrender. (**P**)

29:27 And We bestowed on him [Ibrahim (Abraham)], Ishaque (Isaac) and Ya'qub (Jacob), and ordained among his offspring Prophethood and the Book [i.e. the Taurat (Torah) (to Musa—Moses), the Injeel (Gospel) (to 'Iesa—Jesus), the Qur'an (to Muhammad), all from the offspring of Ibrahim (Abraham)], and We granted him his reward in this world, and verily, in the Hereafter he is indeed among the righteous. (**HK**) And We bestowed on him Isaac and Jacob, and We established the prophethood and the Scripture among his seed, and We gave him his reward in the world, and lo! in the Hereafter he verily is among the righteous. (**P**)

2:144 Verily! We have seen the turning of your (Muhammad's) face towards the heaven. Surely, We shall turn you to a *Qiblah* (prayer direction) that shall please you, so turn your face in the direction of *Al-Masjid- al-Haram* (at Makkah). And wheresoever you people are, turn your faces (in prayer) in that direction. (**HK**) We have seen the turning of thy face to heaven (for guidance), O Muhammad. And now verily We shall make thee turn (in prayer) toward a qiblah which is dear to thee. So turn thy face toward the Inviolable Place of Worship, and ye (O Muslims), wheresoever ye may be, turn your faces (when ye pray) toward it. (**P**)

5:51 O you who believe! Take not the Jews and the Christians as *Auliya'* (friends, protectors, helpers, etc.), they are but *Auliya'* to one another. And if any amongst you takes them as *Auliya'*, then surely he is one of them. Verily, Allah guides not those people who are the *Zalimun* (polytheists and wrong-doers and unjust). (**HK**) O ye who believe! Take not the Jews and the Christians for friends. They are friends one to another. He among you who taketh them for friends is (one) of them. Lo! Allah guideth not wrongdoing folk. (**P**)

8:55–59 Verily, The worst of moving (living) creatures before Allah are *those who disbelieve*,—so they shall not believe. They are *those with whom you made a covenant, but they break their covenant* every time and they do not fear Allah. So if you gain the mastery over them in war, punish them severely in order to disperse those who are behind them, so that they may learn a lesson. If you (O Muhammad) fear treachery from any people throw back (their covenant) to them (so as to be) on equal terms (that there will be no more covenant between you and them). Certainly Allah likes not the treacherous. And let not those who disbelieve think that they can outstrip (escape from the punishment). Verily, they will never be able to save themselves (from Allah's Punishment). (**HK**) Lo! the worst of beasts in Allah's sight are *the ungrateful* who will not believe. Those of them *with whom thou madest a treaty, and then at every opportunity they break their treaty*, and they keep not duty (to

Allah). If thou comest on them in the war, deal with them so as to strike fear in those who are behind them, that haply they may remember. And if thou fearest treachery from any folk, then throw back to them (their treaty) fairly. Lo! Allah loveth not the treacherous. And let not those who disbelieve suppose that they can outstrip (Allah's Purpose). Lo! they cannot escape. (**P**)

5:11 O you who believe! Remember the Favour of Allah unto you when some people desired (made a plan) to stretch out their hands against you, but (Allah) withheld their hands from you. So fear Allah. And in Allah let believers put their trust. (**HK**) O ye who believe! Remember Allah's favour unto you, how a people were minded to stretch out their hands against you but He withheld their hands from you; and keep your duty to Allah. In Allah let believers put their trust. (**P**)

59:2–4 He it is Who drove out the disbelievers among the people of the Scripture (i.e. the Jews of the tribe of Bani An-Nadir) from their homes at the first gathering. ... *That is because they opposed Allah and His Messenger (Muhammad)*. And whosoever opposes Allah, then verily, Allah is Severe in punishment. (**HK**) He it is Who hath caused those of the People of the Scripture who disbelieved to go forth from their homes unto the first exile. ... *That is because they were opposed to Allah and His messenger,* and whoso is opposed to Allah, (for him) verily Allah is stern in reprisal. (**P**)

33:9 O you who believe! Remember Allah's Favour to you, when there came against you hosts, and We sent against them a wind and forces that you saw not [i.e. troops of angels during the battle of *Al-Ahzab* (the Confederates)]. And Allah is Ever All-Seer of what you do. (**HK**) O ye who believe! Remember Allah's favour unto you when there came against you hosts, and We sent against them a great wind and hosts ye could not see. And Allah is ever Seer of what ye do. (**P**)

33:10–11 When they came upon you from above you and from below you, and when the eyes grew wild and the hearts reached to the throats, and you were harbouring doubts about Allah. There, the believers were tried and shaken with a mighty shaking. (**HK**) When they came upon you from above you and from below you, and when eyes grew wild and hearts reached to the throats, and ye were imagining vain thoughts concerning Allah. There were the believers sorely tried, and shaken with a mighty shock. (**P**)

33:12–15 And when the hypocrites and those in whose hearts is a disease (of doubts) said: "Allah and His Messenger promised us nothing but delusions!" And when a party of them said: "O people of Yathrib (Al-Madinah)! There is no stand (possible) for you (against the enemy attack!) Therefore go back!" *And a band of them ask for permission of the Prophet saying: "Truly, our homes lie open (to the enemy)." And they lay not open. They but wished to flee. And if the enemy had entered from all sides (of the city), and they had been exhorted to Al-Fitnah (i.e. to renegade from Islam to polytheism) they would surely have committed it and would have hesitated thereupon but little.* And indeed they had already made a covenant with Allah not to turn their backs, and a covenant with Allah must be answered for. (**HK**) And when the hypocrites, and those in whose hearts is a disease, were saying: Allah and His messenger promised us naught but delusion. And when a party of them said: O folk of Yathrib! There is no stand (possible) for you, therefor turn back. *And certain of them (even) sought permission of the Prophet, saying: Our homes lie open (to the enemy). And they lay not open. They but wished to flee. If the enemy had entered from all sides and they had been exhorted to treachery, they would have committed it, and would have hesitated thereupon but little.* And verily they had already sworn unto Allah that they would not turn their backs (to the foe). An oath to Allah must be answered for. (**P**)

33:25–27 And Allah drove back those who disbelieved in their rage, they gained no advantage (booty, etc.). Allah sufficed for the believers in the fighting (by sending against the disbelievers a severe wind and troops of angels). And Allah is Ever All-Strong, All-Mighty. *And those of the people of the Scripture who backed them (the disbelievers) Allah brought them down from their forts and cast terror into their hearts, (so that) a group (of them) you killed, and a group (of them) you made captives.* And He caused you to inherit their lands, and their houses, and their riches, and a land which you had not trodden (before). And Allah is Able to do all things. (**HK**) And Allah repulsed the disbelievers in their wrath; they gained no good. Allah averted their attack from the believers. Allah is ever Strong, Mighty. *And He brought those of the People of the Scripture who supported them down from their strongholds, and cast panic into their hearts. Some ye slew, and ye made captive some.* And He caused you to inherit their land and their houses and their wealth, and land ye have not trodden. Allah is ever Able to do all things. (**P**)

2:204-205 [Y]et he is the most quarrelsome of the opponents. And when he turns away (from you "O Muhammad"), his effort in the land is to make mischief therein and to destroy the crops and the cattle, and Allah likes not mischief. (**HK**) [Y]et he is the most rigid of opponents. And when he turneth away (from thee) his effort in the land is to make mischief therein and to destroy the crops and the cattle; and Allah loveth not mischief. (**P**)

Chapter 9: The Glorious Quran

15:87 We have bestowed upon you ... the Grand Qur'an. (**HK**) We have given thee ... the great Qur'an. (**P**)

2:23 And if you (Arab pagans, Jews, and Christians) are in doubt concerning that which We have sent down (i.e. the Qur'an) to Our slave (Muhammad Peace be upon him), then produce a *Surah* (chapter) of the like thereof and call your witnesses (supporters and helpers) besides Allah, if you are truthful. (**HK**) And if ye are in doubt concerning that which We reveal unto Our slave (Muhammad), then produce a surah of the like thereof, and call your witness beside Allah if ye are truthful. (**P**)

17:88 Say: "If the mankind and the jinns were together *to produce the like of this Qur'an*, they could not produce the like thereof, even if they helped one another." (**HK**) Say: Verily, though mankind and the jinn should assemble *to produce the like of this Qur'an*, they could not produce the like thereof though they were helpers one of another. (**P**)

52:33–34 Or do they say: "He (Muhammad) has forged it (this Qur'an)?" Nay! They believe not! Let them then produce *a recital like unto it* (the Qur'an) if they are truthful. (**HK**) Or say they: He hath invented it? Nay, but they will not believe! Then let them produce *speech the like thereof*, if they are truthful. (**P**)

11:13 Or they say, "He (Prophet Muhammad) forged it (the Qur'an)." Say: "Bring you then *ten forged Surah (chapters) like unto it*" (**HK**) Or they say: He hath invented it. Say: Then bring *ten surahs, the like thereof, invented*, (**P**)

55:31–45 We shall attend to you, O you two classes (jinns and men)! Then which of the Blessings of your Lord will you both (jinns and men) deny? O assembly of jinns and men! If you have power to pass beyond the zones of the heavens and the earth, then pass (them)! But you will never be able to pass them, except with authority (from Allah)! Then which of the Blessings of your Lord will you both (jinns and men) deny? There will be sent against you both, smokeless flames of fire and (molten) brass, and you will not be able to defend yourselves. Then which of the Blessings of your Lord will you both (jinns and men) deny? Then when the heaven is rent asunder, and it becomes rosy or red like red-oil, or red hide. Then which of the Blessings of your Lord will you both (jinns and men) deny? So on that Day no question will be asked of man or jinn as to his sin, (because they have already been known from their faces either white or black). Then which of the Blessings of your Lord will you both (jinns and men) deny? The *Mujrimun* (polytheists, criminals, sinners, etc.) will be known by their marks (black faces), and they will be seized by their forelocks and their feet. Then which of the Blessings of your Lord will you both (jinns and men) deny? This is Hell which the *Mujrimun* (polytheists, criminals, sinners, etc.) denied. They will go between it (Hell) and the boiling hot water! Then which of the Blessings of your Lord will you both (jinns and men) deny? (**HK**) We shall dispose of you, O ye two dependents (man and jinn). Which is it, of the favours of your Lord, that ye deny? O company of jinn and men, if ye have power to penetrate (all) regions of the heavens and the earth, then penetrate (them)! Ye will never penetrate them save with (Our) sanction. Which is it, of the favours of your Lord, that ye deny? There will be sent, against you both, heat of fire and flash of brass, and ye will not escape. Which is it, of the favours of your Lord, that ye deny ? And when the heaven splitteth asunder and becometh rosy like red hide Which is it, of the favours of your Lord, that ye deny? On that day neither man nor jinni will be questioned of his sin. Which is it, of the favours of your Lord, that ye deny? The guilty will be known by their marks, and will be taken by the forelocks and the feet. Which is it, of the favours of your Lord, that ye deny? This is hell which the guilty deny. They go circling round between it and fierce, boiling water. Which is it, of the favours of your Lord, that ye deny? (**P**)

7:175–176 And recite (O Muhammad) to them the story of him to whom We gave Our *Ayat* (proofs, evidences, verses, lessons, signs, revelations, etc.), but he threw them away. ... So his description is the description of a dog: if you drive him away, he lolls his tongue out, or if you leave him alone, he (still) lolls his tongue out. Such is the description of the people who reject Our *Ayat* (proofs, evidences, verses, lessons, signs, revelations, etc.). (**HK**) Recite unto them the tale of him to whom We gave Our revelations, but he sloughed them off. ... Therefor his likeness is as the likeness of a dog: if thou attackest him he panteth with his tongue out, and if thou leavest him he panteth with his tongue out. Such is the likeness of the people who deny Our revelations. (**P**)

2:185 ... *the Qur'an, a guidance for mankind and clear proofs for the guidance* and the criterion (between right and wrong). (**HK**) ... *the Qur'an, a guidance for mankind, and clear proofs of the guidance*, and the Criterion (of right and wrong). (**P**)

11:114 And perform *As-Salat (Iqamat-as-Salat)*, at the two ends of the day and in some hours of the night [i.e. the five compulsory *Salat* (prayers)]. (**HK**) Establish worship at the two ends of the day and in some watches of the night. (**P**)

17:78–79 Perform *As-Salat (Iqamat-as-Salat)* from mid-day till the darkness of the night (i.e. the *Zuhr, 'Asr, Maghrib,* and *'Isha'* prayers), and recite the Qur'an in the early dawn (i.e. the morning prayer). Verily, the recitation of the Qur'an in the early dawn is ever witnessed (attended by the angels in charge of mankind of the day and the night). And in some parts of the night (also) offer the *Salat* (prayer) with it (i.e. recite the Qur'an in the prayer), as an additional prayer (*Tahajjud* optional prayer *Nawafil*) for you (O Muhammad). (**HK**) Establish worship at the going down of the sun until the dark of night, and (the recital of) the Qur'an at dawn. Lo! (the recital of) the Qur'an at dawn is ever witnessed. And some part of the night awake for it, a largess for thee. (**P**)

20:130 [A]nd glorify the praises of your Lord before the rising of the sun, and before its setting, and during some of the hours of the night, and at the sides of the day (an indication for the five compulsory congregational prayers), that you may become pleased with the reward which Allah shall give you. (**HK**) [A]nd celebrate the praise of thy Lord ere the rising of the sun and ere the going down thereof. And glorify Him some hours of the night and at the two ends of the day, that thou mayst find acceptance. (**P**)

30:17–18 So glorify Allah [above all that (evil) they associate with Him (O believers)], when you come up to the evening [i.e. offer the (*Maghrib*) sunset and (*'Isha'*) night prayers], and when you enter the morning [i.e. offer the (*Fajr*) morning prayer]. And His is all the praises and thanks in the heavens and the earth, and (glorify Him) in the afternoon (i.e. offer *'Asr* prayer) and when you come up to the time, when the day begins to decline (i.e offer *Zuhr* prayer). (Ibn 'Abbas said: "These are the five compulsory congregational prayers mentioned in the Qur'an)." (**HK**) So glory be to Allah when ye enter the night and when ye enter the morning Unto Him be praise in the heavens and the earth! and at the sun's decline and in the noonday. (**P**)

52:48–49 [A]nd glorify the Praises of your Lord when you get up from sleep. And in the night-time, also glorify His Praises, and at the setting of the stars. (**HK**) [A]nd hymn the praise of thy Lord when thou uprisest, And in the night-time also hymn His praise, and at the setting of the stars. (**P**)

76:25–26 And remember the Name of your Lord every morning and afternoon [i.e. offering of the Morning (*Fajr*), *Zuhr*, and *'Asr* prayers]. And during night, prostrate yourself to Him (i.e. the offering of *Maghrib* and '*Isha'* prayers), and glorify Him a long night through (i.e. *Tahajjud* prayer). (**HK**) Remember the name of thy Lord at morn and evening. And worship Him (a portion) of the night. And glorify Him through the livelong night. (**P**)

61:6 But when he (Ahmed i.e. Muhammad) came to them with clear proofs, they said: "*This is plain magic.*" (**HK**) Yet when he hath come unto them with clear proofs, they say: *This is mere magic.* (**P**)

46:7–8 And when Our Clear Verses are recited to them, the disbelievers say of the truth (this Qur'an), when it reaches them: "*This is plain magic!*' Or say they: "*He (Muhammad) has fabricated it."* Say: "If I have fabricated it, still you have no power to support me against Allah. He knows best of what you say among yourselves concerning it (i.e. this Qur'an)! Sufficient is He for a witness between me and you! And He is the Oft-Forgiving, the Most Merciful." (**HK**) And when Our clear revelations are recited unto them, those who disbelieve say of the Truth when it reacheth them: *This is mere magic. Or say they: He hath invented it?* Say (O Muhammad): If I have invented it, still ye have no power to support me against Allah. He is Best Aware of what ye say among yourselves concerning it. He sufficeth for a witness between me and you. And He is the Forgiving, the Merciful. (**P**)

8:31 And when Our Verses (of the Qur'an) are recited to them, they say: "We have heard this (the Qur'an); if we wish we can say the like of this. This is nothing but the tales of the ancients." (**HK**) And when Our revelations are recited unto them they say: We have heard. If we wish we can speak the like of this. Lo! this is naught but fables of the men of old. (**P**)

16:24 And when it is said to them: "What is it that your Lord has sent down (unto Muhammad)?" They say: "Tales of the men of old!" (**HK**) And when it is said unto them: What hath your Lord revealed? they say: (Mere) fables of the men of old. (**P**)

6:93 And who can be more unjust than he who invents a lie against Allah, or says: "I have received inspiration," whereas he is not inspired in anything; *and who says, "I will reveal the like of what Allah has revealed."* (**HK**) Who is guilty of more wrong than he who forgeth a lie against Allah, or saith: I am inspired, when he is not inspired in aught; *and who saith: I will reveal the like of that which Allah hath revealed?* (**P**)

37:34–37 Certainly, that is how We deal with *Al-Mujrimun* (polytheists, sinners, criminals, the disobedient to Allah, etc.). Truly, when it was said to them: *La ilaha ill-Allah* "(none has the right to be worshipped but Allah)," they puffed themselves up with pride (i.e. denied it). And (they) said: "Are we going to abandon our *aliha* (gods) for the sake of a *mad poet?* Nay! he (Muhammad) has come with the truth (i.e. Allah's Religion—Islamic Monotheism and this Qur'an) and he confirms the Messengers (before him who brought Allah's religion—Islamic Monotheism)." (**HK**) Lo! thus deal We with the guilty. For when it was said unto them, There is no God save Allah, they were scornful. And said: Shall we forsake our gods for a *mad poet?* Nay, but he brought the Truth, and he confirmed those sent (before him). (**P**)

21:5 Nay, they say: These (revelations of the Qur'an which are inspired to Muhammad) are mixed up false dreams! Nay, he has invented it! Nay, he is a poet! (**HK**) Nay, say they, (these are but) muddled dreams; nay, he hath but invented it; nay, he is but a poet. (**P**)

100:1–11 By the (steeds) that run, with panting (breath), Striking sparks of fire (by their hooves), And scouring to the raid at dawn And raise the dust in clouds the while, Penetrating forthwith as one into the midst (of the foe); Verily! Man (disbeliever) is ungrateful to his Lord; And to that fact he bears witness (by his deeds); And verily, he is violent in the love of wealth. Knows he not that when the contents of the graves are brought out and poured forth (all mankind is resurrected). And that which is in the breasts (of men) shall be made known. Verily, that Day (i.e. the Day of Resurrection) their Lord will be Well-Acquainted with them (as to their deeds), (and will reward them for their deeds). (**HK**) By the snorting courses, Striking sparks of fire And scouring to the raid at dawn, Then, therewith, with their trail of dust, Cleaving, as one, the centre (of the foe), Lo! man is an ingrate unto his Lord And lo! he is a witness unto that; And lo! in the love of wealth he is violent. Knoweth he not that, when the contents of the graves are poured forth And the secrets of the breasts are made known, On that day will their Lord be perfectly informed concerning them. (**P**)

9:124–125 And whenever there comes down a *Surah* (chapter from the Qur'an), some of them (hypocrites) say: "Which of you has had his Faith increased by it?" As for those who believe, it has increased their Faith, and they rejoice. But as for those in whose hearts is a disease (of doubt, disbelief and hypocrisy), it will add suspicion and doubt to their suspicion, disbelief and doubt, and they die while they are disbelievers. (**HK**) And whenever a surah is revealed there are some of them who say: Which one of you hath thus increased in faith? As for those who believe, it hath increased them in faith and they rejoice (therefor). But as for those in whose hearts is disease, it only addeth wickedness to their wickedness, and they die while they are disbelievers. (**P**)

8:20–22 O you who believe! … [B]e not like those who say: "We have heard," but they hear not. Verily! The worst of (moving) living creatures with Allah are the deaf and the dumb, *those who understand not* (i.e. the disbelievers). (**HK**) O ye who believe. ... Be not as those who say, we hear, and they hear not. Lo! the worst of beasts in Allah's sight are the deaf, the dumb, *who have no sense.* (**P**)

72:1–9 Say (O Muhammad): "It has been revealed to me that a group (from three to ten in number) of jinns listened (to this Qur'an). They said: 'Verily! We have heard a wonderful Recital (this Qur'an)!'It guides to the Right Path, and we have believed therein, and we shall never join (in worship) anything with our Lord (Allah). ... And we have sought to reach the heaven; but found it filled with stern guards and flaming fires. And verily, we used to sit there in stations, to (steal) a hearing, but any who listens now will find a flaming fire watching him in ambush.'" (**HK**) Say (O Muhammad): It is revealed unto me that a company of the Jinn gave ear, and they said: Lo! we have heard a marvellous Qur'an, Which guideth unto righteousness, so we believe in it and we ascribe no partner unto our Lord. ... We had sought the heaven but had found it filled with strong warders and meteors. And we used to sit on places (high) therein to listen. But he who listeneth now findeth a flame in wait for him. (**P**)

37:6–10 Verily! We have adorned the near heaven with the stars (for beauty). And to guard against every rebellious devil. They cannot listen to the higher group (angels) for they are pelted from every side. Outcast, and theirs is a constant (or painful) torment. Except such as snatch away something by stealing and they are pursued by a flaming fire of piercing brightness. (**HK**) Lo! We have adorned the lowest heaven with an ornament, the planets; With security from every froward devil. They cannot listen to the Highest Chiefs for they are pelted from every side, Outcast, and theirs is a perpetual torment; Save him who snatcheth a fragment, and there pursueth him a piercing flame. (**P**)

2:101–103 And when there came to them a Messenger from Allah (i.e. Muhammad Peace be upon him) confirming what was with them, a party of those who were given the Scripture threw away the Book of Allah behind their backs as if they did not know! They followed what the *Shayatin* (devils) gave out (falsely of the magic) in the lifetime of Sulaiman (Solomon). Sulaiman did not disbelieve, but the *Shayatin* (devils) disbelieved, teaching men magic and such things that came down at Babylon to the two angels, Harut and Marut, but neither of these two (angels) taught anyone (such things) till they had said, "We are only for trial, so disbelieve not (by learning this magic from us)." And from these (angels) people learn that by which they cause separation between man and his wife, but they could not thus harm anyone except by Allah's Leave. And they learn that which harms them and profits them not. And indeed they knew that the buyers of it (magic) would have no share in the Hereafter. And how bad indeed was that for which they sold their ownselves, if they but knew. And if they had believed, and guarded themselves from evil and kept their duty to Allah, far better would have been the reward from their Lord, if they but knew! (**HK**) And when there cometh unto them a messenger from Allah, confirming that which they possess, a party of those who have received the Scripture fling the Scripture of Allah behind their backs as if they knew not, And follow that which the devils falsely related against the kingdom of Solomon. Solomon disbelieved not; but the devils disbelieved, teaching mankind magic and that which was revealed to the two angels in Babel, Harut and Marut. Nor did they (the two angels) teach it to anyone till they had said: We are only a temptation, therefore disbelieve not (in the guidance of Allah). And from these two (angels) people learn that by which they cause division between man and wife; but they injure thereby no-one save by Allah's leave. And they learn that which harmeth them and profiteth them not. And surely they do know that he who trafficketh therein will have no (happy) portion in the Hereafter; and surely evil is the price for which they sell their souls, if they but knew. And if they had believed and kept from evil, a recompense from Allah would be better, if they only knew. (**P**)

113:1–5 Say: "I seek refuge with (Allah) the Lord of the daybreak, From the evil of what He has created; And from the evil of the darkening (night) as it comes with its darkness; (or the moon as it sets or goes away). *And from the evil of the witchcrafts when they blow in the knots,* And from the evil of the envier when he envies." (**HK**) Say: I seek refuge in the Lord of the Daybreak From the evil of that which He created; From the evil of the darkness when it is intense, *And from the evil of malignant witchcraft,* And from the evil of the envier when he envieth. (**P**)

3:18 Allah bears witness that *La ilaha illa Huwa* (none has the right to be worshipped but He). (**HK**) Allah (Himself) is Witness that there is no God save Him. (**P**)

2:91–93 And when it is said to them (the Jews), "Believe in what Allah has sent down," they say, "We believe in what was sent down to us." And they disbelieve in that which came after it, while it is the truth confirming what is with them. *Say (O Muhammad Peace be upon him to them): "Why then have you killed the Prophets of Allah aforetime, if you indeed have been believers?"* And indeed Musa (Moses) came to you with clear proofs, yet you worshipped the calf after he left, and you were *Zalimun* (polytheists and wrong-doers). And (remember) when We took your covenant and We raised above you the Mount (saying), "Hold firmly to what We have given you and hear (Our Word)." They said, "We have heard and disobeyed." And their hearts absorbed (the worship of) the calf because of their disbelief. Say: "Worst indeed is that which your faith enjoins on you if you are believers." (**HK**) And when it is said unto them: Believe in that which Allah hath revealed, they say: We believe in that which was revealed unto us. And they disbelieve in that which cometh after it, though it is the truth confirming that which they possess. *Say (unto them, O Muhammad): Why then slew ye the prophets of Allah aforetime, if ye are (indeed) believers?* And Moses came unto you with clear proofs (of Allah's Sovereignty), yet, while he was away, ye chose the calf (for worship) and ye were wrong-doers. And when We made with you a covenant and caused the Mount to tower above you, (saying): Hold fast by that which We have given you, and hear (Our Word), they said: We hear and we rebel. And (worship of) the calf was made to sink into their hearts because of their rejection (of the covenant). Say (unto them): Evil is that which your belief enjoineth on you, if ye are believers. (**P**)

5:14 And from those who call themselves Christians, We took their covenant, but they have abandoned a good part of the Message that was sent to them. So We planted amongst them enmity and hatred till the Day of Resurrection (when they discarded Allah's Book, disobeyed Allah's Messengers and His Orders and transgressed beyond bounds in Allah's disobedience), and Allah will inform them of what they used to do. (**HK**) And with those who say: "Lo! we are Christians," We made a covenant, but they forgot a part of that whereof they were admonished. Therefor We have stirred up enmity and hatred among them till the Day of Resurrection, when Allah will inform them of their handiwork. (**P**)

17:15 No one laden with burdens can bear another's burden. (**HK**) No laden soul can bear another's load. (**P**)

4:140 And it has already been revealed to you in the Book (this Qur'an) that when you hear the *Verses of Allah being denied and mocked at*, then sit not with them, until they engage in a talk other than that; (but if you stayed with them) certainly in that case you would be like them. Surely, Allah will collect the hypocrites and disbelievers all together in Hell … (**HK**) He hath already revealed unto you in the Scripture that, when ye hear the *revelations of Allah rejected and derided*, (ye) sit not with them (who disbelieve and mock) until they engage in some other conversation. Lo! in that case (if ye stayed) ye would be like unto them. Lo! Allah will gather hypocrites and disbelievers, all together, into hell … (**P**)

2:274–281 Those who spend their wealth (in Allah's Cause) by night and day, in secret and in public, they shall have their reward with their Lord. On them shall be no fear, nor shall they grieve. *Those who eat Riba (usury) will not stand (on the Day of Resurrection) except like the standing of a person beaten by Shaitan (Satan) leading him to insanity. That is because they say: "Trading is only like Riba (usury)," whereas Allah has permitted trading and forbidden Riba (usury). So whosoever receives an admonition from his Lord and stops eating Riba (usury) shall not be punished for the past; his case is for Allah (to judge); but whoever returns to Riba (usury), such are the dwellers of the Fire—they will abide therein. Allah will destroy Riba (usury) and will give increase for Sadaqat (deeds of charity, alms, etc.)* And Allah likes not the disbelievers, sinners. Truly those who believe, and do deeds of righteousness, and perform *As-Salat (Iqamat-as-Salat)*, and give *Zakat*, they will have their reward with their Lord. On them shall be no fear, nor shall they grieve. O *you who believe! Be afraid of Allah and give up what remains (due to you) from Riba (usury) (from now onward), if you are (really) believers. And if you do not do it, then take a notice of war from Allah and His Messenger but if you repent, you shall have your capital sums. Deal not unjustly (by asking more than your capital sums), and you shall not be dealt with unjustly (by receiving less than your capital sums).* And if the debtor is in a hard time (has no money), then grant him time till it is easy for him to repay, but if you remit it by way of charity, that is better for you if you did but know. And be afraid of the Day when you shall be brought back to Allah. Then every person shall be paid what he earned, and they shall not be dealt with unjustly. (**HK**) Those who spend their wealth by night and day, by stealth and openly, verily their reward is with their Lord, and there shall no fear come upon them neither shall they grieve. *Those who swallow usury cannot rise up save as he ariseth whom the devil hath prostrated by (his) touch. That is because they say: Trade is just like usury; whereas Allah permitteth trading and forbiddeth usury. He unto whom an admonition from his Lord cometh, and (he) refraineth (in obedience thereto), he shall keep (the profits of) that which is past, and his affair (henceforth) is with Allah. As for him who returneth (to usury)—Such are rightful owners of the Fire. They will abide therein. Allah hath blighted usury and made almsgiving fruitful.* Allah loveth not the impious and guilty. Lo! those who believe and do good works and establish worship and pay the poor-due, their reward is with their Lord and there shall no fear come upon them neither shall they grieve. O *ye who believe! Observe your duty to Allah, and give up what remaineth (due to you) from usury, if ye are (in truth) believers. And if ye do not, then be warned of war (against you) from Allah and His messenger. And if ye repent, then ye have your principal (without interest). Wrong not, and ye shall not be wronged.* And if the debtor is in straitened circumstances, then (let there be) postponement to (the time of) ease; and that ye remit the debt as almsgiving would be better for you if ye did but know. And guard yourselves against a day in which ye will be brought back to Allah. Then every soul will be paid in full that which it hath earned, and they will not be wronged. (**P**)

Chapter 10: The "Satanic" Verses

105:1–5 Have you (O Muhammad) not seen how your Lord dealt with the Owners of the Elephant? [The elephant army which came from Yemen under the command of Abrahah Al-Ashram intending to destroy the Ka'bah at Makkah]. Did He not make their plot go astray? And sent against them birds, in flocks, Striking them with stones of *Sijjil*. And made them like an empty field of stalks (of which the corn has been eaten up by cattle). (**HK**) Hast thou not seen how thy Lord dealt with the owners of the Elephant? Did He not bring their stratagem to naught, And send against them swarms of flying creatures, Which pelted them with stones of baked clay, And made them like green crops devoured (by cattle)? (**P**)

29:61–63 If you were to ask them: "Who has created the heavens and the earth and subjected the sun and the moon?" *They will surely reply: "Allah."* How then are they deviating (as polytheists and disbelievers)? … If you were to ask them: "Who sends down water (rain) from the sky, and gives life therewith to the earth after its death?" *They will surely reply: "Allah."* (**HK**) And if thou wert to ask them: Who created the heavens and the earth, and constrained the sun and the moon (to their appointed work)? *they would say: Allah.* How then are they turned away? … And if thou wert to ask them: Who causeth water to come down from the sky, and therewith reviveth the earth after its death? *they verily would say: Allah.* (**P**)

39:38 And verily, if you ask them: "Who created the heavens and the earth?" Surely, they will say: "Allah (has created them)." (**HK**) And verily, if thou shouldst ask them: Who created the heavens and the earth? they will say: Allah. (**P**)

10:18 And they worship besides Allah things that hurt them not, nor profit them, and they say: *"These are our intercessors with Allah."* (**HK**) They worship beside Allah that which neither hurteth them nor profiteth them, and they say: *These are our intercessors with Allah.* (**P**)

39:3 And those who take *Auliya'* (protectors and helpers) besides Him (say): *"We worship them only that they may bring us near to Allah."* Verily, Allah will judge between them concerning that wherein they differ. (**HK**) And those who choose protecting friends beside Him (say): *We worship them only that they may bring us near unto Allah.* Lo! Allah will judge between them concerning that wherein they differ. (**P**)

3:151 We shall cast terror into the hearts of those who disbelieve, *because they joined others in worship with Allah,* for which He had sent no authority; their abode will be the Fire and how evil is the abode of the *Zalimun* (polytheists and wrong-doers). (**HK**) We shall cast terror into the hearts of those who disbelieve *because they ascribe unto Allah partners,* for which no warrant hath been revealed. Their habitation is the Fire, and hapless the abode of the wrong-doers. (**P**)

6:22–24 And on the Day when We shall gather them all together, We shall say to those who joined partners in worship (with Us): "Where are your partners (false deities) whom you used to assert (as partners in worship with Allah)?" There will then be (left) no *Fitnah* (excuses or statements or arguments) for them but to say: *"By Allah, our Lord, we were not those who joined others in worship with Allah."* Look! How they lie against themselves! But the (lie) which they invented will disappear from them. (**HK**) And on the day We gather them together We shall say unto those who ascribed partners (unto Allah): Where are (now) those partners of your make-believe? Then will they have no contention save that they will say: *By Allah, our Lord, we never were idolaters.* See how they lie against themselves, and (how) the thing which they devised hath failed them! (**P**)

16:28–29 "Those whose lives the angels take while they are doing wrong to themselves (by disbelief and by associating partners in worship with Allah and by committing all kinds of crimes and evil deeds)." Then, they will make (false) submission (saying): *"We used not to do any evil."* (The angels will reply): "Yes! Truly, Allah is All-Knower of what you used to do. So enter the gates of Hell, to abide therein, and indeed, what an evil abode will be for the arrogant." (**HK**) Whom the angels cause to die while they are wronging themselves. Then will they make full submission (saying): *We used not to do any wrong.* Nay! Surely Allah is Knower of what ye used to do. So enter the gates of hell, to dwell therein for ever. Woeful indeed will be the lodging of the arrogant. (**P**)

72:1–2 Say (O Muhammad): "It has been revealed to me that a group (from three to ten in number) of jinns listened (to this Qur'an). They said: 'Verily! We have heard a wonderful Recital (this Qur'an)! It guides to the Right Path, and we have believed therein, and we shall never join (in worship) anything with our Lord (Allah).'" (**HK**) Say (O Muhammad): It is revealed unto me that a company of the Jinn gave ear, and they said: Lo! we have heard a marvellous Qur'an, Which guideth unto righteousness, so we believe in it and we ascribe no partner unto our Lord. (**P**)

34:22–23 Say: (O Muhammad to those polytheists, pagans, etc.) "Call upon those whom you assert (to be associate gods) besides Allah, they possess not even the weight of an atom (or a small ant), either in the heavens or on the earth, nor have they any share in either, nor there is for Him any supporter from among them. *Intercession with Him profits not, except for him whom He permits.* (**HK**) Say (O Muhammad): Call upon those whom ye set up beside Allah! They possess not an atom's weight either in the heavens or in the earth, nor have they any share in either, nor hath He an auxiliary among them. *No intercession availeth with Him save for him whom He permitteth.* (**P**)

17:73–75 Verily, they were about to tempt you away from that which We have revealed (the Qur'an) unto you (O Muhammad), *to fabricate something other than it against Us,* and then they would certainly have taken you a friend! *And had We not made you stand firm, you would nearly have inclined to them a little.* In that case, We would have made you taste a double portion (of punishment) in this life and a double portion (of punishment) after death. And then you would have found none to help you against Us. (**HK**) And they indeed strove hard to beguile thee (Muhammad) away from that wherewith We have inspired thee, *that thou shouldst invent other than it against Us,* and then would they have accepted thee as a friend. *And if We had not made thee wholly firm thou mightest almost have inclined unto them a little.* Then had we made thee taste a double (punishment) of living and a double (punishment) of dying, then hadst thou found no helper against Us. (**P**)

19:16–23 And mention in the Book (the Qur'an, O Muhammad, the story of) Maryam (Mary), when she withdrew in seclusion from her family to a place facing east. She placed a screen (to screen herself) from them; *then We sent to her Our Ruh [angel Jibrael (Gabriel)], and he appeared before her in the form of a man in all respects.* She said: "Verily! I seek refuge with the Most Beneficent (Allah) from you, if you do fear Allah." (The angel) said: *"I am only a Messenger from your Lord, (to announce) to you the gift of a righteous son."* She said: "How can I have a son, when no man has touched me, nor am I unchaste?" He said: "So (it will be), your Lord said: 'That is easy for Me (Allah): And (We wish) to appoint him as a sign to mankind and a mercy from Us (Allah), and it is a matter (already) decreed, (by Allah).'" So she conceived him, and she withdrew with him to a far place (i.e. Bethlehem valley about 4–6 miles from Jerusalem). *And the pains of childbirth drove her to the trunk of a date-palm. She said: "Would that I had died before this, and had been forgotten and out of sight!"* (**HK**) And make mention of Mary in the Scripture, when she had withdrawn from her people to a chamber looking East, And had chosen seclusion from them. *Then We sent unto her Our Spirit and it assumed for her the likeness of a perfect man.* She said: Lo! I seek refuge in the Beneficent One from thee, if thou art God-fearing. He said: *I am only a messenger of thy Lord, that I may bestow on thee a faultless son.* She said: How can I have a son when no mortal hath touched me, neither have I been unchaste? He said: So (it will be). Thy Lord saith: It is easy for Me. And (it will be) that We may make of him a revelation for mankind and a mercy from Us, and it is a thing ordained. And she conceived him, and she withdrew with him to a far place. *And the pangs of childbirth drove her unto the trunk of the palm-tree. She said: Oh, would that I had died ere this and had become a thing of naught, forgotten!* (**P**)

19:34–35 Such is Eesa (Jesus), son of Maryam (Mary). (it is) a statement of truth, about which they doubt (or dispute). It befits not (the Majesty of) Allah that He should beget a son [this refers to the slander of Christians against Allah, by saying that 'Iesa (Jesus) is the son of Allah]. Glorified (and Exalted be He above all that they associate with Him). When He decrees a thing, He only says to it, "Be!" and it is. (**HK**) Such was Jesus, son of Mary: (this is) a statement of the truth concerning which they doubt. It befitteth not (the Majesty of) Allah that He should take unto Himself a son. Glory be to Him! When He decreeth a thing, He saith unto it only: Be! and it is. (**P**)

53:1–23 By the star when it goes down, (or vanishes). *Your companion (Muhammad) has neither gone astray nor has erred.* Nor does he speak of (his own) desire. It is only an Inspiration that is inspired. He has been taught (this Qur'an) by one mighty in power [Jibrael (Gabriel)]. *Dhu Mirrah* (free from any defect in body and mind), *Fastawa* [then he (Jibrael—Gabriel) rose and became stable]. [*Tafsir At-Tabari*]. While he [Jibrael (Gabriel)] was in the highest part of the horizon, Then he [Jibrael (Gabriel)] approached and came closer, And was at a distance of two bows' length or (even) nearer, So did (Allah) convey the Inspiration to His slave [Muhammad through Jibrael (Gabriel)]. The (Prophet's) heart lied not (in seeing) what he (Muhammad) saw. *Will you then dispute with him (Muhammad) about what he saw* [during the Mi'raj (Ascent of the Prophet over the seven heavens)]. And indeed he (Muhammad) saw him [Jibrael (Gabriel)] at a second descent (i.e. another time). Near *Sidrat-ul-Muntaha* [lote-tree of the utmost boundary (beyond which none can pass)], Near it is the Paradise of Abode. When that covered the lote-tree which did cover it! The sight (of Prophet Muhammad) turned not aside (right or left), nor it transgressed beyond (the) limit (ordained for it). Indeed he (Muhammad) did see, of the Greatest Signs, of his Lord (Allah). Have you then considered *Al-Lat*, and *Al-'Uzza* (two idols of the pagan Arabs). And *Manat* (another idol of the pagan Arabs), the other third? Is it for you the males and for Him the females? That indeed is a division most unfair! They are but names which you have named, you and your fathers, for which Allah has sent down no authority. They follow but a guess and that which they themselves desire, whereas there has surely come to them the Guidance from their Lord! (**HK**) By the Star when it setteth, *Your comrade erreth not, nor is deceived;* Nor doth he speak of (his own) desire. It is naught save an inspiration that is inspired, Which one of mighty powers hath taught him, One vigorous; and he grew clear to view When he was on the uppermost horizon. Then he drew nigh and came down Till he was (distant) two bows' length or even nearer, And He revealed unto His slave that which He revealed. The heart lied not (in seeing) what it saw. *Will ye then dispute with him concerning what he seeth?* And verily he saw him yet another time By the lote-tree of the utmost boundary, Nigh unto which is the Garden of Abode. When that which shroudeth did enshroud the lote-tree, The eye turned not aside nor yet was overbold. Verily he saw one of the greater revelations of his Lord. Have ye thought upon Al-Lat and Al-'Uzza And Manat, the third, the other? Are yours the males and His the females? That indeed were an unfair division! They are but names which ye have named, ye and your fathers, for which Allah hath revealed no warrant. They follow but a guess and that which (they) themselves desire. And now the guidance from their Lord hath come unto them. (**P**)

22:52–54 Never did We send a Messenger or a Prophet before you, but; when he did recite the revelation or narrated or spoke, *Shaitan* (Satan) threw (some falsehood) in it. *But Allah abolishes that which Shaitan (Satan) throws in. Then Allah establishes His Revelations.* And Allah is All-Knower, All-Wise: That He (Allah) may make what is thrown in by *Shaitan* (Satan) a trial for those in whose hearts is a disease (of hypocrisy and disbelief) and whose hearts are hardened. And certainly, the *Zalimun* (polytheists and wrong-doers, etc.) are in an opposition far-off (from the truth against Allah's Messenger and the believers). And that those who have been given knowledge may know that it (this Qur'an) is the truth from your Lord, and that they may believe therein, and their hearts may submit to it with humility. And verily, Allah is the Guide of those who believe, to the Straight Path. (**HK**) Never sent We a messenger or a prophet before thee but when He recited (the message) Satan proposed (opposition) in respect of that which he recited thereof. *But Allah abolisheth that which Satan proposeth. Then Allah establisheth His revelations.* Allah is Knower, Wise; That He may make that which the devil proposeth a temptation for those in whose hearts is a disease, and those whose hearts are hardened—Lo! the evil-doers are in open schism—And that those who have been given knowledge may know that it is the truth from thy Lord, so that they may believe therein and their hearts may submit humbly unto Him. Lo! Allah verily is guiding those who believe unto a right path. (**P**)

2:106 Whatever a Verse (revelation) do We abrogate *or cause to be forgotten,* We bring a better one or similar to it. (**HK**) Nothing of our revelation (even a single verse) do we abrogate *or cause be forgotten,* but we bring (in place) one better or the like thereof. (**P**)

Chapter 11: Undistracted by Religion

41:52 Say: "Tell me, if it (the Qur'an) is from Allah, and you disbelieve in it, who is more astray than one who is in opposition far away (from Allah's Right Path and His obedience)." (**HK**) Bethink you: If it is from Allah and ye reject it—Who is further astray than one who is at open feud (with Allah)? (**P**)

9:36 Verily, the number of months with Allah is twelve months (in a year), so was it ordained by Allah on the Day when He created the heavens and the earth; *of them four are Sacred*, (i.e. the 1st, the 7th, the 11th and the 12th months of the Islamic calendar). That is the right religion, so wrong not yourselves therein ... (**HK**) Lo! the number of the months with Allah is twelve months by Allah's ordinance in the day that He created the heavens and the earth. *Four of them are sacred*: that is the right religion. So wrong not yourselves in them. (**P**)

5:2 O you who believe! Violate not the sanctity of the Symbols of Allah, *nor of the Sacred Month*. (**HK**) O ye who believe! Profane not Allah's monuments *nor the Sacred Month*. (**P**)

REFERENCES

Abou El Fadl, Khaled: *The Great Theft: Wrestling Islam from the Extremists*, 2007, HarperSanFrancisco

Ahmad, Leila: *A Quiet Revolution*, 2011, Yale University Press, New Haven

Ali, Abdullah Yusuf: *The Meanings of The Holy Qur'an*, Kindle Edition (also available at www.muslimaccess.com/quraan/translations/yusufali/yusuf_ali.htm)

American Heritage Dictionary, 5th edition, 2011, Houghton Mifflin Harcourt

Arberry, A. J: *The Koran Interpreted*, 1955, Macmillan, New York

Armstrong, Karen: *Muhammad: A Biography of the Prophet*, 2001, Phoenix, London

Aslan, Reza: *No God but God: The Origins, Evolution and Future of Islam*, 2006, Arrow Books

Bhutto, Benazir: *Reconciliation: Islam, Democracy and the West*, 2008, Simon & Schuster, London

Couch, John Andrew: "Women in Early Roman Law," *Harvard Law Review*, Vol. 8, No. 1 (Apr. 25, 1894), pp. 39–50

Encyclopaedia Britannica, 15th edition, (Chicago: Encyclopaedia Britannica, c2005.)

Esposito, John L.: *The Oxford Dictionary of Islam*, 2003, Oxford University Press, Oxford

Hart, Michael: *The 100: A Ranking of the Most Influential Persons in History*, 1993, Simon & Schuster, London

Hashmi, Sohail H.: "The Quran and Tolerance: An Interpretive Essay on Verse 5:48," *Journal of Human Rights*, Vol. 2, No. 1 (March 2003), pp. 81–103

Hilali-Khan (Muhammad Taqi-ud-Din al-Hilali and Muhammad Muhsin Khan): *Translation of the Meaning of the Noble Qur'an in the English Language*, 1426 AH, King Fahd Printing Complex, Madinah

Ibn Ishaq: *The Life of Muhammad* (Translation by A. Guillaume), 22nd impression, 2009, Oxford University Press, Karachi

Maududi, Syed Abul Ala: *Tafhim al-Qur'an—The Meaning of the Qur'an*, 5th edition, 2005, Islamic Publications (Pvt) Limited, Lahore (also available at englishtafsir.com)

Millius, Susan: "Life without Sex," *Science News*, Vol. 163, No. 26 (Jun. 28, 2003), pp. 406–407

Moore, Keith L.: "A Scientist's Interpretation of References to Embryology in the Quran," *The Journal of the Islamic Medical Association*, Vol. 18 (Jan–June 1986), pp. 15–16

Naik, Zakir Abdul Karim: *The Quran and Modern Science: Compatible or Incompatible?* (http://ebookbrowse.com/quran-and-modern-science-zakir-naik-pdf-d164641222) Also: 2007, Darussalam

Pickthall, Mohammed Marmaduke: *The Koran*, 13th printing (US), 1992, Everyman's Library (Alfred A. Knopf), New York

Pritchard, Donald W.: "What Is an Estuary: Physical Viewpoint," American Association for the Advancement of Science Publ. No. 83, pp. 3–5 (Washington, DC: 1967)

Rawls, John: *A Theory of Justice* (revised edition), 1999, Harvard University Press, Cambridge

Roberts, J.M: *The Pelican History of the World*, 1980 (Reprinted in 1984), Pelican Books

Rogerson, Barnaby: *The Prophet Muhammad: A Biography*, 2003, Little, Brown

Rogerson, Barnaby: *The Heirs of the Prophet Muhammad, and the Roots of the Sunni-Shia Schism*, 2006, Abacus

Sagan, Carl: *Cosmos: The Story of Cosmic Evolution, Science and Civilization*, 1995 (Reprinted 1998), Abacus

Weatherford, Jack: *Genghis Khan and the Making of the Modern World*, 2004, Three Rivers Press, New York

Welch, David Mark and Meselson, Matthew: "Evidence for the Evolution of Bdelloid Rotifers without Sexual Reproduction or Genetic Exchange," *Science*, New Series, Vol. 288, No. 5469 (May 19, 2000), pp. 1211–1215

INDEX